Sex, Gender, and Episcopal Authority in an Age of Reform, 1000–1122

The eleventh and early twelfth centuries were a period of intense debate over ecclesiastical reform in western Europe. This book examines the debates from a new perspective, exploring the ways in which contemporary political writers conveyed messages about "public" life through textual and sometimes visual images of the "private" life of the Church. It argues that the images they used – of bishops as husbands of their sees, of the laity as the sons of Mother Church, and of the pope as father of bishops – were shaped not only by intellectual and ritual traditions, but also by contemporary ideas about sexuality and gender. Megan McLaughlin reveals that the boundaries between the "public" and the "private" were extremely fluid in the central middle ages – because of both the realities of political life in that period and the changing nature of life within European households.

MEGAN MCLAUGHLIN is Associate Professor of Medieval History at the University of Illinois at Urbana-Champaign. She has published on the history of ritual in early medieval Europe, most notably in *Consorting with Saints: Prayer for the Dead in Early Medieval France* (1994). Her more recent work focuses on the history of gender and sexuality, especially in the eleventh century.

Sex, Gender, and Episcopal Authority in an Age of Reform, 1000–1122

Megan McLaughlin

University of Illinois

CAMBRIDGE
UNIVERSITY PRESS

CAMBRIDGE UNIVERSITY PRESS
Cambridge, New York, Melbourne, Madrid, Cape Town, Singapore,
São Paulo, Delhi, Dubai, Tokyo

Cambridge Univmersity Press
The Edinburgh Building, Cambridge CB2 8RU, UK

Published in the United States of America by Cambridge University Press,
New York

www.cambridge.org
Information on this title: www.cambridge.org/9780521870054

First published 2010

Printed in the United Kingdom at the University Press, Cambridge

A catalogue record for this publication is available from the British Library

Library of Congress Cataloguing in Publication data
McLaughlin, Megan, 1954–
    Sex, gender, and episcopal authority in an age of reform, 1000–1122 /
    Megan McLaughlin.
       p. cm.
    ISBN 978-0-521-87005-4 (hardback)
    1. Church history–Middle ages, 600–1500.   2. Church renewal–
    Catholic Church–History–To 1500.   3. Women–Religious aspects–
    Catholic Church–History of doctrines–Middle Ages, 600–1500.
    4. Women in the Catholic Church–Europe–History–To 1500.
    5. Catholic Church–Europe–Bishops–History–To 1500.
    6. Europe–Church history–600–1500.   I. Title.
    BX1200.M3 2010
    262′.0240902–dc22   2009053756

ISBN 978-0-521-87005-4 Hardback

Contents

Illustrations

Preface

So long has this book been in the making that graduate students who worked as my research assistants have long since become established scholars in their own right, while others to whom I am indebted have retired from active research or even – alas – from this world. I have undoubtedly forgotten some conversations whose traces can still be found in the chapters that follow, but I would like to acknowledge, to the best of my ability, everyone who helped me through this very long process.

My thanks, first of all, to the late Gerard Caspary, who first introduced me to the Investiture Conflict many years ago. I am also grateful to Gerd Althoff, Mark Angelos, Sharon Farmer, Fiona Griffiths, Kim LoPrete, Jo Ann McNamara, Maureen Miller, Paula Rieder, George Satterthwaite, and Steve Vaughan for stimulating discussions, references, and encouragement. Jim Barrett, Antoinette Burton, Joanna Drell, Caroline Hibbard, Mark Leff, Diane Koenker, Valerie Ramseyer, and Carol Symes all read parts of the manuscript for me, to its great improvement. The anonymous reader for Cambridge University Press also made many helpful suggestions. Of course, any remaining errors are my own.

The staff of the University of Illinois libraries have made it possible for me to locate many of the obscure volumes necessary to this study. I am especially grateful to Karen Dudas and Bruce Swann of the Classics Library for their unfailing kindness and expertise. Special thanks are also due to the Bodleian Library, Oxford; the Biblioteca Apostolica Vaticana, Rome; the Bibliothèque Municipale, Valenciennes; and the Walters Art Museum, Baltimore, for permission to publish the images that appear below.

By rights, this book should be dedicated to my husband, Howard, whose constant encouragement and heroic defense of my work time made it possible. But because the subject of the following pages is a female figure, at once vulnerable and powerful, I offer it instead to the indomitable women in my life: to my sister Lissa, who has given me unfailing love and support for more than half a century, and to my daughters, Antonia Min and Fei Fei, the sources of my deepest joy. Howard will just have to wait for the next book.

Abbreviations

AASS	*Acta sanctorum*, ed. J. Bollandus et al., Antwerp, 1643–
Anselm	*S. Anselmi Cantuariensis archiepiscopi opera omnia*, ed. F. S. Schmitt, 6 vols., Edinburgh, 1946–61; *Epistolae* (vols. 4–5), trans. W. Fröhlich as *The Letters of Saint Anselm of Canterbury*. 3 vols. Cistercian Studies Series, 96, 97, 142. Kalamazoo, Michigan, 1990–94
AQDGM	Ausgewählte Quellen zur deutschen Geschichte des Mittelalters
Briefsammlungen	*Briefsammlungen der Zeit Heinrich IV.*, ed. C. Erdmann and N. Fickermann, MGH, Briefe der deutschen Kaiserzeit, 5. Weimar, 1950
CC	Corpus christianorum
SL	Series latina
CM	Continuatio medievalis
CHFMA	Classiques de l'histoire de France au moyen âge
CSEL	Corpus scriptorum ecclesiasticorum latinorum
CTSEEH	Collection de texts pour servir à l'étude et à l'enseignment d'histoire
DA	*Deutsches Archiv für Erforschung des Mittelalters*
DTC	*Dictionnaire de théologie catholique*, ed. A. Vacant and E. Mangenot. Paris, 1899–1950
FS	*Frühmittelalterliche Studien*
Fulbert	Fulbert of Chartres, *The Letters and Poems of Fulbert of Chartres*, ed. and trans. F. Behrends. OMT. Oxford, 1976
Geoffrey of Vendôme	Geoffrey of Vendôme, *Oeuvres*, ed. and trans. (into French) G. Giordanengo.

	Sources histoire médiévale publiées par l'Institut de Recherche et d'Histoire des Textes. Paris and Turnhout, 1996
Gregory VII, *Register*	*Das Register Papsts Gregor VII.*, ed. E. Caspars. MGH, Epistolae selectae, 2. Berlin, 1920–23. Trans. H. Cowdrey as *The Register of Pope Gregory VII, 1073–1085.* Oxford, 2002
JL	P. Jaffé, *Regesta pontificum Romanorum*, 2nd ed., ed. W. Wattenbach, S. Loewenfeld, F. Kaltenbrunner, and P. Ewald, 2 vols. Leipzig, 1885–88
Lanfranc	*The Letters of Lanfranc, Archbishop of Canterbury*, ed. and trans. H. Clover and M. Gibson. OMT. Oxford, 1979
Liber miraculorum	*Liber miraculorum sancte Fidis*, ed. L. Robertini. Biblioteca di medioevo latino, 10. Spoleto, 1994. Trans. P. Sheingorn, as *The Book of Sainte Foy*. MAS. Philadelphia, 1995
Mansi	Mansi, J., et al. *Sacrorum conciliorum nova et amplissima collectio.* 53 vols. Florence, Venice, Paris, and Arnheim, 1759–1927
MAS	Middle Ages Series
MGH	Monumenta Germaniae Historica
Capit. episc.	Capitula episcoporum
Capitularia	Capitularia regum Francorum
Constitutiones	Constitutiones et acta publica imperatorum et regum
EPP	Epistolae in quarto
LL	Libelli de lite
SRG	Scriptores rerum Germanicarum ad usum scholarum
SS	Scriptores in folio
Norman Anonymous	*Die Texte des normannischen Anonymus*, ed. K. Pellens. Veröffentlichungen des Instituts für Europäische Geschichte, Mainz, 42. Wiesbaden, 1966
OMT	Oxford Medieval Texts
Orderic	Orderic Vitalis, *Historia aecclesiastica*, ed. and trans. M. Chibnall. OMT. 6 vols. Oxford, 1969–80
Papsturkunden	*Papsturkunden 896–1046*, ed. H. Zimmermann. Österreichische Akademie der Wissenschaften,

	Philosophisch-Historische Klasse, Denkschriften, 174, 177. 2 vols. Vienna, 1984–85
Peter Damian	*Die Briefe des Petrus Damiani*, ed. K. Reindel. MGH, Briefe der deutschen Kaiserzeit. 4 vols. Munich, 1983–93. Trans. O. Blum (vol. 6 with I. Resnick), as *The Letters of Peter Damian*. 6 vols. Washington, DC, 1989–2004
PL	Patrologiae, cursus completus, series latina, ed. J. Migne.
Raoul Glaber	Raoul (Rodulfus) Glaber. *Historiarum libri quinque*, ed. and trans. J. France. In *Opera*. OMT. Oxford, 1989.
RIS	Rerum italicarum scriptores
RS	Rolls Series (Chronicles and Memorials of Great Britain and Ireland during the Middle Ages, published under the direction of the Master of the Rolls), 99 vols. London, 1858–96
Settimane	Settimane di studio del Centro Italiano di Studi sull'alto Medioevo
SG	*Studi Gregoriani*
Thietmar	Thietmar of Merseburg. *Chronicon*, ed. R. Holtzmann. MGH, SRG, n.s. Berlin, 1955. Trans. D. Warner, as *Ottonian Germany: The Chronicon of Thietmar of Merseburg*. Manchester Medieval Sources. Manchester, 2001.

Introduction

The archbishop was wavering. Long a supporter of the reforming Pope Gregory VII, now, in the late spring of 1085, Archbishop Hartwig of Magdeburg seemed on the verge of joining forces with the bishops surrounding Gregory's greatest enemy, the excommunicated, but triumphant, Emperor Henry IV. Henry had recently ratcheted up pressure on those who opposed him. At a synod held in Mainz in April, he had deposed all the Gregorian bishops in Germany, including Hartwig. So the archbishop was thinking seriously of a reconciliation with the emperor, one that would allow him to retain his office. It was at this juncture that his mother stepped in. She warned Hartwig that he would offend his father and sin against herself if he joined the Henricians:[1] "O sweetest of sons, continue to do as you have been doing, continue to work as you have been working, continue to protect the maternal inheritance which you have received."[2]

But this was not Hartwig's biological mother speaking. In fact, these admonitions were composed by Bernhard, the learned master of the cathedral school at Hildesheim, who compiled and sent to Hartwig a collection of theological and legal texts soon after the synod of Mainz. Bernhard's *Book of Canons against Henry IV* was designed to prove how wrong it was to be in contact with excommunicated persons such as Henry, to demonstrate that Pope Gregory had justly cast Henry out of the Church, and to show that neither Henry's episcopal supporters nor the synod they had just held had any legitimacy. The texts included in the book were not unusual, although some of them may have been unknown to Hartwig. They came from the writings of Augustine of Hippo, Pope Gregory I, Bede, and others of the Church Fathers, as well

---

[1] Bernhard of Hildesheim, *Liber canonum contra Heinricum IV*, Praefatio, MGH, LL 1: 473. Unless otherwise noted – either in the footnote or in the bibliography – all translations are my own. On Bernhard, see Mirbt (1894), pp. 33–35; Robinson (1978), pp. 107–8. On the political context of this work, see Robinson (1999), pp. 246–49; Althoff (2006), pp. 197–205.

[2] Bernhard, *Liber canonum contra Heinricum IV*, Praefatio, MGH, LL 1: 472.

as from various early medieval compilations of church law – notably the ninth-century collection wrongly attributed to Isidore Mercator (on which more below). What is remarkable about the *Book of Canons* is its narrator. The Church, personified as the Bride of Christ and the Mother of the Faithful, addresses Archbishop Hartwig, urging him not to change sides in this moment of crisis. She reminds him that she was the one who gave birth to him, "with [divine] grace acting as a midwife." The "Father" who will be offended if the archbishop fails in his duty is, of course, God, while the "maternal inheritance" which he must protect is his own see of Magdeburg.[3]

Bernhard attempted an unusual rhetorical move in placing the declaration of church law in the mouth of Mother Church herself. To my knowledge, no other medieval canonist made the Church the *narrator* of a canon law collection. Presumably this move had a practical purpose, giving greater weight to Bernhard's work. Since he himself was no pope, archbishop, or bishop, but merely a scholar and teacher, attributing the statement of law to Mother Church confirmed its validity: "I, your Mother the Church, give you [Hartwig] this bulwark of invincible authority ...".[4] But in treating the female personification of the Church as a central character in his work, Bernhard of Hildesheim was only doing what a great many other clerical authors in the eleventh and early twelfth centuries did. He was viewing ecclesiastical reform through the lens of gender and sexuality, as an attempt to protect and purify the Household of God.

Some seventy years ago, Gerd Tellenbach characterized the Investiture Conflict as a struggle for "right order in the world."[5] That characterization continues to shape our interpretations of the various movements to reform religious communities in western Europe during the eleventh and early twelfth centuries, and our understanding of the complicated conflicts that surrounded and grew out of those movements. Since Tellenbach's time, much effort has been devoted to tracing the many visions of "right order" that prevailed and competed with one another in that period, including the theocratic visions of the Salian emperors and the hierocratic visions of the reforming popes; the rank- and tradition-conscious visions of monastic communities, cathedral chapters, noble families, and individual bishops; and the more utopian, sometimes revolutionary visions of itinerant preachers and participants in popular movements.[6] Many volumes have been

---

[3] Throughout this book, lower-case letters will be used for ordinary, earthly mothers and fathers, while capitals will be used to designate the Church as Mother or God as Father.
[4] Bernhard, *Liber canonum contra Heinricum IV.*, 48, MGH, LL 1: 516.
[5] Tellenbach (1936), p. 1.
[6] Excellent bibliographies may be found in Blumenthal (1982); for discussion of the scholarship on a variety of specific issues, see Hartmann (1993a).

written on the growing power of the papacy, the conflicts between *regnum* and *sacerdotium* (the so-called "Investiture Conflict"), and – especially in recent years – on local reforming efforts in the context of local politics.[7]

A vast scholarly literature exists on all these subjects, because in the central Middle Ages political theories as well as political practices were changing in important ways, with far-reaching consequences for the later history of Europe and, for that matter, America. However, from this very large body of scholarship, gender and sexuality have hitherto been almost entirely missing.[8] While historians have certainly recognized that the Church was often represented in this period as a Mother or as a Bride, and that bishops and popes were sometimes seen as fathers or husbands, no serious effort has yet been made to understand the role of these representations in political discourse during the central Middle Ages, the ways in which they evolved over time, or the emotions they evoked. While scholars have closely examined both efforts to reform the structures of Church and state and efforts to reform marriage in the central Middle ages, they have paid little attention to how "right order" in the world was related to "right order" within the household.

The reason for this is not hard to find. It lies in the impoverished modern notion of the political upon which many scholars continue to rely. From the eighteenth century to the twentieth, political activity was generally understood as something carried on by men in a "public sphere," viewed as distinct from the "private sphere" within which women had their place.[9] Admittedly, some women did appear in the public sphere and participate in public activities, but this was not their normal or expected arena. Moreover, while it was also recognized that "public" men had their "private" side, and engaged in sexual and other intimate behaviors within the family (and sometimes outside the family as well), these private activities were distinguished from politics, except in unusual cases where public scandal arose from them. Despite the efforts of feminist and postmodern scholars to complicate the meaning of "the political," many of those who study the political history of the modern era continue to base their studies on these traditional assumptions.[10]

---

[7] An important critique of the papacy's role was Laudage (1984). But in response to this recent emphasis on local studies, see now Cushing (2005).

[8] The only exceptions thus far have taken the form of brief articles: see McNamara (1994) and (1995); Leyser (1998); McLaughlin (1998) and (1999); Elliott (1999), pp. 81–126; Miller (2003); McLaughlin (2010).

[9] The principal twentieth-century theorists of the public sphere are, of course, Hannah Arendt (1958) and Jürgen Habermas (1962).

[10] Feminist critiques include Brennan and Pateman (1979); Elstain (1981); MacKinnon (1989); Pateman (1989); *Feminists Read Habermas*; Ackelsberg and Shanley (1996); *Feminism, the Public and the Private*. Among postmodern critiques, see especially Foucault (1975) and (1978–86); Lyotard (1984) and (1988).

Medieval politics, of course, operated very differently than do modern politics. There was certainly nothing akin to the "bourgeois public sphere" during the central Middle Ages.[11] "Public" and "private" were distinguished, but only in a very nebulous way – in both practice and theory they tended to flow into one another.[12] It has long been recognized that what we would today consider "public" business was conducted within the households of kings and nobles, while political authority was closely identified with the *mundium* a father exercised over his family. Yet while these peculiarities of medieval politics are well known, most historians of medieval politics and political thought continue to accept without question the modernist assumption that the realm of politics was both male and asexual.[13] Studies of the Investiture Conflict focus on the interactions of important men (and a few "exceptional" women like Agnes of Poitou or Matilda of Tuscany), which are seen as public and therefore political. Sexuality and gender are seen not as integral parts of the field of political action and thought, but rather as essentially private matters, perhaps affected by public politics – as in the campaign to reform Christian marriage and sexuality – but seldom affecting them.

Such a reconstruction of political life in the central Middle Ages is, however, both anachronistic and misleading. Recent research has made it abundantly clear that public business was not only conducted within the household, but often within the most intimate spaces of that household, and in the presence of all its members, male and female, young and old, noble and servile. We know, for example, that matters of state were regularly discussed in the king's bedchamber.[14] A number of scholars have documented the regular and largely unquestioned participation of the wives of kings, nobles, and officials in the business of government and war.[15] And because many of the lower clergy and even a few of the

---

[11] Some scholars have recently argued for the existence of medieval "public spheres" or "spaces": Althoff (1993) and (2003); Masschaele (2002); *Formen und Funktionen*; Symes (2007); Melve (2007).

[12] On the public/private distinction in the eleventh and early twelfth centuries, see the Conclusion, below.

[13] The most egregious example of this tendency may be found in the last works of the great medievalist Georges Duby: (1988), (1995), (1995–96).

[14] Examples of important meetings taking place in the king's bedchamber include: Thangmar, *Vita Bernwardi episcopi*, 19, MGH SS 4: 767; Wipo, *Gesta Chuonradi*, 16, MGH, SS 11: 265 (trans. Mommsen and Morrison, p. 79); Bruno of Magdeburg, *De bello Saxonico*, 62, MGH, SS 5: 350. In literature, this is represented in *Ruodlieb*, 5, pp. 90–91.

[15] Vogelsang (1954); Facinger (1968); Bernards (1971); McNamara and Wemple (1973); Verdon (1973); Leyser (1979), pp. 49–74; Stafford (1983); McLaughlin (1990); Jäschke (1991); Chibnall (1991); Stafford (1994); *Medieval Queenship*; Goez (1995); *Queens and Queenship*; Aurell (1997); Stafford (1997); *Aristocratic Women*; Fössel (2000); *Femmes, pouvoir et société*; Woll (2002); *Capetian Women*; Haluska-Rausch (2005), pp. 155–60 (and see n. 7 to p. 154); LoPrete (2007a) and (2007b).

upper clergy were still married at this time, women helped to conduct the business of the Church as well. This is not to say that women were in any way considered the equals of men; rather it is to recognize that because of the spatial organization of politics in this period, women had direct access to political life, and often exercised authority – if only as deputies for male relatives. Only very gradually, from the late eleventh century on, do we begin to see the emergence of what Jo Ann McNamara has called "woman-less" public spaces.[16]

The absence of a clear distinction between the public and the private does not, however, simply mean that women regularly participated in political life. It also means that in the central Middle Ages the "political" was understood to encompass much more than most modern historians have assumed. The subject of this book is the role of gender and sexuality not in political practice, but in political discourse, from the time when ecclesiastical reform movements were beginning to accelerate, just after the year 1000, to the moment when the most intense phase of conflict over reform (the Investiture Conflict proper) ended with the Concordat of Worms in 1122. The beginning and end points of my study are, of course, somewhat arbitrary, since the representations discussed here were based on earlier precedents and continued to be used for centuries thereafter. Nevertheless, I would argue that in the political writings of the eleventh and early twelfth centuries, ideas about gender and sexuality had greater salience and deeper emotional resonance than ever before.

In those political writings, contestations of sexuality and gender constantly interact with contestations of authority and power. Polemicists in this period represented *Ecclesia*, the Church, in a number of ways – as a city, a dove, a ship, a sheepfold, and notably as the Body of Christ – but by far the dominant image was that of a woman – and a woman of "infinite variety," by turns pure and corrupt, resplendent and abject, commanding and oppressed. Around this central female figure revolved all the other characters in the drama of reform, the popes and emperors, bishops and princes, priests and street mobs – related to her as husbands, as guardians (or corruptors) of Christ's Bride, as faithful (or unfaithful) sons to Mother Church. Earthly women, too, had their roles to play, as wives, mothers, and daughters, although all too often they served merely as foils for the celestial Bride and Mother, with their actions contrasted unfavorably with hers.

What is the significance of such representations, which occur everywhere in political texts from this period? Some historians have referred

---

[16] McNamara (1995).

to them as mere models or metaphors for institutions and authority.[17] Clearly, though, their significance ran deeper. Jérôme Baschet, in his study of the Bosom of Abraham and medieval notions of paternity, has described representations of God as Father or of bishops as fathers as metaphors, but also as something more. He uses the phrase "fantasmes socialement consolidés" to call attention to the ways in which such representations were shaped not only by the traditions of Christian society and by the individual writer's rhetorical concerns, but also by the unconscious.[18] A few scholars have noted the elaborate development of these figures, and their extensive influence in the political and ecclesiological thought of the central Middle Ages. Thus I. S. Robinson argues that "these *allegoriae* are more than metaphors: they are fully developed ecclesiological ideas of great power and complexity."[19] And Tellenbach pointed out long ago that such representations were "more than symbols in our sense of the word," and attributed the highly emotional tone of reform arguments to the fact that "for medieval man there was more truth and clarity in [the image of the Bride] than in abstract expressions of the relation of Christ to the Church."[20]

Yet in treating representations of the Church as Bride or of the bishop as father as mere comparisons, however powerful and complex, even in allowing for the unconscious in their development, there is still something missing – something that Tellenbach and Robinson hint at, but never fully explain. I would argue that for clerical writers of the central Middle Ages, the Church did not just resemble a bride or mother. Rather, she *was* the true Bride and the true Mother – the supernatural prototype for these roles on earth. By the same token, not only was God the prototype of all fathers, but Christ was the truest of bridegrooms. The clerical authors discussed in this book understood the linkage between these human and spiritual relationships to be not arbitrary, not freely chosen by themselves or even by the earlier Fathers on whose works they drew; in short, not simply metaphorical, but truly allegorical in the theological sense – that is, ultimately designed by God, inscribed in Scripture, enacted in the liturgy, and thereby handed down to the faithful on earth.[21]

Medieval clerics, trained in the techniques of scriptural exegesis, believed events and institutions in the world to have hidden meanings, implanted in the world by divine providence as signposts to spiritual truths.[22] References to such hidden meanings occur not only in theology,

---

[17] E.g. Bosl (1975); Fichtenau (1984), pp. 120–32; Schreiner (1990).
[18] Baschet (2000), p. 34, and see p. 352, n. 7
[19] Robinson (1988), p. 252.   [20] Tellenbach (1936), p. 131.
[21] For a modern iteration of this view, see Lubac (1971), p. 39.
[22] Lubac (1959–64).

but also in political polemics, in chronicles, and in many other literary forms. As the historian Raoul Glaber noted, "God, the author of all, distinguished the objects of his creation by many different shapes and forms, so that by means of what the eye sees and the mind perceives, He might raise the wise man to a direct view of God [*ad simplicem Deitatis intuitum*]."[23] After laying out the parallels between various "quaternities" (the four Gospels, four cardinal virtues, four senses, four elements, etc.), Raoul asserts, "God is proclaimed most plainly, beautifully, and silently by this patent chain of correspondences [*evidentissimis complexibus rerum*]; in frozen motion each thing indicates another, and they do not cease to proclaim the original source from which they derive, and to which they seek to return in order to find peace again."[24] Such "correspondences" could work in a variety of ways. Some were "figural," with one historical event foreshadowing another.[25] Others were "tropological," with events and institutions pointing to moral lessons. And still others were "allegorical," in which visible things pointed to invisible truths.[26] (The same word, "allegory," also served as the category encompassing all these types of correspondence.)

Many authors are considered in this book; all were steeped in a variety of textual traditions which authorized their representations of *Ecclesia* in female form, and the correspondences they saw between the life of the Church and the lives of earthly women. The Bride and the Mother both appear in Scripture, which automatically gave these figures a truth-value not granted to ordinary metaphors.[27] Ideas about a feminine Church were also developed to some extent by the Church Fathers, whose ideas about ecclesiastical institutions were essential to the thinking of eleventh- and early twelfth-century writers.[28] The influence of the liturgy, which all medieval clerics regularly performed, was also important, for ritualization – the reiterated re-presentation of *Sponsa Christi* and *Mater Ecclesia* within the context of sacred space and time – underlined the inherent reality of these images in particularly concrete ways.[29] And finally, a very direct source for many of the writers considered below was that peculiar work known today as the "Pseudo-Isidorian Decretals."

This collection of supposedly authoritative texts on church organization and discipline was attributed to the fictitious "Isidore Mercator," but

---

[23] Raoul Glaber, 1.2, pp. 3–4.   [24] Raoul Glaber, 1.3, pp. 6–7.
[25] Auerbach (1938).   [26] E.g. Raoul Glaber, 5.10, pp. 228–31.
[27] On the implications of Biblical exegesis for political thought, see Buc (1994).
[28] Chavasse (1940); Plumpe (1940); Rahner (1944); Bedard (1951), pp. 17–36; Delahaye (1958); Therel (1973).
[29] See below, Chapters Two and Four. On ritualization, see Bell (1992), especially p. 74. My thinking on this subject has also been influenced by Butler (1990) and (1993).

in fact was the creation of a workshop of highly educated clerics, working in northeastern France around the middle of the ninth century.[30] The collection combines authentic material with skillfully forged royal legislation and papal decrees, created in response to the tumultuous situation in the Frankish church during the preceding decades. Pseudo-Isidore was designed to insulate diocesan bishops from interference by archbishops or church councils; it thus emphasized the autonomy of individual bishops and the authority of the (conveniently distant) pope. These characteristics made it extremely useful to many reformers of the eleventh and early twelfth centuries, especially those who supported episcopal independence from lay control and papal claims to supreme authority within the Church. These reformers made extensive use of texts from Pseudo-Isidore in their arguments.[31] In Pseudo-Isidore, however, much more than in earlier texts, the role of bishops was described in terms of family relationships. The correspondences it lays out between the household of God, the household of Church, and earthly households of men and women shaped many of the texts from the central Middle Ages considered in this book.

While representations of the Church as Bride and Mother, or of bishops as husbands and fathers, had earlier precedents, they nevertheless reached a new stage of development in the central Middle Ages. Highly gendered and sexualized representations of the Church, of bishops and popes, of kings and of ordinary layfolk appear everywhere in the large body of polemical pamphlets and books composed to support the concerns of reformers and their opponents from the mid-eleventh century on. They serve as the framework for entire treatises (as in Bernhard's *Book of Canons against Henry IV* or Placidus of Nonantola's *On the Honor of the Church*) or as important recurring themes (as in Ranger of Lucca's *On the Ring and the Staff*[32]). They are elaborated at length and in great detail (as in Peter Damian's *The Debate at the Synod*[33]). The correspondences between earthly, institutional, and heavenly households have their own history, which is intertwined with the histories of theology, canon law, and political thought, and which can be traced by considering how particular formulations are picked up and developed from one author to another.

This book explores the use and development of a specific group of images – it is, in short, essentially, a study of iconography. But in

---

[30] The work has traditionally been dated to around 850: Fournier and Le Bras (1931–32), vol. 1: 183–85; Fuhrmann (1972–73), vol. 1: 191–94. However, Zechiel-Eckes (2001) has suggested a date in the 830s. The collection will be cited below from Projekt Pseudoisidor, available at: http://www.pseudoisidor.mgh.de/.

[31] Fuhrmann (1972–73), vol. 2: 411–62, 586–624.

[32] See below, Chapter 2 .   [33] See below, Chapter 4 .

approaching such a subject, I cannot do better than to follow the lead of art historian Hélène Toubert, who emphasizes how important it is to examine the relationships between images – the commonalities and differences that make it possible to place a particular representation within the "sometimes very lengthy genealogy" of its subject, as well as within the "iconographic repertoire" as a whole. Specific details, Toubert points out, may help to identify an image's immediate source, or clarify the conditions under which it was created.[34] Such techniques, long employed in the study of visual images, can usefully be applied to verbal images as well. Examining the intertextual development of Gregory VII's famous description of the Church as "free, catholic, and chaste," or the story of Noah and his three sons, not only makes the centrality of gendered and sexualized correspondences to political argument in this period clear, but also helps to clarify the relationships among writers, as well as the impact of particular political conditions or religious affiliations on their thought.

One consistent element in all of the texts examined, however, is the unquestioned *reality* attributed to these figures – which brings us back to the distinction made above, between metaphor and allegory. In the political writings of the central Middle Ages, the household of God, the household of the Church, and earthly households are constantly juxtaposed. Sometimes, the authors of these texts made their awareness of the differences between these households clear. They say that they are "comparing earthly to heavenly things," or they state that the Roman Church is "like" a mother, or a bishop is acting "like" a father. Yet even in these cases, the comparisons are nothing like those involved in modern metaphors. Modern metaphors describe the similarities between things, but it is always easy to see where those similarities stop, for the differences are almost as evident as the similarities, and indeed give piquancy to the comparison. In medieval theological allegory (which was ultimately shaped by Christian Neoplatonism, although by the central Middle Ages it had become habitual for most writers), there was an essential unity between the things compared; the difference between them was simply one of degree or dignity. The essence of the earthly household was the same as that of the heavenly household, the two were related as shadow to reality. And this had significant implications for the use of these correspondences in political argument. Perhaps the most remarkable feature of the polemical writings of the central Middle Ages is the way in which the *laws* governing gender, sexuality, and familial bonds are applied directly and unapologetically to ecclesiastical relationships. It

[34] Toubert (1990), p. 9.

was easy for medieval clerics to apply the same laws to human families and to the family of the institutional church, for they believed that both were rooted in archetypal relationships among the members of the divine *familia*: God the Father, Christ, and the Church.

While the writers considered in this book came from all over Europe, and had diverse social and intellectual backgrounds, they also had many things in common. Any reasonably well-educated cleric, regardless of geographical, social, or political position, whether English or Italian, monastic or secular, radical or conservative, would have been familiar not only with the doctrine of correspondences, but also with most of the specific gendered or sexualized correspondences discussed below. These ideas were part of the common intellectual currency of the central Middle Ages. Nevertheless, as we shall see, writers strongly committed to church reform – and especially those radical reformers associated with the circle of Pope Gregory VII in Rome – employed these images more frequently, and developed them more elaborately, than anyone else.[35] As rhetorical devices, the characterization of simony (the buying and selling of holy things, especially church office) as prostitution, and of disobedience to Rome as defiance of one's mother, suited the Gregorians' polemical goals, underlining the heinous nature of those sins. It would be a mistake, however, to understand their deployment of these devices as simply rhetorical. The violent language of rape, incest, and betrayal, the tender language of embraces, kisses, and love, also served to express the reformers' emotional reactions to what was right and wrong in the church of their day. There can be no doubt that they truly recoiled with horror when a church was defiled by the adultery of its bishop, and rejoiced when the faithful supported their rightful spiritual father. At the same time, a careful reading of their works reveals how understanding a bishop as the bridegroom of his church, or a king as the pope's son, helped these thinkers construct their own, often novel, visions of "right order" in the world. If more conservative thinkers sometimes had difficulty refuting the reformers' claims, it was in part because they, too, assumed that such correspondences were real.

The new prominence accorded to images of the Church as Bride or the pope as father in the central Middle Ages can probably be attributed

---

[35] In the past, scholars have sometimes used the term "reformer" in such a way as to imply membership in, or affiliation with, the Roman reformers. Recent scholarship, however, has emphasized how autonomous the various reform movements in different parts of Europe generally were – even if they eventually came to ally themselves with the reforming papacy. In this book, therefore, "reformer" simply denotes anyone engaged in criticism of, or an attempt to change, traditional practices, while "conservative" refers to anyone interested in defending the status quo. Those associated with Gregory VII or his successors are referred to as "Roman reformers" or "Gregorians."

to several causes. The first is simply the multiplication and interaction of texts concerned with fundamental questions about the proper ordering of the church and Christian society. It is hardly surprising that what were already traditional representations would play a more prominent role during this period of intensified debate. Something similar, albeit on a much smaller scale, can be seen in late antiquity, when images of the Church as the Mother and Bride were used by Church Fathers struggling to deal with heresy and schism, and to understand the place of the Church in Roman society. But what made these images even more prominent in the central Middle Ages was the intellectual framework within which the *libelli de lite* and other political texts were composed. This was the world of the "pre-scholastics," in which the tools of logic and grammar were increasingly important, but which was also still powerfully shaped by early medieval monastic theology and spiritual writings. The writers whose works are discussed in this book made use of abstract categories in constructing their arguments, but they also pursued the poetic association of ideas, sometimes to great lengths.[36] In such an intellectual context, which combined reliance on reason with intense appeals to emotion and experience, the feminine figure of the Church struck a deep chord.

But the specific content of these representations is not fully explained by the political and intellectual context within which they developed. I would argue that they were shaped as well by the changing reality of life within European households during the eleventh and early twelfth centuries. Debates about "right order" within the Church and the world had never before been conducted within a society in which household and government were so completely interchangeable. The breakdown of the Carolingian political order had given rise, by the eleventh century, to a situation in which family ties had greater practical importance in struggles for power than ever before. The family was, moreover, under close scrutiny in the eleventh and early twelfth centuries, as clerical efforts to reform the institution of marriage and the sexual behavior of the faithful coincided with the struggle of elite families to consolidate their political position by advantageous marriages and changed inheritance practices. The same clerics concerned about the legitimacy of ordinations performed by simoniacs, or about the pope's ability to excommunicate an emperor, were also deeply interested in problems such as what constituted

---

[36] Researchers have often linked the polemical literature of the eleventh and early twelfth centuries with the beginnings of scholasticism, e.g. Laudage (1984), p. 47 and n. 280. But many of the figures discussed below had their origins in the monastic culture described so beautifully by Leclercq (1957). On the combination of old and new outlooks in the works of Honorius Augustodunensis, see the Conclusion below.

a legitimate marriage, what should be done about adultery, and even what duties children owed their parents. Clerical debates over marriage and family life thus intersected in complicated ways with their debates over episcopal elections, lay investiture, and even papal primacy.

If we are to understand the parallels reformers and their opponents saw between political life and family life, it is important to understand their assumptions about, their expectations for, and even – as far as possible – their emotional associations with, life within the household. Since the 1970s, a large body of research has been devoted to the history of marriage and the family in the central Middle Ages. Most of this work has focused on relatively well-documented issues, for example inheritance patterns and the formation of marriages.[37] Intimate relations within the household, for which sparser evidence exists, have received much less attention. Relatively little has been written about how husbands and wives, parents and children, householders and servants actually interacted with one another, and even less about the affective aspects of those interactions. Hence the structure of this book, which is designed to clarify the relationship between the changing realities of family life during the reform period, and the construction of gendered and sexualized representations of the Church. Each of the three sections examines a particular kind of intimate relationship, first in terms of human practice, and then in terms of ecclesiastical politics.

Thus the first section deals with sexual relationships. Chapter 1 focuses on clerical views of, and concerns about, human marriage, in a period when that institution was the subject of intense reform efforts. Legitimate sexual relationships (marriages) were being redefined and distinguished from illicit liaisons in the eleventh and early twelfth centuries, in response to social, economic, and political pressures, as well as to the demands of theology and canon law. These changes may have heightened perceptions of brides and young wives as vulnerable to violence and exploitation, even as the related campaign for clerical celibacy made it more difficult for clerical writers to express sympathy for sexually active women. Chapter 2 traces the application of legal, theological and societal assumptions about women and marriage to mystical and ecclesiastical relationships. It explores the deployment of the image of the Church as Bride in political writings, and the development of the idea that the bishop was the bridegroom of his church. Together, these two chapters demonstrate how correspondences between earthly unions, the heavenly union of Christ and the Church, and the institutional relationship of the bishop to his see, helped to shape arguments over episcopal elections, simony, and lay investiture in the central Middle Ages.

[37] See below, Chapter 1 .

The second and third sections deal with clerical views of parental authority, which also appear to have been shaped as much by their own experience in society as by Biblical texts. Chapter 3 examines the ambiguous position of mothers in the central Middle Ages. While most mothers could command their children to some extent, maternity was more clearly associated with nurturing than with discipline or firm control. Women were, moreover, extremely vulnerable to wounding through or even by their children during this period. Chapter 4 considers how this understanding of the ambiguities of motherhood helped reshape the traditional image of the Church as Mother during the central Middle Ages. While appeals to filial piety were often deployed to claim the loyalty and obedience of the faithful, at the same time images of *Mater Ecclesia* endangered were increasingly used to elicit support for reform (or sometimes resistance to overly radical reform efforts). These two chapters together show the role linkages between heavenly, earthly, and institutional motherhood played in a variety of polemical contexts, but perhaps most importantly in arguments concerning the relative position of various figures in the ecclesiastical hierarchy, and especially concerning the theory of papal primacy, during the early stages of the "papal" reform.

The final pair of chapters is devoted to fathers. Chapter 5 explores the nexus of ideas that surrounded paternity in the central Middle Ages – affection, discipline, inheritance, and the right to command. It also shows how the authority of earthly fathers could be undermined by appeals to the superior paternity of God. Chapter 6 considers the application of these ideas to the image of the bishop as spiritual father to his flock, and the increasing emphasis on the bishop's paternal power to command in texts from the eleventh and early twelfth centuries. Together, these two chapters demonstrate that correspondences between earthly, divine, and episcopal paternity were crucial to the Gregorian program of exalting spiritual over secular authority, as well as to the development of papal primacy during the later stages of reform.

The central figure in this book is not human but divine: it is *Ecclesia* herself, the Church as Bride and Mother of the faithful. Because of this, my argument focuses on the authority of those most intimately related to *Ecclesia;* that is, bishops (including the bishops of Rome).[38] However, the implications of my findings go beyond the ecclesiastical, to encompass the secular as well. Gender and sexuality impinged, as we shall see, on the authority of kings as well as bishops, on that of emperors as well as popes. Thus my conclusion returns to the question of what was

---

[38] Ott and Jones (2007) provide a useful review of recent scholarship on bishops in the central Middle Ages.

considered "public" and what was "private" in the central Middle Ages, offering a new interpretation of this relationship that could almost as easily apply to the secular as to the sacred realm.

Most of this book is based on old-fashioned research – on the slow and laborious examination of individual texts. In the first of each pair of chapters, I have used a wide variety of sources, in order to get a fuller picture of clerical assumptions about marriage, maternity, and paternity. The second of each pair focuses on political writings, broadly interpreted, and especially on the famous *libelli de lite* – the pamphlets or "little books" composed during the "contest" between reformers and their opponents in the eleventh and early twelfth centuries. Most of these polemics were collected in three volumes of the Monumenta Germaniae Historica in the late nineteenth century, but additional texts have since been added, and new editions have appeared of some of the most important of these works. I have also made extensive use of the letters written by individuals prominent enough (or talented enough as writers) to have had their letters preserved. In particular, my assertions about the papal reformers' changing use of maternal and paternal imagery in Chapters 4 and 6 are based on a comparison of the registers of Pope Gregory I (590–604) and Pope John VIII (872–82), and the letters and privileges issued by early eleventh-century popes (as edited by Zimmermann), with the letters of the reforming popes from 1046 to 1122.[39] However, many other sources have been used in these chapters – chronicles (which in this period are sometimes hard to tell from polemics), sermons, canon law collections, saints' lives, and theological works. Almost any kind of text is relevant to my subject – how clerics in the central Middle Ages imagined the Church and thought about its reform, in relation to life in the household. And indeed, part of my goal in this book is to show that the images and ideas I discuss were not confined to polemics, but permeated clerical culture.

The digitalization of a huge number of medieval texts in recent years has made new kinds of research possible. The searchable Patrologia Latina, Acta Sanctorum, CETEDOC, and Monumenta Germaniae Historica databases empower researchers not only to locate particular words and combinations of words, but also to trace quite easily the changing occurrence of such words and phrases over time. My use of these databases has led me to works I might not otherwise have seen, and has helped to clarify the relationships between texts – for example, how the

---

[39] Gregory I, *Registrum epistularum*; John VIII, *Registrum et epistolae*, MGH, EPP, 7: 1–272; *Papsturkunden*. Most of the letters of the reforming popes are available only in very imperfect editions – they are cited here from the Patrologia Latina. The exception, of course, is the register of Pope Gregory VII (1073–85), carefully edited in the 1920s by Caspar and recently translated into English by Cowdrey.

use of particular Bible verses in the *libelli de lite* played off the common exegesis of those verses. I have indicated in the notes when my assertions about the increased occurrence of a particular phrase or about the "usual" exegesis of a Biblical passage are based on such searches.[40] These can easily be replicated and expanded upon by anyone with access to these databases.

None of the texts used in this book is newly discovered – most, indeed, are very familiar to modern scholars. But they are read here in an unfamiliar way, with a particular focus on phrases and passages that have received little attention in the past. My intention is, frankly, to disrupt the customary scholarly narratives of reform and conflict in the central Middle Ages, by telling the story from a different point of view. New characters take center stage here, while some old characters appear in a new light. Incidents in the usual plots take on a fresh significance, and some different events are added, because of their significance for my new protagonists. Most important, however, is the way my characters communicate with one another – and with us. While logic and close reasoning are by no means absent, the emphasis here is on poetry and pictures, on images – textual and visual – that compelled the emotions as well as the mind, on the flashing association of ideas in the works of highly sophisticated writers. Of course my story does not replace the older ones. It should be seen, rather, as layered on an already very dense scholarly tradition. Examining the role of sexuality and gender in writings about reform does, however, promise to widen, deepen, and enrich our understanding of political thought in western Europe a thousand years ago – and in some unexpected ways.

---

[40] Indicated by "Search for (the particular word or phrase) in (the name of the database)."

1 The reform of marriage

Clerical writers imagined ecclesiastical relationships in terms of sexuality, gender, and kinship in part because these subjects were already much on their minds.[1] In the eleventh and early twelfth centuries, writings on church reform emerged side by side, and in conversation, with writings on marriage, sparked by efforts to transform that institution. Many of the clerics involved in movements for ecclesiastical reform were simultaneously attempting to establish rules for sexual behavior, often amidst vigorous debate, and then slowly, painfully, to put those rules into practice.

One reason why debate was involved was because marital practices were changing in the central Middle Ages, in response to political, economic, and social developments. The long-canonical theory of the "mutation familiale" has come under increasingly harsh attack since the 1990s, but it is worth briefly reviewing here its main points, and how it has held up to criticism. At its core is Karl Schmid's argument that noble families (the only ones for which much documentation exists) underwent a fundamental change around the year 1000, as the extended clans of the early Middle Ages began to give way to the patrilineage.[2] During the Carolingian period, according to this argument, kinship reflected a sense of obligation towards a loosely defined group of relatives on both the male and female side, the *Sippe* or clan. Patterns of inheritance supported this clan structure, for although the children of a property holder normally divided up his or her lands and movables, lateral inheritance – i.e. from brother to brother, or from uncle to nephew – was also relatively common. Thus in the ninth and tenth centuries exchanges of property still cemented links within a wide group of kin.

---

[1] The textual traditions that contributed to these imaginings are discussed in later chapters.

[2] Schmid (1957), (1959), and (1983) – although Schmid based his formulation of the theory on the work of earlier scholars, notably Tellenbach (1939), (1943), and (1957); and Hauck (1954). Schmid's theories were applied to France and widely disseminated through the work of Georges Duby (1953), (1973), and (1981). The complex scholarly literature on this theory is reviewed by Bouchard (2001), pp. 13–38; and Crouch (2006), pp. 99–123.

Around the year 1000, however, the situation began to change, as dynastic considerations gained new importance within the military elite. The "mutationists" generally associate this development with the multiplication of castles, which became evident in most parts of Europe during the last decades of the tenth century. As power was increasingly tied to control of strongholds and the territories around them, at least one member of any family with political aspirations had to have sufficient resources to build castles and maintain the knights to garrison them. And so a shift began to take place from partible to impartible inheritance, which in turn (the theory goes) reinforced awareness of lineage. From the last decades of the tenth century on, a family's most important properties – above all, the castles and lands to support them   came to be conceived of as a single unit, the patrimony, which was not divisible among heirs as in the past, but had to be passed down intact to the next generation. Increasingly, members of the military elite tended to think of themselves as part of a dynasty, which held the same territory over time, rather than as part of an extended clan. A key indicator of this shift, according to the "mutationists," was the growing tendency for individuals to identify themselves by the name of the territory that formed their patrimony.

The theory just outlined has recently been attacked on multiple fronts. One issue is regional differences. One would not expect a model based primarily on German and French sources to work as well, or indeed at all, in other regions. And, in fact, we see very different trajectories in places where different conditions prevailed.[3] It has also become apparent that if a change did take place in the family, it was neither abrupt nor complete. Recent research has shown that signs of what might be called "patrilineal consciousness" can be detected already in the Carolingian period, while dependence upon extended kin persisted into the later Middle Ages.[4] Nevertheless, the core of the "Schmid thesis" has not been completely undermined. It still seems probable that in many (not all) parts of continental Europe, maintaining an undivided patrimony was becoming increasingly important during the central Middle Ages – perhaps to the highest nobility around the turn of the tenth century, but certainly to most members of the military elite by the year 1000.[5] Even if a variety of strategies were devised in different parts of Europe

---

[3] On Italy, for example, see Violante (1977), esp. pp. 118–22; Sergi (1993); on England, see Christelow (1996); Wareham (2001); Crouch (2006), pp. 116–21, 204–5.
[4] White (1988), pp. 86–129; Bouchard (2001), esp. pp. 3–4.
[5] Régine Le Jan has pushed back the formation of what she calls "topolineages" to the beginning of the tenth century, for families holding important *honores*: Le Jan (1995), pp. 414–27, and (2000), pp. 58–61

to protect the patrimony's integrity,[6] it still seems likely that "patrilineal consciousness" was reinforced, if not created, by the move towards impartible inheritance.

Where they occurred, these changes certainly had an impact on marriage and on the position of women in the family. The "mutationists" argue that a wife who failed to provide her husband with a male heir could expect to be badly treated, even shunted aside for a more fertile mate. The heir himself would be obliged to marry for the political advantage of his lineage, regardless of the moral issues this might raise.[7] And, of course, the concentration of a family's resources in the hands of the eldest son meant that little was left for the younger sons or the daughters of a house to inherit. Younger sons who chose not to live off their eldest brother's bounty would have to leave home to seek their fortunes. The violent behavior of these young adventurers often included the rape of heiresses (who could provide these young men with the means for starting their own household) or of any vulnerable female.[8] Meanwhile, their sisters might be denied even minimal inheritance rights, or be married off for purely political advantage.[9]

Many historians now dispute the "mutationist" claim that the move towards impartible inheritance immediately disinherited women. And indeed, the evidence does suggest that women continued to exercise considerable control over property and to wield substantial authority both within and outside the household through the eleventh century and well into the twelfth.[10] Indeed, the political authority of some privileged women may even have grown as their families consolidated power.[11] Nevertheless, even elite women remained susceptible to abuse – to marriage without their consent, to repudiation, and even to rape.[12] And it seems plausible that the political pressure associated with the spread of castles made divorce and adultery, abduction and incest, more common around the turn of the millennium. Increased clerical concern about marriage was probably sparked – at least in part – by an upsurge in behaviors forbidden by ecclesiastical legislation.

Efforts to reform marriage were complicated by the fact that no clear set of sexual norms, no single, widely agreed-upon model of marriage,

---

[6] E.g., Aurell (1995), pp. 44–51; Drell (2002), p. 117.

[7] Aurell (1995), p. 13, on "pitiless" family strategies.

[8] E.g. Orderic, 8.25, vol. 4: 302–3, on the younger sons of Roger of Montgomery. On such "youths," see Duby (1964), focusing on the twelfth century.

[9] E.g. McNamara and Wemple (1973); Duby (1981), pp. 99–100.

[10] See below, Chapter 3.

[11] The well-documented cases of the countesses of Barcelona, of Adela of Blois, and of Matilda of Tuscany are important here. On the first two, see Chapter 3 below.

[12] E.g. Thietmar, 7.45, p. 453; trans. Warner, p. 338; *Briefsammlungen*, p. 24; Orderic, 8.24, vol. 4: 300–1; and see below, on the sad life of Godelieve of Ghistelle.

either lay or clerical, existed in this period.[13] The way layfolk arranged unions for members of their families varied tremendously between classes and regions. The instructions clerics gave to layfolk also varied tremendously. Early medieval canon law did not provide entirely consistent answers to some key questions concerning marriage, as we shall see. As a result, even canonists sometimes disagreed amongst themselves about what was necessary and proper. We should bear in mind as well that the vast majority of clerics – including many bishops – still knew little about canon law, at least in the early part of the eleventh century. Their ideas about marriage were more powerfully shaped by local practice, and by the concerns – about status, wealth, and honor – that shaped their own families' marriage strategies. Small wonder, then, that many aspects of marriage were hotly debated in the eleventh and early twelfth centuries. Nevertheless, almost everyone, lay and clerical, also shared at least some common ground when it came to marriage. It may be as well to begin with these commonalities, before we consider the areas of sexual behavior under dispute.

Making a marriage

A treatise on betrothal and marriage, written in Old English sometime in the late tenth or early eleventh century, lays out the following steps for making a valid marriage: after a man has chosen the woman he wants to marry, and if she and her kinsmen agree, the prospective bridegroom should, "according to God's law and proper secular custom," declare that he wants to marry her and that he will maintain her "as a man should maintain his wife." Then arrangements should be made for remuneration to be paid to those who raised the bride, for a gift to be made to the bride "for her acceptance of his suit," and for her widow's portion – all of these to be confirmed with pledges and sureties. (The widow's portion is to be larger if she bears him children.) After the property transfers are agreed upon, her kinsmen should formally betroth her, and "he who is the leader of the betrothal is to receive the security." Special arrangements have to be made to protect the bride and others if the marriage should take her away from the territory of her own *thegn* or lord. At the marriage proper, "there should by rights be a priest, who shall unite them together with God's blessing in all prosperity." Almost as an afterthought, the anonymous English cleric who wrote the treatise

---

[13] Duby's (1981) thesis about the conflict between "lay" and "clerical" models of marriage has been questioned on precisely these grounds: Aurell (1995), p. 15; Bouchard (2001), p. 43.

notes, "it is also well to take care that one knows that they are not too closely related."[14]

At the very end of the eleventh century, an Italian bishop, Bonizo of Sutri, offered another description of the elements in a valid marriage in his *Book on the Christian Life*, a collection of canon law texts with comments added by Bonizo himself. An ardent reformer, Bonizo begins his account with a discussion of the canonical impediments to marriage, including being too closely related. Only then did he list the other requirements for a valid marriage: the bride and groom must give their consent, then she must be given away by her parents or guardians, she must be properly endowed with wealth in writing (*dotata tabulis*), blessed by a priest, and – accompanied by her attendants – handed over by him to her husband. The two partners should then abstain for the appropriate number of days from intercourse, and only then consummate the marriage.[15]

These two works, written at the two ends of the eleventh century, and at the northern and southern edges of Europe, differ from one another in several important respects. Property arrangements not only figure more prominently in the English account, but they also seem unlike those Bonizo describes in Italy. In England, the bride's family is remunerated for her upbringing, and the bride herself receives a gift for consenting to the marriage, apparently in addition to whatever widow's portion she is promised. But in Italy, only the *dos*, or widow's portion, is mentioned.[16] Impediments to marriage and the issue of consent concern Bonizo much more than the English author. Bonizo also stresses sexual abstinence immediately after the marriage ceremony, while his English counterpart makes no mention of such a custom. In the end, though, both authors basically agree on what constitutes a valid marriage.

Both works emphasize the ceremony of betrothal, during which the bride's kin, those in whose *mundium* she lies, must consent to the union. According to a widely cited text from Pseudo-Isidore, "a marriage cannot otherwise be legitimate unless the wife is sought from those who have lordship over the woman and by whom she is protected."[17] This principle

---

[14] "Concerning the Betrothal of a Woman," trans. Whitelock, in *English Historical Documents, Volume 1: ca. 500–1042*, p. 431. On elite English marriages in this period, see Stafford (1981) and (1997), pp. 66–75.

[15] Bonizo of Sutri, *Liber de vita christiana*, 8.11, pp. 256–57. On this work, see Berschin (1972), pp. 57–75.

[16] Perhaps further evidence for the decline of the *Morgengab* in Italy by this time; see below, Chapter 3.

[17] Projekt Pseudoisidor, Teil I, 1. Evaristus-Brief, p. 139. Available at http://www.pseudoisidor. de/pdf/015_Evaristus_Consulentibus_vobis.pdf. Cited in *Diversorum sententiae patrum*, 271,

held good throughout Europe, in both secular and canon law, and at all social levels (at least those accessible to us through written records). Under these circumstances, the crime of rape was understood, again in both secular and canon law, not as a sexual violation, but as a crime against the parent or guardian's rights.[18] When Margrave Ekkehard changed his mind about his daughter Liutgard's betrothal to Werner, son of another German noble, Werner seized his former fiancée by force from her guardian, Abbess Matilda of Quedlinburg, and carried her off. Rape always created legal problems, the most important being: could the abductor legally marry the woman he had abducted? Secular customs varied, and canon law was inconclusive on this point.[19] Generally, marriage was allowed – so long as the woman's parent or guardian eventually consented. Some canonists, however, explicitly forbade a rapist to marry the woman he had abducted. Werner's case was particularly complex, of course, because the couple had at one point been properly betrothed. In the end, a church council had to be summoned to resolve the issue. It established that Liutgard was willing to remain with Werner. Then the young man was allowed to perform public penance and pay compensation for his crime, and Liutgard was finally allowed to become his wife.[20]

Fathers, mothers, or guardians arranged the betrothal of minor sons as well as daughters, while even grown men often sought parental permission when they contracted their marriages.[21] If parents did not normally allow their children a free choice of marriage partner, and if children generally deferred to their parents' wishes in this matter, it was because marriage was so important to the well-being of the family as a whole, involving crucial political or economic alliances and sometimes major transfers of property.[22] Indeed, lords sometimes intervened for the same reasons, in order to protect their interests.

It was during the betrothal that property arrangements between the soon-to-be allied families (and sometimes their lords as well) were arranged. As both the Anglo-Saxon author and Bonizo of Sutri agreed, this was the moment when the groom promised to endow his wife with

---

pp. 164–65; Ivo of Chartres, *Decretum* 8.4 (PL 161: 584). On marriage in Pseudo-Evaristus, see Reynolds (1994), pp. 391–92.

[18] Brundage (1987), pp. 209–10; Reynolds (1994), pp. 394–401; but see now Hough (1997), Virtue (1998).

[19] Reynolds (1994), pp. 101–8, 394–401. Ivo of Chartres, *Epistolae*, 16 (1094), ed. Leclercq, pp. 64–77, provides evidence of continued confusion on this point.

[20] Thietmar, 4.40–42, pp. 177–80; trans. Warner, pp. 180–81; and see Corbet (1990), pp. 193–96.

[21] E.g. *Ruodlieb*, 14 and 16, pp. 162–67 and 176–79. Compare Aurell (1995), pp. 12–13, 314–15; Drell (2002), pp. 61–65. And see below, Chapters 3 and 5.

[22] E.g. Geoffrey Malaterra, *De rebus gestis Rogerii*, 3.23, pp. 71–72. On royal marriage negotiations, see also Stafford (1983), pp. 32–59.

material wealth. This endowment might take the form of dower or "morning gift" (*Morgengab*), but the purpose was the same: to provide her with support in case of widowhood.[23] Secular law agreed with canon law on this point: a bride had to be properly "endowed": *nullum sine dote fiat conjugium*.[24] Indeed, the lack of such an endowment may have marked the difference between legitimate marriage (*coniugium*) and concubinage (*contubernium*).[25] The other aspects of these financial arrangements, however, varied greatly from place to place. Although neither author mentions it, in some places dowries were beginning to be offered to the new husband by the bride's family during the betrothal ceremony.[26] Elsewhere, something resembling bride-price, or at least some form of remuneration, was transferred from the groom's family to those who had raised the bride.[27] The exact nature of these property transfers was shaped by local custom, by the relative desirability of various candidates for marriage, and by changing political, social, and economic circumstances. But no valid marriage could be concluded without some exchange of goods.

In many parts of Christian Europe during the eleventh and early twelfth centuries, then, there was agreement about at least some of the key elements in marriage. The kin should give consent and property should be exchanged formally and publicly.[28] If possible, a priest should bless the new couple. And, normally, sexual intercourse and children should follow. Nevertheless, there remained considerable disagreement about many aspects of marriage, which led both to theoretical disputes and to heated quarrels over the validity of particular unions. The rest of this chapter examines the theological meaning of marriage, and reviews some of the major controversies related to marriage, and to sexual relationships more broadly, during the eleventh and early twelfth centuries. My intent is twofold: first, simply to remind readers of the general shape of the debates and of their development over time; and second, to examine more closely the rhetoric surrounding the effort to reform marriage – the images, ideas, and emotions associated with various controversial sexual practices – in preparation for the arguments developed in Chapter 2.

Marriage in theology and canon law

While medieval clerics praised virginity most highly, none but the most radical denied the value of marriage for ordinary people.[29] Church

---

[23] Feller (2002).   [24] Corbet (2002).   [25] Reynolds (1994), p. 117.

[26] Hughes (1978). Knowing that their father's estate would be mostly reserved for male heirs, young women saved their own dowries: Peter Damian, 94 and 104, vol. 3: 36–37 and 148; trans. Blum, 4: 39 and 152.

[27] Feller (2002), pp. 6–10.   [28] Reynolds (1994), pp. 401–12.

[29] On the outright rejection of marriage in this period, see Lambert (2002), pp. 22–23, 25, 29, 35.

leaders taught that God had ordained marriage from the time of the creation, which made it inherently good.[30] The fact that Christ was personally present at the wedding at Cana (John 2:1–11) represented further proof that marriage was a blessed state.[31] Its benefits, as delineated by St. Augustine (whose views on the subject profoundly shaped those of medieval thinkers), were threefold: offspring, mutual fidelity, and "sacrament."[32] Marriage allowed for the lawful and orderly generation of children, who not only delighted their parents and provided them with security in old age, but also allowed them to fulfill God's command to "be fruitful and multiply."[33] Marriage prevented fornication, by channeling sexual energy into an acceptable course. Under the appropriate circumstances and with the appropriate intentions, husband and wife could lawfully engage in sexual relations, thus preventing their "unruly members" from drawing them into forbidden activities.[34] Moreover, through intercourse, man and woman became, quite literally, "one flesh," re-creating Adam's original relationship with his wife, Eve, formed from his rib. The peculiar circumstances of Eve's creation were explained specifically in terms of marital affection. "Why did [God form her from Adam's rib]," asked Rupert of Deutz, "if not to show that the love of one's only wife should be firm and indissoluble?"[35] Physical unity between husband and wife forged a bond of fidelity and love stronger (at least in principle) than any other earthly bond.[36] Hence the assumption that a wife would be her husband's most reliable adviser and helper.[37]

The ideal of marital love had an even deeper theological significance, however. Discussing Genesis 2:24: "'For this reason a man shall leave his father and mother and be joined to his wife, and the two shall become one flesh," St. Paul had written, "This is a great mystery [*sacramentum*], but I speak concerning Christ and the Church" (Ephesians 5: 31–32). On Paul's authority, marriage came to be identified as a *sacramentum* in medieval

---

[30] E.g. Rather of Verona, *Praeloquiorum libri VI*, 2.8, p. 53; trans. Reid, p. 71. It is not clear whether this message was publicly preached: see D'Avray (2005), pp. 20–37.

[31] *Recueil des chartes de l'abbaye de Cluny*, 2265, vol. 3: 396; cf. Anselm of Laon, *Sententie*, 10, p. 129.

[32] Augustine, *De nuptiis et concupiscentia*, 1.17 (PL 44: 424). For Augustine's views on sexuality and marriage, see Schmitt (1983); Brown (1988), pp. 387–427; Reynolds (1994), pp. 241–311.

[33] Rouche (2006), pp. 389–99. The importance of procreation, as well as mutual love, in marriage is apparent in a layman's letter to Rome: *Briefsammlungen*, p. 24.

[34] See Brundage (1987), pp. 154–64.

[35] Rupert of Deutz, *De sancta Trinitate et operibus suis, In Genesim*, 2.34, vol. 21: 228.

[36] The prayer *Deus qui in conditione humani generis* describes the affection arising out of this "unity of the flesh": *Sacramentarium Fuldense*, p. 324.

[37] Farmer (1986); and see Eadmer, *Vita sancti Anselmi*, 1.31, pp. 55–57. So ingrained was this assumption that when a man did *not* seek his wife's advice, the situation was worthy of comment: *Liber miraculorum*, Appendix, L3, p. 281; trans. Sheingorn, p. 247.

theology and liturgy.[38] Exactly what medieval writers meant by the word
in this context has been the subject of some scholarly debate, [39] but there is
no doubt that in the eleventh and early twelfth centuries, most of the clergy
(and even, perhaps, some of the more sophisticated members of the laity)
believed that earthly marriage mirrored the true, celestial union of Christ
and the Church. As one thinker put it, "when God first joined the woman,
formed from the man's rib, to the man, he figured the Church, formed
from the side of Christ on the cross, being joined to Him."[40]

But the proper way to translate this understanding into practice was
not always clear. Take, for example, the issue of sexual intercourse. In the
ninth century, Archbishop Hincmar of Reims had stated that "the true
union of legitimate marriage occurs when, between free persons of equal
rank, and with paternal consent, a free woman who has been legitimately
endowed and honoured by public nuptials is joined to a man by sexual
intercourse. It is then that marriage contains the sacrament of Christ
and the Church and that the woman, in whom it is proved that there has
been both sexual union and the nuptial mystery, is known to attain to
matrimony."[41] Apparently, for Hincmar, sex was what finalized the union
that figured Christ's "marriage" to the Church.

In the eleventh century, as well, conjugal unity was often linked with
the act of sexual intercourse. A scholar from Reims, for example, emphasized the role of coitus in the creation of "one flesh." Indeed, to demonstrate the "force of this joining, in which husband and wife marvelously
[*mirabiliter*] move into a unity of flesh," he referred to what physicians
had told him – that if you took blood from a man and a woman who had
had sexual intercourse, and placed it in a container, it would become
indivisibly mixed, whereas if you took blood from a couple who had *not*
had intercourse, and placed it in a container, the two portions of blood
would remain separate.[42] The bond created by sex was thus not simply metaphorical; it was manifested in the very physiology of the two

---

[38] E.g. Anselm of Laon, *Sententie*, 10, p. 129; Hildebert of Le Mans, *Sermo in Carnotensi
concilio* (PL 171: 956); and see the nuptial blessing *Deus qui potestate virtutis tuae* cited
from the Gregorian sacramentary by Reynolds (1994), p. 379. This identification is discussed at greater length below, in Chapter 2.

[39] Godefroy (1926), cols. 2105–09; Le Bras (1926), cols. 2196–2220, 2229–47; Reynolds
(1994), pp. 280–311, on marriage as *sacramentum* in Augustine. But see Toubert (1977),
pp. 268–80; Rouche (1987).

[40] Bruno of Reims (?), *Expositio in epistolas Pauli*, 1 Corinthians 7 (PL 153: 156). Landgraf
believed that this work was not Bruno's, but that it might be that of someone associated
with him: Landgraf (1938), pp. 573–79, 588–90; cf. Williams (1954), pp. 665–69.

[41] Hincmar of Reims, *Epistolae*, 136, MGH, EPP 8: 93.

[42] Bruno of Reims (?), *Expositio in epistolas Pauli*, Ephesians 5 (PL 153: 346). On the relationship between physical union and marital loyalty, see Guibert of Nogent, *De vita sua*,
1.13, pp. 94–96; trans. Benton, p. 72.

partners involved.[43] And because of this, impotence – the inability to consummate a marriage – might be grounds for its annulment.[44]

Yet from the eleventh century on, a small but slowly increasing number of clerics rejected this belief. How could a sacrament depend on what was (for many) an unseemly and dishonorable physical act?[45]

> If they maintain that marriage rests on intercourse, then how is it that the holy canons forbid people to be joined in marriage without public weddings? Do they want the man to mount his wife in public? ... If indeed marriage is made by coitus, then every time a man makes love to his wife no doubt they get married all over again.[46]

An emphasis on coitus also brought into question the legitimacy of the supposedly exemplary marriage between St. Joseph and Mary, perpetually a virgin.[47] By the middle of the eleventh century, some (by no means all) reformers were beginning to see consent, rather than coition, as the essential element in marriage.[48] Some even promoted the idea of "spiritual marriage" – a chaste union more perfect than ordinary marriage.[49]

Those who emphasized consent assumed that a young woman would normally comply with her father's wishes – so that her explicit consent was not required for a valid marriage. However, they also recognized the possibility that she might, under extraordinary circumstances, reject her father's choice of husband.[50] If her objections were reasonable, they had to be respected.[51] Other clerics, including some avid reformers, however, continued to focus on the right of parents, guardians, and lords to make decisions on behalf of those under their *mundium*. Bonizo of

---

[43] On the implications of this belief for the practice of prostitution, see below.

[44] Brundage (1987), pp. 200–3; cf. Burchard, *Decretum*, 19.5 (PL 140: 967); Bonizo of Sutri, *Liber de vita christiana*, 8.11 and 8. 41–45, pp. 256–57 and 264–65; Ivo, *Decretum*, 8.79 and 8.178 (PL 161: 600 and 621). Guibert of Nogent, *De vita sua*, 1.12, p. 76; trans. Benton, p. 64; and see Duby (1981), pp. 141–42.

[45] On marital sex as incompatible with the holy, see *Liber miraculorum*, 1.27, p. 132; trans. Sheingorn, p. 97; *Briefsammlungen*, p. 134.

[46] Peter Damian, 172, vol. 4: 259; this livelier translation by Brundage (1987), p. 189, but see Blum, 6(7): 256.

[47] Peter Damian, 172, vol. 4: 261; trans. Blum 6 (7): 259. On this theme, see Gold (1982); Resnick (2000).

[48] The idea that consent was the sole criterion for a valid marriage had already been broached in the ninth century by Pope Nicholas I, at the time swimming against the tide: Reynolds (1994), pp. 409–10. Progress on this point was slow, despite the growing influence in the eleventh century of Roman law (which also emphasized consent): see Aurell (1995), pp. 306–8.

[49] This model may have been picked up and put into practice by a few couples in this period; it was certainly attributed to certain saintly layfolk by hagiographers: Elliott (1993), pp. 94–131.

[50] Ivo of Chartres, *Decretum* 8.21 (PL 161: 588).

[51] Hariulf of Oldeburg and Lisiard of Soissons, *Vita sancti Arnulfi episcopi Suessionensis*, 1.28, *AASS*, III Aug. (August 15), col. 241.

Sutri mentioned the consent of the bride and groom as one among many elements required for a valid marriage, but Burchard of Worms, Anselm of Lucca, and the anonymous author of the *Collection in Seventy-Four Titles* ignored it completely. In practice, most minor children, male or female, and many adult women as well probably had little say in the matter, and some must have been dragged unwillingly into very unhappy situations.[52]

Clerics also disagreed, surprisingly, on the role of priests in making a valid marriage. By the turn of the millennium, the nuptial blessing was certainly an important part of marriage – often referred to in narrative sources, and treated as essential in all the major canonical collections.[53] In the final part of his *Decretum*, Burchard of Worms provided a list of questions for parish priests to ask their parishioners. One of them was "Have you taken a wife, and not married publicly? Did you and your wife fail to come to church and receive a blessing from the priest, as required by the canons?"[54] If the answer was yes, then penance had to be performed. Fees paid for nuptial blessings were sometimes listed among the revenues of parish churches in this period, suggesting that the clergy regularly played a part in the ceremonies of marriage, even among the lower classes.[55] Their presence was, as Burchard's text suggests, part of what made a marriage "public" and thus legitimate. Nevertheless, a marriage carried out "without benefit of clergy" was still generally considered valid.[56] Indeed, many canonists, while they recognized the legitimacy of second (and maybe even third) marriages, actually forbade clerical participation in them.[57] Second marriages were, then, of necessity often instituted without a priest, although this rule was apparently waived in the case of kings and other powerful members of society, who wanted very public ecclesiastical approval for all of their unions.[58]

During the eleventh century, the canons of earlier church councils, and the letters of earlier theologians and popes concerning matters of ecclesiastical discipline, came to be more widely disseminated than ever before, through the compilations of scholars such as Burchard of Worms, Ivo of Chartres, Anselm of Lucca, and Bonizo of Sutri. The revival of

---

[52] Brundage (1987), pp. 187–88. Consider the daughter forced to marry her father's captor as part of his ransom: Orderic, 8.11, vol. 4: 202–03.

[53] Despite the fact that a priestly blessing was first described as necessary in the ninth century: Reynolds (1994), pp. 402–03. On the liturgy of marriage in Catalonia, see Aurell (1995), pp. 320–24.

[54] Burchard of Worms, *Decretum*, 19.5 (PL 140: 958).

[55] E.g. *Cartulaire de l'abbaye cardinale de la Trinité de Vendôme*, 80, vol. 1: 150–51.

[56] Brundage (1987), pp. 190–91.

[57] Brundage (1987), p. 196; Reynolds (1994), p. 384; D'Avray (2005), pp. 141–44.

[58] E.g. the second marriage of King Henry I of France to Anne of Kiev, celebrated in Reims cathedral in 1051 (see below, Chapter 2).

canon law was undoubtedly a major factor behind the effort to reform marriage. However, if we compare the various canonical collections, it becomes clear how many significant questions related to marriage – such as whether sexual intercourse, consent, or the presence of a priest was required for a valid union – remained unresolved.

And even when everyone agreed that the proper procedures had been followed, could certain unions ever be considered true marriages? Pope Leo I, in an often-cited letter to Bishop Rusticus of Narbonne, had declared,

Not every woman joined to a man is the man's wife, as not every son is the heir of his father. The bonds of marriage are valid among the free-born and among equals. The Lord decided this very matter long before Roman law began. And so, a wife is one thing, a concubine is another, just as a slave girl is different from a free woman. For that reason, also, in order to clarify the difference between these two persons, the Apostle sets forth testimony from Genesis, where it is said to Abraham: "Cast out this bondwoman and her son, for the son of the bondwoman shall not be heir with my son Isaac" [Genesis 21:10; cf. Galatian: 4:30].[59]

The "nuptial mystery" that made earthly marriage a sacrament was lacking in unequal unions. In an age of increasing social mobility, like the eleventh and early twelfth centuries, marriages between the servile and the free were both common and controversial, because the offspring of such unions might claim freedom for themselves.[60] Lords often tried to prevent or to disrupt such marriages, sometimes supported by experts in canon law. Bishop Ivo of Chartres, for example, personally dissolved unions between serfs and freemen, justifying his action by asserting that they were not real marriages, but simply a form of concubinage (*contubernium*).[61] Pope Leo's authoritative statement was applied to other situations of inequality as well. Bonizo of Sutri used it to deny the validity of marriages between Christians and Jews or pagans, or between catholics and heretics, as well as between an abducted woman and her abductor.[62] No matter whether the kin consented, property was exchanged, priestly blessings were offered, and sexual intercourse followed: such relationships always remained illegitimate. And the same was true, as reformers

---

[59] Leo I, *Epistolae*, 167 (PL 54: 1204–05) = JL 544; trans. Hunt, pp. 292–93. Cited by Burchard of Worms, *Decretum*, 9.1 (PL 140: 815); Bonizo of Sutri, *Liber de vita christiana*, 8.12–13, pp. 257–58; Ivo of Chartres, *Decretum* 8.139 (PL 161: 615). On Leo's letter, see Reynolds (1994), pp. 38–39, 162–69.

[60] *Concilium Ticinense* (Pavia) (1022), Mansi 19: 343–56. On this synod, see Denzler (1973), pp. 47 ff.; Herrmann (1973), pp. 10–15, 36 ff.; Schimmelpfennig (1978). The opposite might also be true – the free partner might lose status: e.g. *Liber miraculorum* 3.17, pp. 206–7; trans. Sheingorn, p. 167.

[61] Ivo of Chartres, *Epistolae*, 242 (PL 162: 249–50). On such marriages, see also Sheehan (1988).

[62] Bonizo of Sutri, *Liber de vita christiana*, 8.11, pp. 256–57.

were eager to point out, of sexual relationships between relatives, and those involving clerics in higher orders.

Incest

"Incestuous" marriages had become increasingly common during the early Middle Ages, and the clergy themselves were largely to blame. Gradually, over the course of the period from the seventh to eleventh centuries, regional churches had been moving from a ban on marriage within four degrees of kinship (the number used in Roman law) to a ban on marriage within seven degrees.[63] The change was still far from complete in the eleventh century, which meant that reformers had to argue the case for seven degrees against those who had custom (and often authoritative legal texts as well) on their side.[64] To add to the confusion, the method of calculating degrees of relationship was also in transition. Instead of counting the generations up from one potential spouse to the common ancestor and then back down to the other potential spouse (so that relatives within "four degrees" were first cousins), it became increasingly common to count only the generations up, thus greatly increasing the number of generations within which marriage was forbidden. Constance Bouchard has neatly summarized the drastic consequences of the new rules: "These changes in the number of forbidden degrees and the method calculating them meant that the number of unions considered incestuous increased exponentially; for every increase of one forbidden degree, the number of ancestors a potential couple might share more than doubled."[65]

A further bewildering feature of early medieval incest legislation was the ban on marriage with affines (those related by marriage or indeed by any sexual union) and with spiritual kin. Not only blood relatives, but also their widows or widowers, within the forbidden degrees, along with godparents and baptismal co-sponsors, were all off-limits.[66] A council held in England during the reign of Aethelraed, for example, excluded weddings between relatives within four degrees (the rule of seven was apparently not yet in force in the English kingdom), with wives of dead kinsmen and with godmothers, as well as with nuns and women who had been repudiated by their husbands.[67]

Having tightened the rules on consanguinity, it remained for reforming clerics to enforce them. Dissemination of the rules, presumably

---

[63] See now Corbet (2001).   [64] E.g. Peter Damian, 19, vol. 1: 181; trans. Blum 1: 173.
[65] Bouchard (1981a), p. 270.   [66] Lynch (1986).
[67] *Concilium Aenhamense* (Enham) (1008), Mansi 19: 300.

accompanied by penalties, does seem to have had some effect. By the late tenth and the eleventh centuries, Bouchard has argued, some noble families were modifying their marriage strategies to escape charges of incest. They avoided some politically advantageous marriages, even falling back on marriages with people of lower rank. Encouraged by reformers, the head of a family might have a genealogy drawn up to determine whether he or his children were too closely related to a potential spouse.[68] But the effort to combat incest was far from completely successful. In the middle of the eleventh century, John of Fécamp complained to Pope Leo IX about Duke Robert I of Burgundy and Count Theobald (presumably Theobald III of Blois), who, having repudiated their lawful wives, entered into marriages that were "shameful and tainted by consanguinity."[69] Eleventh-century nobles may have been unlikely to marry first cousins; even marriages between second and third cousins were rare.[70] Yet unions between only slightly more distant relatives may have gone unnoticed, or seemed acceptable, even though they were illegal under the new rules. In his superb study of the marriages of the Counts of Barcelona, Martin Aurell has shown that while the extreme endogamy of the ninth-century counts had given way to unions between more distant kin by the tenth and eleventh centuries, the princely families of Catalonia were still marrying well within the forbidden degrees.[71]

The faithful may have wanted to do the right thing, but if the new rules for calculating consanguinity had been strictly followed, most of them would have been hard-pressed to find appropriate partners. The poor, and especially the peasantry, who lived in small villages and had limited mobility, had only a small range of potential spouses available anyway, and most of these were already related to them by blood, marriage, or spiritual affinity. The elite, on the other hand, had pressing political concerns (the need to create advantageous alliances) and considerations of rank, which they often allowed to trump the strictest laws of the church. As a result, two eleventh-century emperors entered into incestuous unions, despite clerical criticism.[72] And, notoriously, King Robert "the Pious"

---

[68] Bouchard (1981a), pp. 272–86. An example of lay concern about incest occurs in Peter Damian, 17, vol. 1: 165; trans. Blum, 1: 155.

[69] John of Fécamp, *Epistola ad Leonem IX* (PL 143: 799–800). Pope Leo was known for his efforts to combat incest within the nobility: see *Vita Leonis noni*, 2.10, p. 88; trans. Robinson, p. 137.

[70] Bouchard (1981a), p. 272.   [71] Aurell (1995), pp. 29–217.

[72] On Conrad II's marriage, see Raoul Glaber, 4.1, pp. 170–71; Wolfram (2000), pp. 35–36, 46–48; on Henry III's, see *De ordinando pontifice*, MGH, LL 1: 13; Thomas (1977); Parisse (2004b) (which includes a new edition of Siegfried of Gorze's letter to Poppo of Stablò about Henry's marriage).

of France had to be pressured by two successive popes before he finally agreed to separate from Bertha of Burgundy, *consanguineam suam*.[73]

So why did the Church place itself in the embarrassing situation of making rules even the well-intentioned could seldom follow? It has been argued that economic concerns lay behind the change in incest legislation. Jack Goody, in particular, noted that land donated to churches in this period was always subject to ongoing claims by relatives of the donor. Restricting networks of relationship through a drastically extended incest taboo would have helped to limit the number of potential claimants, thus safeguarding the Church's landholdings.[74] But if worldly concerns prompted the move to new rules on consanguinity, the rhetoric used to condemn incest in the eleventh and early twelfth centuries had little to do with wealth and property. It drew, instead, on the Old Testament language of pollution and impurity.

Reforming clerics sometimes distinguished between "carnal" Jewish and "spiritual" Christian attitudes on incest; but in fact, most of their arguments were rooted in Jewish law, as laid out in Leviticus 18, which forbids any sexual approach to those closely related by blood, any "uncovering" of their "nakedness" (*turpitudinem*).[75] In the language of the Old Testament, such actions constituted a "defilement," for which grievous punishment was promised (Leviticus 18:24–25, 29). In the eleventh and early twelfth centuries, incest – however defined – evoked images of shameful and intolerable pollution. Burchard of Worms opened Book 7 of his *Decretum* with a promise to explain why penance should be imposed on those "polluted by the sin of incest."[76] Another canonist, Ivo of Chartres, believed that the illicit marriage between Constance, daughter of the king of France, and Count Hugh of Troyes "polluted" the king's "most noble blood."[77]

Peter Damian uses words like "contagion," "leprosy," and "filth" to describe the sin of incest, and in several of his works he describes its disgusting results. After Robert the Pious married Bertha,

almost all the bishops of France unanimously excommunicated them, namely, the man and his wife. At this decision of the bishops, the people everywhere were so filled with terror, that no one would have anything to do with them,

---

[73] *Concilium Romanum* (998), Mansi 19: 225. On the marriages of Robert the Pious, see Duby (1981), pp. 75–85.
[74] Goody (1983), pp. 48–156, esp. pp. 134–46.
[75] On the Jewish/Christian distinction, see Pseudo-Anselm of Canterbury, *De nuptiis consanguineorum*, 2–3 (PL 158: 557–58).
[76] Burchard of Worms, *Decretum*, 7.1 (PL 140: 779). Cf. Oliba of Vich, *Epistolae*, 4 (PL 142: 602). On Oliba's letter, see Aurell (1995), pp. 298–300.
[77] Ivo of Chartres, *Epistolae*, 158 (PL 162: 164).

except two servant lads who stayed to provide their necessary food. But even these young men considered all the tableware from which the king ate or drank as loathsome, and threw it into the fire. At length, under such pressure, the king followed the good advice of his council, dissolved his incestuous relationship, and was legally married.[78]

In another story, an unnamed man, "degenerate in morals but distinguished by titles of greatness," married a close blood relative. He ignored the excommunication imposed on him, but "as a certain sign of divine anger, it happened that when bread from the nuptial table was thrown into the street for the dogs to eat, they refused to touch it."[79]

Peter Damian was an unusual character, perhaps more obsessed than most of his contemporaries with notions of pollution, but it nevertheless remains true that anxieties about purity and impurity, shaped primarily by Old Testament texts, were central to reformers' thinking about incest. Their efforts to combat consanguineous marriages were not, then, simply a matter of enforcing canon law; rather, they represent a drive for purity in Christian life. Another campaign, based on similar concerns about pollution and purity, and involving many of the same reformers, sought to impose celibacy on the clergy.[80]

Clerical marriage

Some scholars have seen clerical sexuality as a problem *sui generis* – related specifically to the ritual obligations of the clergy. They link renewed efforts during the eleventh century to enforce the ancient rules of clerical celibacy with developments in the realm of sacramental theology, which increasingly emphasized the real presence of Christ in the eucharist, and the need for those who handled His body to be "pure."[81] Without denying such a connection, other historians – in particular Pierre Toubert and R. I. Moore – have recognized the call for clerical celibacy and the demand for a reform of lay marriage as two sides of the same coin – both related to the changes in family structures and property regimes discussed above.[82]

---

[78] Peter Damian, 102, vol. 3: 132; trans. Blum 3: 136.
[79] Peter Damian, 57, vol. 2: 171–73; trans. Blum 2: 375.
[80] Within the massive literature on this subject, see esp. Brooke (1965); Boelens (1968); Denzler (1973); Rossetti (1977); Fornasari (1981); Barstow (1982); Frauenknecht (1997); *Medieval Purity and Piety*.
[81] Frauenknecht (1997), p. 3; Beaudette (1998), pp. 28–29; Jestice (1998), pp. 96–108; Cowdrey (1998b), pp. 282–83.
[82] Toubert (1973), vol. 1: 728–34; Moore (1980), pp. 61–64, and (1998), pp. 192–93. See also Miller (1993), pp. 46–56.

To put their subtle and complex arguments in rather crude terms: as impartible inheritance came into play among powerful families around the turn of the millennium, these families struck a deal with some of their younger sons. If they would enter a monastery or cathedral chapter, and remain "celibate" (that is to say, refrain from producing legitimate children who might have a claim on the patrimony), then the family, for its part, would transfer some of its property permanently to the religious community, supporting it and any future family members associated with it. This arrangement guaranteed younger sons – who might otherwise have been disinherited – a comfortable and honorable lifestyle, while preserving the core of its patrimony for a single heir. This explains why powerful families so often supported efforts to enforce the celibacy of the clergy. Some church leaders promoted those efforts, not so much on theological grounds, as because they realized that married clergy produced children, and children could make claims on their fathers' wealth. Some of the sons of priests might leave the church, taking what would otherwise have been ecclesiastical property with them. Celibacy was, then, of use in keeping the patrimonies of churches, as well as those of powerful families, intact. Some of the earliest eleventh-century legislation against clerical marriage explicitly refers to such economic considerations.[83]

New ideologies were also emerging in this period – in particular, the notion that society consisted of three "orders," each with its own function (working, fighting, or praying). Over the course of the eleventh century, as a result of the broad changes that were reshaping the secular world, as well as in response to specific political situations within the western church, there gradually emerged a new way of thinking about social categories that conflated monks and secular clerics into a single order of "pray-ers" (*oratores*) distinguished from the laity not only by ritual function, but also by a "common life" and the sexual purity that had earlier characterized monks.[84]

This is the social and cultural context within which the multifarious celibacy campaigns of the late tenth and early eleventh centuries unfolded. These were, at first, entirely local affairs. Individual bishops might decide to expel the wives of clerics from their cities;[85] regional synods might choose to impose penalties on married priests and their

---

[83] *Concilium Ticinense* (Pavia) (1022), Mansi 19: 343–56. And see Cushing (2005), p. 99.

[84] Duby (1978); Laudage (1984); Moore (1980) and (1998); Miller (1993), (1998), and (2003); Van Meter (1998).

[85] E.g. Adam of Bremen, *Gesta Hammaburgensis ecclesiae pontificum*, 2.61, Schol. 43, MGH SS 7, 328; trans. Tschan, p. 139. See also Miller (1993), p. 161, on Rather of Verona's campaign against married priests.

wives and children.[86] Popes and emperors were sometimes involved, but before the middle of the eleventh century there was certainly no central direction for these efforts. Only after Henry III's introduction of his own, "reforming" candidates into the see of Rome after 1046 did the papacy began to use its authority actively to promote clerical celibacy.[87] The popes of the second half of the eleventh century not only supported local efforts against what came to be called "nicolaitism," but increasingly demanded that local leaders make such efforts, whether they wanted to or not. Indeed, in 1078, Gregory VII's autumn synod in Rome decreed,

If any bishop shall, with pleas or money intervening, tolerate the fornication of priests, deacons, and subdeacons, or the crime of incest in his jurisdiction, or if he does not assail them with the authority of his office as committed and made known to him, let him be suspended from office.[88]

New techniques were developed in Rome to put pressure on individual clerics: organized lay boycotts of the rituals they performed, and penalties directed against their wives and children.[89]

If such stringent measures were necessary, it was because so many people rejected the demand for clerical celibacy.[90] Conservative religious leaders generally agreed with reformers that celibacy was the best way of life, but they argued that complete abstinence was a virtue granted only to a few individuals; most members of the clergy needed marriage as a sexual outlet, without which they might fall into the "ruin of turpitude."[91] Marriage was an honorable estate – those who said it made the clergy "impure" were denigrating an institution ordained by God. Sometimes clerical marriage was justified with texts from canon law and from Scripture – especially references to the Old Testament priesthood (Leviticus 21:7) and to 1 Timothy 3:2: "A bishop then must be blameless,

---

[86] *Concilium Bituricense* (Bourges) (1031), Mansi, 19: 503–5; "King Ethelred's Code of 1008," and "Extracts from King Ethelred's 1014 Code," trans. Whitelock, in *English Historical Documents, Volume 1: ca. 500–1042*, pp. 406, 413; but compare the "Law of the Northumbrian Priests," 35, *English Historical Documents*, p. 437.

[87] Benedict VIII's legislation at the synod of Pavia against married priests from unfree backgrounds seems to have been a response to a specific situation in Germany and Italy, rather than a general statement of papal policy against clerical marriage: *Concilium Ticinense* (1022), Mansi 19: 343–56. See Laudage (1984), pp. 84–87.

[88] Gregory VII, *Register*, 6.5b, can. 12/28, pp. 405–6; trans. Cowdrey, p. 285.

[89] On the boycotts, see Blumenthal (1998), pp. 242–53; Cowdrey (1998b), pp. 277–80. On priests' sons, see Schimmelpfennig (1978); as yet there is no serious study of the treatment of priests' wives in this period.

[90] The best introduction to the pro-marriage arguments, along with an edition of the relevant texts, can be found in Frauenknecht (1997); see also Barstow (1982), pp. 105–73.

[91] Norman Anonymous, J. 25, p. 206; cf. *Rescriptio beati Udelrici episcopi*, in Frauenknecht (1997), pg. 205.

the husband of one wife."[92] However, it was most often defended simply as established custom. Attempts to eliminate it entirely – and especially the drastic methods adopted by the proponents of celibacy in the second half of the eleventh century – were seen as pernicious innovations, undermining the proper order of society.[93] In many places fierce debate – even violence – met the reformers' efforts.[94]

Hence the need for the reformers to make repeated arguments in favor of clerical celibacy. Some merely refuted their opponents' claims about canon law, or reinterpreted the same Biblical texts.[95] Others offered original arguments, based on their own citations from Scripture. The radical Milanese preacher Ariald asserted that "Christ ... sought and desired such purity in his ministers that he condemned the evil of debauchery not only in their works but also in their hearts, saying 'He who shall have looked lustfully at a woman has already copulated with her in his heart' [Matthew 5:28]."[96] A particularly important New Testament text for reform polemics was 1 Corinthians 6:15: "Do you not know that your bodies are the members of Christ? Shall I then take the members of Christ and make them the members of a harlot? God forbid!" Reformers argued that priests could not conclude a valid marriage, which meant that their wives must really be "concubines" or "whores."[97] But identifying priests' wives as whores also made it possible to equate them with the harlot of Paul's letter. Thus Gregory VII describes how "those who are called priests but are given over to fornication have no shame when singing mass to handle the body and blood of Christ, not heeding what madness or what a crime it is at one and the same time to touch the body of a harlot and the body of Christ ...".[98] The horror expressed in Paul's letter to the Corinthians is also palpable in a text such as this.

---

[92] E.g. Landulf of Milan, *Historia Mediolanensis*, 3.7, MGH SS 8: 78–79.

[93] Sigebert of Gembloux, *Apologia contra eos qui calumpniantur missas coniugatorum sacerdotum*, in Frauenknecht (1997), p. 231; Anonymous, *Tractatus pro clericorum conubio*, ibid. p. 265. And see Conclusion, below.

[94] Violent attacks might be directed against reforming bishops by the married clerics themselves (Orderic, 4 and 12.25, vol. 2: 200–01 and vol. 6: 290–95) or sometimes by their wives: e.g. Nicholas of Soissons, *Vita sancti Godefridi episcopi Ambianensi*, 2.8, *AASS*, Nov. III (November 8), col. 920.

[95] Bernold of St. Blasien, *Libelli*, 1, MGH, LL 2: 7–26.

[96] Andrew of Strumi, *Vita sancti Arialdi*, 4, MGH SS 30.2: 1052. Cf. Peter Damian, 61 and 112, vol. 2: 206–18, and vol. 3: 258–88; trans. Blum 3: 3–13, and 4: 258–85; Gregory VII, *Register*, 2.67, p. 224; trans. Cowdrey, p. 161.

[97] Peter Damian informs the wives of priests that what they thought were valid marriages are actually illegitimate: 112, vol. 3: 282–83; trans. Blum, 5: 280. On the new tendency in the eleventh century to blame (and penalize) women for leading priests into sin, see McNamara (1994); Elliott (1999); Miller (2003.)

[98] Gregory VII, *Register*, 4.11, pp. 310–11; trans. Cowdrey, pp. 220–21. On Gregory's rhetoric, see Cowdrey (1998b), p. 282. Compare Peter Damian 61, vol. 2: 214; trans. Blum, 3: 9.

Both Biblical and canon law texts were employed to represent clerical marriages as filthy.[99] Such marriages could be associated with other sexual sins forbidden under the law of Moses – especially incest, because a married priest could be understood to be committing incest with his own spiritual daughter.[100] However, while both lay incest and clerical marriage were associated with impurity in reforming texts, the two sins carried distinct emotional charges. Disgust is the emotion most often evoked in discussions of lay incest, leading, as we have seen, to the shunning of incestuous couples. But in treatments of clerical marriage, fear of divine anger and of swift punishment predominate.

Writing in 1059, Peter Damian made a series of associations between the fires of lust, of hell, and of immediate divine punishment on earth, prefigured in the punishment of the sons of Aaron, Nadab and Abihu, who offered God "alien fire" and were destroyed by fire from heaven (Leviticus 10:1–2). Those "inflamed with the fire of carnal passion" who do not "fear to participate in the sacred mysteries" will "surely be devoured even now by the fire of God's vengeance.[101] In the early twelfth century, Honorius Augustodunensis similarly evoked Nadab and Abihu, along with other Old Testament figures, to emphasize the sacrilege of combining sexual activity with sacrifice. Of particular interest is his treatment of Uzzah, who was destroyed simply for touching the ark (2 Samuel 6:7), and the sons of Eli (1 Samuel 2:22–34; 4:17), killed for sleeping with women who "assembled at the door of the tabernacle of the congregation." To both of these stories Honorius added elements not mentioned in the Bible: Uzzah was destroyed not just for touching the ark, but because he had slept with his wife the night before, making him ritually impure; the sons of Eli were killed because they had slept with women "dedicated to God."[102] Destruction is associated not just with forbidden, but specifically with sacrilegious sex. The treatment of clerical marriage in reform polemics, then, combines imagery associated with incest with a new and intentionally terrifying emphasis on sacrilege, resulting in violent and sudden death. In the eyes of reformers, the Christian priest who profaned the sacred through his sexual activity could expect to be treated with the same severity as those Old Testament figures guilty of profaning the sacred. Indeed, Peter Damian includes in one of his letters the story

---

[99] E.g. Projekt Pseudoisidor, Teil 3, 2. Innocenz-Brief. Available at http://www.pseudoisidor. mgh.de/html/158.htm. cf. Bonizo of Sutri, *Liber de vita christiana*, 5.37, p. 187. On the rhetoric of clerical marriage, see Cushing (2005), pp. 120–25.

[100] Peter Damian, 61, vol. 2: 214–15; trans. Blum, 3: 10–11.

[101] Peter Damian, 61, vol. 2: 216; trans. Blum, 3: 11–12; cf. 112, vol. 3: 271 ; trans. Blum, 4: 269.

[102] Honorius Augustodunensis, *De offendiculo*, 19 and 47, MGH, LL 3: 44 and 54. On this work, see below, Conclusion.

of a priest struck dead on his wedding night, at the very moment when he reached orgasm.[103]

Sexual relations outside of marriage

Reformers strove to break up marriages involving priests or people too closely related to one another. They also attacked other, less formal sexual relationships, which often coexisted with marriage in the central Middle Ages. Reformers normally described the female partners in these relationships as "concubines" (*concubinae*), to distinguish them from legitimate "wives," but exactly what they meant by the word in any given text often remains unclear.[104] The "concubines" in our Latin sources engaged in a wide range of relationships, and may well have been identified with a number of different words in vernacular languages. In short, all medieval concubines were not equal, even though the modern historian often has trouble telling them apart.

Some appear to have been the more-or-less permanent sexual partners of men not in a position to marry, either because of their lack of social status or because of poverty.[105] Such relationships may have been important for younger sons of elite families, who were discouraged from marrying formally under the new regime of impartible inheritance – unless they could find an unattached heiress to wed. But this type of "concubinage" may also have been common among the poor, who lacked the wherewithal to "endow" wives or pay for nuptial blessings, and among serfs, who were, as we have seen, sometimes excluded from formal marriage entirely because of their unfree status.

The word *concubina* could also be used to describe the secondary wives of powerful men. Such men frequently had a number of more or less permanent sexual partners, with socially recognized status. Normally only one had been formally betrothed and endowed, and publicly handed over by her parents or guardians to her new husband. Others were "taken" less formally – and sometimes by force. Some of these relationships were short-term sexual liaisons, but others were permanent or semipermanent unions.[106] The women involved were of lower rank than the men, but they might still play an important social role, and their children occasionally even attained the same status as their fathers.

---

[103] Peter Damian, 112, vol. 3: 275–76; trans. Blum, 4: 274.

[104] On concubinage in canon law, see Kottje (1975); Brundage (1987), pp. 98–103, 117–18, 145, 183 . On the practice more generally, see Ross (1985); Esmyol (2002) – the latter focuses on the early Middle Ages.

[105] E.g. Dillard (1984), pp. 127–32, on the role of the *barragana* in the frontier regions of twelfth-century Spain.

[106] On royal concubinage in the early Middle Ages, see Stafford (1983), pp. 62–74.

The best documented examples come from tenth- and eleventh-century Normandy. The Norman dukes more or less openly practiced polygyny, contracting official, but (by design?) rarely fertile marriages with women from other exalted families, while simultaneously maintaining more productive unions "in the Danish manner" with women of lower rank. The duke of the next generation was often the son of one of these "concubines" or secondary wives. This was the case with Richard I, the son of William Longsword by Sprota. And of course William "the Bastard" (later "the Conqueror") was the son of Robert "the Devil's" (or "the Magnificent's") well-known mistress, Herleva of Falaise.[107]

It is not clear at what point the notion that marriage should be monogamous became widely accepted within lay society. In northern Europe, especially, the habit of taking multiple wives seems to have been ingrained and difficult to dislodge. As late as the early eleventh century, English reformers were still trying to convince the laity that a man could have only one wife: "By virtue of God's prohibition we forbid that any man shall have more wives than one; and she is to be legally betrothed and wedded."[108] Similarly, Adam of Bremen, writing in the late eleventh century, reported that many men in his part of Germany had more than one wife.[109] So many laymen had multiple sexual partners that Orderic Vitalis considered it worthy of note that Ansold of Maule was "content with lawful marriage."[110]

And many clerics simply accepted this. Narrative sources from the central Middle Ages written by monks or secular clerics contain many references to the sons and daughters of powerful men "by a concubine."[111] Tellingly, the authors usually refer to these individuals and their mothers without comment, suggesting an acceptance of concubinage as a social reality. Efforts to combat concubinage were far less organized than movements against incest or clerical marriage. Relatively little legislation was directed against the practice, and its exact target is often difficult to identify. Reformers certainly criticized the multiple sexual liaisons of kings and noblemen, but the situation becomes murkier as we move farther

---

[107] Searle (1988), pp. 93–97 and 131–42.

[108] "The Law of the Northumbrian Priests," 61, trans. Whitelock, *English Historical Documents, Volume 1: ca. 500–1042*, p. 438. And see Ross (1985).

[109] Adam of Bremen, *Gesta episcoporum Hammaburgensis*, 3.55, MGH SS 7: 358; trans. Tschan, p. 163. Such men were criticized by Othlo of St. Emmeram, *Liber de cursu spirituali*, 16 (PL 146: 199), for living "like brute animals" (*more pecudum*). On the situation in Scandinavia, see Jochens (1987), p. 333.

[110] Orderic, 5.19, vol. 3: 180–83; cf. *Vita Aedwardi regis*, 1.5, p. 32, on Tostig's chastity.

[111] E.g. Raoul Glaber, 3.39, pp. 164–65; Orderic, 8.9 and 10.14, vol. 4: 182–83 and vol. 5: 282–83; William of Malmesbury, *Gesta regum Anglorum*, 5.400, p. 725. On resistance to inheritance by illegitimate children, see Orderic, 4, 6.8 and 7.15, vol. 2: 312–13, vol. 3: 254–55 and vol. 4: 82–85.

down the social scale.[112] We have little evidence that the proponents of marital reform were really opposed to the informal but monogamous unions of serfs or the poor, even though these were sometimes referred to as "concubinage" (*contubernium*).

But even if concubinage was not the target of an organized campaign, neither was it an honorable state. In Latin texts, at least, the word "concubine" always carries connotations of low status, "ignobility," "vileness," and shame.[113] Not only clerical wives, but other women involved in "irregular" unions might find themselves labeled "whores" as well as "concubines." And this makes it difficult to distinguish women involved in informal sexual relationships from actual sex workers, normally identified in Latin texts as *meretrices* or *scorta*, but sometimes also called *concubinae*. The latter were the subject of growing interest during the central Middle Ages.

Writing in the first quarter of the eleventh century, Bishop Burchard of Worms devoted many pages in his compendium of church law, the *Decretum*, to incest, adultery, and fornication. Commercial prostitution, on the other hand, received very little attention, and the few references to it are ambiguous. At one point, Burchard urges bishops, during their visitations, to inquire whether any women in the parish had committed *lenocinium* – but without defining what that crime entailed.[114] In a later section, Burchard does define the term, in a query that the bishop or parish priest was meant to address to laywomen:

Have you practiced *lenocinium* either in yourself or in others; that is to say, have you handed over your body to your lovers for use and defilement, in the manner of a prostitute [*meretricio more*], for a price? Or, what is crueller and more dangerous, have you sold or conceded another's body, that of a daughter or a granddaughter or of any Christian woman, to lovers, or served as a go-between, or advised that any shameful act of violation [*stuprum*] be perpetrated by such means?[115]

For Burchard, then, the primary meaning of *lenocinium* seems to have been prostitution, although the classical meaning – procuring – remains as a secondary definition. Both activities are assigned the same severe penance – six years. Finally, Burchard included in his collection a canon

---

[112] This might prove a dangerous business; witness the confrontation between William of Aquitaine and Bishop Peter of Poitiers: William of Malmesbury, *Gesta regum Anglorum*, 5.439, pp. 782–85. Sometimes, too, the recognized wife's male relatives might act against the husband who took a concubine: see Orderic, 8.23, vol. 4: 284–85.

[113] E.g. Alexander II, *Epistolae*, 1 (PL 146: 1280) = JL 4469; *Liber miraculorum sancte Fidis*, 2.2, p. 156; trans. Sheingorn, p. 118.

[114] Burchard of Worms, *Decretum*, 1.92 (PL 140: 575).

[115] Burchard of Worms, *Decretum*, 19.5 (PL 140: 975).

denying deathbed communion to any man whose wife had committed adultery with his knowledge and consent.[116] This might be a reference to pimping, or it might refer to the noncommercial exchange of women. Altogether, Burchard's treatment of prostitution amounts to only a few paragraphs.

Writing around the year 1100, Bishop Ivo of Chartres devoted much more attention than Burchard to sex workers. In his vast collection of canons (also known as the *Decretum*), the terms of reference are much clearer, and the materials on which he drew more extensive; they included the corpus of Roman law, recently rediscovered in Ivo's day, as well as the decisions of earlier church councils and the writings of the Church Fathers. Ivo offers two definitions of the term *meretrix*, both drawn from the Fathers. According to Jerome, a prostitute was any woman "who is available for the lusts of many men." Augustine, on the other hand, defined *meretrices* as those "whose sexual service [*turpitudo* – literally, "shame"] is publicly for sale."[117] Already in Ivo, then, we find the two major elements characterizing the prostitute in later medieval canon law – public promiscuity and venality. Nevertheless, for Ivo, the commercial aspect seems more salient. He presents a passage from Roman law that defends the prostitute's right to her earnings – while "she does behave disgracefully, since she is a prostitute," yet "she does not accept money disgracefully, being a prostitute." Ivo follows Roman law in understanding the principal meaning of *lenocinium* as commercial pimping – he includes texts from Justinian's *Digest* concerning men who keep prostitutes, as either their main occupation or as a sideline to such businesses as tavern-keeping or bath-managing. In any case, those who sold either the bodies of others (as pimps) or their own bodies (as prostitutes) were not to be given communion, even on their deathbeds, unless they repented.[118]

The increased attention paid to commercial prostitution in Ivo's *Decretum* may simply reflect the larger number of legal texts – and especially of texts from Roman law – available to the Bishop of Chartres around the year 1100, as compared to the Bishop of Worms around 1000. Or it may be that over the course of the eleventh century prostitution had become a more pressing problem for both canonists and pastors. We would certainly expect paid sex work to be on the rise, given urban growth, economic expansion, and the increased availability of money in this period. Other indications – albeit fragmentary and inconclusive – support this

[116] Burchard of Worms, *Decretum*, 9.69 (PL 140: 826); cf. 1.92 (PL 140: 574).
[117] Ivo of Chartres, *Decretum*, 8.297, 8.311 (PL 161: 648, 652). And see Brundage (1976); Karras (1996), pp. 10–12.
[118] On a prostitute's right to her earnings, see Ivo of Chartres, *Decretum*, 8.307 (PL 161: 651); on *lenocinium*, see ibid., 8.304–06 (PL 161: 650–51).

conclusion. First, religious leaders seem to have changed their approach to the problem over the course of the century. Most eleventh-century references to prostitution reveal little sympathy for the prostitutes themselves. They are seen very simply as a danger from which Christian society must be protected.[119] From the second half of the century on, however, a few clerical writers begin to treat them as human beings, deserving spiritual assistance. By the beginning of the twelfth century, we find a number of holy men conducting campaigns not to expel, but to reform prostitutes. The itinerant Norman preacher Vitalis (who later founded the abbey of Savigny) was criticized by some for his ministry to fallen women. He called them his "daughters" (apparently a surprisingly kind form of address), gently admonished them to give up their "disgraceful" work, and then arranged for those who did repent to marry.[120] Likewise, the heretical preacher Henry the Monk, during his sojourn in Le Mans in 1116, called for women of the streets to burn their clothing and their hair; he then took up a collection to buy them new clothes, and called on the young men of the city to accept them in marriage.[121] Does this mean that by the early twelfth century the number of whores had grown so large that new approaches to the social and religious problem of prostitution were needed?

The remarkable growth of the cult of "holy harlots," between the late tenth and the early twelfth centuries, may also owe something to an increase in commercial sex work, although religious factors were probably more important.[122] The best-known cult is that of Mary Magdalene, which underwent, according to Victor Saxer, an "explosion of fervor" during the eleventh century, most notably at Vezelay, but elsewhere as well.[123] Other prostitute–saints also received renewed attention. In the west of France, for example, Marbod of Rennes and Hildebert of Le Mans wrote lives of Saints Thaïs and Mary the Egyptian, while in Saxony, Hrotswitha of Gandersheim composed a play celebrating Thaïs' conversion. In Augsburg, new music was composed for the local cult of St. Aphra.[124]

---

[119] E.g. Othlo of St. Emmeram, *Dialogus de tribus quaestionibus*, 49 (PL 146: 130–31).

[120] Stephen of Fougères, *Vita beati Vitalis*, 9, p. 365. Compare *Vita Annonis archiepiscopi Coloniensis*, 1.12, MGH SS 11: 472.

[121] *Actus pontificum Cenomannis*, pp. 108–14.

[122] On medieval devotion to holy harlots, see Karras (1990).

[123] Saxer (1959), vol. 2: 352; on developments in the eleventh century, see also vol. 1: 59–88.

[124] Hildebert of Le Mans, *Vita beatae Mariae Aegypticae* (PL 171: 1321–40); Marbod of Rennes, *Thaisidis vita altera metrica*. AASS. Oct. IV, cols. 226–28; Hrotsvit (Hrotswitha), *Pafnutius/Conversio Thaidis meretricis*, in *Opera*, pp. 218–44; Hermannus Contractus, *Historia Sanctae Afrae Martyris Augustensis*.

These developments have usually been explained as an outgrowth of penitential consciousness, especially within monastic circles. Prostitutes who achieved sanctity symbolized the liberating power of repentance from even the most profound entanglement in sin, for to celibate monks there could be no worse sin than prostitution.[125] In all probability, though, growth in the number of sex workers in eleventh-century cities was also making the figure of the harlot more salient to clerical writers in this period. And some of the same concerns that fueled ecclesiastical reform in this period – concerns about sexual purity and pollution, and particularly about the corrupting influence of money on social relations – also spurred the growth of these cults.[126]

If the "holy harlots" served as symbols of repentance, common prostitutes served other symbolic purposes as well. They stood, above all, for pollution – so much so that an infant saint might prove his holiness by refusing to suck from the breasts of a prostitute hired as his nurse.[127] But even more importantly, by breaching the boundaries of licit sexuality, prostitutes also symbolized the vulnerability of Christ's body, the Church. St. Paul's words from I Corinthians 6:15–16 – "Shall I then take the members of Christ and make them members of a harlot?" – appeared in eleventh-century admonitions against various forms of sexual misconduct, not only clerical marriage, but incest, fornication, adultery, and so forth.[128] And clerical leaders were aware that the danger was not to the sinner alone.

A remarkable tale reflects not only clerical awareness of commercial prostitution, but also the importance of the prostitute as a "boundary marker" in their mental universe. Peter Damian tells of three prostitutes living in Spain, in a region inhabited by both Christians and Muslims. Because the women were Christians, they only offered themselves to Christian customers. This angered the Saracens in the area, who took the prostitutes to court and demanded sexual access to them, but the women stoutly refused, and were sentenced to death as a result. When an initial attempt at execution failed, the three were remanded to prison for a time. And it was there that one of them – "better than the others" – had a vision of Christ. The Savior urged them not to be afraid: "Today

[125] Saxer (1959), vol. 2: 328–34; Dalarun (1992).

[126] It is certainly no accident that a number of reformers were devoted to the Magdalene's cult. On Leo IX, see *Vita Leonis noni*, 1.16, pp. 54–56; trans. Robinson, pp. 122–24; Brakel (1972), pp. 247, 254–56, 269, 277–78. See also Geoffrey of Vendôme, 73 and 215, pp. 130–38 and 536–42; and Dalarun (1992). On money as a corrupting force in social relationships, see below, Chapter 2.

[127] Marbod of Rennes, *Vita sancti Roberti abbatis Casae-Dei*, 1.1 (PL 171: 1507).

[128] Oliba of Vich, *Epistolae*, 4 (PL 142: 601); Lanfranc, *Commentarius in omnes epistolas Pauli* (PL 150: 174).

I will bring your struggle to an end, and receive you with the crown of martyrdom into the pleasure [*amenitate* – an interesting choice of word within the context of prostitution] of my glory." The prostitutes were brought back into court, maintained their refusal to sleep with Muslims, and were duly executed – "and so martyrs were made out of *meretrices*."[129] Unlike the better known "holy harlots" of the eleventh century, the three prostitutes in Peter's tale earned a heavenly reward not for their repentance, but for their heroic defense of the Christian community's frontiers, within the context of their sex work.[130]

A final form of extramarital sex should be mentioned briefly here, even though it was seldom directly evoked in the political writings that are the focus of this book.[131] Some men certainly engaged in homosexual activities during the central Middle Ages, although it is impossible to tell how common such activities were. What we can say is that a number of reformers considered sex between men even more polluting than other erotic misbehavior.[132] Peter Damian's *Book of Gomorrah* is a notoriously extreme example of this attitude, which may not have been shared by all clerics, or even all reformers.[133] However, Peter was certainly not alone in expressing revulsion. The German reformer Manegold of Lautenbach, for example, in an attack on Henry IV of Germany, accused the king of engaging in "the uncleanness of sodomitical filth" (*sodomitica colluvionis immunditia*). Manegold saw this as even worse than Henry's other crimes, which (he claimed) included adultery, incest, sacrilege, and murder.[134] Concubines, prostitutes, and probably "sodomites" as well were thus a normal part of life in Europe during the central Middle Ages, but for reforming clerics especially (though not exclusively) they also served as potent and contradictory symbols: of the power of repentance, of filth and disorder, and even of the vulnerability of the Body of Christ– that is, the Church– to pollution.

---

[129] Peter Damian, 123, vol. 3: 407; trans. Blum, 5 (6): 19–20.
[130] The prostitute still served as boundary marker in later medieval Spain: Nirenberg (1996), p. 156.
[131] At one point, Humbert of Silva Candida did link simony, effeminacy, and sodomy: see *Adversus Simoniacos*, 2.28, MGH LL 1: 174. A more specific accusation concerning bishops acquiring office through sodomy appears in *Walrami et Herrandi epistolae de causa Heinrici regis conscriptae*, MGH LL 2: 287, 289.
[132] Sex between women was apparently of no interest to the reformers – although it was occasionally listed as a sin: see Boswell (1980), p. 180; Brundage (1987), p. 167 and 213.
[133] Peter Damian, 31, vol. 1: 284–330; trans. Blum, 2: 3–53; see Boswell (1980), Jordan (1997).
[134] Manegold, *Ad Gebehardum*, 30, MGH LL 1: 366; and see p. 338 on similar accusations against the enemies of Gregory VII in general. On Manegold's use of sexual accusations to discredit Henry IV, see McLaughlin (forthcoming).

Divorce and remarriage

Sexual relationships involving prostitutes, concubines, the clergy, or consanguinity were not marriages. They never contained the sacrament of Christ and the Church; neither did they express true love (*veram dilectionem*).[135] Consequently, they could and should be dissolved, and the participants separated.[136] But what of marriages that were legitimate to begin with, but later ran into serious difficulties?[137] Sometimes this was the result of personality conflicts or of extramarital affairs.[138] But structural factors, closely related to the political and economic changes described above, could also contribute to the breakup of marriages, especially among the upper classes and especially around the time of the millennium.

Powerful families had always intermarried with their political allies – those equal in rank traded brides to encourage peaceful relations, while lords sometimes gave their daughters to subordinates to ensure their loyalty. But a lord who changed allegiance might find it necessary to repudiate his old wife, and take a new one. This was nothing new, of course, but as the fragmentation of power and growing competition among castellans led to more rapid shifts in allegiance around the year 1000, disrupted marriages must have increased as well. The move towards patrilineage may also have played a role. As wealth and power were increasingly transmitted from father to son (rather than being disseminated in a variety of directions within the kin-group), men needed and wanted male heirs more than ever. Wives who failed to produce at least one son were likely to be repudiated. A number of noblemen in the eleventh century resorted to what Martin Aurell has called "serial polygamy" – marrying time after time until an heir was finally forthcoming.[139] The most notorious examples were the eleventh-century counts of Anjou, but they were by no means unique. So common, indeed, was the practice that exceptions elicited some surprise. Thus the Burgundian chronicler Raoul Glaber noted approvingly that when Cunigunde failed to provide Emperor Henry II with an heir, he nevertheless "did not repudiate her."[140]

---

[135] Ivo of Chartres, *Epistolae*, 242 (PL 162: 250).
[136] E.g. Orderic 5.13, vol. 3: 132–33, on the annulment, after many years, of the incestuous union between William of Moulins-la-Marche and his wife Aubrée.
[137] On divorce and separation, see Fransen (1977); Brundage (1987), pp. 199–203; Reynolds (1994), pp. 173–238; D'Avray (2005), pp. 74–99.
[138] E.g. Raoul Glaber, 1.3, and 4.20, pp. 16–17, 204–5; *Liber miraculorum* 4.17, p. 249; trans. Sheingorn, p. 206; *Briefsammlungen*, p. 92.
[139] Aurell (2002), pp. 13–14.
[140] Raoul Glaber, 3.1, pp. 94–97. The translator in the edition cited renders *dimisit* as "abandon"; "repudiate" better conveys the sense of the Latin word. Clerical authors often assumed that noblewomen feared repudiation: see Hildebert of Le Mans, *Epistolae*, 6 (PL 171: 149–53); Orderic, 8.20, vol. 4: 260–61.

Divorce was, then, a very real possibility, despite the potential repercussions for such drastic action. The family of the repudiated wife might be irate (unless they had other plans for her), and the clergy would almost certainly disapprove, for a true marriage was supposed to be indissoluble.[141] There were exceptions to this rule. If one's spouse simply disappeared for a long period of time one could eventually take another husband or wife. But at what point did remarriage become possible? In *The Miracles of St. Foi*, Bernard of Angers recounts the tale of a castellan from southern France who was absent from home for some fifteen years. His wife remarried in his absence, which earned her Bernard's condemnation for infidelity. Reading between the lines, however, it becomes clear that her remarriage was considered the normal thing to do. (The fact that she tried to murder her first husband when he reappeared was perhaps less so …) The castellan's friends advised him to take her back – "there was absolutely no disgrace."[142]

The authoritative statement on this subject came from a letter of Pope Leo I. He noted that women whose husbands had been taken captive in war, and who were uncertain of their fate, sometimes remarried "because of their own need and anxiety." But if their husbands should return,

we should of necessity believe that the unions of their lawful marriages should be restored and, after the evils which the hostility brought have been removed, each should have what he lawfully had. However, no one should be judged culpable and considered an intruder into another's right if he married the wife of a husband who was thought no longer to exist. If, however, wives are so enraptured with love for their second husbands that they prefer to live with them rather than return to their lawful union, they are rightly to be censured so that they are deprived of ecclesiastical fellowship until they return to their lawful union.[143]

At the end of the eleventh century, with the beginning of the crusades, the issue of the disappearing spouse became especially important.[144]

Marital separation – as opposed to divorce – was also possible under certain circumstances. Jesus himself had specified the most

---

[141] On the complex politics of royal divorce, see Duby (1981), pp. 75–85; Stafford (1983), pp. 79–86.

[142] *Liber miraculorum*, 2.2, p. 157; trans. Sheingorn, p. 119.

[143] Leo I, *Epistolae*, 159 (PL 54: 1136–37) = JL 536; trans. Hunt, pp. 248–50. The letter was widely cited in the central Middle Ages: Burchard of Worms, *Decretum*, 9.55–58 (PL 140: 824–25); *Diversorum sententiae patrum*, 272, pp. 165–66; Bonizo, *Liber de vita christiana*, 8.53–56, pp. 267–68; Ivo, *Decretum*, 8.190–93 (PL 161: 624). On Leo's letter, see Reynolds (1994), pp. 134–38.

[144] Brundage (1967a) and (1967b). The wife's status when her husband is known to be alive, but has been imprisoned for many years, is discussed by Orderic, 8.23, vol. 4: 282–83.

important: "Whosoever shall put away his wife, except it be for
fornication ... commits adultery" (Matthew 19:9). A man whose wife
had committed adultery could put her aside. (In practice, women had
much more difficulty doing the reverse.) But could a cuckolded man
remarry? Most of the canonists of the eleventh and early twelfth centuries said no – basing their arguments on Scripture, especially Mark
10:11–12 and Luke 16:18. Separation did not end the marital bond.[145]
However, quite a few clerics, including some very highly placed ones,
either remained unsure, or believed – contrary to the canons – that
remarriage was possible. Towards the end of the eleventh century,
Archbishop Thomas of York wrote to Lanfranc of Canterbury on precisely this question. Lanfranc cited the Bible in response, then added,

There are also many patristic opinions on this subject; but where the sun is
shining we need not bring out a candle to give light. In these words of the Lord
it is clearer than daylight that while the husband or wife is alive, neither is permitted to seek a union with anyone else.[146]

Separation was also possible when one of the partners in a marriage
wanted to enter religious life. But could the partner who remained in the
world remarry? This issue was not addressed in Scripture; but according to canon law, neither husband nor wife could enter a religious community without the permission of the other. Otherwise, they would be
denying their partner the only legitimate outlet for sexual desire, leaving
them prey to illicit temptations. Some canons specified that the partner
in the world should promise to remain celibate; others were less clear –
leaving the door open for continued confusion. In the eleventh century,
most canonists agreed that the spouse remaining in the world could not
remarry while his or her partner still lived.[147] In practice, however, men
whose wives were convicted (or sometimes merely accused) of adultery,
or had entered convents, very often did take another wife – in effect,
turning the separation from their first wife into a divorce.

Until they returned to their first wife, or agreed to be celibate, such
men should be excommunicated, the reformers said. It is clear, however, that divorce and remarriage did not automatically lead to excommunication in this period. The canons emphasizing the indissolubility
of marriage had not necessarily reached every part of Christian Europe.

---

[145] E.g. Burchard, *Decretum*, 9.15, 9.72 (PL 140: 817, 827); Bonizo, *Liber de vita Christiana*,
8.64, p. 270; Ivo, *Decretum*, 8.43, 8.200, 8.209, 8.222 (PL 161: 593–94, 625, 627, 631).
[146] Lanfranc, 23, pp. 104–7.
[147] Reynolds (1994), pp. 227–38. In the central Middle Ages, see also Burchard, *Decretum*,
9.45–48 (PL 140: 822–23); Bonizo, *Liber vita christiana*, 8.46–48, pp. 265–66; Ivo,
Decretum, 8.16, 8.131–36, and 8.183–86 (PL 161: 587, 612–14, and 622–23); and see
Anselm of Canterbury, 297, vol. 4: 217–18; trans. Fröhlich, vol. 2: 314–15.

And even clerics who knew that divorce was forbidden may have discreetly ignored the repudiation of wives or illicit second marriages, either because it was to their own advantage to do so, or because they saw it as preferable to the alternative – for the fact is that husbands sometimes killed wives who stood in the way of their remarrying.[148] This was the fate of Godelieve of Ghistelle (later revered as a martyr), whose husband first attempted to repudiate her, and then, when he was forced to take her back, arranged for her murder.[149]

Awareness of this harsh reality may explain why the great scholar Fulbert of Chartres was willing to "bend" the rules of canon law a bit for Count Galeran I of Meulan, despite accusing Galeran of "shamelessness" and mendacity. Galeran's wife had left him. He wanted to enter into a new marriage, but Fulbert would not allow this, because the first marriage was legal, and the count's wife was still alive. Galeran apparently retorted that unless his wife returned, or he was allowed to remarry, the bishop and his wife together were "forcing him to commit adultery." When asked for her side of the story, the (unnamed) wife said she was willing to become a nun, if Galeran would provide the money for her "dowry" to the convent. As Fulbert told the archbishop of Rouen: "I am neither forbidding nor compelling her to become a nun, but neither am I venturing to force her to return to a husband who hates her and so to her death." His expectation was, then, that an unreconciled Galeran would kill his unfortunate wife. Fulbert was willing to allow Galeran to remarry, if his wife died a natural death, or if she became a nun, even though church law normally required that the husband of a woman who became a nun remain celibate until her death. Does this, perhaps, explain why Fulbert, in this letter, claimed he was unable to provide the "appropriate chapters of canon law" on the subject of remarriage? His excuse was that he was "troubled and persecuted by enemies," which may well have been true. But he also may well have been trying to get out of providing any specific legal texts, knowing that they would not support the position he was adopting in this case, apparently out of sympathy for a woman in danger.[150]

Despite Fulbert's flexibility in this case, reformers normally took a strong stand against divorce.[151] And it is remarkable (and perhaps not accidental) that the breakup of a marriage was often represented in

---

[148] This practice was so common in the ninth and tenth centuries that Pierre Toubert referred to it as "divorce à la Carolingienne": Toubert (1986), pp. 333–60.

[149] Drogo of Bergues, *Vita sanctae Godelevae*, *AASS*, II Jul. (July 6), cols. 402–09; on Godelieve, see Nip (1995a), 145–55, and (1995b), pp. 191–209; Kienzle and Nienhuis (2004), 33–61, esp. 45–51.

[150] Fulbert, 93, pp. 168–70.   [151] E.g. Orderic, 8.11, vol. 4: 194–95.

reform texts as an extremely violent event. This was not entirely new, but the language associated with divorce becomes much more dramatic in the central Middle Ages. Did reformers use such language simply to emphasize the problem's significance? Or was it intended to evoke situations of precisely the kind I have just described, to suggest that divorce was just as dangerous as – or even moreso than – an unhappy marriage, and that it should therefore be forbidden, despite the physical threat discontented husbands presented to their wives? The answer must remain unknown. But it is certainly the case that a number of reformers compared divorce to murder, arguing that it involved the destruction of the one marital body formed by the marriage of man and woman.[152] For others, divorce represented physical mutilation. According to Rupert of Deutz, God make woman out of Adam's rib, rather than from the dust of the earth, to show that the love between spouses should be firm and unshakeable. A man cannot reject his rib without injury to his Maker; if Leviticus (21: 17–23) forbids anyone suffering from a deformity to serve as a minister of the altar, how much more should someone who violently removed an entire rib from his body and discarded it be excluded from the altar and from communion. Indeed, such a man is not a man at all, because he is not a whole body, and in the same way, a woman who leaves her husband is not a whole body, but only a body part (*non corpus integrum, vel tota caro, sed pars*) – since she was taken from man in the first place.[153] In reform writings, then, divorce represented homicide, mutilation, deformity: the violent destruction of the physical and spiritual unity between husband and wife.

Women

While sexual practices varied widely from one region to another in the central Middle Ages, clerics throughout Europe shared a belief in the correspondence between ordinary earthly marriage and Christ's union with the Church. When reformers tried to make marriage more Christian, they were not simply trying to make it adhere more closely to canon law, although that was certainly an important element in their thinking. They were also trying to give ordinary marriages the shape that would best serve to maintain this mystical correspondence, while preventing illicit unions from endangering it. In the same way, as reformers fought to reform the Church, the profound spiritual connections between

---

[152] E.g. Rather of Verona, *Praeloquiorum libri VI*, 2.4, p. 48; trans. Reid, p. 65.

[153] Rupert of Deutz, *De sancta Trinitate et operibus suis, In Genesim*, 2.34, vol. 21: 228. More conservative clerics could use a similar argument to criticize efforts to separate priests from their wives: Landulf of Milan, *Historia Mediolanensis* 3.23, MGH, SS 8: 90.

ecclesiastical and marital relationships were never far from their minds. Many of the passages from the canon law of marriage discussed in this chapter will reappear in the next, in the context of ecclesiastical reform. The rich and emotionally charged symbolic language associated here with incest, prostitution, and divorce will reappear as well. Yet despite these important parallels, there is a significant difference in the language used to describe gender and sexuality in writings about church reform, as compared to writings about marriage.

In texts about mortal marriage and sexuality from the central Middle Ages, women remain strangely nebulous figures. Changes in inheritance practices and marriage patterns in this period seem to have made women even more vulnerable than in earlier centuries – if not necessarily to disinheritance, then certainly to repudiation, to rape, and to other forms of violence. Yet in the works examined in this chapter, the focus is almost entirely on the utility and the legitimacy of the marital union. The language of purity and pollution, murder and dismemberment is associated with the relationship, much more than with the individuals involved. Indeed, many discussions are conducted on such an abstract level that neither husband nor wife comes clearly into focus. Clerical authors do reserve a little attention for the status and spiritual well-being of men within marriage. However, the situation of women seems not to interest them.

Reforming clerics, in particular, display little empathy for women in their writings about marriage and sexuality. While the rare individual like Fulbert might express concern for a woman threatened by her estranged husband, in general the reformers' desire to prevent divorce thoroughly trumped any worry about the consequences of preserving unhappy unions. While a few insisted that the bride's consent was essential for a valid marriage, most assumed that her fate should be decided by her kin. The only sexually active women to whom reformers really devote much attention are prostitutes and the wives of priests. The former are treated as symbols of sin (and perhaps repentance) rather than as real women – except perhaps towards the very end of our period – while the latter increasingly become the targets of scorn and hatred as time goes on.[154] The reformers' hostility towards priests' wives in particular, and their lack of empathy towards women in general, are usually understood today as expressions of celibate men's anxieties about their own sexuality and about the sexual temptation presented by women.[155] Deeply concerned

---

[154] Consider Thietmar of Merseburg's savage attack on adulterous women (8.3, pp. 495–96; trans. Warner, pp. 362–63), or the vision of punishment imposed on lascivious women (not men) in the afterlife: Orderic, 8.17, vol. 4: 238–41.

[155] Famously, Peter Damian, 39, vol. 1: 380–81; trans. Blum 2: 106–07; analyzed in Elliott (1999), pp. 81–106.

with reshaping marriage to conform to religious ideals, they were at the same time often eager to avoid not only physical, but perhaps even psychological contact with the very real women whose lives were affected by their efforts at reform.

The Bride of Christ, on the other hand, posed no threat to the celibacy of those who wrote about her. It was, indeed, their duty to love and care about her, to mourn with her if she suffered, to rejoice with her as her Bridegroom approached. Thus the female figure of the Church may have provided clerical writers with an outlet for feelings they could not easily express about ordinary women. It is certainly the case, as we shall see in the next chapter, that they depicted the Bride with far greater sympathy than they did ordinary brides. Her mystical marriage was described in far greater detail than any earthly marriage, and often in highly erotic terms. Paradoxically, too, the language of purity and pollution, of violence and love, which remains on an abstract level in texts about marriage, is highly personalized when applied to the Bride of Christ in writings on church reform.

VOX OPTANTIS XPI ADVENTVM.

S
CV
LE
TVR
ME

osculo orif sui. Apostropha ad sponsū·
Quia meliora sunt ubera tua uino· &
odor ungentorum tuoʒ super omnia aro
mata flagrantia ungentis optimis, oleū
effusū nomen tuum: ideo adolescentulę
dilexerunt te. Vox ecclę ad xpm·
Trahe me post te· curremus in odore
ungentorū tuoʒ. Vox sponsę ad adolescentulas·
Introduxit me rex in cellaria sua· Spon

Figure 1. Valenciennes, Bibliothèque Municipale, MS. 10, f. 113r. Opening of the Song of Songs from the Bible of Alard. Reproduced by permission of the library.

2   The Bride of Christ

Eleventh-century clerics often imagined the Church they served as a woman, and generally as a beautiful and queenly woman, "glorious ... not having spot or wrinkle."[1] Sometimes, though, she took on a very different aspect. Bishop Bruno of Toul, the future Pope Leo IX, dreamed one night that an "ugly old woman," with a frightening face, ragged clothes, and shaggy hair, asked for his friendship. Disgusted by her ugliness, he tried to get away, but she clung to him until finally he marked her face with the sign of the cross. With that, "she fell to the ground like a dead woman but rose up again, her appearance now one of wonderful beauty." Bruno's biographer claimed that the meaning of the dream was clear: "For it is certain that the beauty of the Church, indeed the Christian religion, throughout the various regions of the world had faded to a fearful extent and through Bruno it was, with Christ's help, brought back to its former dignity."[2] In this passage, ecclesiastical reform – which Bruno promoted strongly during his pontificate – was represented in terms of a woman's physical transformation. As we shall see, reform might also be described as the cleansing of a polluted woman, as the reclothing of a ragged woman, or even as the rescue of a captive one.

Representations of *Ecclesia* as a woman were authorized by the Bible and the writings of the Church Fathers, and supported by important liturgical and legal texts. However, they were also shaped by contemporary gender ideology, and by their creators' experiences with real women in the world. In this chapter, I will be examining one of the most emotionally evocative of these images, that of the Church as a beautiful, lovable, but highly vulnerable Bride.[3] This image became central to the eleventh-century debates over simony, episcopal elections, and lay investiture, largely because the most ardent among reforming clerics

[1] Ephesians 5:27. On visual representations of the Church in this period, see Toubert (1990) pp. 37–63.
[2] *Vita Leonis noni*, 2.3, pp. 70–72; trans. Robinson, pp. 129–30.
[3] In addition to the literature cited below, see Robinson (1988), pp. 257–59.

chose to represent these issues in terms of sexualized threats to a feminized *Ecclesia*. More conservative writers were also clearly familiar with such nuptial imagery – indeed, it was so pervasive in eleventh-century clerical culture that they could hardly ignore it. However, it was invoked much less often in their works, perhaps because it was less effective for their rhetorical purposes, but also, perhaps, because it held less emotional resonance for writers who saw no threat to the Church in the status quo.

Let him kiss me with the kisses of his mouth

The image of the Church as Bride was above all the creation of St. Paul, who compared human marriage to the mystical marriage of Christ and the Church in the fifth chapter of Ephesians. Drawing on the text from Genesis in which husband and wife are said to become one flesh, Paul writes, "This is a great mystery, but I speak concerning Christ and the Church." That is to say, he represented the mystical marriage as the one, true marriage, of which human matrimony is only a *figura*, a dim shadow. Later Christian thinkers elaborated on this image in various ways, drawing on other Biblical texts, as well as on their own ideas about marriage, for material. In general, they assumed that the love affair of Christ with his Church began with the Creation – it was figured, as we have seen, in the formation of Eve from Adam's rib – and that the entire history of salvation could be thus understood as different moments in the history of a marriage.

Thus, in commentaries on the so-called "Nuptial Psalm" 45,[4] the act of redemption was often represented as the rescue of the Bride from demonic powers. "Listen, O daughter," reads the psalm, "Consider and incline your ear; forget your own people also, and your father's house." In one text (long attributed to Bede, but more likely the work of the eleventh-century reformer Manegold of Lautenbach), this is seen as an address to the Church. She is urged to forget her people – "that is, the people of Babylon, from whom this King took you in a filthy state [*foedam*], in order to make you beautiful." She is told to forget her father's house – "that is, [the house of] the Devil, who made you filthy, a wicked sinner. And if you do this, then the King will love you, the filthy one, in order to make you beautiful."[5] Interpretations of Ephesians 5, in the light

---

[4] Numbered 45 in the Vulgate; elsewhere sometimes numbered 44.

[5] Pseudo-Bede, *In psalmorum libro exegesis* (PL 93: 721–22). On this text, see Morin (1911); Hartmann (1972), esp. pp. 319–27; Gorman (1998), pp. 214–39, esp n. 5. Cf. Bruno of Würzburg, *Expositio psalmorum* (PL 142: 189). On patristic readings of Psalm 44, see Hunter (2000).

of Genesis 2, literally "fleshed out" the process of redemption, in terms of the creation of the Church from Christ's body:

Adam represents Christ, while Eve represents the Church. What does it mean to say that the Lord first made Adam fall asleep, and then took a rib from his side, from which the woman was formed, unless that first Our Redeemer slept in death, and then from his side blood and water flowed in the sacrament of the Church? Eve was made from the side of a sleeping man; the Church came forth from the side of the Savior, hanging on the cross.[6]

If Psalm 45 and Ephesians 5 shaped medieval clerics' views of redemption, St. John's allusions to the "Marriage of the Lamb" in Revelations 19 and 21 shaped ideas about the final consummation of the relationship between Christ and his Church at the end of time, when the heavenly Jerusalem will come down from heaven, "prepared as a bride adorned for her husband." Hence the hymn sung during the ceremony for the dedication of new churches:

> Blessed city of Jerusalem, called "vision of peace,"
> Built in heaven from living stones,
> Crowned by angels as betrothed companion,
> Newly come from heaven to the nuptial bed,
> Prepared to be joined as Bride to the Lord ...[7]

The promise of eternal life took the form of an invitation to the heavenly wedding feast: "Let all the saints rejoice and make merry and give glory to God, because they are come to the wedding of the Lamb."[8]

More than any other Biblical text, however, the Song of Songs shaped medieval ideas about the mystical marriage. Its erotic images and evocation of desire simultaneously stirred the imagination and exercised the intellect. For it was, of course, necessary to find an acceptable spiritual interpretation for a text that on the surface appeared to be an unabashed celebration of human sexuality.[9] Moreover, the challenge of fitting a scripture with many memorable vignettes but no clear story line into the great narrative of salvation history intrigued medieval interpreters. Ann Matter has counted nearly one hundred fully fledged commentaries and homilies on the Song of Songs written between the sixth and

---

[6] Peter Damian, *Sermones*, 66, pp. 399–400.

[7] *Analecta hymnica medii aevi*, 26737, vol. 2: 73; Ashworth (1956). The Bride also appears in the mass celebrated on the anniversary of a church's dedication: Deshusses (1971), 1264, p. 423. See also Thietmar, 6.60, p. 348; trans. Warner, pp. 278–79; Raoul Glaber, 3.4, pp. 118–19; *Vita Aedwardi regis*, 1.6, p. 48.

[8] Bruno of Segni, *Expositio in Apocalypsim*, 19 (PL 165: 708).

[9] Political writers came to quite different conclusions than did monastic exegetes concerning the relationship between earthly marriage and the marriage of Christ and the Church. On the latter, see especially Turner (1995), pp. 131–56.

the fifteenth centuries; eleven were created in the tenth and eleventh centuries alone.[10] There were, in addition, many shorter treatments of individual passages.

These texts resolved the problem of spiritual interpretation in a variety of ways in these texts. The female figure who opens the Song with the words "Let him kiss me with the kisses of his mouth" could be understood as the soul desiring union with God; the person who announces "I am the flower of the field and the lily of the valley" (Song 2:1) might be the Virgin Mary (an increasingly important interpretation from the end of the eleventh century on).[11] Most often, however, the Song of Songs represented for medieval clerics a portrait of the love between Christ and the Church. And even when it was interpreted in other ways, this ecclesiological sense of the text remained as the background over which other meanings were painted.[12] Hence the magnificent image of Christ and the Church, locked in close embrace, in a Bible created at the monastery of St. Amand sometime around 1100.[13] The two figures – clearly labeled "*Christus*" and "*Ecclesia*" – are so intertwined that it is difficult to tell where one begins and the other ends. Surely the artist was trying to convey the idea that Christ and his Bride, the Church, through their mystical marriage, formed but a single body.

Yet the ecclesiological sense was itself highly complex, for each interpreter highlighted different passages in the Song of Songs, and connected them with different moments in the history of the Church. These choices were shaped by the conditions under which the interpreter worked: by worries about heresy, by pastoral concerns, by changing patterns of piety, and – especially in the eleventh century – by awareness of the need for reform. In the third century, for example, the Church father Cyprian evoked the phrase "My dove, my perfect one, is the only one" (Song 6:9) to emphasize the importance of maintaining unity within the Church and avoiding schism – an interpretation that would prove important during the age of reform.[14]

Eleventh-century authors often evoked contemporary issues in their commentaries. Robert of Tombelaine equated "the flocks of your

---

[10] Matter (1990), p. 3, and see the Appendix, pp. 203–10; on medieval Song commentaries, see also Ohly (1958); Herde (1967).

[11] See Riedlinger (1958), pp. 202–8; Matter (1990), pp. 151–70; Fulton (1996).

[12] Matter (1990), pp. 86–87.

[13] Valenciennes, Bibliothèque Municipale, Ms. 10, f. 113 r. The image fills the "O" of *Osculetur me osculo oris sui* – "Let him kiss me with the kisses of his mouth" – the opening verse of the Song of Songs.

[14] Cyprian of Carthage, *Epistulae*, 69, in *Opera*, vol. 3C: 471–72. In addition to the works cited in the last section of this chapter, see also Peter Damian 28, vol. 1: 255–56; trans. Blum 1: 262.

companions" (Song 1:6) with the "false Christians" of his own day: "These multitudes are rightly called 'flocks' in reproach, since they live like irrational animals, without order."[15] John of Mantua glossed the place-name "Hermon" as "excommunication." The "top of Hermon" (Song 4:8), he claimed, referred to the powerful who had been excommunicated by Gregory VII: "There are many such to be found today, like the bishops of Lombardy and the other adherents of Henry [IV] …".[16]

Bruno of Segni's commentary on the Song of Songs addresses contemporary concerns, while at the same time evoking the apocalyptic expectations shared by many of the reformers.[17] In a beautiful poetic paraphrase of Song 5:2–7, Bruno describes Christ "knocking at the door" to summon the sleeping Church to him. She throws the door open, "that the whole house might lie open to my love / and my mind might most fully see / whom it longs greatly to see," but Christ has already gone away. "Weeping," she says, "I followed that youth / whose hands molded men." And then,

> The watchmen of the City found me,
> they plundered me,
> they took and gave away my cloak,
> they sang to me a new song
> with which I will be led into the palace of the King.[18]

The word "plundered" (*exspoliaverunt*) does not come directly from the Song; rather, for the reformers in Bruno's circle, it must have evoked the many depredations their opponents had committed against church property and privileges. The last two lines of Bruno's poem clearly echo the Book of Revelation: the song of the elect before the throne of the Lamb (14:3), and the final entry into the heavenly city (21). Thus the Bride, suffering in this world, longs for her reunion with the King's Son at the end of time; she charges the apostles to "tell God of her love and desire" (*amorem et desiderium*).[19]

Despite its lack of coherent plot, the Song of Songs was, in the words of Odorannus of Sens, a "drama" – the Biblical text represented the voices of a whole cosmic cast of characters, acting out violence and

---

[15] Robert of Tombelaine, *Commentariorum in Cantica canticorum libri duo* (PL 150: 1368). On this work, see Ohly (1958), pp. 95–98; Riedlinger (1958), pp. 102–4; Quivy and Thiron (1967); Matter (1990), pp. 107–9.

[16] John of Mantua, *In Cantica canticorum tractatus*, p. 92. On this work, see Ohly (1958), pp. 106–9; Riedlinger (1958), pp. 106–8.

[17] On Bruno, see Grégoire (1965); on this work, see also Ohly (1958), pp. 103–6; Riedlinger (1958), pp. 104–6; Herde (1967), pp. 1068–69.

[18] Bruno of Segni, *Expositio in Cantica canticorum*, 5 (PL 164: 1266); trans. Matter (1990), p. 188, who mistakenly attributes the poem to Peter Damian.

[19] Bruno of Segni, *Expositio in Cantica canticorum*, 5 (PL 164: 1266).

vulnerability, longing and expectation, love and desire, both within and outside time.[20] In art, in the liturgy, and in poetry, scenes from this drama were constantly being reenacted, and these reenactments gave solidity to an abstract theological concept: that of the mystical marriage of Christ and the Church, the reality of which human marriage was only a shadow.[21] As a result, the image of the Church as Bride had more immediacy, and probably more emotional resonance, for medieval clerics than did many other religious ideas. The rest of this chapter examines closely the various roles played by the Bride in the polemical writings of the eleventh and early twelfth centuries. Yet before the curtain can go up, one character still needs to make his entrance.

The bishop as bridegroom

Two important weddings took place in the city of Reims in May of 1051. In the first, King Henry I of France married the Russian princess, Anne of Kiev. In the second, a cleric from Cambrai was joined in union with the church of that city, by being ordained as her bishop. In the words of Bishop Lietbert's biographer, Abbot Raoul of Saint-Sépulchre:

A carnal bride is wedded to the King of the Franks, while the holy Church is committed to the Lord Lietbert, bishop of Cambrai, a chamberlain both royal and priestly. How much more holy, how much better was this second union! While the first generates offspring in the flesh, the second produces a holy progeny by adoption; the first in corruption, the second in virginity ... The first [bride] bears children in pain; the second, singing, makes them to be reborn through water and the Holy Spirit. The daughter of an earthly king is brought to the King of the Franks; to our Lord, Bishop Lietbert, is committed the Bride of Christ, King of Kings.[22]

Raoul describes Lietbert's episcopal consecration as a wedding, with the church of Cambrai as Bride, Christ as the Bridegroom, and the new bishop as their "chamberlain" (*cubicularius*).

Representations of the bishop as an attendant at the marriage of Christ and the Church were well established by Lietbert's time.[23] In other eleventh-century texts, the bishop was said to represent a *paranymphus*, one of the attendants who accompanies a bride (in this case, *the* Bride) to her new husband's home; he might also be the "friend of the

---

[20] Odorannus of Sens, *Opera*, 7, pp. 228–30.
[21] Additional liturgical associations may be found in Peter Damian, 17, vol. 1: 157–58 and 161; trans. Blum 1: 147 and 151.
[22] Raoul of Saint-Sépulchre, *Vita Lietberti episcopi Cameracensis*, 20, MGH SS 30/2: 850. On Lietbert, see Ott (2007).
[23] See Herde (1967), pp. 996–1003.

Bridegroom ... who stands and hears him," and "rejoices greatly because of the bridegroom's voice" (John 3:29).[24] More important to the eleventh-century debates over reform, however, was the identification of the bishop as himself the bridegroom, as the spouse of the particular church over which he presided. Within his own diocese, the bishop was the vicar of the heavenly Bridegroom, and thus espoused the local church in His name.[25]

This idea emerged rather slowly, and was not everywhere accepted, even at the end of the eleventh century. It first appeared in the fourth century, within the context of growing controversy over episcopal translation, the movement of bishops from one see to another. In the eastern half of the Roman Empire, translations were sometimes criticized as a form of "divorce," forbidden by Scripture.[26] In the west, however, this identification of the bishop as the spouse of his church was criticized and – perhaps as a result – had very little influence at first.[27] Only in the ninth century were its implications clearly articulated, as Carolingian clerics represented the bishop as bridegroom in discussions of church law and liturgy.

Three forged passages from Pseudo-Isidore devote special attention to this issue, applying the laws of earthly marriage – as spelled out in Scripture – to the bishop's relationship with his church and the breakdown of that relationship – whether voluntary (through translation) or involuntary (through expulsion).[28] Thus, in a letter attributed to Pope Evaristus, we find:

Just as a husband should not commit adultery against his wife, so a bishop should not do so against his church ... And just as a wife is not allowed to dismiss her husband in such a way that she joins herself to another in matrimony while he is still alive, or commits adultery against him ... so a church is not allowed to send away her bishop or to separate herself from him or to accept

[24] Bishops or popes acting heroically in the cause of reform, for example, could be described as "friends of the Bridegroom": Osbern of Canterbury, *Vita sancti Dunstani*, 35, in *Memorials of St. Dunstan*, p. 111; Hugh of Flavigny, *Chronicon*, 2, MGH, SS 8: 434–35.

[25] Tellenbach (1936), pp. 127–32.

[26] Gaudemet (1978), p. 72; Scholz (1992), pp. 5–24. The argument that this was an eastern phenomenon is my own, based on the examples Scholz cites.

[27] Jerome rejected the identification of the bishop as a bridegroom, calling the application of I Corinthians 7:27 to the issue of episcopal translation "forced": see Scholz (1992), p. 23. Except in the proceedings of a single Roman church council (see Scholz (1992), pp. 23–24), the bishop has no bride in the earliest western collections of church law nor in works on episcopal office – for an ambiguous reference in Gregory the Great's *Pastoral Care*, see Herde (1967), p. 997

[28] The context is the same as in the fourth-century writings discussed by Scholz. However, the forgers of Pseudo-Isidore appear unfamiliar with those earlier writings. They are, rather, wrestling in their own way with the breakdown of the bishop's bond with his see. See Gaudemet (1978); Scholz (1992), pp. 105–17.

another while he is alive, but she should either keep him or remain unmarried, that is, she should not accept another bishop while her own is alive ...[29]

Later in the same letter, it becomes clear that what was in question was the intrusion of new bishops into sees from which the previous occupant had been expelled: "Those, indeed, who hold [the expelled bishops'] spouses, that is, the churches, in an adulterous union, we order to be expelled and treated as adulterous and infamous ...".[30]

Neither was it permitted for the faithful to reject their bishop's authority and choose another one, as a letter attributed to Pope Calixtus I makes clear:

Just as someone's wife is not to be made adulterous by another or judged or put away by another, but only by her own husband while he is alive, so the wife of a bishop (by which without doubt is meant his church or parish) is not given up to another to judge or to dispose of or to share her bed, that is, by ordination, while he is alive ... after he dies [the church] is set free. She can then marry whom she will in the Lord, that is, lawfully. But if she marries another while he is alive, she will be judged an adulteress. Likewise, if he willingly takes another spouse, he will be deemed an adulterer and shall be deprived of communion.[31]

In the ninth century, then, the forgers responsible for the compilation of the Pseudo-Isidorian Decretals asserted categorically that bishops were married to their sees. They may have been influenced by the fourth-century texts mentioned above,[32] but they developed the image of bishop as bridegroom much more fully than had their predecessors.

At about the same time that Pseudo-Isidore came into being, the bishop's relationship with his church was also undergoing a ritual reinterpretation. Sometime around the year 823, Amalar of Metz presented to Emperor Louis the Pious the *Liber officialis*, the first sustained spiritual interpretation of the Christian liturgy, and one that was destined to become very influential in the west.[33] Amalar imagines all the clergy participating in the episcopal mass as characters in an allegorical drama. The bishop, of course, is the *vicarius Christi*.[34] He enters the church surrounded by his clerics, who represent prophets (the deacons), the elders or wise men (the subdeacons), and scribes (the acolytes). The choir is imagined as a crowd

---

[29] Projekt Pseudoisidor, Teil I, 2. Evaristus-Brief, p. 139. Available at http://www. pseudoisidor.de/pdf/016_Evaristus_Unum_nos_fratres.pdf.

[30] Projekt Pseudoisidor, Teil 1, 2. Evaristus-Brief, p. 141. Available at http://www. pseudoisidor.de/pdf/016_Evaristus_Unum_nos_fratres.pdf.

[31] Projekt Pseudoisidor, Teil I, 2. Calixtus-Brief, pp. 253–54. Available at http://www. pseudoisidor.de/pdf/036_Calixtus_Plurimorum_*relatu.pdf*

[32] See Scholz (1992), p. 106.   [33] On Amalar, see Cabaniss (1954).

[34] Amalar of Metz, *Liber officialis*, 3.5, in *Opera*, vol. 2: 271, 275, 277.

of young women playing timbrels.[35] The Bride, says Amalar, prays "Let him kiss me with the kisses of his mouth" (Song 1:1), and this prayer is fulfilled when the procession is complete. The bishop's bow before the altar signifies Christ's humbling himself to receive human form, while the kiss of peace given to the ministers on his right and left "is the very kiss by which the Church was reconciled with God."[36] Later Amalar adds that "the kisses of the vicar of Christ correspond [*congruunt*] to Christ's kiss."[37]

It is not clear whether it was the allegorical interpretation of the mass or Pseudo-Isidore's slowly expanding influence that was responsible for changing interpretations of the bishop's ring between the late ninth and the eleventh centuries.[38] Bishops in France and Spain first began to wear a ring as part of their official attire in late antiquity. At first, it was understood simply as a "token of episcopal honor," given (along with the crozier, or pastoral staff) to a new bishop during his consecration and taken away again if he were deposed.[39] In the ninth and tenth centuries, however, the ring began to be associated with betrothal and marriage in some parts of Europe. In the late ninth century, Archbishop Hincmar of Reims described the bishop's ring using a new phrase. He called the ring a *signum ... fidei*, a "token of faith."[40] Hincmar explained this phrase in terms of a prelate's role in explaining religious doctrine and – when necessary – concealing the mysteries of the faith; elsewhere, however, he had used an almost identical phrase to describe a wedding ring – a token of plighted faith between the bride and groom.[41] It may be, then, that this ninth-century archbishop was already identifying the bishop's ring as a kind of engagement or wedding ring.[42] And this may reflect the influence of Pseudo-Isidore, for Hincmar was also one of the first church leaders to make use of the forgeries in his writings.

---

[35] Amalar of Metz, *Liber officialis*, 3.5, in *Opera*, vol. 2: 274–78.

[36] Amalar of Metz, *Liber officialis*, 3.5, in *Opera*, vol. 2: 271–82.

[37] Amalar of Metz, *Liber officialis*, 3.5, in *Opera*, vol. 2: 281. In the early twelfth century, Honorius Augustodunensis repeats much of Amalar's language, but with an even clearer identification of the bishop with Christ the Bridegroom: *Sacramentarium*, 34 (PL 172: 765)

[38] Scholars have not hitherto noticed the link between the development of allegorical readings of the liturgy and changing interpretations of the ring. Gaudemet (1978), 72–73, and Engels (1987), p. 756, link the latter to the political tensions that also resulted in Pseudo-Isidore.

[39] Gaudemet (1978), 72–73; Engels (1987), 754–56. The phrase *signum pontificalis honoris* comes from Isidore of Seville, *De ecclesiasticis officiis*, 2.5 (PL 83: 783).

[40] Hincmar of Reims, *Epistolae*, 29 (PL 126: 188). (This letter is not included in the incomplete edition of Hincmar's letters in MGH, EPP.)

[41] Hincmar of Reims, *Coronatio Judith Caroli filiae* (PL 125: 811).

[42] Normally, in the early Middle Ages, rings appear to have been exchanged as part of the betrothal: see Reynolds (1994), pp. 6, 92, 96, 113–14, 393; on the less common association of the ring with the nuptial blessing, see pp. 369–70.

The association of the episcopal ring with betrothal or marriage was well established on the continent of Europe only a few decades later, as evidenced by a number of *ordines*, or ritual directions, for the consecration of bishops. In one pontifical, we find the formula for the blessing of the ring that was eventually adopted in Rome, for the consecration of the pope: "Receive this ring, the sign of faith [*fidei ... signaculum*], so that, adorned with pure faith, you may preserve without harm the bride of God, namely the holy Church."[43] Clearly, the tenth-century authors of these prayers – which remained in use into the later Middle Ages – now understood the ring to be a wedding ring. However, they still seem to have envisioned it as a sign of the mystical union between Christ and the Church as a whole, not between the bishop and his particular church. In the liturgical context, as in Raoul's account of Lietbert's ordination, the bishop was the guardian of Christ's Bride, rather than her spouse.

The prayers said over the bishop's ring remained unchanged into the eleventh and twelfth centuries, ensuring the survival of this older meaning. But how those prayers were understood was shifting. The interaction of new and old interpretations of the ring is evident in a work by Bruno of Segni:

The ring on a bishop's finger seems to be a sign, through which he is understood to be Christ's vicar, in ruling and in caring for His Bride, which is the Church. Concerning this Bridegroom and Bride, John [the Baptist] said: "He who has the Bride is the Bridegroom" [John 3:29]. But who is the Bridegroom's friend? The bishop is that friend, and the vicar of the Bridegroom; but as vicar, he is also, in some sense, the Bridegroom.[44]

The ring was, then, coming to be seen as the symbol of the bishop's own marriage.

The image of the bishop as bridegroom (rather than as simply the "friend of the Bridegroom") became widespread and familiar in the eleventh century, recurring in many contexts.[45] The introduction of a new bishop to his see, for example, could be represented as a wedding. Odorannus of Sens, in a sermon composed in the vernacular for the ordination of Mainard as Bishop of Troyes, announces to the people of the city that their church has found a new spouse.[46] Outside intervention (even

---

[43] The consecration *ordo* in the pontifical of Aurillac, from around the year 900, includes another formula: "With this ring of faith [*sub hoc anulo fidei*] we commend to you the bride of Christ, [this] church, so that you may keep her holy and immaculate." Both prayers cited from Gaudemet (1978), p. 73; cf. *Le pontificale romain*, p. 149.

[44] E.g. Bruno of Segni, *Tractatus de sacramentis ecclesiae* (PL 165: 1108).

[45] See Herde (1967), pp. 999–1003.

[46] Odorannus of Sens, *Opera,* 9, pp. 247–48. In the autograph manuscript, the sermon is described as *vulgariter pronuntiandus*. See also Adam of Bremen, *Gesta episcoporum Hammaburgensis*, 3.3, MGH SS, 7, p. 336; trans. Tschan, p. 117, on episcopal installation

by the pope) in the affairs of a local church could be condemned: "for each bishop ... is bridegroom of his own see and equally embodies the Saviour, and so none should interfere insolently in the diocese of another bishopric."[47] But it was in the context of the fierce debates raging in this period over issues like episcopal election, simony, and lay investiture that nuptial imagery was most widely and energetically deployed to construct the proper relationship between a bishop and his see.

Naked and for sale and full of confusion

If a bishop was the husband of his church, then the death of a bishop left his church a "widow" – lonely, vulnerable, and subject to the depredations of the wicked. The practical difficulties created by vacancies – the absence of leadership in spiritual affairs, competing claims on church property, and so on – were represented as the sufferings of a weak and powerless human widow.[48] Thus, when the monk Osbern tried to convince Abbot Anselm of Bec to accept the position of Archbishop of Canterbury, he has Christ Himself describe the church of Canterbury's troubles:

> See, this Church has now become the "refuse of the world" [1 Corinthians 4:13], contemptuously trodden by the feet of all walking past ... Those men ... whom I appointed for her for the protection of her chastity, from whom I received the assurance that they would preserve her integrity, not only did they not prepare any defense against those desiring to defile her but they them-selves contemplated the most flagrant kind of corruption. But she, not forget-ting how she had risen to greatness through material possessions, how she had been maintained through laws and finally been endowed with gifts, cried out as she struggled; they, after stripping off her garments of honor, abandoned her naked and for sale and full of confusion ...[49]

What really threatened the archdiocese of Canterbury in the early 1090s was a potential loss of property, but Osbern transforms this into a sexual threat – the Church's "chastity" is in danger. And so Christ, "no longer able to bear the great distress" of his Bride, chooses Anselm to defend her: "I have chosen you, Anselm, out of the host of men and have made you a friend of the Bridegroom to be zealous to me."

Christ himself may have chosen Anselm as "friend of the Bridegroom" in Canterbury, but generally the selection of bishops was a much vexed

---

as marriage. A bishop could also regret dying apart from his "bride": Orderic, 5.3, vol. 3: 14–15.

47 Raoul Glaber 2.7, pp. 64–65.
48 Of course, not all widows in this period were weak and powerless – see below, Chapter 3.
49 Anselm, 149, vol. 4: 6–10; trans. Fröhlich, vol. 2: 11–16. On Osbern, see Rubenstein (1995).

question in the central Middle Ages. Around the year 1000, episcopal elections were conducted in a variety of ways. The legal norm for this process since late antiquity had been election by the clergy and people of the diocese; in addition, the metropolitan had the right to review and approve of newly elected bishops.[50] Yet as bishops were not only spiritual guides, but also political leaders, with large landholdings, and judicial and military obligations, secular rulers also had an important stake in the selection process.[51] The king's right to intervene in the process was already recognized by the seventh century. It eventually came to be justified by the ruler's quasi-priestly character – the ritual of anointing at the time of his accession to power (a ritual introduced in the eighth century in Spain and Frankia) gave him both royal and sacerdotal qualities, like Melchizedek, King of Salem, and like Christ himself.[52] The intervention of nobles was less easy to justify, either legally or theologically; still, as royal powers devolved, first to great, and then to lesser nobles over the course of the late ninth and tenth centuries, such men came to play a major – sometimes an exclusive – role in the selection of bishops.[53] The intervention of nobles could be considered an abuse of power, since they did not possess the same sacral qualities as kings. Yet some canonists were willing to accept their role. In 1021, for example, Bishop Fulbert of Chartres wrote to the Count of Troyes, complaining that he had recently "sold" the bishopric of Troyes; Fulbert noted, however, that if Count Stephen had proceeded "in accordance with the law," he would have supported him in electing a bishop for his city.[54] In any case, as long as the magnates and other bishops of the region accepted the candidate as legitimate, little could be done about such noble interference.

In practice, the process of election varied tremendously over time and from one region to another, depending on local customs and fluctuations in the political situation. Generally negotiations took place between all the interested parties before a final decision was made, because "unanimity" of choice (however contrived) was a valuable guarantee of the new bishop's legitimacy.[55] The clergy might send representatives to the royal court, to ascertain the king's wishes before proceeding with a "free" election. Whoever claimed the right of nomination in a particular area might meet in assembly with other magnates in order to reach consensus on the best

[50] Schmid (1926); Gaudemet *et al.* (1979), pp. 50–104; Kaiser (1981); *Die früh- und hoch-mittelalterliche Bischofserhebung.*
[51] The bishop's varied roles are summarized by Parisse (2004a).
[52] Erkens (1998); Reuter (2000); Hoffmann (2000). On Melchizedek, see Genesis 14:18.
[53] On bishoprics as "proprietary churches" in this period, see now Wood (2006), pp. 292–311.
[54] Fulbert of Chartres, 52, p. 92.   [55] Erkens (1998), p. 27.

candidate – or at least on which candidate to choose. Notoriously, when Count Herbert of Vermandois wanted to install his son Hugh (five years old at the time) as archbishop of Reims in 925, he convoked an assembly that included two bishops, as well as the "clergy and people" of the city in order to validate his choice.[56]

But because the stakes in episcopal appointments were so high and political relations so fluid in the central Middle Ages, disputes often broke out. Different clerical factions might put forward different candidates, the local clergy might refuse to receive a bishop sent to them by the king, and rival secular powers might end up nominating competing bishops.[57] Sometimes prolonged wrangling over who had the right to "elect" or "appoint," and whether the locally recognized procedure had been followed properly, led to intense confusion.

Most notable was the case of the city of Rome in the years from 1044 to 1047.[58] Pope Benedict IX, a member of the powerful Tusculan clan which had controlled the See of St. Peter for several decades, was driven from Rome in the fall of 1044 by an opposing faction within the Roman aristocracy. Early in 1045, this second faction arranged for the election of a new pope, who took the name Silvester III. He in turn was forced from office in March 1045, and Benedict was restored. By May, however, Benedict had voluntarily resigned, and yet a third pope took office as Gregory VI. None of the three popes of 1045 was above reproach. Benedict IX had almost certainly purchased the papal office back in 1032. He is also reported to have been somewhat profligate, although these reports come from later sources and may not have been current in the 1040s. Silvester III's election was clearly irregular. Gregory VI seems to have been regarded as a reform candidate of sorts – with an unblemished personal reputation and the support of many reformers. But the unpleasant fact remained that someone – it is not clear who – paid a large sum of money in bribes to ensure his selection as pope. So his election, too, could be considered invalid.

Silvester's claims to the papacy seem to have been largely ignored after March 1045, but not everyone accepted Benedict's resignation. Thus, when King Henry III of Germany crossed the Alps in September of 1046, hoping to be crowned emperor by the successor of St. Peter, who that might be was by no means clear. A strong supporter of church reform,

---

[56] Flodoard, *Historia Remensis ecclesiae*, 4.20, MGH, SS 36: 411–12; Schieffer (1998), p. 80.

[57] E.g. *Gesta episcoporum Autissiodorensium*, 48, vol. 1: 239–41; on the notoriously disputed election in Reims at the end of the tenth century, see Riché (1987), pp. 111–40; Schieffer (1998).

[58] Zimmermann (1968), pp. 119–39; Herrmann (1973), pp. 151–65; Schmale (1979), pp. 55–103; Blumenthal (1982), pp. 56–57; Cowdrey (1998a), pp. 21–25; Gressel (2007), pp. 33–55.

Henry seems to have recognized Gregory VI as the most acceptable candidate; he is said to have received Gregory "honorably" when they met at Piacenza in November. However, at a synod held at Sutri in December, Gregory was accused of simony and either resigned or was deposed from office, while Silvester III was found to have no legitimate claim. At a second synod, held at Rome a few days later, Benedict IX's resignation was also confirmed, clearing the way for Henry to nominate a new candidate, who – after being duly confirmed by the "clergy and people" of Rome – was consecrated as Pope Clement II. Gregory VI was sent into exile in Germany, accompanied by a young Roman deacon named Hildebrand (the future Pope Gregory VII). Nevertheless, he continued to be recognized in some quarters as the legitimate bishop of Rome until his death in exile in 1047. Meanwhile, Benedict IX continued intermittently to claim the papal office until he in turn died, in 1055/56.

Sometime (probably shortly) after Gregory VI's death, an unknown author wrote an account of these events in a treatise entitled by its modern editor *On Pontifical Ordination*.[59] The provenance of the text is uncertain – it survives in a manuscript now in Leiden and has usually been attributed to a learned cleric working either in lower Lorraine or in some part of France.[60] However, Horst Fuhrmann has raised questions about the writer's location, as well as about his purpose in writing, which may have been less immediately practical than modern scholars have assumed.[61] Regardless of where or why it was written, *On Pontifical Ordination* is of interest for its extended critique of the ways in which popes were made and unmade between 1044 and 1047. The author, a thinker of austere tendencies, presents all of the individuals involved in an extremely harsh light, although he also designates some of the rival popes as preferable to others at various points. His arguments are largely based on canon law, including passages from Pseudo-Isidore, like the ones cited earlier. Significantly, however, some of the canons he uses were not originally intended to regulate a bishop's relationship with his see, but rather a husband's relationship with his wife.

The author apparently considered Benedict IX the most legitimate pope, even after he was driven out of Rome in 1044, for at least he

---

[59] *De ordinando pontifice*, MGH, LL 1: 8–14; reedited in Anton(1982). The passages discussed below are identical in the MGH and the Anton editions, so I have cited the former, which is more easily accessible.

[60] Anton (1982), Introduction, esp. pp. 9–11. An attempt has also been made to identify the author as Adelman, a student of Fulbert of Chartres, see Zieulewicz (1991), pp. 390–401. There is an extended discussion of the work in Melve (2007), vol. 1: 121–71.

[61] Fuhrmann (1992).

had broad support among his fellow bishops. To make this point, he paraphrases a passage from Cyprian's *On the Unity of the Church*:

If it is permitted to compare human to heavenly things ... the Church is the bride of Christ and bishops fill Christ's place. Therefore they are not the bridegrooms of the Church, but her bridegroom ... The number of bishops does not obstruct this [for] their unanimity should make them one. But if they are one, they are the bridegroom. He who falls away from unity is neither the bridegroom nor the bridegroom's friend.[62]

A pope like Silvester III, who did not enjoy the support of his fellow bishops, was, then, no true "bridegroom" of the church.

Benedict IX's relationship with his church did not end with his flight from Rome late in 1044. When he returned, the following spring, he had the right to reclaim his office. This is clear, argues the author of *On Pontifical Ordination*, from a letter of Pope Leo I:

For the venerable Pope Leo, writing to Nicetas, bishop of Aquileia, said, "If a wife, when her husband has been captured, marries another, when [the first husband] returns from captivity, let her be united to her former [husband], and let each man receive what is his. Nor shall he be judged culpable who shared in his marriage in the interim. And if the woman is unwilling to return she is to be expelled from ecclesiastical communion as impious."[63]

This passage makes the same point as Pseudo-Isidore, but does not, remarkably, cite that collection; rather, it refers to a text that had become part of the canon law of marriage. Reformers included it in their canonical collections to ensure the fidelity of wives whose husbands were absent for a long time.[64] Women who remarried in their husbands' absence – like the wife of Raymond (discussed in the previous chapter) – might be reminded of this text if their first husbands returned. Here, however, it is applied to the situation of a church whose bishop had been forced into exile.

On Pontifical Ordination also deploys the canon law of marriage in relation to a third candidate for the papacy, Gregory VI. The author treats Gregory ambiguously: in one passage describing him as preferable to the emperor's choice, Clement II, but in a second characterizing his assumption of the papal title in the spring of 1045 in strongly negative terms, first as theft and then as rape. Because "a lesson may be sought in lesser matters," the author reminds us of the laws requiring the consent

---

[62] *De ordinando pontifice*, MGH, LL 1: 9. Cf. Cyprian of Carthage, *De ecclesiae catholicae unitate*, 5–6, in *Opera*, LL, SL 3: 252–54.
[63] *De ordinando pontifice*, MGH, LL 1: 9–10.
[64] Leo I, *Epistolae*, 159 (PL 54: 1136–37) = JL 536; trans. Hunt, pp. 248–50.

of kin and of the bride in earthly marriage, then applies them to mystical unions:

> But if this happens to the Church, it is much worse because she is of much greater dignity. Who would choose him with whom we are dealing [Gregory VI]? He was not sought out by the "kin" of the Church, who are the bishops. He was not willingly accepted by the Church. Therefore, he is not legitimate …[65]

As we shall see, in seeking "lessons" about episcopal politics "in lesser matters," this author was by no means unique.

From the middle of the eleventh century on, efforts to regularize episcopal elections intensified in various parts of Europe.[66] Encouraged, perhaps, by such unseemly spectacles as the Roman schism of 1044–7, and fueled by the increasing availability of canon law collections, the ideal of the "free" and "canonical" election became more widely accepted. What such an election might actually entail, however, was by no means clear. Even the more radical reformers generally recognized the right of emperors and kings to participate as representatives of the "people." The revised process for the election of the pope agreed upon by Nicholas II and his cardinals in 1059 was intended to limit the influence of the Roman nobility in the choice of the Roman pontiff; the cardinal bishops of the Roman church were to take the lead in elections, so as to prevent further troubled elections. Nevertheless, consideration for the wishes of the emperor was built into this so-called "election decree."[67]

The movement to reform episcopal elections may, in the short run at least, have led to even more disputed elections, as reformers struggled with their conservative opponents for control of strategic sees.[68] During the papal schism of 1061, the reformers elected Alexander II, while the Empress Agnes, acting for her son, selected Cadalus of Parma.[69] Cardinal Peter Damian, one of those responsible for the election of Alexander II, immediately began firing off letters to his pope's rival, accusing Cadalus of illegitimate intrusion into the Roman see. His first letter was fairly mild, but, getting no response, Peter wrote again, in much stronger terms. This second letter depicts the antipope as a sexual predator, an adulterer, and a rapist.[70] His desire for office is represented as a form of lust, which threatens the "chastity" of the Church, and should be punished in the

---

[65] *De ordinando pontifice*, MGH, LL 1: 11.
[66] Gaudemet et al. (1979), esp. pp. 105–6, 108–11.
[67] Jasper (1986).
[68] Gaudemet et al. (1979), pp. 113–18; the *gesta episcoporum* and the *vitae* of saintly bishops also reveal many disputed elections.
[69] On this election, see below, Chapter 3.
[70] Peter Damian, 88, vol. 2: 519, 521, 528–29; trans. Blum 3: 313, 315, 322 and 324. Similar language is used in letter 89.

same way as ordinary sexual misbehavior: "We keep laymen from entering the Church if after abandoning their wives they are married to others; how much meaner is his adultery who, without synodal approval, like a plunderer, invades a church of another's jurisdiction after abandoning his own?"[71] As in *On pontifical ordination*, there is an echo here of Pseudo-Isidore, but Peter also makes direct use of marriage law.[72]

A second papal schism occurred in 1080, when Emperor Henry IV declared Gregory VII deposed, and arranged the election of his own pope, Wibert of Ravenna.[73] Bishop Anselm II of Lucca, a canon law expert, who had himself been expelled from his see by Henry IV's forces, accused Wibert of a "new and unheard-of abomination," for he had "defiled" the Roman Church "from top to bottom" (Jeremiah 2:16).[74] Wibert had committed adultery with her by intruding himself into the papal see, and thus all her modesty was departed – she was "no longer the Bride of Christ but an adulteress, not a free woman, but a slave girl."[75] A few years later, another canonist, Cardinal Deusdedit, composed an entire treatise *Against the Invaders of Churches*, in which he asserted that there will be no salvation for those invaders. The Henrician bishops are rapists, who "seize the wives of others and defile them," and are thus doomed to hell.[76] To the simple notion of adultery laid out in Pseudo-Isidore are added new images of violence, pollution, and degradation.

The violent language of these reformers reminds us that the bishop's marriage to his church was understood as much more than a metaphor in the eleventh and early twelfth centuries. In the works we have just examined, it is envisioned as a true marriage – indeed, a truer marriage than any human one. The sacred laws that govern earthly unions are, if anything, even more relevant to spiritual ones. And breaches of those laws are far graver. As the author of *On Pontifical Ordination* put it, "if this happens

---

[71] Peter Damian 88, vol. 2: 519; trans. Blum 3: 313. He further compares Cadalus' behavior to that of Biblical rapists, including Shechem, the abductor of Dinah (Genesis 34:1–3), and "those foreigners who had stripped off a virgin's veil to defile her, uncovered her thighs to shame her" (Judith 9:2–4).

[72] In a later letter, Peter asks Godfrey of Lorraine whether he would find it acceptable if someone else had sex with his wife; if not, then how can Godfrey accept Cadalus? Peter Damian 154, vol. 4: 69; trans. Blum 6(7): 73–74. Peter also applied the language of adultery and incest to the antipope Benedict X. Peter Damian 58, vol. 2: 193–94; trans. Blum 2: 393 and 393.

[73] Ziese (1982), pp. 54–64, 81–94; Cowdrey (1998a), pp. 201–3, 227–29; Robinson (1999), pp. 198–201, 227–29; Althoff (2006), pp. 171–73, 190.

[74] Anselm of Lucca, *Liber contra Wibertum*, MGH, LL 1: 520. On Anselm and the *Liber contra Wibertum*, see Berschin (1991), pp. 122–24; Cushing (1998), pp. 43–63 and 133–36. Jeremiah was cited in a similar context by Peter Damian, 88, vol. 2: 520; trans. Blum, 3: 313–14.

[75] Anselm, *Liber contra Wibertum*, MGH, LL 1: 521.

[76] Deusdedit, *Libellus contra invasores et symoniacos et reliquos schismaticos*, 2.20, MGH, LL 2: 340.

to the Church, it is much worse because she is of much greater dignity."[77] When modern scholars attempt to explain why irregularities in episcopal elections so disturbed churchmen in this period, they generally focus on the practical implications of improper or disputed elections for good order within the Church and for good behavior within the episcopate. Certainly these were important considerations. But such irregularities also induced, I would suggest, a powerfully visceral reaction, rooted in, and expressed through, concrete textual and visual images of the Church as Bride. Those active in reform movements seem to have been particularly sensitive to the Bride's vulnerability, as if compelled to respond to her desperate need for assistance. This attitude becomes even clearer if we turn to the reformers' rhetorical attacks on simony and lay investiture.

Matter out of place

Gift-giving played a crucial role in eleventh-century social relationships.[78] We have already seen how families arranging a marriage gave one another suitable presents. Rulers exchanged gifts – a beautifully forged sword, a piece of fine jewelry, a falcon – when they concluded a peace treaty.[79] Nobles made donations of land to monastic communities in return for "association" in their prayers.[80] It was thus quite normal for clerics who had dealings with powerful people to exchange gifts and services with them – a bishop might give a fine horse to a king, and receive in return a jeweled chalice for his cathedral. An abbot might offer a copy of his latest book to a noble lady, who would reciprocate by sending her personal physican to care for the abbot when he fell ill. This is how amicable relationships were maintained in this period – by frequent little attentions, and occasional bigger ones, that signaled friendship and a recognition of social position.

However, the potential for impropriety was very great. If the exchange of political favors for gifts is a problem in the twenty-first century, how much more acute was the problem a thousand years ago, when the boundary between acceptable social attentions and bribery was even less distinct. The vigorous eleventh-century campaign against simony – the traffic in ecclesiastical offices and other holy things – was not primarily directed against the relatively small number of cases in which someone purchased a bishopric or abbacy outright.[81] Such behavior was clearly beyond the pale. The more difficult problem was to separate nominations

---

[77] *De ordinando pontifice*, MGH, LL 1: 11.   [78] Fichtenau (1984), pp. 40–42
[79] E.g. Raoul Glaber, 3.8, pp. 108–11; *Ruodlieb*, 5, pp. 68–77.
[80] White (1988); Rosenwein (1989); McLaughlin (1994).
[81] On Wifred of Cerdaña's purchase of the see of Narbonne for his son, see Magnou-Nortier (1974), pp. 351–53 and 463–68. The price of the see of Rimini at the end of the

to office from the ongoing and completely normalized exchanges of property and services at the highest levels of society.[82]

Recent scholarship has attempted to explain why behavior widely accepted in the ninth and tenth centuries became "simoniacal" in the eleventh. The rhetoric used by individual reformers and by reforming church councils in this period indicates several layers of concern. The first is simply legal: St. Peter had denounced Simon Magus (after whom "simony" was named) for his attempt to purchase the gifts of the Holy Spirit; Pope Gregory I had condemned the acquisition of such spiritual gifts through purchase (even if disguised as a freewill offering), through service, or in return for promises of assistance;[83] and a number of later church councils had reiterated Gregory's broad definition of simony (although not always applying it in practice) and these decisions were then incorporated into major collections of canon law, including Pseudo-Isidore.[84] With the revival of canon law in the eleventh century, the decisions of these earlier church councils became more accessible, making failure to comply more reprehensible. Anyone aware of these rules who nevertheless continued to offer gifts in return for appointment to a bishopric was clearly rejecting the established law of the church – hence the use of the phrase "simoniacal *heresy*" to designate those who defended traditional ways of doing things, despite their knowledge that those ways were forbidden.[85]

The second layer of worry was practical. The intrusion of economic considerations into decisions about ecclesiastical appointments was – in the reformers' view – a formula for moral disaster. Candidates chosen primarily because they were willing and able to make gifts were unlikely to be effective spiritual leaders. The undesirable moral consequences of simony were a common theme in reforming diatribes: "As irreligious laxity grows amongst the clergy, a lust for wantonness and incontinence prevails amongst the laity ... Because guilty blindness has crept over the bishops who are the eye of the catholic faith, its people, ignorant of the path to salvation, fall into ruinous perdition."[86]

Yet even if a man of high moral character were (somehow) appointed as bishop under the existing system, and even if he did his best to maintain

---

tenth century was apparently nine hundred pounds in the coin of Pavia: Peter Damian, 40, vol. 1: 479; trans. Blum, 2: 188.

[82] Making it easy to use accusations of simony as a political weapon: see Schieffer (1972); Vollrath (1993).

[83] Gregory defined the three types of simony as *a manu, ab obsequio*, and *a lingua*: *Homiliae in Evangelia*, 1.4.4, p. 31.

[84] For the debate on whether this constituted an "extension" of the definition, see Hirsch (1906); Meier-Welcker (1952/53); Vollrath (1993).

[85] Leclercq (1947); Gilchrist (1965).

[86] Raoul Glaber, 2.12, pp. 72–73; cf. 4.17, 4.25, pp. 196–99, 210–13.

discipline within his flock, his integrity was still compromised. For he always remained obligated to the person who had appointed him, to the proprietors and patrons of the church he served. Timothy Reuter has argued that the extension of definitions of simony in the eleventh century was intended to make bishops and abbots more independent of the lay powers who had hitherto controlled churches: "What the [new] discourse of simony provided was a coded means of renouncing the church's normal gift obligation."[87] The constant reiteration of the phrase "freely you have received, freely give" (Matthew 10:8) in anti-simoniacal writings suggests a reaction against the normal system of gift and countergift, with its expectations of reciprocity and ongoing obligation.

It is, however, the third, symbolic, level of anxiety that particularly concerns us here. The eleventh-century "discourse of simony" drew heavily on a new vocabulary of dirt, defilement, and disgust, which seems to reflect several major cultural shifts occurring around the turn of the century, almost certainly related to the expansion of commerce and the increased circulation of money.[88] Spiritual leaders were becoming concerned with money as a potential source of spiritual danger. Not only simony, specifically, but the sin of avarice, conceived very broadly, now began to receive much more attention than in the past.[89] This was not simply a reaction of the "poor in Christ" (as monastic writers in this period characterized themselves) against the excesses of the rich, and the power they wielded through their wealth. Rather, it seems to reflect an obsession with maintaining the boundaries between what we would call commercial transactions (i.e. those determined by economic motives), and other forms of exchange, which ought to have been shaped by moral and spiritual concerns.[90] It is not an accident that – as we saw in the last chapter – prostitution was now becoming an issue. For sex exchanged for money was, in Mary Douglas' phrase, "matter out of place"[91] – the union of two bodies outside the context of lawful marriage, and without the moral imperative of the marital debt. Commercial sex work, and commerce more generally, are closely associated with simony in reforming polemics.[92] All three activities involved venality and avarice, which made them inherently defiling.

---

[87] Reuter (2001), p. 164.

[88] On pollution concerns and their role in the rhetoric of simony, compare Remensnyder (1992); Cowdrey (1998a), pp. 545–46; Cushing (2005), pp. 111–20.

[89] Little (1978), pp. 31, 70–83; Murray (1978), pp. 59–80.

[90] E.g. Peter Damian 40, vol. 1: 480 and 501; trans. Blum 2: 189 and 206 – on simony as a "commercial deal" and on the dangers of avarice.

[91] Douglas (1966), especially pp. 35–40.

[92] In Humbert's *Adversus Simoniacos* (discussed in more detail below), not only does prostitution appear, but there is also an unfavorable comparison between merchants – who at least sell their own goods – and simoniacs: 2.17, MGH, LL 1: 158–59. On this point, see also Moore (1980), pp. 66–67.

In the letters of reformers and in the *libelli de lite*, simony was linked not only to images of pollution, but often, more specifically, to images of sexual pollution.[93] In question, moreover, was the corruption of the individual soul, as well as of the Church. If the Song of Songs was normally understood to refer to Christ's marriage to the Church, a very important secondary interpretation of the Song was as the epithalamium of Christ and the soul. The image of the soul as bride had already been richly elaborated in the early Middle Ages; it continued to be discussed extensively in a variety of contexts in the eleventh and early twelfth centuries, and of course reached its most beautiful expression in the mid-twelfth, in Bernard of Clairvaux's sermons on the Song of Songs. A full discussion of this theme falls outside the purview of this book. We must, however, give it some consideration here, for in discussions of simony a similar language of pollution was consistently applied to both "brides."

The generation of vipers

The sexually corrupted soul is a theme in the two best-known treatises on simony from this period – Peter Damian's *Most Gratuitous Book* (*Liber Gratissimus*) and Humbert of Silva Candida's *Three Books against the Simoniacs*. Both were written by members of the reforming circle in Rome in the 1050s, but the two authors reached distinctly different conclusions. Peter claimed that the sacraments performed by simoniacs remained valid – for they depended on the gift of God, and not on moral status of those who administered them. Humbert, on the other hand, argued that the heinous nature of simony prevented simoniacs from receiving divine grace, and that therefore they could not confer that grace on others. Nevertheless, both Peter and Humbert understood simony to be intensely polluting to the soul of the simoniac, and both represented that pollution in sexual terms.

In his *Most Gratuitous Book*, Peter Damian argues that the sacraments are always pure, no matter how "contaminated" the person performing them may be.[94] Those consecrated by simoniacs – without themselves paying anything for their office – are therefore true priests. "Often," Peter writes, "a beautiful child is born of an adulterous union, and from the indecent lust of parents an admirable line of offspring comes into being."[95] Thus he evokes the common idea that ordination is a form of

---

[93] Cowdrey (1998a), p. 545; and see below.
[94] The work was originally written in 1051, although Peter later revised it. The extensive scholarly literature on this work is listed in note 2 to Peter Damian, 40, vol. 1: 385; see also Cushing (2005), p. 118.
[95] Peter Damian, 40, vol. 1: 439–41; trans. Blum, 2: 154–56.

generation, an idea normally related to the notion that the bishop is the father of the priest whom he ordains.[96] Here, though, the simoniacal bishop is compared to a sinful *mother*. Specific examples of "beautiful children" born of "adulterous" unions include Pharez, "born of her who played the harlot and sat at the crossroads," and Boaz, the son of Rahab, the harlot.[97] Elsewhere in the *Most Gratuitous Book*, Peter compares the contamination caused by simony to that of a grave or a sewer, and often to that of leprosy.[98] A central image, however, is that of sexual defilement, and specifically the defilement of harlotry.

The association of simony with sexual pollution and prostitution is even more intense in Humbert's *Three Books against the Simoniacs*. He uses the language of filth and disgust, which is further linked to violence, to argue that simony is an impassable barrier to the reception of divine grace. Humbert's treatise on simony, in its present form, consists of three books.[99] In the first, he argues that bishops who purchase their offices are not really bishops at all, because the gifts of the Holy Spirit cannot be obtained through a purchased ordination. The second book is essentially an extended sermon, which outlines the moral failings of simoniacs and the destructive nature of their sin. The third book raises the issue of lay involvement in ecclesiastical appointments. Modern historians have primarily been interested in Book One, in which Humbert provides the theological and canonical authorities to support his radical ideas about simony. Book Three has also attracted considerable scholarly attention, because its attack on lay influence within the Church seems to foreshadow the later Investiture Conflict.

My focus below is primarily on Book Two, which has been little discussed in modern scholarship.[100] I should point out, however, that Humbert's uneasiness with "matter out of place" and his fear of pollution are evident throughout the entire work. In the Preface, for example, he expresses his desire that "the precious and the vile, ... the holy and the profane, the clean and the unclean" should be kept separate.[101] Book One outlines the ways in which catholics should be kept apart from

---

[96] See below, Chapter 6.

[97] Peter Damian, 40, vol. 1: 447; trans. Blum 2: 162. On Pharez, see Genesis 38; the connection of Boaz, from the book of Ruth, with the harlot Rahab is not Biblical.

[98] Peter Damian 40, vol. 1: 521, 424, 440, 453; trans. Blum 2: 139, 141, 155–56, 167.

[99] Elaine Robison's revised edition (Ph.D. dissertation, Princeton University, 1972) is not readily available, so I have cited this work from the MGH. It has been suggested that Book Three was an addition to the original work: see Hoesch (1970), p. 32. Humbert's career in Rome is summarized by Hüls (1977), pp. 131–34; see also Blumenthal (2004b). Relatively recent discussions of *Against the Simoniacs* include Schieffer (1981), pp. 36–47; Laudage (1984), pp. 169–84; Szabó-Bechstein (1985), pp. 130–37; and Struve (1991), pp. 223–24.

[100] An exception is Fliche (1924–37), vol. 1: 284–93

[101] Humbert of Silva Candida, *Adversus simoniacos libri tres*, Praefatio, MGH, LL 1: 100.

heretics.[102] Book Two explains how the faithful can distinguish real from pseudo-bishops.[103] And Book Three stresses the importance of separating the laity from the clergy, their property, and their sacramental office.[104]

For Humbert, simony was a problem for theological reasons, but also, more viscerally, because it broke down the walls of difference, permitting leakage from one category into another. Money was the great solvent: it "made the sacred secular."[105] And this breakdown of difference created pollution: in making the sacred secular, it also made the clean unclean. Pollution might be imagined in terms of disease – most often as leprosy.[106] But for Humbert, an even more potent symbol of the pollution brought on by simony was sexual impurity. Already in his Preface, he equates the simoniac with the harlot of Proverbs 7 and 9, who seduces the simple. The simoniac as prostitute returns in Book Two. Like a merchant, who looks forward to annual fairs in order to fill his empty purse, so the simoniac (the seller of offices) looks forward to ordinations.[107] But the money he gains from these transactions will do him no good – even if he expends it on almsgiving or pilgrimage – for God rejects the simoniac's wealth. According to Deuteronomy 23:18, "You shall not bring a prostitute's fee, nor the price of a dog into the house of the Lord thy God in payment for any vow, for both are an abomination unto the Lord thy God." And if divine law spurns what an earthly prostitute earns for corrupting her own and another person's flesh, how much more will be rejected the fee the simoniac earns, for prostituting his own soul and those of many others?[108]

Thus Humbert, like Peter Damian, associates simony with prostitution. But he also develops another, far more horrifying, image in the second book of *Against the Simoniacs*. This passage depends heavily on a poem by the early Christian poet Prudentius (d. *ca* 405), which examines, in very similar terms, the destruction of the soul by mortal sin.[109] Prudentius, in turn, drew his imagery from the *Physiologus*, that curious compilation of natural history lore, combined with allegorical interpretations of (sometimes quite imaginary) animal behavior.[110] *Physiologus* became increasingly

---

[102] Humbert, *Adversus simoniacos*, esp. 1.11, MGH, LL 1: 116–18.
[103] Humbert, *Adversus simoniacos*, esp. 2.39–40, MGH, LL 1: 188–90.
[104] Humbert, *Adversus simoniacos*, 3, MGH, LL 1: 196–253.
[105] Humbert, *Adversus simoniacos*, 1.14, MGH, LL 1: 123.
[106] Humbert, *Adversus simoniacos*, Praefatio; 1.16–17; 3.13, MGH, LL 1: 100, 128, 215.
[107] Humbert, *Adversus simoniacos*, 2.21, MGH, LL 1: 164; cf. 2.26, p. 171.
[108] Humbert, *Adversus simoniacos*, 2.21, MGH, LL 1: 165.
[109] Prudentius, *Hamartigenia*, ll. 581–636, pp. 92–96. Cf. Gregory I, *Moralia in Iob*, 15.15, vol. 143A: 759–60; Isidore of Seville, *Etymologiae*, 12.4.10 (PL 82: 443).
[110] On *Physiologus*, see Lauchert (1889); Goldstaub (1899–1901); McCulloch (1962); and Henkel (1976).

popular in the eleventh century, and must have been circulating among the reformers in Rome.[111] Humbert draws from it directly, as well as indirectly through Prudentius, in Book Two of *Against the Simoniacs*.

In a lengthy passage, he describes the sex lives of vipers, which are the "worst of all beasts," just as simoniacs are the worst of heretics.[112] According to the *Physiologus*, Humbert says, a female viper conceives by coming at her mate with an open mouth. When he, "mad with lust," places his head in her mouth, she promptly bites it off and swallows it. Thus she conceives from her mate's death. When it is time for her to give birth, she perishes in her turn, for the young vipers gnaw their way out of her sides. "Thus these, the worst of all beasts, perish – the male when they mate, the female when she gives birth. The male is killed by the female, the female by her children – who will themselves meet their parents' fate not long after."[113] This excursion into natural history is not irrelevant, for "nothing in the world occurs without reason." Considered typologically (*typice*), the mating of vipers "fits very well" with two spiritual situations – the general case of the heretic's soul falling into mortal sin (this is closely related to Prudentius' theme), and the more specific case of the simoniac (Humbert's primary concern). The ensuing discussion plays off the traditional notion of the human soul as the Bride of God: for both mortal sinners and simoniacs, that spiritual marriage is so hideously perverted that the end result is not spiritual rebirth, but destruction.

Money functions here as the moral equivalent of the vipers' sexual desire.[114] In the would-be buyer of church office, the natural movement of his soul towards God is "corrupted," so that his goal becomes, instead, the purchase of honor. Like the female viper, he pursues a "mate," someone from whom he can acquire the desired office (this person becomes, like the Devil in the previous section, the "adulterer"). The "female" simoniac opens her mouth to reveal the money within. Next, her mate, "insane with the love of money," inserts his head by submerging his most important characteristics, his faith and reason, in the infidelity and irrationality of the other. This leads to his death, for by offering him money in return for office, "she" has taken away his faith, his most important part.

The seller loses his grace, nor does the buyer gain it, but the wrath of God horribly reaches them both. Thus they mutually kill each other with their tongues,

---

[111] Peter Damian made extensive use of *Physiologus* in his Letter 86, vol. 2: 459–504; trans. Blum 3: 255–98.

[112] Humbert, *Adversus simoniacos*, 2.11–13, MGH, LL 1: 151–54. The phrase "worst of beasts" (p. 152) probably derives from Ambrose, *Hexaemeron*, 5: 7 (PL 14: 213).

[113] Humbert, *Adversus simoniacos*, 2.12, MGH, LL 1: 152.

[114] The connection may have been suggested by Ambrose, *De Tobia*, 12 (PL 14: 774–75), who compared moneylenders to vipers.

like vipers, because – made heretics, this one by asking, that one by offering grace venally – they perish. And since both are venomous, only venomous children are born to them.[115]

While Peter Damian had argued that "beautiful children" could be born of "adulterous" parents, Humbert concludes that only "venomous children" could be born from such vipers as the buyers and sellers of church offices.

To both Peter and Humbert, then, simoniacs are disgusting and effeminate – like harlots or female vipers.[116] But Humbert, even more than Peter, underlines his disgust through the violence of his language. In the mating of the unfaithful soul with the Devil, or the joining of the buyers and sellers of church office, the boundaries between sexual partners are violently invaded and exploded, with deadly results. But the horrors of simony go beyond its effects on the soul of the simoniac. According to the best-known Latin text of *Physiologus*, with which Humbert seems to have been familiar,

Our Savior compared the Pharisees to vipers [Matthew 3:7; Luke 3:7]. Just as in the latter, the generation [of offspring] kills father and mother, so too that godless people [kills] its father, Jesus Christ, and mother, the earthly Jerusalem. And how will they flee from the wrath to come? Our father Jesus Christ and Mother Church will live forever, but they, living in sin, are [already] dead.[117]

Not the attempted killing of the Church, but her pollution horrifies Humbert. As simoniacs themselves "fornicate," through their infidelity to Christ, so, too, they "stain" and "ruin" the Church, who ought to be "without spot or wrinkle." They contaminate her with the contagion of their uncleanness, so that her Bridegroom has to warn her not to wander among the "flocks" of her "companions" (cf. Song 1:7), that is, among the heretics. Christ warns the Church to remember who she is, and how she is obliged to him, lest he give her a bill of divorce (*libellum repudii*). Let her not endanger her chastity amid the lust and wantonness of the "goats" (the simoniacs), which threatens to "defile her from top to bottom" (Jeremiah 2:16) by admitting adulterers into the bridal chamber.[118] Thus, in Book Two of *Against the Simoniacs*, the Church is represented as in some sense complicit in her own "ruin."

---

[115] Humbert, *Adversus simoniacos*, 2.13, MGH, LL 1: 153.
[116] Peter also used the image of the viper in the *Most Gratuitous Book*, but only briefly. Peter Damian 40, vol. 1: 473; Blum 2: 182.
[117] "Physiologus Latinus, versio Y," 12, p. 110.
[118] Humbert, *Adversus simoniacos*, 2.32, MGH, LL 1: 180–81. A similar reference to Jeremiah 2:16 occurs in Anselm of Lucca, *Liber contra Wibertum*, MGH, LL 1: 520; cf. Anselm's letter in *Briefsammlungen*, p. 17.

Presumably this was because Book Two deals with the faults of the clergy (identified with the Church). A very different picture emerges in Book Three, where the Bride is depicted as the helpless victim of lay abuse. Here, laymen use their wealth to claim for themselves what should belong to the "household of the Church" (*familiae ecclesiasticae*).[119] This makes them not only thieves, but rapists – and here Humbert cites both canon and secular law on abduction and marriage. "If some wicked person seizes another man's bride along with her trousseau [*supellectilum*], by giving (or promising) money to her treacherous and avaricious guardian, couldn't money truly be said to have overcome her and all her possessions?" Under canon law such a crime would be punished by lifelong excommunication, under secular law by death or perpetual exile for her abductor, her guardian, and all their accomplices. This demonstrates just how desperate the Church is, how little consideration is given to her: "for no one can be found who mourns her injuries, no one who defends her chastity – which is prostituted, sold, and bestowed on sacrilegious rapists [*sacrilegis raptoribus prostitutam, venditam et addictam*]. No one [can be found], even, who will take her back from them, and return her, however defiled [*constupratam*], to her Bridegroom." No ecclesiastical or lay official, laments Humbert, pays any heed to Jesus' bitter complaints concerning his abducted Bride – they should fear his vengeance for the "despicable rape of his Bride" (*raptus suae sponsae quamlibet abjectus*).[120]

Based on the manuscript tradition alone, one might think that Humbert had little influence on his contemporaries.[121] Only one full copy of *Against the Simoniacs*, containing all three books, survives; fragments appear in only two other manuscripts. Yet even if few people actually read *Against the Simoniacs*, Humbert's ideas on simony almost certainly circulated by word of mouth within the Roman curia and beyond.[122] Certainly some of his violent imagery had a rhetorical afterlife. After Humbert's younger colleague, Hildebrand, became Pope Gregory VII, some of Humbert's images resurfaced in his letters. One described the iniquities of Bishop Juhel of Dol, who had acquired his see from Count Alan of Britanny in return for numerous gifts. To make things worse, after Juhel became bishop he married: "so that he who had already prostituted his soul to the debaucher of souls by his simoniacal trafficking might likewise dedicate his body in shame to the devil by his lewd and foul lust."[123] While Gregory did not represent simoniacs as fornicating vipers in this letter, his rhetoric plays on the same idea of the simoniac's soul united sexually

---

[119] Humbert, *Adversus simoniacos*, 3.5, MGH, LL 1: 203.
[120] Humbert, *Adversus simoniacos*, 3.5, MGH, LL 1: 203.
[121] Schieffer (1981), pp. 41–47.   [122] Leyser (1994), vol. 2: 3.
[123] Gregory VII, *Epistolae vagantes*, 16, pp. 44–47.

to the devil.[124] Gregory also echoes Humbert very directly when he writes to the faithful in Lombardy that Archbishop Godfrey of Milan had

> presumed to buy, like a base slave-girl, the church which formerly ... shone forth among the other churches of the Lombards for religion, liberty, and especial glory; now, in an attempt to prostitute the bride of Christ to the devil and to separate her from the catholic faith, he has striven to besmirch her with the offence of heresy.[125]

The "heresy" in question being that of defending simoniacal transactions.[126]

Towards the end of his life, when Gregory sought to sum up his goals as a reformer, he chose a very concrete image: he wanted to ensure that the "holy Church, the Bride of Christ, our Lady and Mother" would be "free, chaste, and catholic" (libera, casta, et catholica).[127] Insofar as this formula has received any scholarly attention, the focus has largely been on the image of the Church as "free," in relation to other references from this period to the "freedom of the Church."[128] The other two elements in the formula – catholicity and chastity – have been almost completely overlooked, perhaps because they seem self-explanatory. The Church had to be catholic – that is, unified, in the true faith, neither schismatic nor heretical. And she had to be chaste – that is, pure, undefiled by abuses such as simony or clerical marriage.

The term "chaste," however, does not denote purity in general so much as it does a specifically sexual, and highly gendered, purity. While men (especially clerics) could and perhaps should be chaste, abstinence from unlawful sexual contact was the central virtue for women in the central Middle Ages, as in earlier and later centuries. Gregory VII, then, was imagining the problem of reform in sexualized and gendered terms, as Humbert had done.[129] His formula, which was repeatedly restated by his successors, would not have seemed inappropriate even to clerics far from Rome, for they already associated bridal imagery with the Church. In northern Europe, however, only one reformer followed Humbert and Gregory in linking simony with the prostitution of the Church.

[124] Cf. Archbishop Gerard of York to Anselm (Anselm, 373, vol. 5: 316–17; trans. Fröhlich, vol. 3: 124).
[125] Gregory VII, Register 1.15, pp. 23–25; trans. Cowdrey, pp. 15–17.
[126] Gilchrist (1965).
[127] Gregory VII, Epistolae vagantes 54, pp. 128–35. On the circumstances, see Cowdrey (1998a), pp. 677–82.
[128] On the "freedom of the Church," see especially Tellenbach (1936), pp. 126–61; Szabó-Bechstein (1985); and now Cowdrey (1998a), pp. 536–39. Remarkably, however, neither Tellenbach nor Szabó-Bechstein pays much attention to Gregory's formulation.
[129] Cf. Gregory VII, Register, 2.55 and 2.67, pp. 200–1 and 223–25; trans. Cowdrey, pp. 148–49, 160–61.

Abbot Geoffrey of Vendôme's preoccupation with this theme was probably fueled in part by his personal interest in the symbolic value and legal status of prostitutes. Like other churchmen in the west of France during this period, Geoffrey was devoted to the cult of the "holy harlot," Mary Magdalene.[130] However, he also had very close ties to Rome, and was strongly influenced both by the Roman reformers' ideas and, it is clear, by their rhetoric.[131] Gregory VII's formula – *catholica, libera et casta* – was extremely important to Geoffrey's conception of the Church and his understanding of why reform was needed.[132] Some variant of it appears in at least twelve of his letters, dating from 1101 to the mid-1120s, and he developed the ideas it encapsulates in a variety of ways over the years.[133] But Geoffrey chose to focus much more than Gregory had on the "chastity" of the church, which he imagined to be seriously threatened by simony and by lay investiture.[134] His rhetoric is, in fact, highly reminiscent of Humbert's, although it seems unlikely that he had any direct knowledge of *Against the Simoniacs*. Perhaps the powerful images Humbert had used half a century earlier were still circulating in Rome in Geoffrey's day.

In 1101–2, Geoffrey attempted to prevent the elevation of the underage and irregularly elected Renaud of Martigné to the see of Angers.[135] His letters accuse Renaud of simony – "the first and greatest" of heresies, which "presumes to defile the chastity of the church with the foulest pollution."[136] Renaud's election threatens to turn Christ's Church – which should be completely chaste and free – into the "concubine and slave of worldliness" (*secularitatis concubinam et ancillam … constituistis*). Geoffrey would rather be "burned alive" than consent to such an "abomination."[137] All his efforts were in vain, however, and he had to resign himself to Renaud's episcopacy. Early in 1102 he wrote to the new bishop of Angers (whom he now called his "dear friend"), encouraging him to fulfill his role with courage and integrity. If he weakens in defense of his church, she who was "confided to his care chaste and free" will become "a harlot and a slave-girl"

---

[130] See Dalarun (1992). And see Geoffrey of Vendôme, 73 and 215, pp. 130–38, 536–42.

[131] On Geoffrey's links with Rome, see Johnson (1981), pp. 114–20; Giordanengo's introduction to Geoffrey's works, esp. pp. VIII–XIII and XXI.

[132] Probably he knew of the formula not directly from Gregory's encyclical of 1084 (although it did circulate in France), but from its reiteration at the Council of Clermont, which Geoffrey personally attended: *Councils of Urban II, Volume I: Decreta Claromontensia*, p. 90.

[133] Geoffrey of Vendôme, Nos. 14, 19, 28, 111, 112, 126, 134, 142, 153, 176, 189, 203.

[134] On lay investiture, see below.

[135] On the election in Angers, see Hildebert of Le Mans, *Epistolae*, 2.4, 2.5 (PL 171: 211–13). Cf. Hauréau (1870); Bienvenu (1968), pp. 151–55; Guillot (1972), vol. 1: 260–62.

[136] Geoffrey of Vendôme, 14, p. 28. Cf. Humbert, *Adversus simoniacos*, 2.21, MGH LL 1: 164.

[137] Geoffrey of Vendôme, 19, p. 36.

(*meretrix efficietur et ancilla*).[138] This letter seems to echo Humbert's attack on the iniquitous guardians of the Bride, who, far from protecting her, sold her off like a slave.[139]

In the prostitute, Geoffrey of Vendôme saw a powerful symbol, with complex associations.[140] If he used it extensively to describe the corrosive effects of simony, it was because it pulled together his awareness of the sin's especially polluting nature, and his horror (shared with Humbert) of the corrupting role of money.[141] These ideas are all present in a short, but extremely dense, treatise, addressed to Pope Calixtus II, on what made the Church "catholic, free and chaste." She is catholic, Geoffrey wrote, because she should be neither sold nor bought; free, because she should be subject to no secular power; chaste, because she should not be corrupted by gifts. She loses her (catholic) faith, when she is sold or bought, because what God made beyond price, man thinks he can put a price on. Someone who sells a church imitates the cupidity of Judas, and someone who buys it follows the Jews in avarice.[142] When the Church is made subject to a secular power, she who was the mistress before becomes a mere slave. On the cross, with his own blood, Christ wrote a "charter of liberty" for his Bride, the Church, to turn men who had been slaves to the devil into the free offspring of a free mother.[143] But the Church, when corrupted by gifts, loses her chastity entirely, and instead of the chaste and virginal Bride of the Lord becomes "like a common woman" (*quasi mulier publica*).[144] "For this is the nature of a whore," Geoffrey notes, "that she is always sold for a price" (*Hoc enim est proprium meretricis ut semper sub precio redigatur*).[145]

Geoffrey warns Calixtus about the terrible implications of heresy, lay investiture, and simony. If the Church is no longer catholic, free, or chaste, she can no longer be called the Bride of Christ: "For Christ, the good shepherd, seeks a faithful wife and scorns the unfaithful; he takes the free to himself and rejects the slave; he loves the chaste and hates the impure." Like Humbert, who wrote about the Bridegroom offering his

---

138 Geoffrey of Vendôme, 28, p. 50.
139 Another significant occurrence of harlot imagery occurs in Geoffrey of Vendôme, 134, pp. 274 and 278.
140 Geoffrey of Vendôme, 142, p. 302.
141 Geoffrey of Vendôme, 199 and 203, pp. 494 and 508.
142 Cf. Humbert, *Adversus simoniacos*, 2.20–21, MGH LL 1: 163–65.
143 See Chapter 3 below.
144 The phrase *mulier publica*, drawn from classical usage, became the most common designation for the prostitute in later medieval Europe: see Karras (1996), p. 138.
145 Geoffrey of Vendôme, 176, p. 406. We know that Geoffrey was familiar with Ivo of Chartres's canon law collections – could he have been influenced by Ivo's views on prostitution? (See above, Chapter 1.) Compare also Humbert, *Adversus simoniacos*, 2.21, MGH, LL 1: 164.

faithless Bride a "bill of divorce,"[146] Geoffrey envisions a chilling scenario in which Christ rejects the corrupted Church.

The abbot of Vendôme's depiction of the prostituted Church probably owes something to Geoffrey's own preoccupation with the figure of the fallen woman; it certainly borrows directly from Gregory VII's formula, and also, I would argue, echoes directly or indirectly Humbert's rhetoric of simony. Like these Roman reformers, Geoffrey was transforming an ancient idea to reflect the concerns of his own day. The Church had long been represented as a whore in Biblical exegesis – especially in commentaries on the Old Testament prophets, who excoriated Israel (identified by Christian exegetes with the Church) for "whoring after foreign gods." Following this exegetical tradition, which viewed "harlotry" as a matter of promiscuity, of infidelity to God, early medieval writers had viewed heresy or schism as the cause of the Church's meretricious behavior. These traditional ideas were given a new twist by Humbert and his successors. Reformers in the central Middle Ages saw the Church's chastity compromised not simply by promiscuity, but by the exchange of money for what might be called "spiritual sex" – the acquisition of ecclesiastical office. In their writings, a complex nexus of ideas about the corrupting influence of money, ideas that apparently arose out of the changing economic environment of the time, turned the Church from a simple whore into a "common woman," abandoned as well as defiled, because she was sold by her guardians "for a price."

Catholic, chaste, and free

"Investiture," in a medieval context, refers to the transfer of a variety of physical symbols – generally denoting some kind of authority, a particular office, or rights over property – from one person to another. The person who invests is thought to hold the authority or to control the office or land in question, and to be transferring it, by means of the symbol, to the person invested. A pervasive ritual in the Middle Ages, investiture could occur in a variety of situations and take a variety of forms.[147] Sometimes, however, it involved powerful rulers or nobles granting the symbols of ecclesiastical office to bishops, abbots, or abbesses.[148] "Lay investiture" is the phrase historians commonly use to describe this phenomenon. The phrase is, of course, problematic, because it implicitly accepts the contention of the more radical reformers that emperors and

---

[146] Humbert, *Adversus simoniacos*, 2.32, MGH LL 1: 181.   [147] Keller (1993).

[148] Because my focus in this book is on episcopal authority, I will not be discussing the investiture of abbots and abbesses.

kings were "merely" laymen – a contention emperors, kings, and their followers often vehemently denied. Nevertheless, it provides a convenient shorthand for a set of practices that originated in the ninth-century Carolingian heartland, spreading to other parts of Europe (and to a much wider social stratum) by the beginning of the eleventh century.

Carolingian rulers had begun granting the pastoral staff to new bishops as a way of signaling approval of their election.[149] The ritual paralleled that by which they granted control over land or office to their secular vassals, by means of a staff or wand. As control over episcopal churches gradually devolved into the hands of nobles over the course of the tenth century, they, too, began investing the holders of those churches with the staff. The episcopal ring, on the other hand, had no secular equivalent; it remained for a time a purely ecclesiastical symbol, conferred on the new bishop by the other bishops present at his consecration. Only in the eleventh century, and then only in certain parts of Europe, did rulers begin investing bishops with the ring as well as the staff, before their consecration. The chronology is not entirely clear, but investiture with the ring seems to have originated in the Holy Roman Empire, in conjunction with the development of the emperor's theocratic claims to authority. Henry II is the first emperor we know of to invest with both ring and staff.[150] It is normally assumed that other western European rulers began investing with the ring as well in this period.[151] In fact, though, it is not at all clear whether this was the case.

What is clear is that, before the last quarter of the eleventh century, few churchmen were troubled by either the practice of lay investiture or the introduction of the ring into the process. Some, notably Cardinal Humbert, grumbled a bit, but the first general prohibition of "investiture by laypersons" was not issued until 1078.[152] Over the next few decades, councils issued similar decrees more than twenty times, but not nearly as often as decrees against simony or nicolaitism.[153] Most reformers devoted relatively little attention to lay investiture until 1100, when Archbishop Anselm of Canterbury refused to accept investiture from the new king of England, Henry I.[154] Ironically, Anselm had been peacefully invested by Henry's predecessor, King William Rufus, seven years earlier. Now, however, the archbishop had changed his position. Having been present

---

[149] Keller (1993), pp. 61–66.   [150] Keller (1993), pp. 60–61.
[151] E.g. Engels (1987), p. 758.
[152] See Schieffer (1981), pp. 153–76; Engelberger (1996) and (1998); Cowdrey (1998a), pp. 103–08, 546–50. Blumenthal (2001), pp. 172–78, provides an excellent discussion of the issue.
[153] Beulertz (1991), pp. 4–25, 83–84, 158–60.
[154] On the conflict between Anselm and Henry I, see Brooke (1931), pp. 147–74; Cantor (1958); Southern (1963) and (1990); Vaughn (1980); Blumenthal (1982), pp. 142–59; on the king's role in the English church, see now Green (2006), pp. 254–83.

at a Roman synod in the spring of 1099, during which Urban II reissued earlier prohibitions against clerics doing homage to laymen or receiving investiture from them, Anselm apparently felt bound to follow its policy. The result was a prolonged quarrel between king and archbishop, which led the former to confiscate the revenues of the see of Canterbury, and the latter to go into exile. Only in 1107, after a compromise had been brokered between them, did Anselm return to England.

The subject of lay investiture was canvassed in letters among the principals, in historical narratives, and in a few treatises composed by Anglo-Norman writers. For our purposes, however, what is most striking about these works is their *lack* of nuptial imagery. Anselm himself never mentions the bishop's marriage to his church nor identifies the ring as a symbol of that marriage; he also devotes much less attention to the image of the Church as Bride than either Humbert or the later Italian writers Ranger of Lucca or Placidus of Nonantola.[155] Anselm's biographer, Eadmer, our major source of information on the archbishop's quarrel with Henry I, also seems uninterested in this aspect of the subject. Hugh of Fleury, a conservative writer who generally supported the king in this dispute, mentions the bishop as bridegroom only a single time, in passing, and within the context of a discussion of episcopal dignity, rather than investiture.[156] Only one Anglo-Norman writer, the profoundly conservative "Norman Anonymous" – a staunch defender of lay investiture – pays much attention to the Bride, and then only in a very idiosyncratic way.[157]

Her absence from Anglo-Norman writings on investiture can probably be ascribed to differences in ritual traditions between England (and perhaps Normandy as well) and the imperial territories. To begin with, it is by no means clear that the Anglo-Norman kings ever invested new bishops with the ring.[158] Most modern scholars have assumed that they did, perhaps because the ring plays such a prominent role in continental works on the subject. However, when Eadmer describes how Anselm accepted investiture from William Rufus, he refers only to the staff. The Norman Anonymous' discussion of investiture likewise focuses on the staff.[159] The absence of investiture with the ring would certainly have eliminated

[155] Even during the period of his quarrel with Henry, the Bride is mentioned only very briefly in Anselm's letters: Anselm 235, 248, 249, 262, vol. 4: 143, 159, 177; trans. Fröhlich, vol. 2: 211, 232, 233, 259.
[156] Hugh of Fleury, *De regia potestate et sacerdotali dignitate*, 10, MGH, LL 2: 478.
[157] See below in this chapter.
[158] Vogtherr (1998), pp. 316–17 has misinterpreted the ritual of consecration; the *Accipe* was pronounced by the consecrating bishops, not by the ruler.
[159] The ring does make a few brief appearances in the works of these two writers, but this is as likely to have been suggested to them by Pope Pascal II's intervention in the quarrel between Anselm and Henry as by the normal practice within the English kingdom.

the crucial motive for deploying nuptial imagery in discussions of lay investiture. However, even if Anglo-Norman kings did grant new bishops their rings, this still would not have suggested the use of nuptial imagery to Anglo-Norman writers, for in England and Normandy the episcopal ring was never identified with marriage anyway. The new prayers for the consecration of the bishop apparently never made their way to these regions: in English and Norman liturgies, the ring continued to be identified simply as a sign of honor, dignity, or faith.[160] Neither the ceremony of investiture, nor the liturgy of episcopal consecration, then, would have suggested to English or Norman writers the use of nuptial imagery in their polemics.[161]

The situation was very different within the Holy Roman Empire, where the emperor did invest with the ring, and where the ring itself had come to be very clearly associated with the bishop's marriage to his church.[162] Imperial territories produced most of the surviving polemics dealing with lay investiture, and nuptial imagery figures largely in these works. In Book Three of *Against the Simoniacs*, for example, Humbert asks: how does it pertain to laypeople to bestow either ecclesiastical symbols (*sacramenta*), like the staff and the ring, or the grace of office? Humbert, writing half a century before Anselm's quarrel with Henry I, was one of the first to layout in detail the meaning of the two *sacramenta*. The meaning of the episcopal staff is straightforward: it is a shepherd's crook, representing the pastoral care of the faithful. The ring, however, receives a more complex interpretation, presumably because Humbert was familiar with a variety of liturgical texts for its blessing and conferral. On the one hand, he identifies it (as in the older liturgical texts) as a *signaculum* – a sign of faith (but also perhaps a signet ring, representing the "sealing" of heavenly mysteries). As such, it symbolizes the bishop's preaching function, his duty to open up the hidden wisdom of God to the perfect, and to keep it "sealed up" (*signatam*) or hidden from those who are yet imperfect. On the other hand, as in the ordination prayers that began circulating from the tenth century on, the ring is an engagement ring, a pledge of faith

---

[160] See the *Sacramentary of Ratoldus* (a continental manuscript that incorporates a tenth-century English pontifical), p. 40; *Two Anglo-Saxon Pontificals*, p. 11; a reference to the Bride on p. 127 is, significantly, a later interpolation (see p. 127 n. 25). The Norman Anonymous (pp. 163–64) confirms the evidence of liturgical books on this point.

[161] The one place where we might see the influence of those continental liturgical texts is in Osbern's letter to Anselm, urging him to accept the office of archbishop: Anselm 149, vol. 4: 6–10; trans. Fröhlich, vol. 2: 11–16. Yet Osbern concluded that Anselm would be the friend of the Bridegroom, rather than a bridegroom himself.

[162] Compare the works cited above with the letters which Pope Pascal II sent to England concerning lay investiture: e.g. Pascal II, *Epistolae*, 49 (PL 163: 71) = JL 5868. Pascal's letters are almost certainly the source of the nuptial imagery in a letter of Gerard of York, in Anselm 373, vol. 5: 316–17; trans. Fröhlich, vol. 3: 124.

between Christ and the Bride, granted to the new bishop as a "friend of the Bridegroom."[163]

No layman, but the clergy, and specifically other bishops, should give the new prelate these sacred symbols.[164] To paraphrase Humbert, whoever grants the ring and the staff to the new bishop is claiming episcopal authority for himself – yet metropolitans and primates stand by when secular rulers invest new bishops, not even daring to murmur against the practice. What a position these ecclesiastics are in! They are forced to witness the adultery of their wives – God's curse on those who fail to obey His commandments (Deuteronomy 28:30). "Thy wife shall be an harlot in the city, and thy sons and thy daughters shall fall by the sword," wrote the prophet Amos (7:17), and this applied as well to bishops who accepted lay investiture. For "beyond a doubt, the wife of a priest is violated whenever his church is administered or ruled by laymen, to whom she does not belong."[165]

Modern scholars who have discussed Humbert's views on lay investiture have generally focused on his innovative – one might even say idiosyncratic – use of legal texts to attack the practice. But Humbert's approach is really much more theological than legal, deeply rooted in Scripture and liturgy, and particularly reliant on domestic imagery, in relation both to the mystical marriage of Christ and to contemporary concerns about marriage, divorce, adultery, and even prostitution.[166] And it remains unclear how much immediate influence his ideas really had. The first conciliar decrees against lay investiture were issued more than a decade after his death, and it would be several decades more before another polemicist engaged so deeply with the symbolism of ring and staff.

Indeed, it was only in the early twelfth century that lay investiture emerged as a truly central issue in the conflict between the reforming papacy and the Holy Roman Emperor.[167] When Pascal II repeated his prohibition of lay investiture at the synod of Guastalla in 1107, Bishop Ranger of Lucca responded by composing an extended critique of the practice, in verse.[168] The choice of verse is significant: it suggests that the argument being advanced, while it draws on legal precedents, is essentially mystical in nature, carried on within the realm of symbols. It is thus best addressed in

[163] Humbert, *Adversus simoniacos*, 3.6, MGH, LL 1: 205.
[164] Humbert, *Adversus simoniacos*, 3.15, MGH, LL 1: 217.
[165] Humbert, *Adversus simoniacos*, 3.11, MGH, LL 1: 211–12.
[166] Further domestic and nuptial imagery appears in Chapters 5 and 26 of Humbert's third book: MGH LL 1: 203–04, and 231.
[167] Beulertz (1991), pp. 158–60.
[168] Blumenthal (1978a), pp. 32–73; Servatius (1979), pp. 200–5; Beulertz (1991), pp. 16–17, 76, 137–39. Concerning *On the Ring and the Staff*, see Servatius (1979), pp. 221–23.

poetry. At the heart of *On the Ring and the Staff* lies the distinction – foreshadowed in Humbert's work and more recently sharpened among Gregorian writers – between clergy and laity, between those who can administer the sacred sacraments and those who cannot. For Ranger, a ruler like the current Emperor Henry V is only a layman, and though he may wear "purple, gems, and gold," he nevertheless holds a lower rank within the spiritual realm than any cleric.[169] While a king or emperor has authority over the laity, he has none over the clergy, who are subject only to Christ.[170] It is obvious that he cannot invest bishops with a spiritual office which he himself does not hold.[171] And the claim made by Henry's supporters that investiture with ring and staff is only intended to confer the temporalities of the see is ludicrous.[172] For, as Ranger reminds his readers in both the opening and the closing lines of his work, "the ring and the staff are two sacred signs, by no means to be accepted from the hands of the laity."[173]

These lines suggest that ring and staff are equally sacred: both symbols of Christ, held by the bishop as Christ's representative. Yet Ranger accords them quite different treatment. Ranger's discussion of the pastoral staff is almost perfunctory; it is really the episcopal ring that lies at the heart of his argument. Of course, as a relative innovation, and one that had no parallel in secular practice, investiture with the ring was a far easier target to attack. Yet Ranger probably devoted more attention to the ring primarily because he attached more profound symbolic meaning to it. The central image in *On the Ring and the Staff* is Christ's marriage to the Church. The ring belongs to the Bridegroom, and is given to the Bride. Its gem, moreover, represents the Bride, while its gold represents the Bridegroom; the gem is the flesh and the gold the divinity of Christ. The two elements come together in the ring, just as Bride and Bridegroom merge in the mystical marriage – just as a man leaves his mother and father and cleaves to his wife, and the two become one flesh.

Ranger further links the ring to the history of salvation. In the "bridal chamber" of Mary's womb, the Word of God joined "naturally" with the flesh, never again to be separated.[174] In other works from this period, the

---

[169] Ranger of Lucca, *De anulo et baculo*, ll. 130–32, MGH, LL 2: 511–12.

[170] Ranger, *De anulo*, ll. 1143–48, MGH, LL 2: 513–14, ll. 225–28; 533.

[171] Ranger, *De anulo*, ll. 597–610, MGH, LL 2: 521–22.

[172] Ranger, *De anulo*, MGH, LL 2: 522–23, ll. 649–60. Such an argument had already been attacked by Abbo of Fleury, *Apologeticus* (PL 139: 466–67) and by Humbert, *Adversus simoniacos*, 3.26, MGH LL 1: 231. See also Tellenbach (1988), p. 170; Robinson (2004), pp. 295–301.

[173] Ranger, *De anulo*, ll. 1–2, 1159–60, MGH, LL 2: 509, 533.

[174] Ranger, *De anulo*, ll. 3–10, 15–32, MGH, LL 2: 509. The gold of the ring represents divinity joined with the "gem" of the flesh, in a giant (*gigas*) of "twinned nature" (*geminae naturae*). Cf. Kantorowicz (1957), pp. 42–86 on the "twinned nature" of kings.

mystical marriage occurs at the Crucifixion, but for Ranger the critical moment is the Incarnation, when Christ "wed" human nature, a moment regularly reenacted by bishops and priests during the mass.[175] The conferral of the ring is also, in a sense, a reenactment of the Incarnation: it is God himself who consecrates the bishop, and it is He who gives the new pontiff the ring, the symbol of his own marriage to the flesh.[176] The final consummation of the mystical marriage, however, will occur only at the end of time. In a passage based on Song of Songs 2:3, humanity (literally, "the flesh") becomes the Bride, "the most beautiful of women," seeking her beloved; fatigued by the heat of the day, she rests in the shade of a tree, and eats its fruit. The Tree, with its fruit, represents the New Law of Christ; the shade, the Old Law (which "foreshadows" the New). Neither satisfies her completely, however – after she has rested, she continues on her way, seeking her husband, that she may enjoy his love, not "in a glass darkly," but "face to face" (*Non iam per speciem, sed magis ad faciem*).[177]

For Ranger, then, the episcopal ring is primarily a symbol of Christ's marriage to the Church, as it plays out throughout history. The bishop's bond with his see receives less attention, and its exact nature remains ambiguous. On the one hand, Ranger invokes the words of John the Baptist, identifying the bishop as the Bridegroom's friend, the *medius sponsi*; yet he is also the *maritum sponsae*, the husband of the church.[178] During his consecration, the bishop receives the ring, "so that he may know himself to be the Bridegroom, and may love the Church joined to him – or rather, not to him, but to Christ."[179] But regardless of whether the bishop properly holds the title of "bridegroom," Ranger insists that no layman, not even the emperor, has any place in this solemn ritual. The emperor is not joined in marriage (*non est iunctus sponsaliter*) to the Church, so possession of the ring simply makes a mockery of him (*anulus ecclesiae ludibrio fit ei.*)[180]

My dove, my perfect one

"When a man sees someone honoring or scorning his bride, he can most truly claim that this is done to himself, the bridegroom."[181] Four years after Ranger of Lucca wrote *On the Ring and the Staff*, Placidus, a monk of Nonantola, near Modena, composed another work *On the Honor of the*

---

[175] Cf. Ranger, *De anulo*, ll. 345–56, MGH, LL 2: 516.
[176] Ranger, *De anulo*, ll. 49–50, MGH, LL 2: 510.
[177] Ranger, *De anulo*, ll. 999–1016, MGH, LL 2: 530.
[178] Ranger, *De anulo*, ll. 33–40, 49–52, MGH, LL 2: 509–10.
[179] Ranger, *De anulo*, ll. 859–62, MGH, LL 2: 527.
[180] Ranger, *De anulo*, ll. 83–84, MGH, LL 2: 511.
[181] Placidus of Nonantola, *Liber de honore ecclesiae*, 3 and 5, MGH, LL 2: 576. On Placidus, see Cantarella (1983); Büsch (1990), pp. 1–40.

Church. He begins his treatise with a question: "What is the Church?" His response? The Church is Christ's Bride, and therefore "he who honors Her, also honors Christ, and he who scorns Her, also scorns Christ." Honor – scorn – mockery – longing – anger – shame: such highly charged words electrify reform rhetoric during the central Middle Ages. Writers like Humbert, Geoffrey of Vendôme, Ranger of Lucca, and Placidus of Nonantola present their demands for ecclesiastical reform with legal precedents attached, but above all with heartfelt pleas for the relief of the suffering Bride. The sympathy they fail – for whatever reason – to express for ordinary wives, they pour out for the *Sponsa Christi*. It is impossible to see their images of a Bride abandoned by her lawful defenders, plundered, raped, prostituted, so defiled that she is in danger of being repudiated by her own Spouse, as simple rhetorical devices. They want their readers to respond personally and intensely to their call for reform, and their own emotions are clearly involved.

At the same time, these representations are much more than simple expressions of outrage. They are meticulously constructed, drawing not only on well-established traditions of Biblical exegesis, common liturgical performances, and authoritative legal texts, but also on the contemporary understanding of marriage, to represent the desperate state of the Church. And they were, ultimately, highly successful. While the identification of the Church as Bride had been clear since antiquity, the identification of the bishop as bridegroom took longer to develop; it was still not accepted everywhere as late as the first decades of the twelfth century. The association of disputed elections, simony, and lay investiture with the Bride's sufferings was also made only gradually. Once formulated, however, these reforming iconographies proved surprisingly difficult to resist. Conservative thinkers might deny particular legal precedents, or refute particular theological points, but they seldom criticized the reformers' stingingly poetic and emotionally persuasive representations of the Bride.

Conservatives were certainly familiar with the allegory of the Church as Bride of Christ, and were willing to deploy it, and occasionally even the image of the bishop as bridegroom, for specific purposes – when, for example, they wanted to criticize Gregorian bishops for deserting their sees. On the whole, though, they avoided nuptial imagery. They use it less often, and much less elaborately, in their works than the reformers do.[182] And when they do invoke the Bride, conservatives must often rework established assumptions, or play with traditional associations, to limit potential damage to their arguments.[183]

---

[182] E.g. Hugh of Fleury; see above p. 82. [183] See below, on the Norman Anonymous.

The one context within which conservative writers regularly deployed nuptial imagery with success was that of schism. In a series of texts, dating from the 1070s to 1111, they repeatedly accused reformers of forcing a divorce between Christ and his Bride.[184] In the summer of 1111, for example, a monk of the imperial abbey of Farfa, near Rome, wrote a defense of his community's support for the emperor. He claimed that he and his fellow monks were simply obeying the teachings of Christ and the apostles, and following established custom. Those who criticized Farfa, on the other hand, were introducing new and unheard-of rules, resulting in scandal and schism.[185] In this work, the Church appears not only as a Bride, but as a Queen, adorned with gorgeous virtues decorating her various "members."[186] This trope suggests a further image, central to this text, and to many others from this period – that of the Church as the Body of Christ, made up of various parts or "members," each with its own, specific role to play.[187]

By linking together the two images of the Church – as Bride and as Body of Christ – the monk of Farfa created further associations. Their marriage on the cross turned Christ and the Church – like any man and wife – into "one body," with the Bridegroom as the head, commanding his Bride's obedience. And here the monk faces a dilemma. He should identify the emperor – who, in imperialist ideology, represents Christ on earth – with the Bridegroom. There was, however, no clear precedent for such an identification, whereas legal and liturgical tradition by this time supported the image of the bishop as bridegroom. But casting the bishop in this role would make him the vicar of Christ, and thus the emperor's superior. The monk of Farfa resolves this problem ingeniously. He claims that when the Church announces, in the Song of Songs (8:3), that "his left hand is under my head and his right hand embraces me," she means that royal power (*regnum*) functions as the left hand, and priestly authority (*sacerdotium*) as the right hand; both must work together harmoniously if the dignity of the Christian body is to be maintained.[188] Those who deny the emperor's right to confirm episcopal elections cause schism and

---

[184] In the 1070s, an anonymous author warned that a too-vigorous campaign against clerical marriage might pluck the Sunamite away from Christ, her Spouse, by an "irremediable divorce": *Rescriptio beati Udelrici episcopi*, in Frauenknecht (1997), p. 215.

[185] *Orthodoxa defensio imperialis*, 1, MGH, LL 2: 535. Boynton (2006), p. 151 and n. 32 provides a summary of scholarly views concerning Gregory of Catino as author of this text. On the events in Rome during the spring of 1111 that led to its composition, see below, Chapter 6.

[186] *Orthodoxa defensio imperialis*, 2, MGH, LL 2: 536.

[187] All references to the Christian Body in medieval texts contained certain common elements, drawn from I Corinthians 12: thus Christ was always its "head," and the members – however they might be identified – owed him due obedience, and one another charity.

[188] *Orthodoxa defensio imperialis*, 3, MGH, LL 2: 536–37.

dissension, trying to "cruelly cut off the left hand of Christ from under the Church's head."[189] The intense violence of this image is very similar to that found in discussions of divorce in this period.

Only implicitly, then, does the monk of Farfa reject the reforming image of the bishop as bridegroom. He chooses to identify Christ as the bridegroom, with *regnum* and *sacerdotium* serving as the two arms with which the Savior embraces the Church. Thus the two forces become almost equal in dignity – though we should note that the left arm (here identified as the *regnum*) is "under the head" of the Church. And since Christ is always represented as the head, this brings the emperor directly under Christ, in a somewhat superior position to the clergy.

If the monk of Farfa implicitly rejected the identification of the bishop as bridegroom, other conservatives were willing to accept that identification and make their own uses of it. In the early 1090s, another unnamed monk, this one from Hersfeld, in Germany, composed a fierce attack on the Gregorians and their policies, criticizing them for rending the Church asunder.[190] In *On Preserving the Unity of the Church*, the monk of Hersfeld depicts individual Gregorians as bad husbands to their individual churches. Thus he argues that the Roman church was never truly Gregory VII's bride, since he had usurped the see.[191] The church of Würzburg was promised to "one husband, as a chaste virgin to Christ," but her bishop, Adalbero, has deserted her.[192] Herman of Metz has also deserted his bride, even though, in the ceremony of ordination, bishops are told to remember always their betrothal to their church (*ut memor sic sit semper sponsionis et desponsationis ecclesiasticae*).[193] Bishop Adalbert of Worms is also urged to return to his see, in a complex play on Ephesians 5:29–31, which urges husbands to love their wives as their own bodies.[194] But notice that these ideas remain only embryonic in conservative texts. Allusions to the Song of Songs, if repeated, are brief and undeveloped. There is little elaboration of nuptial themes. The most evocative image comes from the monk of Farfa – and it consists of only a few sentences. Most conservative thinkers in the eleventh and early twelfth centuries seem oddly hesitant to advance their own visions of the mystical

---

[189] *Orthodoxa defensio imperialis*, 6, MGH, LL 2: 538.

[190] See, in particular, *De unitate ecclesiae conservanda*, 2.3, 2.15, and 2.42, MGH, LL 2: 215, 227, and 275–76.

[191] *De unitate ecclesiae conservanda*, 2.6, MGH, LL 2: 217. On this work see Robinson (1978), pp. 91–98, 138–43, 171–73; Melve (2007), vol. 2: 423–550.

[192] *De unitate ecclesiae conservanda*, 2.29, MGH, LL 2: 254. Here the monk of Hersfeld is deliberately playing on the reformers' insistence that bishops were irrevocably wedded to their churches: e.g. John of Lodi, *Vita beati Petri Damiani*, 5.29, *AASS* Feb. III (February 23), col. 422.

[193] *De unitate ecclesiae conservanda*, 2.30, MGH, LL 2: 256.

[194] *De unitate ecclesiae conservanda*, 2.37, MGH, LL 2: 265.

marriage. Perhaps this was because the reformers had been so successful in associating their own political agenda with nuptial imagery, making it less effective for conservative rhetorical purposes. But it may also have been the case that the image of the Bride simply held less emotional resonance for writers who saw no threat to the Church in the status quo.

There was one exception – the so-called "Norman Anonymous" – whose idiosyncratic writings nevertheless serve to prove the general rule.[195] A mysterious figure, about whom we know only that he wrote within the Anglo-Norman realm around the beginning of the twelfth century, the Anonymous was fascinated by the figure of the Bride – not altogether surprising, considering his love of arguments based on allegorical correspondences. However, his interpretations are highly unusual, to say the least. Sometimes the Anonymous seems to be offering his own construction of that relationship, in direct refutation of what had become, by this time, widely accepted ideas. He employs nuptial imagery, usually briefly, to attack the reformers' lack of charity, to accuse them of fomenting schism, and to deny the primacy of Rome.[196] He also refers explicitly to the Gregorian formula, that the Church should be "catholic, chaste, and free," then offers his own definitions of those qualities: "catholic in faith, and in the communion of the saints, chaste in sobriety and continence, and free through the presence of the Holy Spirit, dwelling within her."[197] In short, without rejecting it outright, he has stripped the formula of all its reform content.

While the monk of Farfa delicately undermines the reforming image of the bishop as bridegroom, by depicting *regnum* and *sacerdotium* as Christ's two arms, the Norman Anonymous explicitly denies any claim that the bishop could be married to his see. In a brief treatise in defense of clerical marriage, he scornfully rejects the argument that "some" have put forward, that a bishop who married must be an adulterer, because he is already married to his church. The Anonymous points out that there is no scriptural support for such an idea. "Holy Church," he says, "is not the Wife or Bride of the priest, but of Christ."[198]

An alternative introduction to his most famous work, the treatise on the consecration of bishops and kings (J24), contains an even more radical development of this idea. Here, the Anonymous reminds his reader

---

[195] On the Norman Anonymous, see Williams (1951); Pellens (1973); and Hartmann (1975).

[196] Norman Anonymous, pp. 7–8, 11, 43, 60; and see Williams (1951), pp. 137–43. Oddly enough, a very similar argument is made by the normally pro-reform author Raoul Glaber – although in this case he is criticizing Roman intervention into local affairs, much as the Norman Anonymous is. Raoul Glaber, 2.4, pp. 60–65.

[197] Norman Anonymous, p. 146.

[198] Norman Anonymous, p. 205; and see McLaughlin (1998), pp. 221–22.

that Holy Church is the Bride of Christ, the true king and priest, but only insofar as he is king, not priest (*non secundum hoc, quod sacerdos est, sponsa eius dicitur, sed secundum hoc, quod rex est*).[199] She is called "queen" (not "priestess") in Psalm 45, and her "royal nuptials" are mentioned in an antiphon for the feast of Epiphany. "And therefore," the Anonymous concludes, "the sacrament of these nuptials better befits the royal than the sacerdotal dignity, and so kings, who present the image of Christ the king [*qui Christi regis imaginem preferunt*], are more suited to these nuptials."[200] This alternative introduction provides a new nuptial framework for the main argument of the treatise, which justifies the practice of kings investing bishops on the grounds that the king is the true *typus Christi*, and therefore has the right to distribute ring and staff.[201]

But why, in the one surviving manuscript (possibly autograph) of the Anonymous' works, is this introduction separated from the rest of treatise J24? The manuscript does include alternative introductions to, or passages from, several of his works, so perhaps the Anonymous simply could not make up his mind about which draft worked best. But it is also possible that this particular introduction made its author uneasy. For while he was correct that Scripture never clearly described the bishop's mystical union with his church, canon law certainly did offer a basis for representing the bishop as bridegroom – as he knew very well.

We know that the Norman Anonymous was familiar with Pseudo-Isidore, for he cited the collection a number of times in his writings, probably because it offered excellent support for the arguments he developed in other treatises against the interference of metropolitans in local dioceses.[202] As we have seen, however, Pseudo-Isidore was an important source for the idea that the bishop was married to his see. Several of its passages directly contravened the Anonymous' claim. And perhaps this is why the introduction was kept separate from the rest of treatise J24. In the end, even this fiercely argumentative conservative found it difficult to resist the reformers' representations of the bishop, for they had been cleverly constructed, if not on the basis of Scripture, then at least on the basis of many other authoritative texts.

---

[199] Norman Anonymous, p. 196.   [200] Norman Anonymous, p. 197.
[201] Williams (1951), pp. 174–98, discusses the Norman Anonymous' views on kingship.
[202] See esp. Norman Anonymous, pp. 7–18, 35–45.

3 The ambiguities of motherhood

We have seen how political writers shaped their visions of the mystical marriage of Christ and the Church in accordance with the marriage practices of their own time. In the same way, social reality shaped their understanding of the Church's maternal role. Educated clerics in the central Middle Ages associated motherhood with a complex set of meanings, ranging from tenderness, generosity, honor, and authority to weakness, vulnerability, loss, and sorrow. They shared with their contemporaries a notion of maternal authority rooted in mutual affection between mother and child, as well as in cultural expectations about how both parties would behave. Their assumption was that women should love and care for their children, and that children should – in turn – feel gratitude and love for, and therefore respect the wishes of, the women who gave them life. Nevertheless, clerical writers also understood maternal authority to be situational, open to negotiation, difficult to enforce, and therefore limited in important ways.

The child's gender made a difference here. Daughters spent more time with their mothers growing up, and were socialized to be humble and obedient; it was the cultural norm for daughters to obey their mothers, just as wives were to obey their husbands. (This does not mean, of course, that daughters always did what they were supposed to do.) Sons, on the other hand, were increasingly separated from their mothers as they grew older, drawn by their fathers into the world of men. Anxious to achieve the autonomy associated with adulthood, sons often clashed with their parents – mothers as well as fathers.[1] This was more excusable in a son than in a daughter, for manhood virtually required freedom from female control.[2] Sometimes, indeed, a son's disobedience might be depicted as positively virtuous.

---

[1] On the father–son relationship, see below, Chapter 5.
[2] Hence the implied critique of Bernard, who, ashamed of his baldness, withdrew from society – "He wanted only his mother to take care of him, just as if he were a little boy": *Liber miraculorum*, 3.7, p. 192; trans. Sheingorn, p. 153.

Life stages also made a great difference – in the lives of both children and mothers. Maternal authority over young children was virtually complete – limited only by the potential interference of husbands, who normally left the care of the young in female hands. As children grew older, however, the situation became more complicated. Not only did husbands interfere more often (especially in the rearing of sons), but children themselves grew more fractious. The death of her husband sometimes gave a widow almost paternal control over children – if she was their legal guardian. Even if she was not, the absence of another parent probably gave her advice greater weight. On the other hand, she almost certainly had more trouble than a father in managing older children – again, especially sons. Legal support for her authority was limited, so much probably depended on her social skills, on her ability to maintain a superior position diplomatically, when dealing with grown, or nearly grown, children.

While mothers could sometimes exercise considerable power (depending on the circumstances), they were also highly vulnerable, in ways that fathers were not. The deep affection they were assumed to feel for their children made them liable to pain, when the dangers of the world led – as it very often did – to loss. Images of grieving mothers were widely deployed in eleventh-century texts, to illustrate the horrors of a military campaign or the despair caused by famine, and in critiques of particular policies. Even worse, competing interests might pit mother against ruler, mother against husband, sometimes even mother against child, and generally to the woman's detriment. Women's dependent position in medieval society left them ill-equipped to compete effectively, opening them to further losses, to alienation, even to betrayal by those they loved best. In clerical texts from the central Middle Ages, then, mothers were represented in ambiguous terms – as potentially powerful yet at the same time deeply vulnerable.

Maternal authority

The scholarly literature on medieval motherhood is limited,[3] and what work has been done casts little light on the issue of maternal authority.[4] To trace the shifting parameters of a mother's control over her children, detailed

---

[3] Among works on maternity in the early and central Middle Ages, see Bynum (1982); Stafford (1983); Atkinson (1991); *Sanctity and Motherhood*; Gradowicz-Pancer (1996); *Medieval Mothering*; Claussen (1996); Skinner (1997); Stafford (1997), pp. 75–81; Heene (1997); Dockray-Miller (2000); Sheridan (2005).

[4] An exception is Felice Lifshitz's article on the authority of early medieval abbesses: Lifshitz (1996). While much of the article is excellent, I disagree with Lifshitz's claim (see especially pp. 119–20, 122) that abbesses had to function as honorary fathers because maternal authority was not recognized in late antiquity and the early Middle Ages. Compare Claussen (1996).

studies of different classes, regions, and periods are still needed.[5] We do know, however, that in the central Middle Ages, throughout Europe, clerical writers *expected* children to care for their mothers, and mothers to exercise significant influence over their offspring. How these writers describe the relationship between mother and adult son – that is, the child least likely to accept her authority without question – provides our best evidence. If they represent submission to maternal authority as appropriate for grown sons, then presumably it was appropriate for other children as well.

Chroniclers and letter writers assumed that provision for a mother's support in life, and for her burial and commemoration after death, was the duty of a good son, who would also try to rescue her from danger – even if she had earlier betrayed him – or at least avenge her death.[6] Good sons showed their mother deference. Queen Emma's sons received a letter purported to come from her "with honor, as a gift from their parent [*genetricis*]."[7] Likewise, when the hero of the Latin poem *Ruodlieb* returned home from the king's court to his mother's house, he left the highest seat in the hall for her, acting rather as a guest in her house.[8] We have many accounts from the eleventh and early twelfth centuries of sons listening to their mothers' advice.[9] After Hartacanute took over the kingdom of England, he was said to have "attended to his mother's counsel in all things [*maternis per omnia parens consiliis*]."[10] Mothers often played an important role in their adult sons' lives – selecting their brides, for example, and even, on at least one occasion, standing in for the young man during the actual wedding ceremony.[11] Such meddling undoubtedly chafed many young men, and some maternal actions must have enraged them. The redoubtable Countess Adela of Blois actually disinherited her eldest son (after he had reached his majority!) and replaced him with his younger brother.[12] Nevertheless, filial obedience to a mother's wishes

---

[5] An excellent example of such a focused approach is Stafford (1983), pp. 143–74, on queen mothers.

[6] On provision, see Orderic, 5.19, vol. 3: 180–81; on burial and prayer, see Thietmar, 4.15, p. 150; trans. Warner, p. 162; on rescuing, see Thietmar, 7.41, p. 336; trans. Warner, pp. 335–36.

[7] *Encomium Emmae*, 3.4, pp. 42–43.

[8] *Ruodlieb*, 13, pp. 156–57; cf. 16, pp. 174–77.

[9] As he lay dying, Ansold of Maule told his wife to lead their children to salvation through her exhortations. Orderic, 5.19, vol. 3: 196–97.

[10] *Encomium Emmae*, Argumentum, pp. 6–7. And see Thietmar, 4.10, p. 142; trans. Warner, pp. 157–58, on Theophano's influence over Otto III.

[11] Peter Damian 56, vol. 2: 160; trans. Blum, vol. 2: 367; *Ruodlieb*, 5, pp. 92–93; Cf. *Briefsammlungen*, p. 92, where a mother consents to the dowering of her daughter-in-law.

[12] LoPrete (1996) and (2007a), pp. 153, 156, and 215–19. Other women disinherited children by their first marriages to provide for the children of a second (still using the first husband's property), e.g. Countess Richilde of Hainaut: Nicholas (1999), p. 115.

was treated as highly praiseworthy by most clerical writers. According to Orderic Vitalis, Ansold of Maule never failed to obey his mother, "as a faithful son should."[13] And Guibert of Nogent described his own relationship with his saintly mother in the following terms: "I was in such submission to her that my will was one with hers."[14]

The appearance of the phrase *auctoritas materna* in our sources (albeit only rarely) indicates that the concept was familiar to medieval writers.[15] And indeed, when it does appear, it is usually employed in a straightforward way, with neither irony nor explication. Abbot Geoffrey of Vendôme is one of the few writers from the central Middle Ages to address the subject directly – and he actually uses the even stronger term, *imperium matris* – the mother's "power to command." Explicating the Virgin's intervention at the marriage at Cana, he briefly alludes to the relationship of mothers to their powerful (here the *most* powerful of) sons: "This is indeed what maternal law decrees regarding sons great in dignity – that if mothers very often beseech their sons, insofar as they are lords, they also sometimes almost command them [*eis etiam aliquando quasi imperent*], insofar as they are sons."[16] For Geoffrey, then, a mother's *imperium* may be qualified, but it is nevertheless real.

The extent and force of maternal authority in the central Middle Ages is difficult to define. Surviving secular law codes generally ignore mothers, providing them with nothing comparable to the Roman *patriapotestas* or its barbarian equivalent. (Widowed mothers, serving as guardians for their children, were the one exception – on which more below.) There is no indication that customary law made any provision for mothers trying to control their children. Neither, for that matter, did canon law. A mother's *imperium* appears, then, to have been based not on law, but on two, generally unstated, cultural assumptions – first, that a woman could act as her husband's delegate and thus exercise his authority over the household; and second, that children owed their mother some degree of obedience in return for her efforts on their behalf.

By social custom (and, of course, only according to her husband's wishes), a wife exercised a derivative authority – based on his *patriapotestas* or *mundium* – over the members of her household, both children and servants. Only to this extent did legal custom recognize a mother's power – insofar as it was an extension of the father's. Her own autonomous authority over her children had a much more nebulous basis. It

---

[13] Orderic, 5.19, vol. 3: 180–81.

[14] Guibert of Nogent, *De vita sua*, 1.16, p. 122; trans. Benton, p. 83.

[15] E.g. Goscelin of Canterbury, *De sancta Wereburga virgine*, 3, *AASS* Feb. I (February 3), col. 388. And see *Ruodlieb*, 8, pp. 130–31, on maternal *potestas*.

[16] Geoffrey of Vendôme, 147, p. 318.

was grounded in her love and care for her child, which in turn inspired the child's affection for, and gratitude towards, the mother. Despite the arguments of scholars like Philippe Ariés, considerable evidence exists that children loved their mothers. One interesting strand comes from saints' lives, in which saints have visions of their deceased mothers in heaven. St. Anskar's mother died when he was still a young child. When the little boy saw her in heaven, he tried to run to her, as he had done while she was alive.[17] St. Dunstan, on the other hand, had his vision in adulthood. Nevertheless, he, too, found real solace in the sight of his beloved mother amidst the joy of the heavenly kingdom.[18] Of course, not all mothers were nurturers – some must have been indifferent or even cruel. By the same token, not all children were loving or grateful. But even in the absence of these emotions, society still expected behavior in keeping with them.

In the late eleventh century, Alfanus of Salerno – scholar, physician, poet, and eventually archbishop – wrote an account of the early Christian martyr Christina, who, converting to Christianity in defiance of her parents' wishes, was imprisoned and executed by the Roman state. Christina's relationship with her father will be discussed below, but Alfanus' text also includes an extended discussion of the saint's interactions with her mother.[19] At one point a group of "matrons" accuse Christina of ingratitude, reproaching her for causing such pain to the mother who bore her (*quae te genuit matrem tu magni causa doloris facis esse*). They urged her to "desist from such impiety" (*ab hac impietate desistere*).[20] Here an eleventh-century text invokes the ancient Roman virtue of *pietas*, deference towards one's parents, on behalf of a mother.

Maternal affection might find expression simply in the suffering of childbirth and in physical care for the child, or extend beyond this to encompass provision for the child's future. A woman's authority over her children could be bolstered by her ability to use family connections or wealth to help them. Such authority might still be derivative, depending on the support of her husband's relatives, or the distribution of his family's resources to the children, according to his wishes. Yet it might also be independent, for women in this period frequently called on their own relatives to assist their children. They also not uncommonly had property of

[17] Rimbert of Hamburg, *Vita Anskarii*, 2, MGH SRG, 55, pp. 20–21.
[18] See the lives of St. Dunstan by Osbern and William of Malmesbury, in *Memorials of St. Dunstan*, pp. 117–18 and 315–16.
[19] On Alfanus' career and writings, see Acocella (1958) and (1959); Cowdrey (1983), pp. 22–23; Ramseyer (2007). On the archbishopric of Salerno in this period, see Ramseyer (2006), pp. 125–58. On the relationship between Christina and her father, see below, Chapter 5.
[20] Alfanus of Salerno, *Vita et passio Sanctae Christinae* (PL 147: 1277).

their own, and could choose to bestow or withhold it, according to their personal desires. It would be an ungrateful child indeed who scorned the source of such substantial benefits.

A final factor contributing to maternal authority in the central Middle Ages was religious sanction. Indeed, Scripture provided the only authoritative texts explicitly supporting such authority. The law of Moses directed children to "honor" their mothers as well as their fathers; many other passages from Scripture enjoined obedience and love. What practical impact these texts had remains unclear, but for clerical writers they were critically important as statements of divine will – even though, as we shall see, these writers did not always apply them primarily to earthly mothers.

Materfamilias

Our sources generally tell us little about women's role in the household when their husbands were still alive. From what little evidence we have, we do know that a wife normally exercised authority as her husband's deputy when he was away, and even when he was present at home. Just as the *paterfamilias* ruled over his *familia*, so the *materfamilias* (a term often used for wives in the sources) regularly gave orders on his behalf to members of his household – vassals in elite families, servants in most, and children in all.[21] Exceptions occurred in troubled families, but for the most part the rule held that failure to obey the wife was an affront to the husband. As Placidus of Nonantola stated: "When a man sees someone honoring or scorning his bride, he can most truly claim that this is done to himself, the bridegroom."[22]

The role of the *materfamilias* is easiest to observe, of course, at the highest levels of society. Famously, in the late ninth century, Hincmar of Reims described how court officials answered at times to the queen as well as to the king, and how she was responsible for "the good management of the palace, and especially the royal dignity, as well as the gifts given annually to the officers ...".[23] In the eleventh and early twelfth centuries, the names of queens regularly appeared in royal documents, and narrative sources describe their frequent interventions in royal affairs.[24] It is not surprising,

---

[21] Eadmer, *Vita sancti Anselmi*, 1.1, p. 4: the saint's mother fulfills the role of a "good *materfamilias*" by taking charge of her household. Cf. *Liber miraculorum* 2.16, p. 166; trans. Sheingorn, p. 128. Guibert of Nogent, *De laude sanctae Mariae*, 10 (PL 156: 565) speaks of *matronae imperium*.

[22] Placidus of Nonantola, *Liber de honore ecclesiae*, 5, MGH LL 2: 576. Yet when a man suddenly died, his wife might lose her influence. Orderic, 8.24, vol. 4: 292–95.

[23] Hincmar of Reims, *De ordine palatii*, 5, pp. 72–74.

[24] Vogelsang (1954); Dhondt (1964–65); Facinger (1968); Stafford (1983), pp. 93–142; Turner (1990); Jäschke (1991); Chibnall (1991); Erkens (1991); *Medieval Queenship*;

under the circumstances, that empresses held the title of the emperor's "consort in the wedding bed and in the kingdom," and truly acted as such. In his study of this title, Vogelsang suggested that the power of the empress was waning, as the institutions of imperial government expanded in the eleventh century.[25] Certainly the title did become less common towards the end of the eleventh century. Recent research, however, indicates that as late as the early twelfth century empresses were still very powerful figures. When her husband had to return to Germany to deal with a rebellion in 1118, for example, the very young Empress Matilda was left with the imperial army in Italy, to serve as regent there.[26] She who was "of one body" with her royal husband continued to be his reliable deputy.

At a less exalted level, wives played a similar role – organizing feasts and gift-giving on their husband's behalf, sometimes marshalling troops in defense of his strongholds, commanding both his servants and his children.[27] Noble wives, like royal ones, appeared in their husband's documents – either acting with him or serving as witness. The evidence of narrative sources suggests considerable independence in these endeavors, with women using household resources according to their own judgment and wishes (albeit subject to their husband's ultimate approval).[28] In the central Middle Ages, then, a "lady" (domina) could approach a lord in power.[29] After her husband's death, the widow often retained her role, taking over as head of her husband's household and as legal guardian for his minor children.[30] And her dependents treated her much as they would a father. When Abbot Poppo of Stablò's widowed mother followed him into the religious life, all her other children, along with her servants, begged her to return, because they had lost the "solace of their only mother and lady."[31]

Law codes and legal customs only paid attention to mothers when they were widows. Late Roman law allowed women to serve as the legal guardians of their minor children, and to manage their husband's property on

    Queens and Queenship; Stafford (1997); Fössel (2000); Woll (2002); *Capetian Women* (2003); Baumgärtner (2004); Erkens (2004).

[25] Vogelsang (1954), pp. 40–58; more nuanced discussions by Fössel (2000), pp. 373–87; and Erkens (2004).

[26] Chibnall (1991), pp. 33–34; Fössel (2000), 56–66.

[27] Bernards (1971); McNamara and Wemple (1973); Leyser (1979); Stafford (1983); McLaughlin (1990); Goez (1995); Haluska-Rausch (2005), pp. 155–60; LoPrete (2007a) and (2007b).

[28] E.g. Eadmer, *Vita sancti Anselmi*, 2.3, p. 65.

[29] LoPrete (2007a) on Adela of Blois. Cf. Odilo of Cluny, *Epitaphium Adalheidae*, 11 (PL 142: 989) on a *potens comitissa*; compare Orderic, 11.4, vol. 6: 38–39, on the epitaph of Countess Sibyl.

[30] Santinelli (2003), pp. 357–77.

[31] Everhelm, *Vita Popponis abbatis Stabulensis*, 10, MGH SS 11: 299.

behalf of his heirs, as long as they did not remarry. From Roman law, via the Visigothic *Liber Judiciorum*, this rule passed into the customary law of Catalonia, in force in the eleventh and early twelfth centuries.[32] In Italy, a further refinement was added by the *Eclogue* of the Byzantine emperor Leo III, which stated that a widow who remained as head of her household and guardian of her children was entitled to all due respect.[33] The customary law of northern Europe was not recorded in writing until much later. Nevertheless, the evidence of narrative and diplomatic sources clearly shows that in northern France, England, and Germany, widows frequently continued to exercise authority as their husbands' deputies.[34]

Clerical writers drew on their own experiences with mothers, but also on literary models of maternal authority within the household. The Biblical prototype of the *materfamilias* was Sarah, the wife of Abraham and mother of Isaac. Her story demonstrated to clerical interpreters both the reality and the derivative nature of maternal authority. Before her son was born, the aged Sarah, despairing of ever conceiving, told her husband to have sex with her slave Hagar. Once pregnant, Hagar became contemptuous of her mistress, who then complained to Abraham. His response was, "Your slave-girl is in your power; do to her as you please" (Genesis 16:6). Sarah treated Hagar so harshly that she ran away, but eventually returned to her mistress and gave birth to Ishmael. Some time later, Sarah, despite her age, bore her own son, Isaac, at which point she was no longer willing to tolerate the presence of rivals in her household: "So she said to Abraham, 'Cast out this slave woman with her son; for the son of this slave woman shall not inherit with my son Isaac'" (Genesis 21:10). Despite his own distress, Abraham bowed to his wife's wishes, and sent Hagar and Ishmael away. In Genesis, Sarah's position as legitimate wife gives her the right to exercise authority over Hagar – but only with her husband's consent.[35]

The authority of mothers without living husbands is somewhat clearer. An especially interesting case comes from a play by Hrotswitha of Gandersheim, which recounts the martyrdom of Faith, Hope, and Charity, the three daughters of Wisdom. The figures in this drama are allegorical, but their martyrdom is represented as historical fact. In the play, when the Emperor Hadrian tries to persuade the young women to sacrifice to the gods, their mother, Wisdom – who seems to be a widow – says, "O my daughters, do not listen to the serpentine allurements of this Satan, but loathe them along with me." To this, Faith replies, "We do

---

[32] Dixon (1988), p. 65; Compare *Usatges of Barcelona*, Appendix 3, C4, p. 101.
[33] Cited in Skinner, (1997), p. 395.   [34] Santinelli (2003), pp. 357–77.
[35] On the rich exegetical tradition concerning this story, see Chapter 4 below.

loathe these worthless [arguments] and despise them in our hearts."[36] Later, awaiting execution, Wisdom tells her daughters that this is what she raised them for, to give them to a heavenly rather than an earthly bridegroom, and Faith, again, replies, "We are ready to die for the love of this Bridegroom."[37] Here and elsewhere, the daughters indicate their willingness to do as they are told by echoing their mother's words. Charity baldly announces, "We willingly comply with your maternal admonitions."[38]

Notice that Wisdom claims the right to give her daughters in marriage, and that her daughters implicitly recognize it. Likewise, in the prayer that ends the play, Wisdom claims that she has offered her daughters to Christ to be slain, again suggesting authority.[39] Yet the *Martyrdom of Faith, Hope, and Charity* also suggests some limits to maternal control: at several points during the martyrs' interview with their Roman captors, Wisdom actually solicits her daughters' opinions on how to proceed. In other words, she seems tentative in her leadership, needing their confirmation for her decisions. It would seem, then, that early medieval mothers – unlike fathers – were expected to rule by consensus rather than by *fiat*.

A much more unusual, but equally telling, description of female domestic authority comes from the *Conversion of St. Aphra*. The text of this story is actually Merovingian, but was incorporated verbatim into an eleventh-century account of the cult of the holy Bishop Narcissus, suggesting that its image of an independent female household head was still comprehensible by the standards of the central Middle Ages.[40] The *Conversion* tells the story of a complex group of women, all without husbands, who accept the Christian faith simultaneously sometime during the first few centuries of the Church. Aphra is a temple prostitute, dedicated to the service of the goddess Venus by her mother, Hilaria. Fleeing persecution, Bishop Narcissus and his deacon seek refuge in Aphra's home. Narcissus offers to baptize her and her household, and the idea appeals to Aphra, but she calls together her servants (*puellae*) and asks them what they think. The language of their response is remarkable: "You are our lady [*domina*], and if we have followed you into the pollution of sin, should we not follow you in the forgiveness of sin? You are our head [*caput*] and wherever you go, [we] your members,

---

[36] Hrotswitha, *Sapientia*, in *Opera*, p. 248.   [37] Hrotswitha, *Sapientia*, in *Opera*, p. 253.
[38] Hrotswitha, *Sapientia*, in *Opera*, p. 257.
[39] Hrotswitha, *Sapientia*, in *Opera*, pp. 264–65. The daughters are here described as the "flowers of my womb." A father is notably absent from this play, which revolves around maternity.
[40] Oliba of Vich, *Conversio beatae Afrae* (PL 142: 593–98). The earlier text and a discussion of its origins can be found in MGH Scriptores rerum merovingicarum, 3: 41–64.

must follow."[41] This last line echoes two different passages from Paul's first letter to the Corinthians. In 1 Corinthians 12, Paul discusses the unity of the various members of the Body, and the importance of avoiding schism. In the same way, Aphra's servants, by describing themselves as her "members," agree to maintain the unity of her household by joining her in conversion. Because of Aphra's profession, however, the text would have also reminded the educated reader of 1 Corinthians 6, which warns Christians to avoid sexual immorality: "Do you not know that your bodies are members of Christ? Shall I then take the members of Christ and make them members of a harlot?" If Aphra and her *puellae* wish to join the Body of Christ, they will have to give up prostitution. In this passage from the *Conversion*, the relationship of head and members echoes both Roman political theory and early Christian thought. Remarkably, Aphra stands in the same relationship to her household as Christ does to the Church – she is the head, the figure of authority.[42] And yet, as in Hrotswitha's play, the authority of this *materfamilias* is curiously hobbled. Rather than simply deciding to convert to Christianity on her own, Aphra turns to her servants for their opinion. True, they defer to her wishes, characterizing her as their "lady" and "head," but her need to consult with them suggests an uncertain, and thus ultimately negotiable, authority. It is difficult to imagine a pagan *paterfamilias* consulting his servants about the prospect of conversion.

Alma mater

If some clerical writers attributed to mothers the potential to command and discipline their households, motherhood was more often associated in our sources with love, affection, and nurturing.[43] It is clear that most women in the central Middle Ages eagerly desired children. Miracle collections are full of anecdotes concerning individual women (as well as couples) asking for heavenly assistance in obtaining a child – one noblewoman actually promised St. Foy her golden bracelets if she would help her conceive a son.[44] Of course, self-interest contributed to this eagerness. As we have seen, the woman who failed to bear sons risked repudiation by her husband.[45]

---

[41] Oliba of Vich, *Conversio beatae Afrae* (PL 142: 593–94).

[42] Aphra's deference to her own mother is also emphasized in this text. Asked to hide Bishop Narcissus and his deacon from the Roman authorities, Aphra goes to Hilaria to ask if they can be moved from her own house to that of her mother for greater safety: "If you so command, Lady Mother [*domina mater*], I will bring them here." Oliba of Vich, *Conversio beatae Afrae* (PL 142: 595)

[43] Geoffrey of Vendôme (79, p. 150) and Anselm (158, vol. 4: 25–26; trans. Fröhlich, vol. 2: 39) both contrast the "piety" of mothers with the "discipline" of fathers.

[44] *Liber miraculorum*, 1.19, p. 120; trans. Sheingorn, p. 85.   [45] See above, Chapter 1.

Moreover, her best security for the future lay in those same sons. If she out-lived her husband, they would (she hoped) take over the role of protecting and providing for her. This helps to explain why Emma, the widow of King Aethelraed, refused to become the bride of the Danish conqueror Canute, "unless he would affirm to her by oath, that he would never set up the son of any wife other than herself to rule after him ...".[46] But clerical writers did not see maternal love as primarily self-interested; they assumed, rather, that such love was instinctive – sometimes even irrational.[47]

When a small boy became seriously ill, "his anguished mother ... ranted and raved uncontrollably and snatched up her son in her arms. Then, filling the entire area around the crossroads with her great cries," she rushed to the shrine of St. Foy at Conques. The unnamed mother told the saint that she was "overcome by immense grief because [her] only child [was] dying," and that her grief filled her "whole body." "I fly," the child's mother said to St. Foy, "to your feet, distraught because the child of my own womb is dying ... Do not deprive me of the sweetness of my son, whom I love in the depths of my heart more than all my desire to live."[48] Such intense maternal love was normally inherent in the female condi-tion, and could thus be found in the animal kingdom as well. According to Peter Damian, the mother eagle abandons any of her offspring whose eyes cannot withstand the rays of the sun, "as though it were low-born and unworthy of such high honor and, as one disinherited and bastardized." The common coot, on the other hand, adopts the abandoned eaglets "with truly maternal instinct," and raises them with her own young.[49] For Peter, then, (and he was not alone in this assumption), maternal instinct called forth a deep, abiding, and unconditional love, even for the young of another species or family.

Although the mother who took her son to St. Foy called him the "child of my own womb," contemporary science assigned mothers little influence on the fetuses they carried. Constantine the African may have been a Muslim from North Africa; if so, he converted to Christianity and ended his career as a monk at the monastery of Monte Cassino around the end of the eleventh century. His medical writings – which in time became highly influential – combine western monastic lore about human bodies with material which he brought with him from the world

---

[46] *Encomium Emmae*, 2.16, pp. 32–33. On this passage, see Stafford (1997), pp. 33–34.

[47] E.g. *Liber miraculorum*, 1.34, p. 145; trans. Sheingorn, p. 110.

[48] *Liber miraculorum*, 3.20, p. 210; trans. Sheingorn, p. 170. Yet immediately after she utters this speech, the woman is informed that her husband needs her, and so she leaves her son at the shrine of St. Foy in the care of his nurse in order to hasten home. The anony-mous author simply reports this, apparently with no irony.

[49] Peter Damian, 86, vol. 2: 480; trans. Blum, 3: 274–75. Peter acquired his animal lore indirectly from the *Physiologus*, via Ambrose's *Hexaemeron*.

of Arabic medicine. As Joan Cadden has shown, Constantine's discussions of reproduction smoothed over a number of inconsistencies in his sources; nevertheless, like other medieval scientists, he emphasized the male role in the production of offspring, claiming that sperm was to menstrual blood as a craftsman is to his material. He did recognize that the uterine environment might have some influence on the sex of the fetus, but in general he emphasized the role of male seed in shaping the future child.[50] Constantine's is one of the few scientific voices we have from the eleventh century, and it is unclear how widely diffused such views were. It is the case, however, that eleventh-century writers seldom describe the mother's relationship with, or impact on, the fetus *in utero*.[51]

What they do associate maternity with is breast-feeding. A computer search for the adjective *materna* in eleventh-century texts from the Patrologia Latina database brings up a very large number of references to *ubera*, or breasts. Many of these references are metaphorical: a young scholar has "suckled at the breasts" of his alma mater, the school where he studied; a monk remembers with fondness the "milk of spiritual life" his abbot had fed him. But many others are literal, for women did indeed normally suckle their own babies. There were exceptions, of course. Elite women, especially in northern Europe, often employed wet nurses.[52] While clerical critics sometimes blamed female vanity or lust for this practice, the fact is that women of high rank often had to travel or had other duties that made nursing their children themselves impractical. Many clerics understood this, and even accepted the possibility that a deeply loving mother might choose to have her children nursed by someone else.[53] Still, the noblewoman who refused to use a wet nurse might be singled out for praise. According to her hagiographer, Ida of Boulogne feared that a nurse's milk might pass on bad habits to her children, and therefore insisted on feeding them herself.[54]

Feeding her child was a mother's joy, but also a heavy burden. Contemporary science declared that a nursing mother shared with her infant her very life's blood, concocted into milk. Even those ignorant of science recognized the physical demands nursing made on a woman, and the element of self-sacrifice involved. And indeed, self-sacrifice – in a variety of forms – was central to the nexus of ideas associated with

---

[50] Cadden (1993), pp. 57–65; cf. MacLehose (1996).
[51] The only exception I have found is *Liber miraculorum*, 4.13, p. 244; trans. Sheingorn, p. 201.
[52] Skinner (1997) suggests that wetnursing was less common in the Mediterranean region than in the north.
[53] *Liber miraculorum*, 3.20, p. 210; trans. Sheingorn, pp. 170–71.
[54] *Vita sanctae Idae comitissae Boloniensis*, 1.4, *AASS*, Apr. II (April 13), col. 142.

maternity in this period. This is expressed most clearly in Orderic Vitalis' famous account of the rebellion of William the Conqueror's son, Robert Curthose. When William forced Robert into exile, and the young man ran out of money, his mother Matilda used to send him "large sums of silver and gold and other valuables without the king's knowledge." When William learned what his wife had done, he told her to stop; when she continued, he accused her of being a "faithless wife." Matilda's response justifies her apparent infidelity in terms of the intensity of her maternal love:

O my lord, do not wonder that I love my first-born child with tender affection. By the power of the Most High, if my son Robert were dead and buried seven feet deep in the earth, hid from the eyes of the living, and I could bring him back to life with my own blood, I would shed my life-blood for him and suffer more anguish for his sake than, weak woman that I am, I dare to promise. How do you imagine that I can find any joy in possessing great wealth if I allow my son to be burdened by dire poverty? May I never be guilty of such hardness of heart; all your power gives you no right to demand this of me.[55]

Matilda's privileging of her son over her husband is left unstated here – perhaps because it would have been difficult to defend. The focus of the passage is, instead, on blood-sacrifice, which paralleled that of breast-feeding.

It was the nature of mothers to sacrifice not just blood, but also their sleep and their health to raise children. Guibert of Nogent's mother offered up, in expiation for her dead husband's sins, the sleep deprivation that resulted from caring for an adopted infant.[56] Mothers went on long and arduous pilgrimages to beg the saints to cure their ailing children, daughters as well as sons.[57] But their efforts went far beyond physical nurturing.

They continued to serve as sources of emotional support for their children well into adulthood. Thus, when Queen Emma of France lost her husband in 986, she turned to her mother: "Let an affectionate mother sense the distress and grief of a daughter full of sorrows. Inwardly, I would not wish to be, but that the Divinity has left my mother as a comfort. O when shall I see her, when speak with her?"[58]

Mothers labored to advance their children's status and protect their interests in a wide variety of ways, by managing their property for them

---

[55] Orderic, 5.10, vol 3: 102–05.

[56] Guibert of Nogent, *De vita sua*, 1.18, pp. 154–58; trans. Benton, pp. 96–97.

[57] E.g. Osbern of Canterbury, *Miracula sancti Dunstani*, 6, in *Memorials of St. Dunstan*, pp. 133–34; *Historia inventionis sancti Wulfranni*, 2.13, *AASS*, Mar. III (March 20), col. 154; Odilo of Cluny, *Epitaphium Adalheidae*, 11 (PL 142: 989–90). And see Quirk (2001).

[58] Gerbert, *Die Briefsammlung Gerberts von Reims*, 97, p. 127; trans. Lattin, p. 119.

while they were young, arranging for their education or setting up advantageous marriages.[59] A militant mother sometimes went to war to defend a son's inheritance – as did Richilde of Hainaut, captured on the battlefield at Cassel in 1071 – or engaged in a lawsuit on his behalf.[60] A mother might also undertake to rule in her son's stead if he departed on crusade or pilgrimage.[61] Many children recognized the sacrifices their mothers made for them, and tried to express their gratitude, sometimes in words – as did both Guibert of Nogent and Herman "the Lame," whose epitaph for his mother is included in his chronicle – and sometimes in deeds, through their own love and obedience. This was, perhaps, most likely when the mother had contributed directly to her child's financial welfare.

Maternal inheritance

The movement in the central Middle Ages towards impartible inheritance favored one son over all the other children in a family. The remaining siblings might be offered a small part of the family wealth to start them off in life, but they were sometimes left with no alternative but to stay at home, dependent on their brother, or (in the case of young men) to go off adventuring in hopes of finding their own fortune. As patrilineage became more important among elite families, property was increasingly moving in the male line, from father to son. But this change was very far from complete in the eleventh and early twelfth centuries. In many parts of Europe, some property continued to move in the female line as well. Many women possessed their own economic resources, and sometimes, at least, they were able to make their own choices about how to dispose of them.[62]

---

[59] Thietmar, 4.8 and 6.94, pp. 141 and 387; trans. Warner, 155, 299–300. The widowed Agnes of Poitou (on whom more below) betrothed her son, the future Emperor Henry IV, at an early age and then fostered his bride-to-be until the wedding could take place: Bühler (2001). On widows as managers of their children's patrimony, see Santinelli (2003), pp. 338–49.

[60] On Richilde, see McLaughlin (1990), p. 200; Nicholas (1999), pp. 115–17. Grassenda, wife of Bernard "the Hairy," sued the abbey of Conques for an estate that had been the property of her first husband, and so should belong to his (and her) son. *Liber miraculorum*, 1.12, p. 109; trans. Sheingorn, p. 73. Godila paid two hundred talents to secure her son's inheritance. Thietmar, 6.86, pp. 377–78; trans. Warner, p. 294. Mothers might support their children in other ways as well; see Santinelli (2003), pp. 377–87.

[61] *Chronicon sancti Petri vivi Senonensis*, p. 163.

[62] Within the growing body of literature on this subject, see especially Christelow (1996); Livingstone (1997); Stafford (1997), pp. 123–42; *Aristocratic Women in Medieval France*; Drell (2002), pp. 76–89; *Dots et douaires*. Hellmuth (1998) looks at women's control of property before the middle of the tenth century.

Women acquired property from various sources. They often inherited something from their fathers – even when most of his property went to one or more sons. In France and Catalonia, and increasingly in Italy – daughters were entitled to a dowry, which would be transferred, when they wed, from their birth families to the new household established by the marriage. Eventually the dowry was usually absorbed into the patrimony of her husband's family.[63] But in the short term, the wife normally retained some control over it. Occasionally she was allowed to use it for her own purposes; even if not, the dowry normally could not be alienated without her consent, giving her some say in its disposal.[64]

Women also acquired property from their husbands, as *Morgengab*, as dower, or simply as gift. The ancient Germanic practice of *Morgengab* still prevailed in many areas during the central Middle Ages. [65] This "morning gift" was conferred upon a new wife by her husband, the night after the marriage was consummated, and it often became hers absolutely, to dispose of it as she chose.[66] When Wulfric married the sister of the archbishop of York in the early eleventh century, for example, he gave her, among other things, "the estate at Alton, to grant and bestow on whomsoever she pleased during her lifetime or after her death."[67] *Morgengab* was beginning to die out in this period, but this did not mean that the husband made no financial provision for his new bride. The bride's family would normally negotiate a marriage settlement with her husband-to-be before the wedding took place. This settlement provided her with a dower, property intended to support her in the case of her husband's death.[68] Dower was similar to *Morgengab* (indeed, they are sometimes hard to tell apart in the sources), but it was a more tightly regulated property transfer. Normally, a dower would revert back to the husband's family after the wife's death or sometimes after her remarriage. However, some widows were allowed (or simply chose) to use it in their own way. Thus, for example, the widowed Gisla, whose grandson established the abbey of Gembloux, endowed the new foundation with property she had acquired from her husband as

---

[63] Feller (2002), pp. 17–18; Magnani Soares-Christen (2002), pp. 133, 136–39, 146; Amado (2002), p. 161; Aurell (2002), pp. 176–82; Santinelli (2002), pp. 251–53; Bougard (2002), pp. 74–87.

[64] Bauduin (2002), pp. 446–48; Amado (2002), p. 151.

[65] E.g. Thietmar, 5.36, p. 262; trans. Warner, p. 229. On the survival of *Morgengab* in Italy, see Kreutz (1996); Skinner (1999), pp. 62–64; Bougard (2002); Bartoli Langeli (2002).

[66] Elsewhere, a woman's right of disposal might be more limited.

[67] "Old English Marriage Agreement between Wulfric and Archbishop Wulfstan's Sister," trans. Whitelock, in *English Historical Documents, Volume 1: ca 500–1042*, p. 547; cf. Bremmer (1995), p. 60.

[68] Magnou-Nortier (2000), pp. 169–72; Fössel (2000), pp. 67–80; Magnani Soares-Christen (2002), pp. 133, 139–42; Aurell (1995) and (2002), pp. 172–75, 179–82; Bauduin (2002); Le Jan (2002).

dower.[69] The dower was normally a set portion of the husband's wealth (often a third), but some men left their wives control of their entire estate until they died or remarried.[70] In addition to these formal settlements of property at the time of marriage, a woman might also benefit from gifts made to her by her husband over the course of the marriage – clothing, household items, jewelry, and so on. These were almost always movable objects rather than land (the ultimate source of wealth in this agricultural society), but nevertheless their value might be quite substantial.[71]

Women who acquired property through inheritance, *Morgengab*, dower, or other gift could sometimes grant it to other people, although they might need their husbands' or other relatives' permission to do so. Many records survive of women making donations to religious communities during the eleventh and early twelfth centuries, thereby becoming enmeshed in the complex webs of social relationships among lords, vassals, neighbors, monks, and nuns that were marked by such property exchanges, and that offered these female donors prestige as well as religious merit.[72] However, women – like men – were probably most likely to transfer property to other members of their families, and especially to their children and grandchildren.[73]

In order to marry, young women often needed a dowry of some sort, and sometimes this was provided by their mothers.[74] An aspiring nun might also obtain from her mother the "dowry" that allowed her to enter a convent.[75] Sometimes young men depended on their mothers, rather than their fathers, for the wealth and influence needed to give them a start in life.[76] Gerard, the future bishop of Cambrai, was raised by Archbishop Albero of Reims, partly on account of kinship, but also because of the property the young man had received by inheritance from his mother.[77]

---

[69] Sigebert of Gembloux, *Vita Wicberti*, 5, MGH SS 8: 510. Or perhaps Sigebert is using the early twelfth-century word "dower" to describe what was really a *Morgengab* in the tenth century.

[70] See the case of Basil Isabrus and his wife Eufimia, cited by Skinner (1997), p. 393.

[71] Magnou-Nortier (2000), p. 172; Santinelli (2002), pp. 253–59. Exceptionally, in 989, after twenty years of marriage, William of Poitiers offered Emma, the wife with whom he had recently reconciled, a large addition to her original dower, including land and control over churches. She was specifically granted the right to do "whatever she wishes" with them. Carpentier (2000), pp. 211–12.

[72] E.g. *Historia inventionis sancti Vulfranni*, *AASS* Mar. III (March 20), col. 149, in which a *matrona* finances the rebuilding of the abbey church at Fontanelle in the early eleventh century. Her husband is never mentioned.

[73] Sometimes even to their husband's natural children: e.g. the case cited by Drell (2002), p. 133.

[74] Some widows reused dower lands to provide dowries. Santinelli (2003), p. 339.

[75] Aselbod of Utrecht, *Vita S. Walburgis*, 2 (PL 140: 1095).

[76] Count Hugh V acquired Maine by inheritance through his mother. Orderic, 8.11, vol. 4: 194–95.

[77] *Gesta episcoporum Cameracensium*, 3.1, MGH SS 7: 465.

Even if a mother was not the sole source of wealth for her child, she might still make a significant contribution. Bishop Lietbert of Cambrai, for example, started in life with "a multiform inheritance of paternal and maternal possessions."[78]

Economic dependence tends to ensure, if nothing else, a certain level of deference, which may have been reflected during the early Middle Ages in naming patterns. A number of scholars have noted the widespread use of matronymics to identify men as well as women in the late tenth and early eleventh centuries.[79] Men's willingness to be identified as "son of [their mother] or [their grandmother]" appears to be correlated either with inheritance of property once held by the woman named, or with the desire to be associated with a woman of particularly high rank.[80] By the second half of the eleventh century matronymics were becoming less common – perhaps because inheritance through the female line was becoming less important. Nevertheless they were still occasionally employed, probably both as a practical way of identifying the source of an individual's wealth, and as a means of honoring that source as well.

The greater her economic contribution, presumably, the more powerful the leverage a mother had over her offspring. In pursuing this calculus, however, we must take into account not only a woman's own property, but also that held by other people over whom she had influence. Presumably mothers lobbied their husbands to provide for a particular child, but they might also intervene with their own blood relatives.[81] Doda, for example, left her daughter's son "great wealth and high social position"; we can probably assume that this was because the daughter was on good terms with her and could ask for help for her son.[82] Women might also, however, turn to their brothers and sisters for help. The sibling bond was often very close in this period – so close that Thietmar of Merseburg's mother agreed to send her son as a hostage in place of her brother, Siegfried, who had been captured by pirates and had no son of his own to take his place.[83] By extension, a woman's siblings might be closely involved with her children. In the eleventh-century life of St. Gudila, her maternal aunt served as her godmother and introduced her to learning and the religious life.[84] Maternal

---

[78] Raoul of Saint-Sépulchre, *Vita sancti Lietberti Cameracensis episcopi*, 3, MGH SS 30/2: 844. And see Thietmar, 6.44, p. 328; trans. Warner, p. 268; Sigebert of Gembloux, *Gesta abbatum Gemblacensium*, 6, MGH SS 8: 526.

[79] Herlihy (1962), pp. 92–96; Skinner (1999a); Amado (2002), pp. 158–60.

[80] Herlihy (1962), pp. 96–113.

[81] On the significance of maternal kin, see Leyser (1970).

[82] *Liber miraculorum*, 1.11, p. 107; trans. Sheingorn, p. 72.

[83] Thietmar, 4.24, p. 160; trans. Warner, pp. 168–69. Another brother left his wealth to his sister. Thietmar, 6.76, p. 366; trans. Warner, p. 288.

[84] Hubert, *Vita sanctae Gudilae*, 1.5, *AASS*, Jan. I (January 8), col. 515.

uncles, in particular, played an important role in the lives of their nieces and nephews in medieval Europe, as in many traditional societies.[85] They might help to arrange suitable marriages for young women, or placement in a cathedral chapter for a young man.[86] They provided refuge for children forced into exile.[87] And crucially, when they had no heirs of their own bodies, these uncles often left their property to their sisters' children instead. So common was this practice, that when King Rudolf III of Burgundy died childless, his two sisters' sons both used their relationship to justify their claims to the kingdom.[88] The sources seldom tell us how such interventions came about, but they were probably not automatic. Normally it would have been the mother who went to her brother for help – and we can assume that she would not have done so if her children had been disobedient or disrespectful.

The economic and even the political importance of maternal support could be very considerable indeed. When Duke Godfrey "the Hunchback" of Lorraine was assassinated in 1076, leaving no child from his loveless marriage with Matilda of Tuscany, he was already grooming his sister's son, young Godfrey of Bouillon, to be his successor. Presumably Duke Godfrey's sister, the sainted Countess Ida of Boulogne, had played a role in establishing a relationship between the two Godfreys.[89] Twenty years later, in 1096, Ida helped her son finance his expedition to the east, by selling some of her own property to religious houses.[90] And of course, as a result of this expedition, Godfrey of Bouillon became the first ruler of the crusading kingdom of Jerusalem. Without the support of his mother and her blood kin, the meteoric rise of this most famous of all crusading knights would have been impossible.

In her excellent study of motherhood in imperial Rome, Suzanne Dixon has argued that while Roman law did not grant mothers much legal power, Roman matrons nevertheless exercised considerable influence over both sons and daughters through their right to bequeath property to the obedient and disinherit the disobedient.[91] A similar dynamic seems to have been at work in Europe during the eleventh and early twelfth centuries. Certainly her customary role in the household as *materfamilias* ensured a woman some deference from her children, which

---

[85] Kupper (2004).
[86] Thangmar, *Vita beati Bernwardi*, 1, MGH SS 4: 758; cf. Peter Damian, 125, vol. 3: 412; trans. Blum, 5 (6): 26.
[87] As in the case of Robert Curthose. See Orderic, 5.10, vol. 3: 102–03.
[88] The nephews were Henry II of Germany and Odo of Blois. Raoul Glaber, 3.37, pp. 160–61; Thietmar, 8.7, p. 501; trans. Warner, p. 366. On Henry II's claim, see Wolfram (2000), pp. 65–66; on Odo's, see Santinelli (1999), p. 80.
[89] On Ida, see Huyghebaert (1981); Nip (1995b), pp. 209–18.
[90] Tanner (2004), p. 135, n. 27.   [91] Dixon (1988), pp. 53–67, 168–203.

would have been augmented by their gratitude for her love and care. Nevertheless, it was probably those women who commanded economic resources of their own who could also command the most respect from their offspring.

Honor thy mother

A final and crucial element in the equation of maternal authority during the central Middle Ages was the influence of Scripture – obviously of great importance to our clerical authors. The most important of the Biblical admonitions concerning mothers is, of course, the Fourth Commandment: "Honor your father and your mother, that your days may be long in the land that the Lord your God is giving you" (Exodus 20:12), but a number of other important passages, in the Apocrypha as well as in the canonical books, also come to mind. Most of these texts are cited in a letter sent by Peter Damian to a nobleman named Albert (otherwise unidentified).[92] Albert and his wife did not get along with his mother; they found her quarrelsome and annoying, and so failed to show her the deference that was her due. It is not clear how Peter came to hear of the situation, but sometime between 1061 and 1071 he fired off a rather curt reminder to the nobleman that "one who makes little of honoring his parents stands in contempt of the commands of the Law of God. One who does not obey those who bore him will not receive a share of the inheritance in the land of the living." The child who defers to his parents will receive God's blessings; the defiant child will be cursed. And one important aspect of those blessings (or curses), according to Peter, will be their effect on the child's own children, for obedience breeds further obedience. Filial piety will be passed down through the generations, as will its opposite.[93] Hence the letter's final warning: "We must beware that in offending our parents we do not destroy the children who will come after us."[94]

Filial piety, based on such Biblical passages, was also a topos in a number of saints' lives from the eleventh and early twelfth centuries. Thus, for example, in the *Life* of Bishop Hugh of Grenoble, the saint remains with his mother until her death, despite his desire to enter religious life, thus "fulfilling the manifest obedience that God ordained

---

[92] Peter Damian, 85, vol. 2: 455–59; trans. Blum 3: 250–54. In addition to Exodus 20:12, and Leviticus 20:9, Peter cites Sirach 3:6–9.

[93] Cf. Raoul Glaber, 3.35, pp. 156–57.

[94] Peter Damian 85, vol. 2: 456; trans. Blum, 3: 252.

in the Mosaic Law, saying 'Honor your father and mother ...'."[95] Yet injunctions to honor one's mother constantly warred in clerical writings with reminders that loyalty to God must come before loyalty to any parent. Jesus had said, "He who loves father or mother more than me is not worthy of me" (Matthew 10:37).[96] And this text, too, often occurs in accounts of saintly behavior. When a group of Roman matrons criticizes the martyr Christina for causing her pagan mother grief, Christina replies with a reference to Matthew 10:37, along with her own redefinition of filial piety: "The piety which you urge me to show towards my mother makes me an impious servant to the Lord, and thus, this kind of 'piety' is esteemed true impiety by those who examine it closely."[97]

Defying a mother who failed in her own Christian duty could be considered acceptable, even praiseworthy. Peter Damian, the very man who urged Albert to honor his mother, praised another son's rudeness. Waldericus (who "died as an outstanding martyr while fighting the heretics") once visited his mother, and found a poor man at her door, complaining that he had a bunch of greens, but could not season them because lady of the house wouldn't give him any salt:

After the holy man had entered his mother's house and found salt in a container, he became very angry. He took the bottle and poured the salt in the street as an affront to his mother, saying that what through greed had been denied to Christ must not be consumed by a Christian.[98]

The salt cellar was later miraculously refilled, but Peter treated the insult to the mother's honor as entirely justified. Thus both Scripture and other Christian teachings treat maternal authority equivocally. Children should honor their mothers – but maternal honor always takes second place to the honor of God.

Vulnerability

Cultural norms dictated that women protect and care for their young children, and grown children protect and care for the women who gave them birth – supposedly making for a happy and satisfying relationship. The actual depth of these emotional attachments varied widely, of course. But a medieval mother could never be completely indifferent to her offspring, for her own fate was entangled with theirs. Her standing within family and

---

[95] Guigo of La Chartreuse, *Vita S. Hugonis Gratianopolitani*, 1 (PL 153: 764); but compare the grudging acquiescence to his mother's wishes exhibited by Desiderius, the future abbot of Montecassino: *Chronica monasterii Casinensis*, 3.1–4, MGH, SS 34: 364–66.

[96] The implications of this text for paternal authority are considered below, in Chapter 5.

[97] Alfanus, *Vita et passio sanctae Christinae* (PL 147: 1277).

[98] Peter Damian, 110, vol. 3: 237; trans. Blum, 4: 240–41.

society depended on her ability to bear children (especially sons), and on her relationship with those children (again, sons especially) after they grew up. For her own sake, then, she had to concern herself with her children's physical survival, their social status, and their political success; if she truly loved them, she also worried about their happiness and their salvation.

A mother's many concerns for her children made suffering almost inevitable. Guibert of Nogent noted that his mother opened herself up to misery and mourning when she gave birth to an evil son like him.[99] (Guibert always characterized himself as a great sinner.) But danger might also come from outside the family, as is evident from the touching letter of the widowed noblewoman Beatrix, to her brother, Bishop Udo of Hildesheim. Beatrix appeals to Udo because her son has been forced into exile and her daughter threatened with a shamefully unequal marriage. She herself has been despoiled of her wealth, simply because she had children (presumably in line to inherit the property her enemy wanted): "Gold, silver, clothing – at various times he has taken all these things from me. He was not ashamed to persecute a woman, and for no other reason except that I had given birth to such children."[100] Motherhood, in short, made women vulnerable.

A child in danger aroused anxiety in both mother and father. Sigebert of Gembloux reports that when a young girl was bitten by a snake, "the father mourned inconsolably, the mother didn't know how to temper her maternal anguish."[101] When a child died, both parents grieved.[102] In the surviving texts from the central Middle Ages, however, it is always the mother's agonies which are most emphasized. The Feast of the Massacre of the Innocents on December 28 served as an annual liturgical reminder of maternal loss. According to Honorius Augustodunensis, the usual joyful chants (the Alleluia, Gloria in Excelsis, and Te Deum) were omitted from mass on that feast, in imitation of the sadness of those mothers whose babies had been slaughtered by Herod's men.[103] (No mention is made of the fathers – presumably because the Biblical reference, Matthew 2:16–18, focuses on mothers as well.) The sorrow of a mother whose child had died was proverbial in medieval society: "Indeed, there is no greater sorrow for a mother than to see or hear of the death of a most dear son."[104] When chroniclers wanted to depict the evils of war, a common topos

[99] Guibert of Nogent, *De vita sua*, 1.12, p. 84; trans. Benton, pp. 67–68
[100] *Briefsammlungen*, p. 66
[101] Sigebert of Gembloux, *Vita Sancti Maclovii*, 22 (PL 160: 743).
[102] E.g. *Liber miraculorum*, 3.8, pp. 193–94; trans. Sheingorn, pp. 154–55.
[103] Honorius, *Gemma animae*, 3.14 (PL 172: 647). And see Nolan (1996).
[104] *Encomium Emmae*, 3.6, pp. 44–45.

was the image of the mourning mother. Maternal laments were, too, an acknowledged poetic form – so much so, that the plaints of mothers over sick or dead children in saints' lives and miracle tales were often expressed in verse.[105] If not as final as death, exile had the same practical effect of removing any possibility of direct contact between mother and son. Exile led, then, to a similar kind of maternal mourning.[106]

Injuries to her children – the illness of a daughter, the death or exile of a son – were painful wounds for a mother. But those inflicted on her by her children themselves were, perhaps, even worse. What deeper humiliation could there be than a lack of recognition from the child in whom she had invested so much? Even small indignities could be intolerable. In 1054, in southern Italy, Constantina took the drastic step of disinheriting her adopted son Peter Boukarinos. He had agreed to support her in her old age, but instead had become "insolent and scornful and full of reproaches." In retribution, she declared: "I annul my previous dispositions in his favour and exclude him completely from any claim to my lands."[107] Not surprisingly, financial tensions often underlay rifts between mother and child. Children were supposed to support their parents in old age. But, as King Lear discovered, children and parents do not always agree on what is appropriate support. And so the details of the arrangement might have to be spelled out in a contract. In 1004, a widow from Gaeta in southern Italy, named Matrona, handed over her property to her daughter Euprassia in return for a promise of support for the rest of her life. The document details that Euprassia would provide her mother twenty modia of grain, ten modia of beans and peas, and thirty jars of wine a year, along with a slave to work for her and any clothes Matrona might need.[108] There is no way of knowing what personal history lay behind this document, but it certainly does not suggest that Matrona had complete confidence in her daughter. In discussing the relationship between two women, and not of a particularly exalted social status, this document is unusual. Most surviving records of mother–child conflict focus on sons and property relations within the social elite.[109]

Hildeburge, the widow of Robert, castellan of Ivry, devoted her final years to a pious life attached to the (male) monastery of Saint-Martin of Pontoise. She also made a number of donations to the community. In

---

[105] E.g. *Liber miraculorum*, Appendix, L, 6, pp. 293–94; trans. Sheingorn, pp. 259–60. The enigmatic Old English poem "Wulf and Eadwacer" has been interpreted as a mother's lament for her illegitimate son. See Tasioulas (1996).

[106] E.g. *Ruodlieb*, 1 and 5, pp. 30–31 and 78–79.

[107] Skinner (1997), p. 399.   [108] Skinner (1997), pp. 400–1.

[109] E.g. the well-known case of Queen Constance of Arles. Adair (2003), pp. 15–21.

particular, she repeatedly asked her son, Goel, to grant Pontoise a piece of property at Jouy, which appears to have come from her own dowry – his permission was required because he was her heir. Goel refused to approve the grant, but after persistent nagging he agreed that the monks have Jouy during his mother's lifetime and for a year after her death. Hildeburge died and was buried at Pontoise, and for a year the monks held the property in peace. At the end of the year, however, as Goel was preparing to reclaim the property, he had a dream. He saw his mother in the abbey church, washing the feet of three paupers, while he himself held the basin and towels. In the dream, his mother turned to look at him, and spoke to him in a fury, accusing him of stealing the donation she had wanted to make to Pontoise. She then attempted to stab him with a white-handled knife, crying, "Unless you return my inheritance to me, you will die!" Nor surprisingly, Goel woke up in a sweat, told his wife about the dream, and promptly made the gift to Pontoise permanent.[110]

Hildeburge died probably in the second decade of the twelfth century. This text comes from her *vita*, which was apparently read at Pontoise during an annual anniversary service of commemoration, and intended to demonstrate her sanctity. The scene with the knife, however, seems out of keeping with such an intention. Similar threats of violence – used to defend a monastic community's property or privileges – do occur in other works of hagiography, but normally the threatening saints are male. Hildeburge's behavior conflicted not only with cultural expectations about women's weakness, but also with assumptions about the nature of mothers. Hildeburge's use (or promised use) of violence might seem to open her up to criticism on the grounds of unfeminine and unmaternal behavior. For this reason, I would discount the possibility that the story was simply the monastic hagiographer's invention. More likely, it represents Goel's actual experience, as reported to the monks. And if so, it says something about his relationship with his mother – who must have been a very forceful character, and of whom, apparently, he was at least a little afraid.

Other forceful mothers also quarreled violently with sons over property and power in this period. The most notorious was Countess Ermessende of Carcassonne (*ca.* 975–1058), whose interactions with son and grandson over many decades entailed both hostility and cooperation.[111] When Ermessende's husband, the powerful Ramon Borrell, who controlled three counties in the Pyrenees, died in 1017, she took

---

[110] *Vita Hildeburgis viduae, AASS.*, I Jun. (June 3), p. 363. Another mother whose wishes were ignored appears in Thietmar, 4.17, p. 152; trans. Warner, p. 163. In this case, the son was criticized, but not threatened.
[111] Aurell (1995), pp. 226–32.

over his lands and ruled them on behalf of her minor son, Berenguer
Ramon I. When he came of age, his mother refused to relinquish her
power – and the two eventually went to war over control of Ramon
Borrell's patrimony. After two years of fighting, mother and son were
reconciled, and went on to work together fairly amicably. The pattern was repeated after Berenguer Ramon died in 1035. His widow
remarried, leaving Ermessende – now sixty years old – to rule again, on
behalf of her young grandson, Ramon Berenguer I. When he reached
his majority, she again refused to give up her control. War raged again
in Catalonia from 1041 to 1043, with the local nobility choosing sides,
until eventually the aged countess was forced to give up most of her
claims, and even pledge fidelity to her grandson. In 1054, however, she
fomented a new quarrel – questioning Ramon Berenguer's admittedly
uncanonical liaison with Almodis, the wife of the count of Toulouse.
Ermessende appealed to Rome, arranging for her grandson and his new
partner to be excommunicated. However, this time he outmaneuvered
her, rallying the local bishops to his side and eventually convincing the
pope to annul his and Almodis' previous unions, so that they could
marry. In 1057, Ermessende – now in her eighties – sold her remaining
rights in her husband's patrimony to her grandson, and even pledged
fidelity to his new wife. A year later, just before her death, she drew up
a will, in which she asked Ramon Berenguer and Almodis to look out
for the welfare of her soul, "because God knows that I have loved you
more than any other of your kin, as I have proven by all that I have done
for you." In later sources, Ermessende was sometimes depicted as an
"unnatural" mother, who took advantage of her son and grandson. And
indeed, Ermessende's struggles with her son and grandson are unusual
in being so protracted and socially destructive. Nevertheless, they were
far from unique.

   All too often, relations between elite mothers and sons were embit-
tered by disputes over property. Sometimes, as in Ermessende's case,
or that of Adela of Blois, the widowed mother blocked her son's access
to full control over his patrimony.[112] Sometimes, however, the son tried
to add to that patrimony property that his mother either owned outright or had the use of during her lifetime, thus increasing his own
resources, but depriving her of her livelihood. And here sons did run
afoul of the law. Women had clear rights to their *Morgengab* or dower,
and sometimes to their dowry as well, although the precise nature of
their rights was not always clear in particular situations. They could
appeal to the courts to protect their property, even though they might

---

[112] LoPrete (2007a), pp. 153, 156, and 215–19.

need to find male assistance against their recalcitrant sons. The surviving records of such cases often reveal women as tough-minded as any of those described above.

In England, during the reign of King Cnut, Edwin sued his mother for control of two estates. Her kinsman Thurkil agreed to represent her in court, but when she heard about the lawsuit, she declared that her son had no claim to any of her property. She called in Thurkil's wife, Leofflaed, and granted her "after my death ... my land and my gold, and my clothing and my raiment, and everything that I possess." She then told the messengers sent by the shire court to "act like thegns and announce well my message to the meeting before all the good men, and inform them to whom I have granted my land and all my possessions, and to my own son never a thing!"[113]

Another lawsuit was threatened almost a century later, in Flanders. In 1112, the widowed Countess Clemence of Flanders quarreled with her adult son, Count Baldwin VII, over her dower and other property granted to her by her husband. Clemence arranged for Bishop Lambert of Arras to write to her son about giving up his claims. "We ask your excellency," wrote Bishop Lambert,

not to provoke your mother to wrath, but – in keeping with the Lord's command to "Honor your father and your mother so that you may have a long life upon the land which the Lord God shall give to you" – that you should mildly agree to let her possess them peacefully and without scandal, so that, through the Lord, you may live upon the land as a long-lived and a peaceful prince.

In this case, the Biblical reference to "the land" was particularly pointed. The bishop further stated that if Baldwin did not give up his claims on her dower, then his mother would take him to court.[114]

Elite women like Hildeburge, Ermessende, Edwin's mother and Clemence were unwilling to let their sons obstruct their plans for disposing of what they considered their own property. Nevertheless, their struggles against recalcitrant sons, while dramatic, were not desperate. Even if they failed, an honorable retirement, whether in the world or in a convent, remained an option. For other women, a child's betrayal of trust could be literally fatal. Struggling to feed her brood without a husband's assistance, the poor widow epitomized for the clerical culture of the central Middle Ages maternal vulnerability. She it was who suffered most from political turmoil – the lands and

---

[113] "Old English Record of a Family Lawsuit," trans. Whitelock, in *English Historical Documents, Volume 1: ca. 500–1042*, 135, p. 556. And see Bremmer (1995), p. 67.

[114] Lambert of Arras, *Epistolae*, 126 (PL 162: 693); see also Nicholas (1999), p. 119.

livestock she held taken away, her freedom and that of her children lost.[115] Whatever authority she had when her children were young dissipated as they became older and had to fend for themselves. And her vulnerability was only intensified if her grown children turned out ungrateful. A daughter's refusal to care for her in her old age, a son's attempt to seize whatever dower she had, left the poor widow, unlike her wealthier sisters, entirely bereft, searching desperately for the charity that would allow her to survive.

Agnes

The ambiguities of motherhood in the central Middle Ages are best summed up, however, not in the lives of poor widows (about whom we generally have only limited information), but in that of Agnes of Poitou. While Agnes was very far indeed from being a "typical" mother, her widely discussed, and therefore well-documented, relationship with her son illuminates particularly well the authority attributed to mothers, the difficulties they had in maintaining control over their children, and their susceptibility to suffering as a result. Agnes was born in 1025, her mother, also named Agnes, a daughter of the Count of Mâcon, and her father Duke William V of Aquitaine. We know almost nothing about her childhood, although, from what we know about the court of Aquitaine and about Agnes' later activities, there is reason to think that she learned to read, and may have been fairly well educated by lay standards. In 1042, when she was seventeen, the most powerful ruler in western Europe, the Salian king of Germany, Henry III, began negotiating for her hand. The next year they were formerly betrothed, Agnes was crowned queen at Mainz, and finally the wedding itself took place, in November of 1043. Probably this sequence of events can be explained by the king's desire to allow the German nobles to give their formal approval to his choice by ritually acclaiming their new queen, before the union was permanently sealed by marriage.

From 1043 to 1056, Henry occupied himself with the consolidation of his power in Germany, and the promotion of church reform. Agnes shared in her husband's activities to some exent.[116] Her name appears with his on a number of royal diplomas – especially those confirming grants of property and privileges to churches. She was also with him in 1046 when he entered Italy, presided over the synod at Sutri, and was crowned emperor by his new pope. (Agnes was crowned empress at the

---

[115] Peter Damian, 70, vol. 2: 314–15; trans. Blum, 3: 105.
[116] Black-Veldtrup (1995), pp. 7–21.

same time.) However, most references to Agnes in narrative sources from this period have to do with her childbearing capacity. She was producing children at regular intervals, including, in 1050, the long-awaited male heir, who was given his father's name.

Only with the death of Henry III in 1056 does Agnes begin to emerge in the sources as a figure in her own right.[117] Young Henry was only six years old, so Agnes accepted the regency, ruling the empire in her son's name from 1056 to 1062. In the past, historians often treated "the minority of Henry IV" as a time of political weakness for the Salian house, as the German nobility encroached on royal rights, and the Roman reformers moved towards a more radical understanding of the relationship between secular and spiritual authority. Older scholarship generally attributed these developments to Agnes' ineptness as a ruler. More recent research, however, has revealed Agnes to be a fairly astute politician. She enlisted the support of influential men like Abbot Hugh of Cluny, and made some excellent appointments to important offices, allowing her to pursue her husband's policies with considerable success for at least several years after his death.[118] A number of contemporary chroniclers – while not necessarily disinterested observers – felt they could at least plausibly praise her competence, her prudence, and her ability to manage the fractious nobles, already making trouble for Henry III before he died. Her young son, who was often by her side at court, also remembered her regency positively – at least to judge by the way his "authorized" biographer later described it: "Agnes, the most serene Empress, a woman of manly disposition, sustained greatly this happy state of the kingdom, she who together with her son with equal right governed the commonwealth."[119]

Still, the regency did end in debacle. In the summer of 1061, the reformers in Rome, led by Archdeacon Hildebrand (the future Pope Gregory VII), elected Bishop Anselm of Lucca as their new pope. Without waiting for the imperial assent traditionally required, Anselm was enthroned as Pope Alexander II. The conservative bishops of Lombardy, as well as many of the leading citizens of Rome (who had their own candidates in mind) were unhappy with this election, and turned to the court of the empress for help. On the advice of the imperial chancellor for Italy and

---

[117] On her regency, see Bulst-Thiele (1933), pp. 33–83; Black-Veldtrup (1995), pp. 22–36.

[118] Compare Bulst-Thiele (1933) with Black-Veldtrup (1995); Robinson (1999), pp. 31–36; Althoff (2006), pp. 44–51.

[119] *Vita Heinrici IV.*, 2, MGH SRG, 58: 13; trans. Mommsen and Morrison, p. 106. Cf. Lampert of Hersfeld, *Annales*, a. 1056, in *Opera*, MGH SRG, n.s. 38: 69; Frutolf of Michelsberg, *Chronicon*, a. 1056, p. 72.

her other counsellors, Agnes designated Cadalus, bishop of Parma, as pope at an imperial diet held in October 1061.[120] Cadalus had a respectable reputation, and was a loyal servant of the empire; apparently Agnes believed that she was simply making another judicious appointment.[121] It soon became clear, however, that she had made a terrible mistake. The reformers refused to accept Cadalus as pope, and a schism resulted, with most of the churches of western Europe recognizing Alexander II, while many Italian and German churches clung to Cadalus. Agnes seems to have been profoundly shaken by these events, apparently seeing them as her own fault. Not only did she publicly repudiate Cadalus, she also did penance for the sin of fomenting schism, taking the "veil of chastity" (perhaps meaning she vowed never to remarry) and adopting a more ascetic lifestyle.

However, the political damage was already done. The schism had exacerbated the existing divisions within the German church and nobility, and Agnes' retreat from political involvement into private devotion allowed an opposition party to develop. In April 1062, a group of powerful church leaders and nobles managed to kidnap young Henry from his mother.[122] Some later chroniclers claimed that this, rather than the regency itself, was the root of the kingdom's later troubles.[123] Agnes made no attempt to resist the coup, or to get her son back.[124] Perhaps she saw the kidnapping as divine punishment for her role in the schism, and felt that it would be wrong to resist. In any case, she retired without protest from her position as regent, and devoted the rest of her life to devotional exercises, good works, and the cause of reform.[125] She spent much of her time in Italy, becoming the patron and protector of the increasingly radical reform party surrounding Hildebrand/Gregory VII.[126]

This, however, put her in an extremely difficult position, as the conflict between her son, now an adult, and Pope Gregory heated up in the 1070s. Trying to serve as a peacemaker between the two, Agnes traveled back and forth between the royal (Henry IV had not yet been crowned emperor) and papal courts. However, when it became obvious that a

---

[120] On the "Cadalan schism," see Herberhold (1947); Schmidt (1977), pp. 104–33; Cowdrey (1998a), pp. 49–51; Robinson (1999), pp. 36–45; Tabacco (2004), pp. 84–85.

[121] Miller (1993), pp. 74–76.

[122] See Robinson (1999), pp. 36–45, on the politics behind the coup.

[123] Frutolf, *Chronicon*, a. 1056, p. 72.

[124] Lampert of Hersfeld, *Annales*, a. 1062, in *Opera*, MGH SRG, n.s. 38: 80–81.

[125] The exact date is debated: Struve (1985); Black-Veldtrup (1995), pp. 347–51, 376–77. On Agnes' retirement, see also Sansterre (1999); on the retirement of early medieval queens generally, see Stafford (1983), pp. 175–90.

[126] Black-Veldtrup (1995), pp. 37–61.

breach was unavoidable, she stuck grimly to her religious principles. She was even present and gave her assent when Gregory excommunicated Henry for the first time in 1076.[127] Yet she continued to work for a reconciliation, and her efforts were apparently rewarded when the opponents met at Canossa in January of 1077. Their conflict was later renewed, but Agnes was not to know that. She died soon after the meeting, in what Southern has called "the false after-glow of Canossa."[128]

Was Agnes the kind of affectionate mother to inspire love in her young son? She certainly struggled to help him during her years as regent, and he appears to have cared as much for her as for anyone in his life. In his only surviving letter to his mother, written sometime between 1074 and 1076, Henry calls Agnes "the mother of blessing and well-being," and sends her "love from [our] whole heart and whatever is better and beyond." This traditional royal rhetoric does not necessarily express the emotion Henry really felt, but later in the letter Henry uses less formulaic terms. He recognizes Agnes' right to information about what is happening in Germany, not because she is a former ruler, but "inasmuch as you are our dearest mother." He asks her to intervene in Rome on his behalf, and promises, in return, that she will receive "whatever we can grant to your love."[129] The king also chose to represent himself as a dutiful and loving son in a number of his diplomas, where he claims to be acting in deference to his mother's wishes.[130] Particularly suggestive of real affection is the language of a document dated to 1083, six years after Agnes' death, in which he confirmed a donation she had made: "We also give and confirm all these things to this church of Tortona, because we know that our mother, the Empress Agnes, gave them ...".[131]

Whether he truly loved her or not, Agnes does seem to have retained some influence over her son. We know that Gregory VII sent her to Henry's court to negotiate on his behalf in 1074, and afterwards wrote to her praising her efforts: "your counsels and your merits have brought great benefit to your ... son."[132] However, contemporary writers

---

[127] Black-Veldtrup (1995), p. 54. Agnes' letter to Altmann of Passau about the excommunication was cited by Manegold of Lautenbach, *Ad Gebehardum*, 27, MGH, LL 1: 358–59, and Hugh of Flavigny, *Chronicon*, a. 1076, MGH SS 8: 435.

[128] Southern (1953), p. 77.

[129] Henry IV, *Briefe*, 15, pp. 21–22; trans. Mommsen and Morrison, pp. 155–56.

[130] Henry IV, *Urkunden*, 79, 85, 95, 119, 144, MGH Diplomata, 6.1: 102–04, 110–11, 123–25, 157–58, 186–88.

[131] Henry IV, *Urkunden*, 352, MGH Diplomata, 6.2: 465.

[132] Gregory VII, *Register*, 1.85, p. 122; trans. Cowdrey, pp. 89–90. Lampert of Hersfeld reports that the empress came back from Italy to Germany in 1072, in order to defend Rudolf of Swabia (who had married one of her daughters) against charges of treason (*Annales*, a. 1072, in *Opera*, MGH SRG, n.s. 38: 137–38). Unless she expected to have some impact on Henry's decision, the journey would have had no point.

represented Agnes' influence as more or less effective depending on their views of Henry IV and whether they were primarily trying to damn the king or praise his mother. Bruno of Magdeburg, the Saxon propagandist, who saw Henry as a criminal, claimed that Anno of Cologne took the boy away from his mother back in 1062 because she could not control her wicked son.[133] Similarly, the chronicler Bertold claims that when, "as his adviser and corrector," using "maternal discipline," the empress tried to get her adult son to reform, he complied for a while, but then grew worse then ever. Bertold reports that Agnes gave up in despair and returned to Rome.[134] On the other hand, Gregory VII's biographer, Paul of Bernried, says about her legation to Germany that "after she had spent some time with [Henry], she restored him completely to the affections of holy mother Church."[135] Bonizo of Sutri portrays a furtive Henry secretly meeting with the excommunicated Lombard bishops, out of fear that his mother will find out.[136] In short, even in the case of the empress, a mother's authority over her son remained uncertain.

Her vulnerability to suffering was much clearer. Lampert of Hersfeld describes both mother and son as weeping when Henry was kidnapped from Agnes at Kaiserwerth in 1062.[137] Bertold reports that Agnes, present at the Roman synod that excommunicated Henry in 1076, was "wounded in her soul" by the "sword of his condemnation."[138] And the imperialist chronicler Sigebert of Gembloux, attacking Gregory VII for seducing many from their loyalty to Henry, reports that the pope even "alienated his mother Agnes" from him.[139] Even at the very highest levels of society (perhaps especially at these levels), then, the bond between mother and child could generate anguish as well as honor.

---

[133] Bruno, *De bello Saxonico*, 1, MGH SS 5: 330.
[134] Bertold, *Annales*, a. 1077, MGH SS 5: 304.
[135] Paul of Bernried, *Vita sancti Gregorii VII*, 63 (PL 148: 66–67); trans. Robinson, p. 307. Paul posits two trips to Germany, but according to Black-Veldtrup (1995), pp. 96–97, Agnes only made one trip, in 1074.
[136] Bonizo of Sutri, *Liber ad amicum*, 8, MGH LL 1: 610; trans. Robinson, pp. 241–42.
[137] Lampert, *De institutione Hersveldensis ecclesiae*, 2, in *Opera*, MGH SRG, n.s. 38: 353.
[138] Bertold, *Annales*, a. 1076, MGH SS 5: 283.
[139] Sigebert, *Chronica*, a. 1076, MGH SS 6: 363.

Figure 2. Rome, Biblioteca Apostolica Vaticana, MS. Barberini lat. 592. Mother Church from the Montecassino Exultet Roll. Reproduced by permission of the library.

4 The Mother of the Faithful

Sometime around the year 1000, an anonymous author – identified in the manuscript only as "B." – composed the first *Life* of Archbishop Dunstan of Canterbury (d. 988). The work includes an account of a remarkable vision: Dunstan was sleeping one night when he saw his own mother – "she who gave birth to him" – being married to a great king, with the king's princes as witnesses and with a written endowment for the bride. Before he moved on to the rest of Dunstan's life, the author decided to give his own interpretation of what the archbishop saw. Dunstan's mother, "B." asserts, represents Holy Church, who, "in a maternal manner, regenerated him and countless others in the spiritual womb of holy baptism." She is joined – "as a bride to her spouse" – to Christ, the Highest King, through knowledge of the true faith and in the embrace of divine love. "This same holy Mother Church cries out, in the Song of Songs, 'the King has brought me into his chamber … Stay me with flagons, comfort me with apples, for I am sick of love … His left hand should be under my head and his right hand shoud embrace me … '."[1] In this daring interpretation, then, the mother who physically gave birth to Dunstan stands in for *Mater Ecclesia*, Mother Church – that is, the Church as a whole.[2] But she had another, more specialized, meaning. "In another sense," Dunstan's mother could be seen as his own church of Canterbury – "which he received from the hand of the eternal king, from Christ the Lord, as the guardian and preserver of his mother's pure virginal integrity." "B." evokes Christ's words on the cross, when He commended Mary to St. John: "Behold your mother" (John 19:27), thus connecting the idea of the bishop as the "friend of the Bridegroom,"

---

[1] "B.", *Vita sancti Dunstani*, 29–30, in *Memorials of St. Dunstan*, pp. 40–43. Various verses from the Song of Song are combined in the passage cited. On the author of this work, see Lapidge (1992).

[2] How daring this interpretation was may be deduced from the fact that Dunstan's later biographers, who borrowed wholesale from the *vita* of "B.", included this vision, but either omitted entirely, or toned down, his interpretation of it. Compare the versions by Osbern and Eadmer, in *Memorials of St. Dunstan*, pp. 117–18, 205–06, and the life by William of Malmesbury, in his *Saints' Lives*, pp. 284–87.

as the guardian of his see on Christ's behalf, with the idea of a son's responsibility for his mother.

In the central Middle Ages, the Bride of Christ was also understood to be the Mother of the Faithful, who gave birth to Christians through the sacrament of baptism.[3] Because of their many imperfections, ordinary, earthly women were seldom compared directly to Mother Church – "B.'s" text is highly unusual in that regard. Nevertheless, they shared the same maternal attributes: many texts from the central Middle Ages emphasize the Church's ability to give birth, and her love and care for her spiritual children. At the same time, her vulnerability was often stressed, especially in the context of demands for reform. My special concern in this chapter, however, is with constructions of the Church's maternal authority, especially as these were deployed in arguments about hierarchy within the Christian community. *Mater Ecclesia* appears regularly in this period, both in debates about the relationship between the laity and the clergy, and in discussions of the relative positions of different bishops within the ecclesiastical hierarchy. Above all, she plays an important role in assertions of (and sometimes in resistance to) papal primacy.

The mother rejoices

The image of the Church as Mother, like that of the Church as Bride, was ritualized in the Middle Ages, made real through repeated references within sacred time and space.[4] This was most clear in the liturgy of the Easter vigil, in the ancient prayer, known as the Exultet, which the deacon pronounced over the paschal candle:

> Rejoice now, angelic choir of the heavens,
> let the divine mysteries rejoice
> and for the victory of such a king
> let the trumpet of salvation sound …
> Let Mother Church, too, be glad, adorned with the brightness of
> such splendor;
> and let this hall resound with the great voices of the people …[5]

The rejoicing expressed in the Exultet has a double cause: first, Christ's victory over sin and death, and second, the entry of new members into the Christian community, to share in his triumph. In the ancient church, catechumens were baptized during the Easter vigil, their personal regeneration

---

[3] In addition to the works cited below, see Robinson (1988), pp. 259–60.
[4] In the liturgy of Christmas, for example, the Church, like Mary, suffers labor pains. Peter Damian, 118, vol. 3: 332; trans. Blum 4: 334. Compare the sermon of Herbert of Losinga, Bishop of Norwich, cited by Brett (1975), p. 116.
[5] Translated by Kelly (1996), p. 32.

timed to coincide with the annual regeneration of the cosmos. The Exultet was probably composed – perhaps in two stages – sometime between the fifth and the seventh century,[6] at a time when infant baptism soon after birth was rapidly replacing the baptism of adults on Holy Saturday. Nevertheless, even in the central Middle Ages, in many parts of Europe, the Easter vigil was still regarded as the most appropriate moment for baptism. The prominence of Mother Church in the text was probably intended to remind the faithful of her role in their spiritual rebirth.

The Exultet was used throughout Europe in the Middle Ages,[7] but in southern Italy it gave shape in the tenth and eleventh centuries to the exquisite Exultet rolls, illustrated with scenes from the prayer.[8] The Exultet rolls offer some of our most beautiful medieval representations of *Mater Ecclesia*. In particular, one of the six surviving rolls from the abbey of Montecassino – this one prepared for Abbot Desiderius, the reformer who became Pope Victor III in 1087 – is justly celebrated for its image of Mother Church. In this manuscript, a figure clearly labeled "Mater Ecclesia" spreads her arms wide in a gesture both powerful (she seems to be supporting the columns of the church building) and welcoming. On either side, "clergy" and "people" run to join her – clearly for the ritual of baptism, since a baby is being carried in by its father.[9] Like the blessing itself, the image of Mother Church in this Exultet roll concretizes the female figure of the Church, making her literally visible – whether to the faithful as a whole or simply to the bishop seated nearby – as a real person.

The Church was, for medieval clerics, the archetypal mother – of whom earthly mothers were only faint shadows. Biblical passages about maternity applied more truly to her than to any ordinary woman. Indeed, their application to carnal mothers might be problematic, precisely because of the passages' primary association with the Church. In his explication of Exodus 21:17 ("He that curses his father, or his mother, shall surely be put to death"), Cardinal Bruno of Segni wrote,

Although it may indeed be a great sin to strike one's [earthly] father and mother, yet I understand this to mean something greater. I suppose that by "father" and "mother" what is meant is God and the Church. Those who deride them, or strike them with a "blow of the tongue" by blaspheming, will be subject to a sentence of death. For that is what happens to him who curses his father or

---

[6] Kelly (1996), pp. 50–53.
[7] E.g. Raoul of Saint-Sépulchre, *Vita sancti Lietberti Cameracensis episcopi*, 13, MGH, SS 30.2: 848.
[8] See especially *Exultet: Rotoli liturgici del medioevo meridionale*.
[9] Bibliotheca Apostolica Vaticana, Barberini Lat. 592. On this roll, see Kelly (1996), pp. 245–47.

mother, and if this is not understood in terms of God and the Church, it seems to be a very severe sentence ...[10]

The extreme penalty threatened in Exodus 21 only makes sense to Bruno if the mother in question is really the Church.[11] Because the spiritual was more important than the physical, the Church was the essential mother for Christians, just as God was their most important father. Earthly parents were linked with heavenly ones, as figures to reality, but the latter were immeasurably superior. As Tertullian had noted, centuries earlier, Christ, "by a repudiation of carnal kinship," had pronounced the Church "a mother of higher significance" than any mortal one.[12]

The identification of the Church as Mother of the Faithful was, as this allusion to Tertullian suggests, very ancient. Its most important source, the fourth chapter of Paul's letter to the Galatians, reinterprets the story of Hagar and Sarah as an allegory of the two covenants, the old and the new. Hagar represents the old law of bondage, while Sarah is the heavenly Jerusalem, which is the "mother of us all" – that is, she represents either the new law, or the Church, formerly barren like Sarah, but now become fertile (Galatians 4:26–27). Christians, writes Paul, are not the children of the bondwoman, but of the free (Galatians 4:31). The Church Fathers drew on this and on other passages from Scripture to develop richly the allegory of the Church as Mother.[13] By the eleventh century, the figure of *Mater Ecclesia* had become central to Biblical exegesis and therefore to theology, as well as to political thought.

For medieval exegetes, the Church's maternal body signified many aspects of religious life – the womb could represent the baptismal font or the cemetery in which the faithful were buried, or even the "precepts of truth."[14] Baptism was universally represented as a form of birth – or better, rebirth – in which the Mother brought forth her children into a new life.[15] Mortal sin or heresy, on the other hand, could be viewed as a kind

---

[10] Bruno of Segni, *Expositio in Exodum* (PL 164: 286–87).
[11] The Norman Anonymous (p. 32) interpreted Exodus 21 in a similar way: "Your mother is the heavenly Jerusalem [cf. Galatians 4:26, where the heavenly Jerusalem is called "the mother of us all"] ... by whose labor, by whose care, by whose ministry you were born and nourished ... if you do an injury to your carnal mother, the injury redounds to that mother, the heavenly Jerusalem."
[12] Tertullian, *De carne Christi*, 7.13, p. 889. On the maternity of the Church in Tertullian, see Plumpe (1943), pp. 45–62.
[13] Plumpe (1943); Delahaye (1958); Lubac (1971), pp. 47–71; Therel (1973).
[14] On the baptismal font as womb or mother in antiquity, see Bedard (1951), pp. 17–36; medieval references occur throughout this chapter. On the cemetery as womb, see Gerard of Cambrai, *Acta synodi Atrebatensis*, 7 (PL 142: 1295); on the "precepts of truth," see Pseudo-Bede, *In psalmorum libro exegesis* (PL 93: 784).
[15] E.g. Peter Damian, 40, vol. 1: 398; trans. Blum, 2: 118; Rupert of Deutz, *Anulus sive dialogus inter Christianum et Judaeum*, 1 (PL 170: 571).

of abortion, when the Church expelled sinners from her womb.[16] Her maternal breasts were powerful symbols of spiritual nourishment. Most often they represented the Old and New Testaments,[17] but sometimes they were also described as offering two kinds of nourishing liquid – the milk of simple doctrine for the ordinary faithful, the inebriating wine of higher truths for the wise.[18] Sometimes the Church fed Christians first with the milk of doctrine, and later with the "solid food of Scripture."[19] The Church's breasts could also symbolize ecclesiastical justice.[20]

Before the advent of Christ, the Church had been barren, but with the Incarnation she became the "joyful mother of many sons" (Psalm 112).[21] She became, indeed, a *materfamilias*, exercising great authority over her household. Bruno of Segni devoted one of his theological *sententiae* to a discussion of the various women in the Bible who might be considered *figurae* of the Church. Among them was the "virtuous woman" of Proverbs 31, who "lays her hand to the spindle and her fingers hold the distaff." "In this," writes Bruno,

is manifested the wisdom of the Church, which disposes so well of all things. Her hands – that is, those who are stronger and wiser – she puts to her greater affairs, making them rectors and bishops. Her fingers hold the distaff, for she assigns those who are more imperfect and less experienced to minor matters.[22]

Later in the same text, Bruno identifies the Church with the matriarch Sarah, "who was earlier called Sarai, which means 'my prince'." That name was not appropriate, however: this "prince and mother of all" should really have been called "*our* prince," "because in the son that she bore, all people were blessed." Sarah's authority, then, was not only maternal, but princely.[23]

Others identified Hagar with the Synagogue, which obeyed God "carnally," from fear of the "servile law," and her son Ishmael with "false Christians and heretics."[24] Sarah and Isaac, on the other hand,

---

[16] Bruno of Würzburg, *Expositio in psalmos* (PL 142: 224); Ivo of Chartres, *Sermones*, 13 (PL 162: 581).

[17] E.g. Peter Damian, 135, vol. 3: 460; trans. Blum 5(6): 80–81.

[18] E.g. Bruno, *Expositio in Cantica canticorum* (PL 164: 1280).

[19] Rupert of Deutz, *Anulus*, 1 (PL 170: 571); cf. Peter Damian, 65, vol. 2: 236; trans. Blum, 3: 29; Conrad of Brunweiler, *Vita Wolphelmi* (PL 154: 412).

[20] Geoffrey of Vendôme, 74 and 117, pp. 138–40 and 226.

[21] Bruno of Würzburg, *Expositio in psalmos* (PL 142: 414). The psalm in question is numbered 112 in the Vulgate; elsewhere sometimes 113. On Mother Church's care for her sons, see also Thietmar, 6.35, p. 317; trans. Warner, p. 261; on maternal forgiveness, see Peter Damian, 88, vol. 2: 516; trans. Blum, 3: 309–10.

[22] Bruno of Segni, *Sententiae*, 1.5 (PL 165: 889).

[23] Bruno of Segni, *Sententiae*, 1.5 (PL 165: 891). Added emphasis.

[24] Peter Damian, 84, vol. 2: 454–55; trans. Blum, 3: 248–49.

prefigured the Church and her sons, "who will in the future inherit eternal glory."[25] For these authors, as for Paul, an important aspect of the Church's authority was her power of discernment, her ability to divide true Christians from false, thus ensuring that her sons, and not those of the "bondwoman," would "inherit" – this quality became important in discussions of schism. Also essential was her ability to discipline the faithful. In a letter examining whether force could properly be used against heretics, Augustine of Hippo had discussed Sarah's legitimate right to discipline her "stubborn servant" Hagar.[26] As we shall see, eleventh-century political thinkers made extensive use of this image of maternal discipline.

Yet in all these texts, the Church's authority is always understood as derivative, delegated to her by her heavenly Spouse, just as the power of an earthly *materfamilias* depended on that of her husband.[27] A sermon preached on Ash Wednesday by Bishop Ivo of Chartres probably refers to the ancient practice, still in use for sinners of certain types during the central Middle Ages, of physically excluding penitents from the church at the beginning of Lent and then absolving and readmitting them at Easter.[28] "Today," proclaimed Ivo, "Mother Church corrects her children *with paternal severity*, so that she can gather them together *with maternal piety*, once they have been reformed by medicinal abstinence …".[29] While the bishop's call to repentance is authorized by Mother Church, notice that the disciplinary role is not naturally hers – she must use "paternal severity" to correct sinners, before returning to her accustomed mercy and forgiveness. The threat of paternal wrath, then, backed up the Church's commands. In the third century, Cyprian of Carthage had written (in a passage often cited in the eleventh century), "He cannot have God as Father who does not have the Church as Mother."[30] Those who failed to obey Her ran the risk of offending Him.

Stubborn and rebellious sons

In the year 1050, the citizens of Osimo did something quite common in the central Middle Ages, even though it was contrary to canon law. At the death of their bishop, they looted his belongings and destroyed episcopal

---

[25] Bruno of Würzburg, *Expositio in psalmos* (PL 142: 652–53).
[26] Augustine of Hippo, *Epistulae*, 93, vol. 34.2: 450.
[27] As Placidus of Nonantola put it (*Liber de honore ecclesiae*, 6, MGH LL 2: 577): "many of the faithful willingly hand over themselves and their property to the Church, that is to the Bride of Christ, as God's representative [*vice Dei*]."
[28] Mansfield (1995); Hamilton (2001).
[29] Ivo of Chartres, *Sermones*, 13 (PL 162: 579). Emphasis added.
[30] Cyprian of Carthage, *De ecclesiae catholicae unitate*, 6, in *Opera*, CC, SL 3: 253.

property. Peter Damian wrote on behalf of Pope Leo IX to curb this "unlawful venture":

If indeed, the honoring of our parents is called the First Commandment with a promise, that cursing our father or mother is to be punished by death, what should the sentence of chastisement be for those who undertake to persecute not their natural parents, but like vipers attempt to destroy their mother, the Church, in which they were reborn by water and the Holy Spirit?[31]

Peter critiqued the looting not by invoking the law, but by drawing a picture of a household in disorder.[32] In attacking church property, the people of Osimo were acting like murderous young vipers rather than proper children of the Church; they were breaking a commandment, and could thus expect to be punished by God. (Possibly Peter made this argument because he realized they would never be punished any other way.)

Images of "unnatural" children appear in many critiques of lay misbehavior – including the misbehavior of kings, increasingly labeled by the more radical reformers as laymen – in this period. Bad sons were, for example, a major theme in Pope Pascal II's letters concerning lay investiture in England. To Archbishop Anselm, exiled from his see because of his refusal to do homage to, or be invested by, King Henry I, Pascal complained that lay investiture impaired the honor of the Church, as well as weakening ecclesiastical discipline:

It is not for laymen to hand over the Church nor for sons to defile their mother by adultery. He who has polluted his mother by adultery is rightly to be deprived of his patrimony; and he who pursues her by wicked attacks does not deserve the fellowship of ecclesiastical blessing. It is the duty of laymen to protect the Church, not to hand her over.[33]

Because the Mother of the Faithful was also the Bride of Christ, and (secondarily) of her bishop, to "hand her over" to an unsuitable candidate was to force her into adultery. The pope used similar language in his letters to Henry:

You see then, O King, how shameful, how dangerous it may be for the mother to be adulterously defiled by her own sons. If, then, you are a son of the Church, as indeed every catholic Christian is, allow your mother to enjoy lawful marriage, so that the Church may be joined to her lawful husband not by a man but by Christ, the God-man.[34]

Lay investiture is conflated in these letters with lay selection of bishops. Bad sons enslaved their Mother the Church, by forcing her into a union

---

[31] Peter Damian, 35, vol. 1: 337–38; trans. Blum 2: 62.
[32] Cf. Orderic, 8, vol. 4: 158.
[33] Pascal II, *Epistolae*, 85 (PL 163: 106) = JL 5928.
[34] Pascal II, *Epistolae*, 49 (PL 163: 70–71) = JL 5868.

with a bishop she had not chosen herself, while true sons allowed her to enjoy a "lawful marriage."

A passage in the twenty-first chapter of Deuteronomy deals with the "stubborn and rebellious" son who refuses to obey his father and mother; the parents are to take him before the elders of the city, and declare his disobedience – and then the men of the city are to stone him to death. Writing in the early twelfth century, Bruno of Segni interpreted this to mean that priests and bishops, "who are the spiritual fathers and mothers of all others," should excommunicate and thereby condemn to eternal death those of their sons who refused to obey their admonitions and the teachings of Scripture.[35] This was indeed how the more radical reformers of the period imagined the proper relationship between clergy and laity.

The Gregorians in Rome, in particular, often depicted the laity as children, and the Church as their Mother or the clergy their fathers.[36] Layfolk who refused to obey their spiritual parents should be excommunicated, or – in the case of rulers – even deposed. Yet how much this hierarchical view was actually conveyed to the laity is unclear. In 1113, Pope Pascal II urged a group of citizens in Arras to act as arbitrators in a dispute between the monastery of Saint-Vaast and the cathedral clergy. "We have heard that you are good men" the pope writes, "and therefore we confidently issue the orders that should be ordered to you, as good sons of the Church.[37] But even such a mild demand for obedience was rare. Reformers like Pascal generally appealed to the faithful's affection for Mother Church, rather than explicitly asserting her maternal authority. In other words, they depicted her more often as the helpless victim of her children's oppression than as an imperious "prince." The Church's ability to discipline her children, her power to excommunicate, is seldom invoked in letters to the laity – probably because the surviving letters were mostly directed to high-ranking nobles, accustomed to deference from the clergy. Only in the most extreme circumstances, and then primarily in exchanges among church leaders themselves, was maternal authority directly invoked. This interplay of deference and command is most clearly visible in the deeply troubled relationship that developed over the course of the late eleventh and early twelfth centuries, between Rome and the German emperors.

The emperor's mother

When the Empress Agnes, acting on behalf of her young son Henry IV, appointed Cadalus of Parma as pope, she set off the chain of events

---

[35] Bruno of Segni, *Expositio in Deuteronomium* (PL 164: 520).
[36] On the clergy as fathers, see below, Chapter 6.
[37] Pascal II, *Epistolae*, 373 (PL 163: 335) = JL 6366.

that brought her regency to an end. This was the context within which Cardinal Peter Damian wrote *The Debate at the Synod*, intended to undermine the German court's support for Cadalus, and to justify the election of Alexander II by the Roman reformers.[38] Peter creates two characters – the Royal Advocate and the Defender of the Roman Church – who represent the perspectives of the young King Henry IV and his mother, on the one hand, and the reform party in Rome (identified here simply as the Roman Church), on the other. Needless to say, in this imaginary dialogue the arguments of the Defender of the Roman Church (i.e. the reform party) ultimately prevail.

The central issue in the debate is that of the king's role in papal elections – a role which had varied considerably in the past and which had been left undefined in the controversial election decree of 1059.[39] The Royal Advocate contends that Alexander II's election was improper, because carried out without royal consent. The Defender of the Roman Church agrees that, like his father before him, Henry IV is entitled to some role in papal elections. However, he also argues that Agnes' regency for her minor son created a special situation in 1061.

The Defender's argument depends on the assumption that the Church – in this case, the Roman Church – is a Christian's true mother. He points out that the Roman Church, as the king's spiritual Mother, far excels his physical one:

The Roman Church is a mother of the king much more noble and sublime than a mother of flesh. If the latter [i.e. Agnes] bore him so that through her stock he should return to dust, the former gave birth to him in order to make him a co-heir of the Christ who reigns without end.[40]

This neatly undercuts Agnes' claim to be acting on her son's behalf.

In electing Alexander II, the Defender says, the reformers – who represent the Roman Church – were simply acting in the maternal role, as guardian for a king still too young to act on his own behalf: "What evil, then does the Roman Church do, if she undertakes the office of guardian [*tutor*] to her son while he is still young, when he still lacks a guardian, and exercises the right which is his. For who does not know that a boy does not know how to elect a priest?" The suggestion is that Henry IV had no guardian to act on his behalf in 1061, which is why the Roman

---

[38] The *Debate* in its current form is contained within a public letter addressed to Cadalus. Peter Damian, 89, vol. 2: 531–72; trans. Blum, 3: 336–69. The editor of Peter's letters, Kurt Reindel, reviews the literature on this work in note 26 to p. 541.

[39] See Jasper (1986), p. 1, n. 2, for a brief review of the extensive modern literature on the election decree and the role of the emperor in papal elections.

[40] Peter Damian, 89, vol. 2: 548; trans. Blum, 3: 343; cf. 64, vol. 2: 227; trans. Blum, 3: 21–22. And see Maccarrone (1974), p. 67.

Church had to step in. Peter Damian has neatly erased Henry's earthly mother (Agnes) from the scene, a rhetorical technique which serves the double purpose of avoiding overt criticism of a still very powerful woman and allowing the reformers in Rome to assume her maternal authority.

To make it clear that the reformers are not usurping young Henry's inherited right to have a say in papal elections, the Defender invokes Roman law and everyday practice:

Often a mother will intrude upon a judge's tribunal, receive witnesses, call together the clerks for consultation, and thus by the testimony given and confirmed, together with the written evidence, guarantee to her son all the rights to his property. In the meantime, however, until he has reached his majority and is capable of handling his own affairs, she controls and manages everything, and thus disposes as she sees fit of that which belongs to another through inheritance. Can such a mother on this account be said to withhold those things that have been granted to her son? It is rather more true to say, I think, that she is fulfilling her maternal duty, because what her inexperienced son might otherwise destroy or squander, she preserves, in that his goods were properly handed over to her for safekeeping and reasonable management.[41]

This is what an earthly mother would do for her minor son – indeed, what Agnes was already doing for Henry. But the Defender ignores the empress, transferring her position to the Roman Church: "Thus as a natural mother assists her son in earthly matters, should Mother Church not render help to her son, the emperor, in the matter of his spiritual gifts?"[42]

Who, exactly, is "Mother Church" in this text? Clearly not the pope, since his election is the issue at hand. Presumably Peter Damian had in mind the reforming cardinals (including himself) who had been given new authority to choose the pope in the Election Decree of 1059. Whoever represented her, Mother Rome here exercises the same kind of tentative, essentially situational authority as any earthly mother. Peter's language is surprisingly deferential, to imperial rights and even to Agnes herself, even as he tries to construct a convincing claim against them.

Peter's language in this treatise was not unprecedented. The first description of a ruler as a "son of the Roman Church" occurs in the second half of the eighth century.[43] Yet in the early eleventh century,

---

[41] Peter Damian, 89, vol. 2: 548–49; trans. Blum, 3: 343.
[42] Peter Damian, 89, vol. 2: 549; trans. Blum, 3: 343.
[43] Pope Paul I appears to have been the first to use the phrase in correspondence with Frankish rulers, and it was then applied to Charlemagne and his successors. Conte (1971), pp. 608–17; Hauck (1977); Delogu (2000), 218–19. See also Angenendt (1980). This development is, of course, related to the more overt assertion of Rome's maternal authority in the eighth and ninth centuries (see below).

Mother Rome seldom appears in papal letters directed to secular rulers. Other clerics did sometimes use maternal language to describe the relationship between the emperor and the Church, but the emphasis is on affection much more than on filial duty. *The Debate at the Synod*, then, constructs a much more overt hierarchy than did earlier documents. This was possible because the emperor was only a child and therefore more naturally subject to maternal authority than a grown man. The primary victim of Peter's rhetoric, however, was Agnes, not young Henry.

For the most part, however, the first reformers in Rome, like their predecessors, did not use claims of maternal authority to command obedience from lay rulers. As late as the beginning of Gregory VII's pontificate, the pope's use of maternal language was often quite deferential, especially when addressing the emperor directly.[44] When Gregory thought of joining an expedition to bring help to eastern Christians, he wrote to Henry IV (now ruling independently), "if by God's favour I shall go thither, I am leaving to you, after God, the Roman Church so that you may both guard her as a holy mother and defend her to her honour."[45] Not Mother Church, but Henry was in the superior position here.

However, in letters directed to people *other* than the emperor, Mother Rome was already flexing her muscles, claiming obedience from her most exalted son.[46] In 1073, Gregory VII informed countesses Beatrice and Matilda of Tuscany that he was sending envoys to Henry's court, "by whose admonitions ... we may avail to recall him to the love of the holy Roman Church which is his mother, and to instruct and adorn him in a befitting manner of life for receiving the imperial office."[47] By 1076, the pope was asking the faithful within the empire to aid him in the task of recalling Henry "to the bosom of our common mother which he has tried to rend."[48] A few months later: "Let him no longer think holy church to be subject to him as a handmaid but set over him as a lady."[49] When Henry's opponents elected an anti-king, Rudolf of Swabia, in 1077, the faithful in Germany had trouble knowing whom to obey. Gregory agreed to travel north of the Alps to help mediate, but if either king tried to hinder him on his journey or refuse to accept the pope's decision, that candidate, "having been rendered disobedient by

---

[44] On the importance of maternal language in Gregory's letters, see Maccarrone (1974), pp. 82–91; Cowdrey (1998), pp. 596–607. Neither author clearly breaks down the pope's usage according to the recipients of his letters.

[45] Gregory VII, *Register*, 2.31, p. 167; trans. Cowdrey, p. 123. Cf. *Register* 3.3, p. 246; trans. Cowdrey, 176.

[46] On the importance of obedience in Gregory's thought, see Benz (1990).

[47] Gregory VII, *Register*, 1.11, p. 19; trans. Cowdrey, pp. 11–12.

[48] Gregory VII, *Register*, 4.1, p. 291; trans. Cowdrey, p. 207.

[49] Gregory VII, *Register*, 4.3, p. 298; trans. Cowdrey, p. 212.

resisting the holy and universal mother church," would lose his claim to the throne.[50]

The most elaborate use of maternal language against Henry IV comes, however, not in texts sent to the laity, but in Gregory's second letter to Bishop Herman of Metz, written in 1081. Rulers, Gregory tells Herman, should obey the Church's commands: "let those whom holy church of her own will summons by deliberate counsel to kingship or empire ... show humble obedience;" such rulers should certainly "not seek to subject or to subdue holy church to themselves like a handmaid."[51] The emperor, however, has denied Rome's maternal authority; he is, "in truth, a treader underfoot, so far as in him lies, of his mother the church."[52] This justifies his excommunication, in keeping with the Old Testament laws which command believers "to obey our fathers and mothers after the flesh," and threaten those who "curse father or mother" with death.[53] Significantly, this new and overtly hierarchical language was directed to another bishop. Even Gregory was not audacious enough to speak in this way to the emperor's face. In addressing powerful rulers, a more diplomatic approach was required.[54]

After Henry IV's death (still excommunicate) in 1106, his son, Henry V – who had deposed his father with the blessing of Pope Pascal II – enjoyed a brief "honeymoon" with the Roman see.[55] But by 1111, the relationship had soured again. The issue of lay investiture, already hotly debated in England, now became a subject of contention within the empire as well. Henry V sent delegations to meet with the envoys of Pope Pascal II at Guastalla in 1106, at Châlons-sur-Marne in 1107, and finally at Rome in 1109, in an effort to resolve the dispute. Apparently, by 1109 Henry was willing to agree not to invest bishops with ring and staff; however, he insisted on his right to use some other symbol to invest them with the *regalia*, the possessions they held from the king. Negotiations repeatedly broke down over the question of what, precisely, these encompassed – was it all the possessions of the imperial churches? Or more specific governmental rights and revenues, ultimately derived from the king's authority? Compromise seemed out of reach.[56]

---

[50] Gregory VII, *Register*, 4.24, p. 337; trans. Cowdrey, pp. 237–38.
[51] Gregory VII, *Register*, 8.21, p. 562; trans. Cowdrey p. 395.
[52] Gregory VII, *Register*, 8.21, p. 551; trans. Cowdrey p. 389.
[53] Gregory VII, *Register*, 8.21, p. 562; trans. Cowdrey p. 395. On the use of paternal language in this letter, see below, Chapter 6.
[54] One Gregorian writer, Anselm of Lucca, did remind King William I of England that Rome was his *caput* and *mater. Briefsammlungen*, p. 17.
[55] On the deposition of Henry IV, see below, Chapter 5.
[56] Compromise had, of course, already been reached in England and France.

Arriving in Rome to be crowned emperor, Henry held secret negotiations with Pascal, which did finally lead to an agreement in February of 1111.[57] However, the radical solution – by which Henry would abandon investiture entirely if the imperial bishops gave up all their specifically regalian rights and revenues – was vehemently rejected by the German princes gathered in Rome for the coronation. Both ecclesiastical and lay princes saw the solution as irreconcilable with good order within the kingdom, and, perhaps, even as heretical. When the agreement collapsed, Pascal refused to crown Henry emperor. And Henry, reasserting his father's claim to invest with ring and staff, seems to have lost both his temper and all sense of what might work politically. When the pope refused to allow his claim, Henry took him prisoner. At first the imprisoned pope held firm, but in April 1111, fearing not so much for his own life (which was probably never in danger) as for the lives of his cardinals and curia, he succumbed. Pascal agreed to crown Henry emperor and granted him the right to invest bishops with ring and staff before consecration; he also pledged never to excommunicate him.

In investing with the traditional symbols of episcopal office, Henry argued, he was simply granting bishops the temporal possessions of their sees, not the spiritual office itself. However, this claim was no longer viable. The kings of France and England had already abandoned investiture in 1107. Their actions bolstered the argument, made most explicitly by Ranger of Lucca in *On the Ring and the Staff*, that the objects in question really were "sacred symbols," not to be conferred by "laymen."[58] Consequently, the result of Henry V's second "agreement" with the pope was an outcry from every part of Europe against him, and against the pope for granting such a concession. In the end, a synod held at the Lateran in 1112 revoked the privilege Pascal had granted Henry, labeling it a *pravilegium* or "wicked privilege. Henry was excommunicated.

The events of 1111 unleashed a torrent of criticism directed at Henry V. One anonymous author from northern Europe wrote,

The mouth of the Lord has spoken: "whoever shall curse his father or mother shall die the death" [Exodus 21:17] … But King Henry, the enemy of the Church, ignoring divine law … curses his Mother, when he destroys the liberty of Holy Church, whose son he should be, and spits in her face when he goes against her by resisting what has been instituted by the holy fathers.[59]

---

[57] On the events of 1111, see Servatius (1979), pp. 214–52; Chodorow (1989). Cantarella (1987), pp. 13–40, provides a valuable discussion of source problems.

[58] Ranger, *De anulo et baculo*, MGH LL 2: 509, 533

[59] *Disputatio vel defensio Paschalis papae*, MGH LL 2: 665. On this work, see Cantarella (1987), pp. 41–91; on the polemics of this period generally, see Servatius (1979), pp. 278–96.

As in the commentary of Bruno of Segni, cited above, which dates from roughly the same period, the "ungrateful" son, who "spits in the face" of Mother Church, is condemned both to death and to "disinheritance" – certainly the loss of the heavenly inheritance of salvation, but also, perhaps, the loss of his earthly kingdom.

In comparison, the language used by Placidus of Nonantola in *On the Honor of the Church* (composed late in 1111) seems mild. Placidus describes this long treatise, full of references to canon law, as "a little book in defense of the honor of Mother Church." A recurring theme is the proper relationship between the emperor and his spiritual Mother: "The emperor should not dominate the Church, but rather guard and preserve her, as a most pious son does his most revered mother."[60] And again:

The most pious emperor should not oppress the church, but rather serve her most devoutly, as his spiritual mother. He is not anointed with holy oil in order to dominate the church, but rather so that in serving Christ the King, he would protect His Bride with human power from the plots of the wicked.[61]

There can only be peace between *regnum* and *sacerdotium*, Placidus concludes, when the emperor, "out of love for his spiritual Mother," allows proper elections, investiture with ring and staff by metropolitans, and only then his own investiture with the property of the Church.[62] Placidus does not depict Henry V as an "ungrateful son"; instead, he spells out what a good son's behavior should be. Nevertheless, for him, as for the anonymous author just mentioned, the relationship between the emperor and the Church is overtly hierarchical, much more so, indeed, than it was in Peter Damian's treatise, written fifty years earlier.

As their understanding of the relationship between *regnum* and *sacerdotium* changed, in the face of continual strife with the emperors, the reformers' position hardened, both in Italy and in northern Europe. In the late eleventh and early twelfth centuries, writing among themselves, reform-minded clerics quickly replaced the deferential language of the early Middle Ages with claims that the emperor, like other laymen, should submit to *Mater Ecclesia*. In addressing powerful laymen directly, the claims of Mother Church generally remained more subdued. Yet here, too, a change in tone is apparent – if not in letters to the emperors, at least in those to other rulers. In 1121, Calixtus II reminded King Louis VI of France of his ancestors' devotion to the Roman Church: "nor did it seem sufficient to them to venerate their Mother in their own day,

---

[60] Placidus, *Liber de honore ecclesiae*, 19, MGH LL 2: 580. On this work, see Cantarella (1983); Büsch (1990).
[61] Placidus, *Liber de honore ecclesiae*, 82, MGH LL 2: 605.
[62] Placidus, *Liber de honore ecclesiae*, 93, MGH LL 2: 615.

but they bequeathed reverence, obedience and love towards her to their descendants, by a kind of hereditary law [*jure quodam haereditario*]." Louis, born of the same royal line, has succeeded them on the throne and also – by divine grace – acts as their "free-born heir" (*haeres ingenuus*) both in "probity of morals" and in "devotion" to his Mother.[63] Strikingly, Louis's obedience to the Roman Church is here depicted as an aspect of his obligations to his own lineage.

Mater et magistra

If maternal language came to play an important role in the construction of clerical–lay hierarchy in the central Middle Ages, it was partly because precedents already existed for that role. Similar language had long been used in the construction of hierarchies *within* the clergy. And here we must return, briefly, to the early Church. During the first three centuries of the Common Era, bonds of charity, much more than institutional ties, linked together the Christian communities of the Roman Empire. While the traditions of the older, "apostolic" churches – those with apostolic origins – were considered especially authoritative, their leaders received no more than honor and deference from their fellow bishops. It was only in the fourth and fifth centuries that an ecclesiastical hierarchy began to develop. At this time, our sources begin to speak of ecclesiastical "provinces," normally paralleling the provinces of the Roman Empire, which encompassed a number of local churches. One bishop in each province was given the title of "metropolitan," and the charge of organizing his fellow bishops for synods, the elections of new bishops, and so on.[64] In the same period, a small number of bishops (eventually the number settled at five) began using the title "patriarch" (and in Rome, the title "papa"), and exercising a similar supervisory function over several provinces.[65]

In late antiquity, the patriarchs and metropolitans were still essentially just the "first among equals." They were often deferred to in matters of doctrine and discipline, and they helped organize their fellow bishops, but they had no real juridical authority over them. They did not yet judge legal cases, or transfer or depose bishops without the other bishops of the province acting with them as colleagues. Only in the ninth century

---

[63] Calixtus II, *Epistolae*, 161 (PL 163: 1225) = JL 6936; cf. Urban II, *Epistolae*, 4 (PL 151: 287) = JL 5351.

[64] Lesne (1905), pp. 1–8; Kempf (1978), pp. 28–33.

[65] On the use of these titles in Rome, see Schieffer (1991). By the eighth century, the title "archbishop" was coming into general use, although at first it sometimes referred to patriarchs and sometimes to lower-ranking metropolitans. Kempf (1978), pp. 47–50.

did these higher-ranking bishops really begin to exercise much control over their suffragans – and only in the ninth century was this relationship really clarified in church law.[66] Paradoxically (given what we know about the limited legal basis of maternal authority), the more nebulous, nonjuridical relationships of the fourth and fifth centuries were sometimes described using paternal imagery – "patriarchs," "papa" – while the canon law collections of the ninth century increasingly defined the ecclesiastical hierarchy in legal terms by reference to the relationship between mothers and their daughters.[67] Although I can only sketch the outlines of this development here, this is a subject that would certainly reward further investigation. It is not yet clear why this development took place, where it began, or how it spread.

The change is most evident if we examine the claims of the Roman see to superiority over other churches, for here we have the most consistent series of sources. The bishops of Rome had a special "significance" within the Christian community from a very early date, first, because the tradition of the Church of Rome was seen as the most authentic, and second, because St. Peter – according to legend the founder of the see of Rome – had been designated by Christ himself as the keeper of the keys of heaven. The popes themselves aggressively asserted their primacy in theological disputes from the fourth century on. They presented themselves as the "successors of St. Peter," and sometimes used the language of both Roman and Christian political theory, describing themselves as the "head" in the overall body of bishops.[68] Seldom, however, did the popes of the fifth or sixth centuries claim that the Roman Church was the "mother" of any other church.[69] The application of such domestic imagery to Rome seems to have begun in the seventh century, when two different writers, one a pope, the other a Byzantine theologian, independently referred to the Roman Church as the "mother of all churches."[70] The fact that two such different figures used this specific phrase may suggest that it was already in common use in the seventh century, but in the surviving sources it does not appear again until the ninth century.

[66] With considerable conflict: see Lesne (1905), pp. 185–293; Kempf (1978), pp. 38–45.

[67] On paternal imagery, see below, Chapter 6.

[68] Within the massive literature on papal primacy in the early Middle Ages, see Maccarrone (1960); Angenendt (1989); Schatz (1990), pp. 1–38; *Il primato di vescovo di Roma*.

[69] Koch (1930), pp. 71–90, finds the earliest such reference in a letter of the fifth-century pope Hilarus, and few other references in the sixth century. Plumpe (1943), pp. 126–29, notes that in earlier centuries, Roman writers had been reluctant to identify the Church, even in the abstract, as mother.

[70] Maccarrone (1960), pp. 704–6; Conte (1971), pp. 173–77; and see Maccarrone (1974), p. 26, n. 14. On the papal position in the seventh and eighth centuries more broadly, see Delogu (2000).

By that time, both the popes and other writers were regularly referring to Rome not only as the "mother" but also as the "mistress" (*magistra*) of all churches; sometimes the two designations are joined in the same phrase: *mater et magistra*.[71] In short, maternal authority is clearly being claimed for Rome. In papal letters, it is evoked variously, to demand the reinstatement of a bishop deposed by his colleagues, to prevent the invasion of a kingdom, to criticize troublesome nobles, and to assert Rome's primacy over the see of Constantinople during the Photian schism.[72] Other writers referred to the "mother of all churches" to assert Rome's right to decide "dubious or obscure" matters of doctrine.[73] In Pseudo-Isidore, the phrase appears repeatedly, in support of the argument that Rome can hear appeals from the decisions of provincial synods. As Pseudo-Zepherinus noted, bishops can always appeal their cases to Rome, "as to a mother at whose breasts they are nourished ... A mother neither can nor should forget her son."[74]

Pseudo-Isidore undercut the interference of metropolitan bishops in the lives of their suffragans by asserting the primacy of Mother Rome. However, in exactly the same period, metropolitans were themselves claiming maternal authority within their provinces.[75] In the 840s, Agnellus, a cleric of Ravenna, described his own metropolitan see as "the mother of all" – in reaction against the claims of the Roman see.[76] And a few decades later, Hincmar, archbishop of Reims, engaged in a quarrel with his nephew, the bishop of Laon, wrote that "according to the holy canons, the care of the whole province belongs to the metropolitan." He urged the younger Hincmar to "come back humbly and diligently and obediently to [Reims], as to a mother, to suck salubrious doctrine from her catholic breasts."[77] Like Agnellus, Hincmar was well aware of Roman

---

[71] Maccarrone (1974), pp. 26, 29. (There were earlier precedents for this usage in the area immediately around Rome; see Maccarrone (1960), p. 645.) On ninth-century papal claims to primacy, see Congar (1967) and (1968); Scholz (2006), pp. 146–239. On relations between popes and metropolitans, see Kempf (1978), pp. 45–57.

[72] E.g. Nicholas I, *Epistolae*, 71, 84, 99, MGH EPP 6: 398, 441, 578 = JL 2785, 2690, 2812; Hadrian II, *Epistolae*, 16–17, MGH EPP 6: 718–19 = JL 2917–18; John VIII, *Epistolae*, 107, MGH EPP 7: 99 = JL 3142/3143. On papal letters in this period, see Jasper and Fuhrmann (2001), pp. 110–31.

[73] Maccarrone (1974), p. 26, n. 15. The phrase echoes Paul's reference to the heavenly Jerusalem as "the mother of us all" (Galatians 4:26).

[74] Projekt Pseudoisidor, Teil 1, 1. Zepherinus-Brief, p. 240. Available at http://www.pseudoisidor.de/pdf/033_Zepherinus_Divinae_circa_nos.pdf.

[75] On the role of metropolitans in this period, see Lesne (1905), pp. 87–184; Foreville (1974), pp. 277–80; Kempf (1978). On critiques of papal interference within provinces, see Fuhrmann (1991), pp. 726–28.

[76] Agnellus of Ravenna, *Liber pontificalis* (PL 106: 619, 671, 739).

[77] Hincmar of Reims, *Epistolae*, 52 (PL 126: 275). Cf. Hincmar of Reims, *Opusculum LV capitulorum*, 44, in *Die Streitschriften Hinkmars von Reims*, MGH Concilia 4, Sup. 2: 321.

claims to be the "mother of all churches," and while he was much more willing to accept those claims, it is possible that he, too, was subtly asserting the autonomy of Reims.

That ecclesiastical hierarchies were being imagined in a new way in the ninth century is evident if we compare a passage from a work written by Hrabanus Maurus, a monk of Fulda (and later archbishop of Mainz) sometime between 814 and 822, with its seventh-century source. In the first book of *On Clerical Institutions*, Hrabanus lists the different kinds of bishop and explains their different titles, in a passage based on a similar one in the famous *Etymologies* of the seventh-century bishop Isidore of Seville.[78] But whereas Isidore had said that the word "metropolitan" meant "the measure of cities," Hrabanus says that "the metropolitan is so called on account of the city over which he presides, which is like a mother to the other cities in the same province. And therefore, in Greek, 'metropolis' means 'mother of cities'."[79] Already in the first part of the ninth century, then, metropolitan authority has come to be seen as related to maternal authority, in ways that Agnellus and Hincmar would later pick up.

Maternal imagery soon came to be used further down the ecclesiastical hierarchy as well. By the tenth century, the cathedral church was coming to be called the "mother church" of the diocese, to which the parish churches, as daughters, owed obedience (and, of course, a portion of their tithes).[80] This term may have developed directly from notions of the Church as Mother of the faithful, or it may be a variation on *ecclesia matrix* – a term that apparently emerged in the late ninth century to designate the church to which chapels were subordinated.[81] But the cathedral was not only described as the "mother church" in a financial context. Increasingly, from the late tenth century on, in saints' lives and in the "deeds of the bishops," the loyalty of the canons or monks to their

---

On Hincmar's view of metropolitan authority, see Lesne (1905), pp. 171–84. On this quarrel, see Morrison (1964), pp. 99–115.

[78] Isidore, *Etymologiae*, 8.12.10 (PL 82: 291).

[79] Hrabanus Maurus, *De clericorum institutione*, 1.5 (PL 107: 301); this passage was later cited by Honorius Augustodunensis, *Gemma animae*, 1.186 (PL 172: 601).

[80] One of the earliest examples I have found is Rather of Verona, *Briefe*, 33, MGH, Briefe der deutschen Kaiserzeit, 1: 183; trans. Reid, pp. 527 (although he translates simply as "the church").

[81] A search in the PL and MGH databases for *ecclesia matrix* and variants reveals no instance earlier than the late ninth century: Hincmar of Reims, *Capitulae*, 2, MGH Capitula episcoporum, 2: 45. Probably *ecclesia matrix*, in turn, derives from *ecclesiae matricula*, a charitable institution funded by a bishop for the care of the poor; see Rouche (1974). Hincmar requires all the *ecclesias matrices* in his diocese to maintain some registered paupers (*matricularios*). *Capitulae*, 2.17, MGH Capitula episcoporum, 2: 50.

cathedral was described as that of sons to a mother – as in B.'s life of St. Dunstan.[82]

By the year 1000, then, maternal imagery had become commonplace, in a variety of contexts related to hierarchy and authority within the western churches, and was available for use by political thinkers. As a result, in the *libelli de lite* and other polemical works of the central Middle Ages, this language is everywhere apparent. Whole treatises were written in the name of, or about, Mother Church – including Bernhard of Hildesheim's canon law collection, composed in a maternal voice, and directed to an archbishop, and Placidus of Nonantola's "little book for the honor and defense of Holy Mother Church."[83] *Mater Ecclesia* was, as we have seen, increasingly important in discussions of the laity's relationship with the clergy. It was also critical to discussions of relationships among bishops, and – above all – of the primacy of the Roman see.

Mothers and daughters

The city of Arras, although an important urban center, had not had its own bishop for many years. It had grown up not around a cathedral church, but around the famous monastery of Saint-Vaast; both monastery and city belonged to the diocese of Cambrai. Nonetheless, in 1093, the clergy of Arras, supported by Count Robert of Flanders, King Philip of France, and Pope Urban II, took advantage of a vacancy in the episcopal see of Cambrai to elect their own bishop, the reformer Lambert.[84] From the point of view of Cambrai, of course, the breakdown of the long-standing ties between Cambrai and Arras was a disaster – and it was treated as such by the author of the *Deeds of the Bishops of Cambrai*, who called it an "incalculable evil" to the "mother church" of Cambrai.[85]

In electing Lambert as their bishop, the clergy of Arras made a "head" out of someone who should have been a "member" of the church of

---

[82] E.g. Peter Damian 84, vol. 2: 453–54; trans. Blum, 3: 247; Landulf of Milan, *Historia Mediolanensis*, 2.34, MGH SS 13: 69–70; Ivo of Chartres, *Epistolae*, 195 (PL 162: 204); Raoul of Saint-Sépulchre, *Vita sancti Lietberti Cameracensis episcopi*, 6, MGH SS 30.2: 845.

[83] An anonymous exegete (perhaps Manegold of Lautenbach) considers the words of Psalm 4 to be written in the voice of Mother Church. Pseudo-Bede, *In psalmorum libro exegesis* (PL 73: 501).

[84] See Delmaire (1994), vol. 1: 39–60. An account of these events, traditionally said to have been compiled by Lambert himself with accompanying documents, has survived: *Gesta quibus Atrebatensium civitas ... in antiquam reformatur dignitatem* (PL 162: 627–48). It is perhaps worth noting that the language of maternity and filiation is never used in this collection of documents. Instead, Lambert elevates Arras to the same rank as other episcopal sees by referring to her as their "sister."

[85] *Gesta Galcheri Cameracensis episcopi*, p. 13.

Cambrai. In the same way, "they struggled so that a widowed mother would be deprived of her daughter; they labored so that a mistress would be abandoned by her servant." In short, the establishment of an independent episcopal see at Arras turned not only the existing ecclesiastical hierarchy, but also the domestic discipline of the household of God, and even the order of Christ's body, upside down. The people of Cambrai worried that a "horrible injury" would be done "with great dishonor" to their mother church. Moved by "shame, decency, and sadness," they sought to prevent their "lady" (*domina*) from losing her "right to be honored" (*honoris privilegia*).[86] In this text, composed soon after the events it described, the breakup of the diocese of Cambrai invoked not anger over potential loss of power or wealth, but concerns about "dishonor" and feelings of "shame." What was endangered was the well-being of a person, more than the success of an abstract institution.

Over the course of the tenth century, many bishops lost control over at least part of their dioceses, while some metropolitans exercised little authority within their provinces. Within any given diocese, there might be many parishes only nominally subject to the bishop, with real control in the hands of exempt monasteries or individual proprietors. A similar confusion of relationships existed at the provincial level. When the Emperor Henry II established a new bishopric at Bamberg in 1007, for example, he arranged for it to be under the pope's special "protection" (*mundiburdio*), although "obedience" was also owed to the local metropolitan. The new see was later referred to as a "special daughter" of Mother Rome.[87] The ideal hierarchies described in Carolingian texts may never have had much reality, but by the year 1000 they certainly bore little relationship to the exercise of ecclesiastical authority "on the ground."

Over the course of the eleventh century, however, increasing efforts were made to clarify the hierarchy among churches, to affirm a bishop's control over his diocese, and – somewhat later – an archbishop's control over his province (the latter in complex dialogue with papal claims to primacy). And in these efforts – not always successful (as the case of Arras shows) – the language of maternal authority played an important role. An interesting case in point is that of the church of Canterbury. Ever since Pope Gregory I sent his mission to Kent in 597, the metropolitan see then founded had enjoyed the greatest prestige within the Anglo-Saxon territories. It was not the only such see in England – from the eighth century on, York had also served as the site of an archdiocese – but

[86] *Gesta Galcheri Cameracensis episcopi*, p. 14
[87] *Papsturkunden*, 435, vol. 2: 830–33 = JL3954. Gregory VII called Bamberg Rome's "special daughter": *Register* 2.76, p. 239; trans. Cowdrey, p. 172.

Canterbury had the largest territory and the most influence. Only in 1070, however, did Archbishop Lanfranc begin to claim "primacy" within England, asserting that Canterbury was the "mother of the whole kingdom."[88] Lanfranc enjoyed not only great personal prestige but also the strong support of the new king, William the Conqueror. Archbishop Thomas of York, on the other hand, presided over a province that had suffered greatly from William's ferocious response to the northern rebellion of 1069. So impoverished was his church that he had to beg Lanfranc for financial assistance. Under the circumstances, he could not possibly resist Lanfranc's claims. In a letter to Lanfranc, Archbishop Thomas depicted the "daughter" church of York making a "filial entreaty" to Canterbury that her "mother's" wealth help her own indigence.[89]

Nevertheless, Canterbury's claims had no substantial legal foundation, and when Lanfranc's successor Anselm quarreled with King Henry I, the archbishops of York took advantage of the situation to deny the primacy so recently established. Gerard of York refused to make a profession of loyalty to Anselm, as did his successor, Thomas II. After his return from exile, Anselm ordered Thomas, archbishop-elect of York, to come to Canterbury to profess obedience and be consecrated:

I have in all charity instructed you more than once to come to your mother, the church of Canterbury, to receive your blessing and to do what you ought, and you have not come. So, still with the same love, I once more instruct you to be with your mother on November eighth ...[90]

Lanfranc's claim that Canterbury was the "mother of the whole kingdom" was repeated by Anselm's biographer, Eadmer.[91]

The popes had not always supported the efforts of bishops and archbishops to control the churches under their jurisdiction; in the tenth and early eleventh centuries, in fact, the popes had quietly expanded their influence outside of Italy by establishing links with monasteries which they exempted from the authority of local bishops. The most famous of these was Cluny, established in 910, but other monastic communities also came to be designated, like the diocese of Bamberg, as "special daughters" of the mother church of Rome.[92] Mother Rome asserted herself to

---

[88] Lanfranc, 3, pp. 40–41. On the primacy in England, see Barlow (1963), pp. 235–36. On papal relations with metropolitans generally, see Foreville (1974), pp. 281–312; Servatius (1979), pp. 95–100, 115–19, 122–35; Cowdrey (1998a), pp. 596–604; Blumenthal (2001), pp. 220–25.

[89] Lanfranc, 12, pp. 80–81.

[90] Anselm 455, vol. 5: 404; trans. Fröhlich, vol. 3: 244. Cf. Anselm 464, vol. 5: 413; trans. Fröhlich, vol. 3: 256.

[91] Eadmer, Vita Anselmi, p. 64. And see Brett (1975), pp. 63–100.

[92] Cowdrey (1970), pp. 12–32; Robinson (1990), pp. 226–31; Rosenwein (1999), pp. 156–83.

defend these monasteries from the encroachment of local bishops. Thus, when Archbishop Leotheric of Sens burned the papal privileges granted to the monastery of Fleury, Pope John XVIII fired off a letter accusing him of "dishonoring the Holy Mother Church of Rome."[93] Twenty years later, John XIX confirmed the privileges of Cluny, stating that if any bishop infringed them, he should know that he lacked the power to do so; let such a bishop not contradict his mother, the Roman Church, from whom he got his ecclesiastical power.[94] This was a reference to Bishop Gauzlin of Mâcon, then engaged in a struggle with Cluny over his role in the ordination of monks. In another letter, the pope accused Gauzlin directly: "inflamed by inextinguishable cupidity, you scorn your mother," i.e. Rome.[95]

After 1046, the reforming popes continued to use their maternal authority to support exempt monasteries, while also using the direct link between the popes and local bishops spelled out in Pseudo-Isidore against metropolitans, especially those who opposed reforming measures. Thus Urban II warned Archbishop Reynaud of Reims that – in attempting to re-try a bishop who had already been absolved of his crime by the pope – he had "raised his hand against [his] mother, the Roman church," and was, thus, worthy of the greatest censure.[96] Pascal II confirmed that the see of Orvieto was subject only to the apostolic see, "as the head and mother of all," promising that she would help him against any metropolitan's attempt to force him into submission.[97]

What is new in the second half of the eleventh century is the papacy's deployment of maternal imagery to support the claims of metropolitans. The reforming popes now recognized archbishoprics as "mothers" in their own right. Gregory VII ordered the people of Britanny to recognize the church of Tours as their "mother and metropolis."[98] Calixtus II went even farther, naming Trier the "mother and mistress" of her province.[99] Behind this metropolitan authority, however, always lay that of Mother Rome. Pascal II told Gerard of York that in failing to make his profession of loyalty to Anselm of Canterbury, he acted against the pope, "or rather against your mother, the holy Roman church."[100] In 1121,

---

[93] *Papsturkunden* 439, vol. 2: 839 = JL 3959. See Cowdrey (1970), pp. 29–32; Fuhrmann (1991), p. 730.
[94] *Papsturkunden* 570, vol. 2: 1083–85 = JL 4079.
[95] *Papsturkunden* 573, vol. 2: 1088 = JL 4082. On this controversy, see Cowdrey (1970), pp. 32–36.
[96] Urban II, *Epistolae*, 115 (PL 151: 388) = JL 5522.
[97] Pascal II, *Epistolae*, 157 (PL 163: 168) = JL 6039.
[98] Gregory VII, *Register*, 7.15, p. 489; trans. Cowdrey, p. 345.
[99] Calixtus II, *Epistolae*, 60 (PL 163: 1149) = JL 6798; cf. *Epistolae*, 82, 165 (PL 163: 1171, 1230) = JL 6827, 6944.
[100] Pascal, *Epistolae*, 87 (PL 163: 107) = JL 5930.

Calixtus II wrote to the clergy and princes of the crusader states, urging them to love, honor, and venerate their new patriarch, and to obey their Mother, the Roman Church – "she who, by the grace of God, liberated your Church with the blood of many of her sons, and she who every day labors for you on both sides of the Alps."[101]

By framing the situation in these terms, the reforming popes lent their support to the establishment of a clearly defined ecclesiastical hierarchy, running from the parish at the bottom to the pope at the top. The "papal monarchy" emerging in this period was, then, constructed in large part through the language of maternity. And at the center of that monarchy was Rome – the "mother of all churches."

The mother of all churches

Among the patriarchs who came to be disinguished from ordinary bishops in late antiquity, the bishop of Rome was clearly the most highly respected. The successors of St. Peter held "primacy" among the bishops of the Christian Church in late antiquity – although not yet in any juridical sense.[102] The "pope" was simply the bishop whose views held the most weight among all those whose opinions had to be considered about matters of discipline and belief. He was often consulted when these matters were in dispute, but as the history of the great church councils of this period shows, his opinion was by no means always accepted without question, especially by other patriarchs.

The collapse of the Roman Empire in the west over the course of the fifth century had a tremendous impact on not only political, but also ecclesiastical structures. Over the course of the next six hundred years, a widening gap came to separate the churches within the eastern Roman (Byzantine) Empire, and the churches of the west. Differences in religious practice and in some of the finer points of belief between east and west became sources of increasing tension, leading to disputes, and sometimes to schism. The bishop of Rome's opinion, while still valued in the east, had less and less relevance to religious developments shaped more by political, social, and intellectual changes internal to the Byzantine Empire. From the perspective of the eastern bishops and patriarchs, papal primacy remained what it had been in late antiquity – a primacy of honor only.

Something very different occurred in the barbarian kingdoms of the west. If the splintering of the Roman Empire led to increasing tensions

---

[101] Calixtus II, *Epistolae*, 148 (PL 163: 1217) = JL 6922.
[102] Schatz (1990), esp. pp. 31–38.

with the east, it also allowed the bishops of Rome greater influence, and eventually greater juridical authority, over the churches of the west. As contact with the eastern churches, and even contact among themselves, became more difficult, the western churches looked to Rome for help in maintaining unity. No other church in the west could rival Rome's authority, no other bishop that of the successors of St. Peter. And so Rome became the final voice in theological debates, and the final court of appeal in disputed legal cases. The popes began to issue decisions in such cases that soon came to be accepted – in the west – as decretals or "decrees," with the same legal force as the decisions of church councils. These were further augmented by the "false decretals," forged and collected under the name of Isidore Mercator in the middle of the ninth century.[103]

The political problems the bishops of Rome faced within Italy, combined with the increasing difficulty of communication with other parts of Europe during the age of Viking, Magyar, and Saracen raids, kept the popes from developing their claims further between the late ninth and the early eleventh centuries. However, neither did they concede any ground, and after Henry III introduced reformers into the Roman see in 1046, the assertion of papal primacy became more vigorous than ever.[104] The reforming popes and their supporters envisioned themselves restoring the ancient status of the Roman Church (though in fact many of their claims were either new, or framed in new ways). One result of this new papal assertiveness was the schism of 1054, which – although no one realized it at the time – was never to be healed, creating a permanent separation between the western and eastern churches. Meanwhile, within the west, the primacy of Rome was realized more concretely than ever before, through an increased flow of letters from the papal chancery, regular use of papal legates, and more frequent councils called by and sometimes in Rome.[105]

As we have seen, the popes began using maternal imagery to assert their primacy in the seventh century. During the Photian schism of the ninth century, John VIII used the claim that Rome was the "mother of all churches" (which must have astonished eastern Christians) to assert his authority over the Bulgarians.[106] Meanwhile, the language of maternity was being increasingly deployed to support Roman primacy in the west

---

[103] Maccarrone (1960); Angenendt (1989); Schatz (1990), pp. 61–75; *Il primato di vescovo di Roma*.

[104] On Rome's primacy in the tenth century, see Maccarrone (1974), pp. 30–32; Fichtenau (1983); Zimmermann (1991); Scholz (2006), pp. 267–423.

[105] Southern (1970), pp. 105–9; Hartmann (1993b).

[106] E.g. John VIII, *Epistolae*, 192, 198, 308, MGH EPP 7: 154, 159, 267 = JL 3261, 3265, 3379. And see Scholz (2006), pp. 233–34.

as well.[107] By the early eleventh century, the popes were even criticizing interference by local bishops in the affairs of exempt monasteries as affronts to Mother Rome. After 1046, however, maternal imagery became still more ubiquitous, employed in a wider range of situations, and developed in greater detail. This was evident already in the events of 1054.[108]

The ostensible issue dividing east and west in that year was the use of leavened or unleavened bread in the Eucharist. Much more important, however, was the patriarch of Constantinople's disregard for papal authority. Writing to Pope Leo IX, Patriarch Michael Kerularios claimed for himself the title of "ecumenical patriarch," and addressed Leo as "brother" rather than "father." Humbert of Silva Candida, the papal secretary, composed a response in which the theme of Rome as the "mother and mistress of all churches" is elaborately developed – the duty of filial obedience dramatically evoked – in order to emphasize Leo's authority over Michael.[109] "Do you really think," Humbert wrote to the patriarch, "that the apostolic see of Rome, which gave birth to the Latin church in the west through the Gospel, is not also the mother of the church of Constantinople in the east?"[110] Humbert contrasted an old and careworn Mother Rome, who had weathered many persecutions while remaining constant in the faith, with her spoiled and dissolute daughter, Constantinople. He argued that Constantinople should be offering her aged mother her hand and her shoulder in support, rather than afflicting her (by questioning her customs). Citing the now familiar passages from Scripture warning against mistreatment of earthly mothers, Humbert asks what the penalty should be for someone who scorns his spiritual mother.[111] Constantinople has "spit in the face" of her venerable mother by trying to separate the faithful of the east from her.[112] Whoever tries to weaken the Roman Church is really attacking all of Christendom, for "if the One Mother is strangled, by whose compassion and aid will her oppressed daughters ever be able to breathe again?"[113]

A few months after he wrote these words, Humbert was sent to Constantinople with two other papal legates to negotiate with Michael.

---

[107] E.g. Nicholas I, *Epistolae*, 34, 113, MGH EPP 6: 305, 628 = JL 2774, 2743; John VIII, *Epistolae*, 32, 264, MGH EPP 7: 32, 234 = JL 3079, 3329.

[108] On the "schism" of 1054, see Michel (1924–30), vol. 1: 7–42; Runciman (1955); Dvornik (1964); Petrucci (1973); Krause (1983); Stiernon (1991); Chrysos (2004).

[109] Michel (1924–30) was the first to identify Humbert as the author of the relevant letters. see especially vol. 1: 43–65. On Humbert's claims for Roman primacy, see Maccarrone (1974), pp. 42–49.

[110] *Acta et scripta*, 23, p. 78.   [111] *Acta et scripta*, 26–27, pp. 79–80.

[112] *Acta et scripta*, 29, p. 80.

[113] *Acta et scripta*, 36, p. 83. Later popes also saw Rome as mother to the Greek church. Gregory VII, *Register*, 1.18 and 8.1, pp. 29 and 513; trans. Cowdrey, pp. 20 and 363.

The patriarch, however, refused to meet them. Finally, on the afternoon of Saturday, July 16, 1054, as Michael Kerularios was preparing to celebrate the liturgy in the great church of Holy Wisdom in Constantinople, the three legates marched up to the altar and laid on it a document declaring the patriarch excommunicate. They then stalked out of the church, ostentatiously shaking its dust from their feet. A deacon hurried after them, urging them to take the document back, but they refused and left the city to return to Rome. A week later, Patriarch Michael called together a synod which, in turn, excommunicated the three legates. The breakdown of communion between east and west begun in 1054 endures to this day.

The Byzantine patriarchs may not have agreed with the papal claim that Rome was the "mother of all churches," but within the west that claim was widely (if not universally) accepted. Certainly the reforming popes used it to assert their authority in a wide variety of situations. Gregory VII summarized his own claims to primacy in his second letter to Herman of Metz (already cited above):

The holy fathers … have called the holy Roman church the universal mother alike in general councils and also in their other writings and deeds. And just as they have received her teachings in confirmation of the faith and instruction in sacred religion, so too they have received her judgements, thereby consenting and as it were by one spirit and by one voice agreeing that all greater matters and especial items of business as well as the judgments of all the churches should be referred to her as to the mother and head, that appeal should never be made against her, and that her judgements neither should nor can be revised or rejected by anyone.[114]

To review the very large number of texts in which the reforming popes and their advocates construct primacy using maternal language would be tedious. It may be useful, however, to consider the range of situations in which such language occurs.

Most obviously, the authority of the "mother of all churches" was invoked against simony, clerical marriage, or lay investiture. Sent to "clean up" the church of Milan in 1059, Peter Damian claimed that the see of Milan had originally been established by the orders of saints Peter and Paul: "and since the founders of your salvation handed down to the present the discipline of the Roman church, it follows, according to all justice, that the Roman Church is the Mother, and the Ambrosian Church [of Milan] is the daughter."[115] In this case, a mother's authority was used to force the Milanese clergy to give up their wives and avoid

---

[114] Gregory VII, *Register*, 8.21, p. 388; trans. Cowdrey, p. 388. On the maternal language in this letter, see Congar (1961), p. 203; Cowdrey (1998a), p. 522.
[115] Peter Damian, 65, vol. 2: 235–36; trans. Blum, 3: 28.

simony. On the other hand, to simply encourage well-disposed clerics to aid in reform efforts, appeals to filial love and reverence might be more effective: "If love and reverence for your mother the holy Roman church shall make you careful instead of negligent and warm instead of luke-warm, you will undoubtedly win the favour of our common fisherman [i.e. St. Peter] and our own love…".[116]

Much of the work of reform was done at local councils or at synods held in Rome. Those considered guilty of some crime were expected to attend these councils for judgment. In 1078, for example, Gregory summoned Wibert of Ravenna and his suffragans to Rome, to answer for their "offence and disturbance to blessed Peter the apostle and to his holy Roman church as your mother" – that is, for their support for the emperor. Gregory promised forgiveness:

> But since to sin is human and it is God's way to bestow pardon on converted sinners, this same church … still as a mother awaits your return to her bosom; for in no way does she desire to revel in your death, but rather she wishes to assist in your salvation.

Acting on behalf of God and "the Roman church which is the mother of all," Gregory urges them to attend the synod.[117] More harshly, Gregory warns another archbishop, Manasses I of Reims, to attend the council to be held by his legate at Lyons. He declared that Manasses would be deposed "if perchance you shall not go to the aforesaid council, and shall not incline an ear of due obedience to your mother the Roman church."[118] Reforming popes summoned friendly archbishops and bishops to councils by appealing to their love for Mother Rome: "indeed, if either the memory of earlier love had survived or proper affection for the Roman church as mother had remained in your mind," Gregory VII wrote to Archbishop Lanfranc in 1079, "nothing … ought to have held you back from our sight."[119]

An issue closely related to the campaign for church reform was that of liturgical unity. While most of the churches of western Europe celebrated some form of the Roman liturgy already by the eleventh century, Spain was different. Most of the churches there celebrated the liturgy according to the Mozarabic rite. The language of the prayers was distinct, and sometimes smacked of ideas that Rome considered heretical. So was the music

---

[116] Gregory VII, *Register*, 1.79, p. 113; trans. Cowdrey, p. 83. Cf. Pascal II, *Epistolae*, 498 (PL 163: 423) = JL 6558.

[117] Gregory VII, *Register*, 5.13, pp. 366–67; trans. Cowdrey, pp. 258–59.

[118] Gregory VII, *Register*, 7.12, p. 476; trans. Cowdrey, pp. 337–38. Cf. Gregory VII, *Epistolae Vagantes*, 51, p. 122–25.

[119] Gregory VII, *Register*, 6.30, p. 443; trans. Cowdrey, pp. 312–13.

of the chants different, suggesting a lack of concord within the Church as a whole. Alexander II had already begun pressing for the adoption of the Roman rite in Spain, and by 1071 had convinced King Sancho I of Aragon to begin instituting it within his kingdom. Gregory VII pursued the campaign, writing repeatedly to Spanish kings.[120] He pointed out to Sancho of Aragon that his identity as a "son of the Roman Church" depended on the extent to which he promoted the Roman liturgy in his kingdom.[121] He exhorted Alfonso VI of Léon-Castile and Sancho IV of Navarre "as most dear sons that ... you recognize the Roman Church as truly your mother ... and that you receive the order and office of the Roman Church, not of the Toledan [i.e. Mozarabic] or any other."[122]

In 1076, Gregory wrote to a Spanish bishop, Simeon of Orca-Burgos, who supported the proposed reform. Gregory praised Simeon for the "faith and devotion" he showed towards the Roman Church:

> The Roman Church wishes you to know that she does not wish to feed the sons whom she brings up for Christ with different breasts or with different milk, so that according to the Apostle, they may be one and there shall not be schisms among them [cf. I Corinthians 1:10]; otherwise she would be called not mother but schism-maker."[123]

Yet the liturgical reform did not progress quickly enough for Gregory. Three years after his first correspondence with the Spanish kings, he wrote to them, more sternly: "We do not believe your wisdom to be ignorant that the holy and apostolic see is the head and universal mother of all the churches and peoples ...".[124] Finally, at the synod of Burgos in 1080, Alfonso of Léon-Castile and his prelates agreed to adopt the Roman liturgy. The following year, Gregory praised the king for having celebrated in his kingdom "the liturgical order of the mother of all, the holy Roman church."[125] In letters to both kings and bishops in Spain, then, Gregory cemented his case for liturgical reform with maternal imagery.

The Roman reformers often used similar imagery to encourage support for reform candidates in disputed elections. In *The Debate at the Synod*, Peter Damian addressed the bishops from northern Italy and Germany who questioned the election of Alexander II: "you who are not just ordinary sons of the Roman Church, but her more noble and outstanding offspring, must demonstrate love and compassion for your mother, and decide whether she should be destroyed for having chosen

---

120 On Gregory's relations with the Spanish kings, see Cowdrey (1998a), pp. 468–80.
121 Gregory VII, *Register*, 1.63, p. 92; trans. Cowdrey, p. 67.
122 Gregory VII, *Register*, 1. 64, p. 93; trans. Cowdrey, p. 68.
123 Gregory VII, *Register* 3.18, p. 284; trans. Cowdrey, p. 202.
124 Gregory VII, *Register*, 4.28, p. 343–47; trans. Cowdrey, p. 242–45.
125 Gregory VII, *Register*, 9.2, p. 570; trans. Cowdrey, p. 399.

her own pontiff."[126] But love and compassion should also provoke resistance to the "wrong" candidate. To encourage the bishops of southern Italy to oppose Wibert of Ravenna, Gregory VII wrote,

You, therefore, most beloved brothers, should have in mind the innocence of your common mother the holy Roman church and should consider how much the devil may employ his members to inflict disturbance upon the aforesaid Roman church; as is fitting and as the debt of your office requires, devote pains and zeal to prayers and to other means by which help should be brought to a mother in travail, so that it may appear that you are her legitimate sons and that by sharing with us a diligence in toiling you feel from the heart for the effrontery against her.[127]

Support for reform was, then, supposed to come "from the heart." It was also, however, a matter of maternal discipline. At the height of the dispute over the see of Milan, Gregory wrote to its suffragans, warning them not to support Henry IV's candidate for archbishop: "Take thought, therefore, for how circumspectly you should walk; for, just as it is hard to kick against the goad [cf. Acts 9:5], so it is grievous to go against the holy Roman church, to which you should always be obedient as to a mother."[128]

Maternal imagery played, then, a critical role in the construction of papal primacy in the central Middle Ages. A number of scholars have examined the image of Mother Church in Gregory VII's writings, and indeed, Gregory made greater use of that image than any other pope from the period.[129] However, it would be a mistake to think his ideas about Rome's maternity unique. On the contrary, similar – if usually less well developed – rhetoric can be found in the writings of the reforming popes and of those associated with them from the middle of the eleventh century through the reign of Calixtus II and beyond.[130] Moreover, while references to Rome's maternal authority are concentrated in writings by Roman reformers, they can also be found everywhere in texts from the central Middle Ages – in letters, in narrative histories, and in polemics from many parts of Europe. The French abbot Geoffrey of Vendôme wrote, "To obey this universal mother of all Christians is useful and honorable; not to obey her is criminal. She always strives to offer love [*servare dilectionem*] to the obedient,

---

[126] Peter Damian, 89, vol. 2. 512 13; trans. Blum 3: 337–38. Alexander II further developed the idea of certain individuals (especially bishops) as "sons of the Roman Church." Maccarrone (1974), pp. 59–60. And see below, Chapter 6, on "sons/daughters of St. Peter."

[127] Gregory VII, *Register*, 8.5, p. 523; trans. Cowdrey, p. 371 . See also Gelasius II, *Epistolae*, 6 (PL 163: 491) = JL 6637.

[128] Gregory VII, *Register*, 3.9, p. 263; trans. Cowdrey, p. 187.

[129] Congar (1961), pp. 202–3; Meulenberg (1965), pp. 19, 53–71; Maccarrone (1974), 81–101; Cowdrey (1998a), pp. 520–29.

[130] Shaffern (2001).

and to render punishment to the disobedient."[131] Even the opponents of reform generally accepted Rome as the "mother of all churches." However, her maternity often meant something very different to them.

A blessed persecution

As we have seen, the church of Arras seceded from the diocese of Cambrai in 1093 or 1094. The aftermath of that separation was bloody. In Cambrai, a certain Manasses, acceptable to the reformers and with close ties to France, was elected bishop in 1093. However, Henry IV quickly replaced him with Walcher, a more strongly imperialist candidate – and one who had taken a very hard line on the separation of Arras from the diocese. Those in the region who supported reform (or who at least opposed the emperor) continued to push for installation of Manasses – with the support of their metropolitan, the archbishop of Reims and of the pope. When Count Robert of Flanders returned from the First Crusade, he used his military power on Manasses' behalf. The resulting war between Robert's troops and those of the emperor devastated the diocese of Cambrai.[132] In the aftermath of Robert's campaign, Pope Pascal II wrote a letter to the count, praising him for his attack on Cambrai and encouraging him to act in the same way against the "pseudo-clerics" of nearby Liège, another imperialist stronghold: "It is indeed just that those who separate themselves from the catholic church should be separated by catholics from ecclesiastical benefices." He also promised Robert and his troops remission of the temporal penalties for their sins – the same promise made to crusading knights – if they would attack Liège.[133]

Several reformers in this period advocated the use of military force against excommunicated heretics and schismatics – exactly how Pascal characterized the clergy of Liège. Anselm of Lucca, for example, used the image of Sarah and Hagar in a treatise against Henry's antipope, Wibert of Ravenna. Henry, Wibert, and their supporters are "schismatics" and "parricides" who persecute Mother Church. They need to be punished until they repent and return to the bosom of the Church. If the Church persecutes them, however, it is a "blessed persecution," for she is acting like Sarah disciplining Hagar. Quoting a letter of Augustine against the Donatists, Anselm contends that Sarah was persecuted more by Hagar's contempt than Hagar was by Sarah's coercion. Hagar did her mistress

---

[131] Geoffrey of Vendôme, 131, p. 270.
[132] Kupper (1981), pp. 393–400; Robinson (1999), p. 316.
[133] Pascal II, *Epistolae*, 88 (PL 163: 108) = JL 5889.

an injury, whereas Sarah imposed (proper) discipline on the proud.[134] The same kind of thinking lies behind a chilling letter of Pope Urban II written sometime between 1088 and 1095. Urban declared that those who, "while burning with zeal of the Catholic Mother," "happened" to kill some excommunicates (*zelo catholicae matris ardentes, eorum quoslibet trucidasse contigerit*), should not be considered guilty of homicide. Presumably they were simply doing Mother Church's disciplinary work. Nevertheless, in order to preserve the "discipline of this same Mother Church," they should perform a suitable penance, according to their state of mind when they acted – not apparently because they needed it, but in order to prevent scandal.[135] In treating Robert of Flander's military action as itself a form of penance, then, Pascal II had simply modified an existing policy.

But his action outraged conservative clerics. Sigebert of Gembloux's *Letter of the People of Liège against Pope Pascal* describes recent events in Flanders from Liège's point of view. Referring to Pascal's letter to Robert of Flanders, Sigebert wrote, "In this, darkness overwhelms me, not so much from fear of danger, as because of the horrible novelty of the matter – that a mother could write such a lamentable letter against her daughters, however sinful."[136] Liège condoles with Cambrai out of "sisterhood" (both churches being daughters of the same mother),[137] then quotes the passage from Pascal's letter cited above. How can it be just, Liège responds, for "my mother, the Roman Church" to "raise the sword of killing" over my own sons (i.e. the clergy and people of Liège), whom I have given birth to and nurtured with the milk of faith and confirmed with the bread of truth?[138] In her own maternal *persona*, the church of Liège steps into Mother Rome's role: "I do not act for the king [i.e. Henry IV], but for the mother of churches, on whose behalf I fear for us, her daughters."[139] At the very end of the letter, Sigebert returns to this theme, as the church of Liège prays for her mother's reformation: "May God free you, O Mother, from all evil!"[140]

---

[134] Anselm of Lucca, *Liber contra Wibertum*, MGH LL 1: 522–23; citing Augustine, *Epistulae*, 93, vol. 34.2: 450. On the issue of coercion in Anselm's work, see Cushing (1998), pp. 122–41. Cf. Bernhard of Hildesheim, *Liber canonum contra Heinricum IV.*, 31, MGH LL 1: 501; Bonizo of Sutri, *Liber ad amicum*, 1, MGH LL 1: 572; trans. Robinson, p. 158.

[135] Urban II, *Epistolae*, 122 (PL 151: 394) = JL 5536.

[136] Sigebert of Gembloux, *Leodicensium epistola adversus Paschalem papam*, 2, MGH LL 2: 452.

[137] Sigebert, *Leodicensium epistola*, 4, MGH LL 2: 454.

[138] Sigebert, *Leodicensium epistola*, 5, MGH LL 2: 456.

[139] Sigebert, *Leodicensium epistola*, 10, MGH LL 2: 461.

[140] Sigebert, *Leodicensium epistola*, 13, MGH LL 2: 464.

So well established was Rome's claim to be the "mother of all churches," that even conservative thinkers, many of whom resisted the reforming popes' new demands and occasional violence, could not reject her maternal authority. They could criticize papal policies on other grounds, but they could not deny their filial obligations. The best they could do, then, was criticize the Roman Church as a "bad" mother. This was Sigebert's tactic, as well as the tactic used by Archbishop Wibert of Ravenna just before Henry IV raised him to the papal throne. Wibert wrote indignantly, "Let the mother, the Roman Church, do no injury to her daughter, the Church of Ravenna, nor let the daughter oppose her mother, but let each possess her own dignity."[141] However, in the face of constant papal demands for submission, such dignity was hard to maintain.

Only one conservative writer refused outright to accept Rome's maternal claims, and that was the highly eccentric Norman Anonymous, whose unusual views on the Bride's earthly spouse have already been discussed. A staunch defender of episcopal autonomy against the claims of both metropolitans and the papacy, the Anonymous launched a ferocious attack on the authority of the archbishop of Lyons within France, based on the argument that all sees are equally the Bride of Christ.[142] His critique of Rome's demands, on the other hand, came from a denial of her maternity. Those who try to interfere in the affairs of the archdiocese of Rouen, he writes, sometimes claim that they do this by Roman authority. They say Rome is the "mother and mistress" of all churches, and that her bishop is the highest of all bishops.[143] But Jerusalem, not Rome, is the true "mother of all churches"; Rome can claim that title only as an "imitation or figure" of Jerusalem. And the claim itself is improper: it is "indecent and unjust for a daughter to take precedence over her mother, or a disciple over her mistress." [144] Rome's superiority, the Anonymous contends, is simply based on earthly considerations – the support of imperial power and the dignity of the city. Her prelature does not come from Christ or from the apostles.[145] Indeed, before Peter arrived, Rome was the "head of error, a bloody city devoted to excess and lust, a purple-clad harlot."[146] Conversion to Christianity made her a city of light and faith – but that faith arose in Jerusalem on earth, which still stands for the heavenly Jerusalem, the Bride of Christ, the Queen of Psalm 45.[147]

---

[141] Wibert of Ravenna/Clement III, *Epistolae*, 3 (PL 148: 830–31) = JL 5322.
[142] Norman Anonymous, pp. 7–18, 35–45. And see Williams (1951), pp. 132–37.
[143] Norman Anonymous, pp. 40–41. Cf. pp. 84 ff.
[144] Norman Anonymous, p. 41.   [145] Norman Anonymous, p. 42.
[146] Norman Anonymous, p. 87.   [147] Norman Anonymous, p. 89.

Ultimately, Rome is only a daughter, not a mother at all. On this point, however, the Norman Anonymous is just as inconsistent as he was in arguing about who marries the Church – for here, too, the evidence of Pseudo-Isidore was against him. And his attack on Roman primacy was no more influential than his other arguments. It remains an anomaly, a fascinating example of a stubborn thinker pushing against the tide.

The Mother sighs

Over the course of the eleventh and early twelfth centuries, as debates over hierarchy and authority multiplied, so too did references to Mother Church. Her image was used at the local level, to demand better behavior from members of the laity and a share in parochial offerings for the episcopal church. It was also used at the provincial level, to obtain professions of loyalty and resist the creation of new dioceses. And finally, the papacy used it to criticize the behavior of rulers and to enforce episcopal attendance at reforming councils. Maternal language was useful in defining relationships of hierarchy in this age of reform thanks primarily to its roots in an ancient tradition of depicting the Bride of Christ as the Mother of the Faithful, and also because precedents for its deployment could be found in legal texts of the ninth century. It was also rhetorically valuable in political discussions, because it drew upon important cultural norms of deference to mothers, and because it evoked powerful emotions. Nevertheless, relying on the language of maternity could be problematic, for a number of reasons.

First, as we saw in Chapter 3, in the central Middle Ages motherhood was heavily associated with vulnerability. And the vulnerability of Mother Church is obvious in writings from this period, especially in those composed by the very same reformers who touted her authority. Reforming clerics used images of a suffering Mother Church much as they used images of a wronged Bride, to criticize intrusions into episcopal sees, simony, and lay investiture. Indeed, bridal and maternal rhetoric are intermingled in their writings, as, for example, in Humbert of Silva Candida's attack on simony. Humbert argues at one point in *Against the Simoniacs* that bishops were responsible for the well-being of Christ's Bride, but if they failed her, lay princes should step in:

But if [the clergy] do not make an effort to resist evil advice, let the lay power in the end not act like degenerate sons of a free and beloved mother, who learn that her chastity has been captured by adulterers. Let them arm themselves without delay to avenge her, even if their father [i.e. the bishop], having been told what has happened, neglects to seek vengeance for such an intolerable evil done to himself. Guarding against a stain on their family and the defamation of their name, even if the father makes no effort, let the good sons never stop punishing the injuries done to their mother.[148]

But laymen who intervene against simoniacal bishops must never themselves sell churches:

If she has been captured by adulterers, and they do not restore her to her legitimate marriage, but rather prostitute maternal purity to their lust, are they not worse and more detestable than any adulterers? Would it not be more tolerable for her not to be defended by others, than for them to usurp and assign her defense to themselves in this way? I ask Christian princes and laymen to consider this with Christian piety and finally to be aware of how much more shameful they would be, if they defend their spiritual mother in such a way that they do not restore her to their father, but themselves make her into a prostitute.[149]

Notice that Humbert establishes lay–clerical hierarchy here by placing bishops in the role of fathers, through their marriage to the Church, and the laity in the role of sons. When their spiritual Mother is endangered by the sale of ecclesiastical office, it is the duty of these sons to defend her sexual purity.[150]

Some of the very writers who sought to extend the authority of Mother Church constantly encouraged reform by reference to her degradation. The most obvious examples here are Peter Damian and Gregory VII, in the passages cited above. Such "mixed" references still made sense, for they evoked the mystical language of paradox so important to Christian thought in general, and to the reformers' thought in particular.[151] In the kingdom of heaven, the last shall be first, and the first last (Matthew 20:16). The barren wife can become the joyous mother of many sons, the former slave can become the mistress. But is it possible to argue effectively and consistently for the commanding power of a figure whose weakness you have just highlighted? All too often in texts from this period, the "mother and mistress" devolves into the "slave-girl." And this brings us to a second issue.

While the law of marriage could be used to define the relationship of a bishop with his see, hierarchical relationships within the Church could not be regulated in a similar way. The texts used to support

[148] Humbert, *Adversus simoniacos*, 3.11, MGH LL 1: 212. Similar language about the duty of sons to protect their mother from sexual pollution occurs in Peter Damian, 58, vol. 2: 194; trans. Blum, 2: 393.

[149] Humbert, *Adversus simoniacos*, 3.11, MGH LL 1: 212.

[150] Cf. Humbert, *Adversus simoniacos*, 2.33, MGH LL 1: 182.

[151] On religious paradox in the eleventh century, see Lesieur (2003); on the use of gender in such paradoxes, see McLaughlin (1991).

the maternal claims of popes, metropolitans, or the Church, in the abstract, were usually scriptural – the commandment to honor one's mother or the warning against cursing her. But how, precisely, were "honoring" and "cursing" to be defined, within the context of ecclesiastical politics? The vagueness of these references left the exact nature of the relationship between pope and emperor, metropolitan and suffragan, bishop and parish priest equally vague. With very rare exceptions (Peter Damian's *The Debate at the Synod* is one), secular law was not deployed to shore up the authority of Mother Church – for relevant secular law simply did not exist. As Chapter 3 demonstrated, maternal authority had very little legal basis in the eleventh and early twelfth centuries. Consequently, polemicists could not evoke legal penalties for unfilial behavior towards Mother Church; the best they could do was label those who mistreated her "illegitimate sons," or condemn their "shameful" behavior.

Finally, there was the complicated problem of identifying the person or group who could legitimately speak for Mother Church. In the political writings of the central Middle Ages, authority was frequently attributed to an invisible female figure, on whose behalf men spoke. The person who gave voice to Mother Church might be an intellectual like Bernhard of Hildesheim, a monk like Placidus of Nonantola, a bishop like Ivo of Chartres, a cardinal like Peter Damian, or a pope, but who actually wielded her authority was not always clear. The only church for which this issue has been much studied is the Roman Church, which is, of course, a highly unusual example. Nevertheless, briefly considering the Roman case may prove instructive.

In the early Middle Ages, the bishop of Rome was considered the *rector* of the "holy Roman church," but the Church itself consisted of all the clergy of the city; her authority was never vested exclusively in the pope. By the middle of the eleventh century, the Roman Church was increasingly identified with the pope and the cardinals, acting together.[152] Nevertheless, when the apostolic see was vacant, the cardinals might be the voice of "Mother Rome," as in Peter Damian's *The Debate at the Synod*, while at other times the pope spoke on her behalf, as Gregory VII did in his letters. During the papal schisms of the eleventh century, including the long-lasting Wibertine schism, the authority of the "mother of all churches" could still be asserted, even when the legitimacy of particular popes or cardinals was in question, because she was distinct from the men who acted for her. But by the same token, it was easy to question the ability of particular individuals to speak on her behalf.

---

[152] Carpegna Falconieri (2002), pp. 48–50.

After Henry IV expelled Gregory VII from Rome, and installed Wibert of Ravenna as Pope Clement III, the Gregorians made haste to underline the distinction between Mother Rome and the person who physically occupied the chair of St. Peter in Rome. One of their methods was to represent Wibert as his mother's oppressor. Anselm of Lucca fired off a treatise criticizing Wibert's installation, this "new and unheard-of abomination," in highly sexualized terms. The Bride (i.e. the Roman Church) has been defiled "from top to bottom" (Jeremiah 2:16): "Now she is not the Bride of Christ, but an adulteress, not free, but a slave girl."[153] Wibert himself is guilty of adultery and incest – and in this case, not the kind of marriage between cousins so often criticized in this period, but of something much more serious. He is the son who has "invaded the marriage bed" of his mother and father, that is, the Roman Church and Pope Gregory.[154]

Wibert's supporters could just as easily characterize Gregory and his successors as the "bad sons," and themselves as the Roman Church's true representatives. The anonymous author of *On Preserving the Unity of the Church* argues that while the Gregorians claim that "Holy Mother Church" is on their side, that cannot be true, because they cause death and schism, while the true "sons of God" are the peacemakers (Matthew 5:9).[155] He further declares that Mother Rome was never Gregory's bride, because Gregory usurped the see of Rome.[156] That is why "she who is truly the Roman Church, the mother of all churches," chose Wibert instead. The schismatic cardinal Beno, who supported Wibert, addressed a letter to "the most revered Mother, the holy Roman church," from "her devoted son and humble servant, Beno ...".[157] Wibert himself wrote to another schismatic cardinal, Hugh Candidus, telling him to be mindful of his mother, the Roman Church: "the sighs of [her] sons should mingle with those of the sighing mother." Hugh should be prepared to suffer for her, just as earlier "sons of this church" did.[158] Both sides in the Wibertine schism, then, could construct arguments claiming the authority of Mother Rome for themselves.

The well-documented case of Rome suggests the outlines of a problem which must have been much more widespread. Given the frequency of long vacancies, disputed elections, and even simple quarrels between bishop and cathedral chapter in Europe during this period, the exact

---

[153] Anselm of Lucca, *Liber contra Wibertum*, MGH LL 1: 520–21.
[154] Anselm of Lucca, *Liber contra Wibertum*, MGH LL 1: 527. And see below, Chapter 6.
[155] *De unitate ecclesiae conservanda*, 2.2, MGH LL 2: 213.
[156] *De unitate ecclesiae conservanda*, 2.6, MGH LL 2: 217.
[157] *Benonis aliorumque cardinalium schismaticorum contra Gregorium VII. et Urbanum II. scripta*, 1, MGH LL 2: 369.
[158] *Benonis ... scripta*, 7, MGH LL 2: 408.

location of Mother Church's authority often shifted alarmingly.[159] (Some papal letters were actually intended to identify where it could be found.[160]) Under the circumstances, it is understandable that political writers – and again, especially those interested in promoting change in the status quo – began searching for other ways to characterize different positions in the ecclesiastical hierarchy. Traditional maternal imagery continues to describe ecclesiastical authority throughout the reform period – and indeed, throughout entire Middle Ages. However, another kind of language, unburdened by the problems just described, came into play, at first very tentatively, then with increasing confidence, from the second half of the eleventh century on. This is the language of paternity.

[159] In the same letter, Geoffrey of Vendôme could praise obedience to Mother Rome (the pope), while also asserting his filial duty to criticize his mother's (the papal legate's) injustices: 131, pp. 268–70.
[160] E.g. Gregory VII, *Register*, 2.38, pp. 174–75; trans. Cowdrey, pp. 128–29.

5   Fathers and sons

At the heart of medieval notions of authority stood the image of the father.[1] Presiding over his household, the *paterfamilias* was not only a crucial social force in reality, but also served regularly to represent other forms of power in the medieval imagination.[2] Most obviously, the image of the father provided a way of comprehending the relationship of God to humanity. The heavenly *paterfamilias* treated his human sons and daughters with affection, but also with sternness, thus preparing them for their inheritance of salvation in the afterlife. References to God as father were so pervasive in texts from the central Middle Ages, and so often developed in theological discussion, that they, in and of themselves, offer considerable information on how "fatherhood" was understood in that period. But paternity was also widely used to describe other relationships. "If you do the works of anyone, you are called his son," wrote William of Malmesbury;[3] conversely, a man who provided advice and help might be identified as a "father."[4] In particular, "spiritual" fatherhood (involving religious caretaking or leadership) was extremely important in the central Middle Ages; this will be the subject of the next chapter. But paternal imagery could be used in other situations as well.

It was, for example, central to descriptions of political relationships. In the *Life of Edward the Confessor*, written for the Confessor's wife, Edith, her own father, Earl Godwin, is also repeatedly referred to as a "father" to the

[1] Yet medieval fatherhood has received remarkably little attention from modern scholars. Among the few works on the subject, see Schieffer (1990) and (2002b); Claussen (1996); Goez (1996); Aird (1998); McLaughlin (1999); Baschet (2000). The original edition of the *Histoire des pères et de la paternité* pays little attention to the Middle Ages; I have not been able to consult the second edition.

[2] So much so that Thietmar of Merseburg could approve of a son who obeyed his father rather than the emperor: 7.17, p. 418; trans. Warner, p. 318.

[3] William of Malmesbury, *Vita sancti Wulfstani*, 2.15, in his *Saints' Lives*, p. 92 – the context was a spiritual one, the distinction between sons of God and sons of the devil, but the aphorism presumably had more general application.

[4] *Vita Aedwardi regis*, 1.1, p. 11: here the new king of the Danes chooses Edward as his father and submits to him "in all things as a son."

English people.[5] In Italy, Peter Damian wrote to Duke Godfrey of Lorraine, the husband of Beatrice of Tuscany, as if he were a father to his subjects:

Do not be overcompassionate. For just as by unrestrained justice the irresolute are broken, so under too much compassion the spirit of license will boldly run to unbridled insolence. Was indiscreet kindness in evidence in the words, "If you take the stick to your son, you will preserve him from the jaws of death" [Proverbs 23:14]? Or again, "A father who spares the rod hates his son" [Proverbs 13:24] And elsewhere, "A man who loves his son will whip him often" [Sirach 30:1] And that other advice, "An unbroken horse turns out stubborn, and an unchecked son turns out headstrong. Pamper a boy and he will shock you; play with him and he will grieve you. Do not share his laughter, for fear of sharing his pain. You will only end by grinding your teeth" [Sirach 30:8–10]. So, if a father should use correction and the rod on an only son, how much more should this be true of a prince with his people, so that a great number of them may not perish in their attempt to act with unbridled liberty.[6]

Peter could have explained Godfrey's duty by drawing on Biblical texts relating to kings or princes; instead, he chose to use texts about fathers. Paternal imagery continually reinforced kingship in the central Middle Ages. References to a king as the "father of his country" echoed classical political rhetoric, as did claims that kings served as fathers to the weak or helpless, especially widows and orphans who had no fathers in their households to protect them.[7] However, the paternal association went beyond classical precedents, to become an aspect of the theology of kingship. In his treatise *On Royal Power and Priestly Dignity*, Hugh of Fleury compared kings to God the Father, and bishops to Christ the Son.[8]

So tight was the association between paternity and authority, that the breakdown of the relationship between father and son could readily serve as a sign of more general social chaos in texts from the central Middle Ages. What bond could hold, if that most intimate and sacred tie failed? Writing in the 1140s, Bishop Otto of Freising, a grandson of Emperor Henry IV, described the rebellion that ended Henry's reign in precisely these terms. Here is Otto's account of the dramatic face-off between the armies of Henry IV and his son Henry V across the river Regen in the fall of 1105:

You might have seen the lamentable and pitiable preparations, you might have seen the world betraying in its deeds more clearly than the sunlight its

---

[5] *Vita Aedwardi regis*, 1.1, 1.4 and 1.5, ed. Barlow, pp. 6, 9, 25, 26, and 30.
[6] Peter Damian, 68, vol. 2: 290; trans. Blum, 3: 80. Cf. Raoul Glaber, 1.21, pp. 36–37: the early Norman dukes treated pilgrims and the poor "with that constant care with which fathers treat sons."
[7] Orderic, 7.16, vol. 4: 100–01; Thangmar, *Vita Bernwardi*, 25, pp. 318–20; *Vita Aedwardi regis*, 1, p. 41.
[8] Hugh of Fleury, *De regia potestate et sacerdotali dignitate*, 1.2–3 and 2.4, MGH LL 2: 468 and 490.

contempt for itself because, forsooth, contrary to the law of nature a son was rising against his father, contrary to the standard of justice a soldier was preparing to do battle against his king, a slave against his master, brother stood opposed to brother, kinsman to kinsman, and each was planning to shed the blood of the sharer in his own blood.[9]

For Otto, writing several decades after the fact, the rebellion of the younger Henry was a tragedy; it illustrated how ambition and greed might overturn the very laws of nature. For Otto, as for the polemicists in the late eleventh and early twelfth centuries, the event was also part of a broader narrative of authority – within the household, within the kingdom, and ultimately within the cosmos.

Paternal authority

The power of paternal imagery in the medieval imagination was rooted in the experience of everyday domestic life, where the father almost always reigned supreme. The emotions of love and fear that clerical writers associated with paternity may well have been reflections of their own childhoods, as much as of the cultural expectations of their times. Love – because fathers in the eleventh and early twelfth centuries did normally love and care for their children. Fear – because the paternal role, much more than the maternal one, involved the ability to command obedience and punish disobedience. The intense desire for children, if not for their own sake, at least to maintain the family line, was reflected in men's willingness to seek the help of the saints if their marriage remained childless, as well as in the less admirable custom of repudiating infertile wives.[10] Men longed for children, identified as the "dearest consolation" of their lives, and met their births with joy.[11] Doubtless not all fathers demonstrated "paternal affection," but the expectation was that they would treat their children lovingly. A father's "tender care" for his children was normally expressed in the provision of food and protection for them, but a father might also act much as a mother did – caring for his children when they were sick, and grieving deeply for them if they died.[12]

---

[9] Otto of Freising, *Chronica sive Historia de duabus civitatibus*, 7.9, MGH SRG, pp. 319–20; trans. Mierow, pp. 413–14.

[10] On invocations of the saints, see *Liber miraculorum sancte Fidis*, 3.9, pp. 196–97; trans. Sheingorn, p. 157. On repudiation, see above, Chapter 1. That sons were needed to preserve family property is explicitly stated in *Ruodlieb*, 16, pp. 174–75.

[11] *Liber miraculorum sancte Fidis*, Appendix, Ms. A, 1, p. 295; trans. Sheingorn, p. 233.

[12] Fathers caring for sick children appear in many saints' lives: e.g. Marbod of Rennes, *Vita sancti Roberti abbatis Casae-Dei*, 2.12–14 (PL 171: 1528–30). Hagiographers also often depict paternal grief: e.g. *Liber miraculorum sancte Fidis*, 4.1, and Appendix, Ms. A, 4, pp.

In the exercise of authority, however, mothers and fathers differed considerably. Paternity, unlike maternity, was powerfully associated with fear and discipline.[13] Geoffrey of Vendôme urged Robert of Abrissel to deal with the nuns of Fontevrault as "a mother in piety, a father in discipline."[14] It was a father's duty to provide his children with moral teachings, and to punish them if they misbehaved.[15] What distinguished a "real" father from a false one, for Peter Damian, was his willingness to discipline, especially physically.[16] So strong was this association that God's punishment could be said to be "like a father's whip."[17] We know that fathers did enforce their commands with blows.[18] It is not surprising, then, that the anonymous author of Book IV of the Miracles of St. Foy described a young boy who lost one of his father's cows as so "thoroughly terrified of his father's most merciless sternness" that he did not dare let anyone see him enter the house.[19]

Conrad II, first emperor of the Salian line, died at Utrecht in the spring of 1039. His corpse was disemboweled, the viscera buried at Utrecht, and the remainder carried in solemn procession through the heartland of his realm to Speyer, where it was finally laid to rest in the cathedral. Wipo, Conrad's biographer, reported,

> The son of Caesar, King Henry, bent his shoulders under the body of his father [as pallbearer] with very humble devotion at every entry into a church and finally at the entombment. And the king showed most zealously to his dead father all this – not only what the son owes to the father in perfect love, but what the servant owes to his lord in holy fear.[20]

In the funeral of Conrad II, then, the future emperor Henry III enacted publicly and dramatically before the princes of the realm the role of dutiful son, coincident in many respects with that of a servant – for in the central Middle Ages a son owed his father submission and obedience, as well as love. In fact, children were often treated like servants in this period – expected to obey their fathers without hesitation and subject to

221 and 303; trans. Sheingorn, 178 and 239; and see Orderic, 5.19, vol. 3: 204–05. In a letter of consolation to a bereaved couple, Peter Damian describes how God has now received their son "with a father's love." Peter Damian, 15, vol. 1: 151–52; trans. Blum, 1: 140–42.

[13] McLaughlin (1999), pp. 31–33, 39–40.
[14] Geoffrey of Vendôme, 79, p. 150; cf. Anselm, 158, vol. 4: 25–26; trans. Frohlich, vol. 2: 39.
[15] Orderic, 5.10, vol. 3: 110–11: "Correct your child when he errs."
[16] Peter Damian, 54, vol. 2: 141–42; trans. Blum, 2: 347.
[17] Orderic, 5.19, vol. 3: 202–03.
[18] E.g. Raoul Glaber, 1.5, pp. 12–13.
[19] *Liber miraculorum sancte Fidis*, 4: 1, p. 220; Sheingorn, 178.
[20] Wipo, *Gesta Chuonradi II imperatoris*, 39, MGH SS 11: 274; trans. Mommsen and Morrison, p. 98. On Wipo's political ideas, see now Bagge (2002), pp. 189–230. On Conrad's death and burial, see Wolfram (2000), pp. 343–47.

punishment if they failed.[21] Sons, especially, owed a wide range of services to their fathers, from going into battle with them or on their behalf,[22] to serving as hostages for them,[23] to guiding them to the shrine of a saint,[24] to seeking their salvation.[25] They could be expected to continue their father's work.[26] Nevertheless, children were distinguished from servants in the household, and within medieval culture, in two important ways.

First, a child's obedience to his or her father was supposedly rooted in affection – though fear might also play a part. It was thus expected to continue even after the father's death, when he was no longer in a position either to reward or to punish. Sons buried their fathers, and provided suitable tombs for them.[27] They took revenge, if their father had been killed.[28] They remembered their fathers and emulated them.[29] Filial love even extended to buildings associated with the parent. A son might hate the castle where his father had been killed, while a daughter might love the monastery where her father was buried.[30] Obviously not all children loved their fathers, any more than they did their mothers, and some might have performed their duties purely out of social obligation. Nevertheless, the expectation was that a deep emotional attachment compelled children to serve.

The other major distinction between children and servants – or at least between sons and servants, for the situation of daughters was somewhat different – was that after the father's death, the son could expect to inherit his property and step into his place. The result was an identification with the father that strengthened love, and a desire for inheritance that reinforced obedience. For indeed, the most severe penalty for a son's disobedience was disinheritance.[31] The centrality of inheritance in the father–son relationship (and perhaps in that between father and daughter as well) meant that changes in inheritance practice had powerful implications for that relationship. Expectations concerning paternal

---

[21] *Liber miraculorum*, 3.9, p. 197; trans. Sheingorn, p. 157. Some sons, however, tricked their fathers into giving them permission to do as they liked; see *Vita Guidonis abbatis Pomposiani*, 1, *AASS* Mar. III (March 31), col. 912.

[22] Peter Damian, *Vita beati Romualdi*, 1, pp. 14–15.

[23] Thietmar, 4.24, p. 160; trans. Warner, p. 168: here a man who has been kidnapped is forced to rely on his nephews to arrange his release, because he has no sons.

[24] *Liber miraculorum sancte Fidis*, 3.6, p. 190; trans. Sheingorn, p. 151.

[25] Raoul Glaber, 5.5, pp. 250–53. Cf. McLaughlin (1999).

[26] Peter Damian, 120, vol. 3: 391; trans. Blum, 4: 394.

[27] Thietmar, 5.8, pp. 229–30; trans. Warner, p. 211; Orderic, 8.1, vol. 4: 110–11.

[28] Thietmar, 7.39, p. 446; trans. Warner, p. 335; Peter Damian, 80, vol. 2: 410; trans. Blum, 3: 194–95.

[29] Lanfranc, 31, pp. 118–19; cf. Orderic, 8.1, vol. 4: 110–11.

[30] *Liber miraculorum sancte Fidis*, 3.15, p. 203; Sheingorn, p. 164; Geoffrey of Vendôme, 57 and 110, pp. 102 and 212.

[31] Peter Damian 56, vol. 2: 161; trans. Blum, 2: 368.

authority and filial obedience may not have been much affected, but the way in which authority and obedience actually worked in practice probably changed significantly.

The growing importance of patrilineage – at least in some parts of Europe – during the eleventh century seems to have raised the emotional and social temperature of the relationship between fathers and their sons.[32] On the one hand, it tightened the bond between the *paterfamilias* and his heir – linking them in the joint enterprise of strengthening and perpetuating their dynasty and its patrimony. And it heightened the importance of filial obedience, by associating it not only with duty towards the father but also with the survival and prosperity of the lineage. Yet the rise of patrilineage also placed additional stress on the father–son bond in those parts of Europe. Younger sons, who could no longer expect a share of the patrimony, wrangled with their fathers for support and sometimes used force to acquire elsewhere the wives and establishments their fathers denied them. Georges Duby explored one social implication of the move to patrilineage: the rise of "youths" as a particularly turbulent element in family and society.[33] Drawing on Duby's model, W. M. Aird has recently pointed out the gendered implications of the change: in the eleventh century, full manhood was not acquired simply by growing older, but rather by displaying – and having society recognize – the attributes associated with being an adult male.[34] For the elite, this involved having access to power, establishing an independent household, and being recognized as its head.[35] Few sons, then, really became "men" during their father's lifetime. Not only the younger brothers, but the heir himself – regardless of his age – might be trapped in a perpetual state of incomplete masculinity until his father's death. Under the circumstances, he might easily become fractious, frustrated by delay in the acquisition of adult status – all the more so if his father's actions threatened in any way the patrimony the younger man expected someday to be his.

While it is obviously impossible to identify the real motives of rebellious eldest sons, the authors of narrative sources commonly pointed to such frustrations.[36] Writers in the eleventh and early twelfth centuries assumed not only that sons should obey their fathers, but also that heirs whose inheritance was delayed might very well resist him. In the voices of "bad counselors" (most often other youths) urging young princes to demand their rights, chroniclers expressed contemporary concerns about the loss of status that might result from such "perpetual adolescence."

---

[32] Which is not to say that that relationship had not already been heavily freighted in earlier centuries; see especially Schieffer (1990).

[33] Duby (1964).   [34] Aird (1998), p. 43.

[35] Aird (1998), p. 44.   [36] Raoul Glaber, 3.32–33, pp. 152–53.

The anonymous author of the *Life of Henry IV* has the emperor's enemies tell his son "they were amazed that he could suffer so harsh a father, that he was no different from a slave, since he tolerated everything a slave did."[37] Other writers associated the heir's failure to acquire independence with disgrace, a loss of manly honor. Orderic Vitalis attributed the following speech to the retainers of young Robert Curthose, the eldest son of William the Conqueror:

> Your father's minions guard the royal treasure so closely that you can scarcely have a penny from it to give to any of your dependents. It is a great dishonour to you and injury to us and many others that you should be deprived of the royal wealth in this way. A man deserves to have wealth if he knows how to distribute it generously to all seekers. How sad that your bounteous liberality should be thwarted, and that you should be reduced to indigence through the parsimony of your father who sets his servants or rather your servants over you … It is not fitting that you should continue to allow those who are born your slaves to lord it over you, and to deny you the riches of your inheritance as if you were a nameless beggar.[38]

In short, the heir's very status *as* heir was threatened by a prolonged delay in inheritance.

It is within this context that we might consider the difficult relationship of Count Fulk Nerra of Anjou and his eldest son, Geoffrey Martel. According to William of Malmesbury – writing a century after the fact – as Fulk grew old, he ceded territory to Geoffrey to govern, but the son grew arrogant, treated his subjects badly and finally took up arms against his own father. The wily old count quickly subdued his son, and then forced him to walk for several miles, carrying a saddle on his back. Afterwards, as Geoffrey lay on the ground before his father, Fulk nudged him with his foot and repeated three or four times, "You are conquered – You are finally conquered!" But there was still some spirit left in the young man, who replied, "I am conquered by you alone, Father, since you are my father. By everyone else, I am unconquered!" Mollified, Fulk gave him back his lands, advising him to behave better in the future.[39]

This rich text illuminates Geoffrey's ambiguous position as a "youth" – how his efforts to function as a fully adult male were frustrated by his father, who chose a particularly humiliating way to enforce his authority, effectively reducing his heir to the status of conquered enemy or even slave, prone on the ground. But the repartee between the two also demonstrates the power of the bond between them: though Geoffrey recognizes Fulk's power, he still asserts his own unconquered spirit, inferior only to his

---

[37] *Vita Heinrici IV.*, 9, p. 29; trans. Mommsen and Morrison, p. 122.
[38] Orderic, 5.10, vol. 3: 96–99.
[39] William of Malmesbury, *De gestis regum anglorum*, 3, vol. 2: 292.

father's. Even in this moment of conflict, father and son are agreed on the superiority of the Angevin dynasty to all its competitors – it is Geoffrey's appeal to dynastic solidarity and assertion of dynastic character that ultimately reconciles the older man and leads him to reinstate his heir.

The details of Geoffrey's humiliation in this story, written so long after the events they describe, might appear William of Malmesbury's invention, perhaps designed to demonstrate the savage temper of the Angevins. Precedents for Fulk's action, however, make the account more plausible. As Mayke de Jong has shown, in the Carolingian empire a penalty known as *harmiscara* was sometimes imposed on those found guilty of egregious crimes – robbery, rape, oppression of the poor, usurpation of church property, conspiracy, or sedition.[40] Only one text from the ninth century actually describes *harmiscara*. The *Constitutio de expeditione Beneventana* of 866 decrees that a free man who steals while on military campaign will be punished with the *harmiscara*; that is, he will be ridden (*dirigatur*) by his lord before the king with a saddle on his back, which is to be kept there at the king's discretion. If the lord fails to enforce this penalty, he must himself suffer it.[41] The origins of *harmiscara* are unclear, but it seems likely that the Carolingians attempted to turn it into a royal monopoly (indeed almost the only early sources to mention it are the capitularies).[42]

By the eleventh century, however, its use had been usurped by ambitious nobles in the West Frankish realm. Those who sought pardon from the dukes of Normandy in the late eleventh century placed a saddle on their shoulders – voluntarily abasing themselves in a manner that confirmed the duke's high status.[43] Even if not strictly contemporary with the events it describes, then, William of Malmesbury's story has the ring of truth. And if true, it seems likely that Fulk imposed this penalty on Geoffrey not only to discipline a rebellious son, but also to claim traditionally royal privileges for himself and his lineage. Such a claim would have been fully in keeping with other aspects of Fulk's political agenda; Geoffrey himself might have applauded the move – had he not been the victim of his father's wrath.[44]

The law of the fathers

If the obligations of children to their fathers were rooted in the experience of life in the household, and reinforced by social custom and cultural

---

[40] De Jong (1992), pp. 46–47.
[41] *Constitutio de expeditione Beneventana* (a. 866), c. 9, MGH Capitularia, 2: 96.
[42] De Jong (1992), p. 49 and n. 76.
[43] William of Jumièges, *Gesta Normannorum*, 5.16, 6.4, vol. 2: 39, 51; Bates (1982), p. 163; cf. Bachrach (1993), pp. 234–36, on supposed Roman precedents for this ritual.
[44] Dunbabin (1985), pp. 184–87.

expectations, they also found explicit justification in law – secular as well as divine. And this is the other major distinction between mothers and fathers in the central Middle Ages: while maternal authority had very little legal support, paternal authority had a great deal. In Roman law, which was undergoing a revival in the eleventh century, the household (*familia*) was defined as "several people ... naturally or legally subject to the power [*potestate*] of a single person ... Someone who exercises authority within his household [*qui in domo dominium habet*] is called the head of household [*paterfamilias*]."[45] Medieval writers drew on Roman tradition to assert that sons were "naturally" subject to their fathers, and that fathers had the right to command their dependents' obedience, to discipline the wayward, ultimately even to disinherit those who persisted in resistance. The idea that paternal authority was undergirded "by law" and "by nature" occurs frequently in texts from the central Middle Ages. The direct or indirect influence of Roman law meant that rebellion against the father could be represented not just as illegal, but as unnatural – even monstrous.

Even more consistently, eleventh- and early twelfth-century writers drew on passages from scripture which represented honoring one's parents as an expression of God's will. The most obvious text here is the fourth commandment, which offers a reward for such behavior: "that thy days may be long upon the land which the Lord thy God giveth thee." In contrast, harsh retribution is promised elsewhere to disrespectful children. In Exodus 21:17, and Leviticus 20:9 – two texts often cited in the *libelli de lite* – the penalty for "cursing" or "reviling" one's parents is death, the same penalty due for the crime of "uncovering the nakedness" of one's father (Leviticus 18:7). Another important text also deals with "uncovering." In Genesis 9:20–27, Noah becomes drunk and lies uncovered in his tent. His son Ham sees "the nakedness of his father" and tells his two brothers, Shem and Japhet. They take a garment, walk backwards so that they can not see their father, and cover him up. When Noah awakes, he blesses Shem and Japhet, but curses Ham for his unfilial behavior: "lowest of slaves shall he be to his brothers."[46] The New Testament, too, underlines the obligation of children towards their parents, although without imposing any punishment for disobedience. In Ephesians 6:1, Paul writes simply, "Children, obey your parents in the Lord, for this is right."

Medieval exegetes explained paternal authority by associating earthly fathers with God, the Father par excellence. As we have already

---

[45] Justinian, *The Digest*, 50.16.195.2, p. 950.
[46] Spiritual interpretations of Noah and his sons are discussed below, Chapter 6.

seen, the Norman Anonymous provided a spiritual interpretation of Exodus 21:17:

The name of "father" is a great mystery ... Your father in the spirit is God ... Secondarily, your father in the flesh, through whom you were born in the flesh and came into this world, is also your father. He carried you in his loins ... And so, because the name of "father" is so sacred and so venerable, whoever shall curse his father or mother shall be put to death ... And it behooves you, as the apostle says, to be grateful to your parents [cf. 1 Timothy 5:4?]. For if you dishonor your carnal father, this is an affront to your spiritual father.[47]

Because the authority of the earthly father resonated mysteriously with that of the Father in heaven, disobedience was not just wrong and sinful, but impious, nearly blasphemous.

Medieval clerics considered the story of David and his son Absalom the most forceful illustration of this point. Absalom claimed his father's kingdom, and even slept with the concubines whom David had left behind him to keep house after he fled from his son's army. The rebellious young man finally got his head caught in an oak tree as he was riding under it, leaving him hanging in the air, which allowed Joab and his men to kill him. Yet when news of his death was brought to David, all the king could do was weep, saying, "Would I had died instead of you, O Absalom, my son, my son!" (2 Samuel 15–18). For medieval exegetes, David represented the God of mercy, who forgave even disobedient human sons. Absalom, on the other hand, represented treachery – indeed, his story foreshadowed that of Judas the betrayer of Christ:

... Absalom, which means "the father's peace," Absalom, I say – son and enemy, or rather, not son but enemy, from before whose face his father fled – represents mystically [in mysterio] Judas the traitor, the false peace of his Father and Master, whom he betrayed with the sign of a kiss ...[48]

When chroniclers and polemicists wanted to criticize filial disobedience in their own time, the story of Absalom, with all its mystical associations, readily came to mind.[49]

But New Testament texts could also be used to undercut the identification of earthly and heavenly fathers. Jerome Baschet has argued that Christianity broke from the ancient Jewish tradition in which God's authority unequivocally supported paternal authority. The early Christians were already promoting a "God the Father" who replaced the "God of the Fathers," depriving earthly patriarchs of their religious role,

---

[47] Norman Anonymous, p. 32.

[48] Rupert of Deutz, *De sancta Trinitate et operibus suis: in libros Regum*, vol. 22: 1286; Peter Damian, 90, vol. 2: 574–75; trans. Blum 3: 372–73.

[49] Search in the PL database for "Absalom" and variant spellings.

devaluing the earthly family in relation to the spiritual one.[50] The change was a slow one. During the central Middle Ages the dominant discourse of fatherhood remained one of untroubled continuity between different forms of paternity – whether divine, biological, political, or spiritual – and one of unquestioned paternal authority. Nevertheless, insistence on the sanctity of paternal authority had come to coexist with another discourse – one which justified rebellion against the earthly father in obedience to the higher authority of God.

Of particular importance here are Matthew 10:37, and Luke 14:26. The first reads, "He that loves father or mother more than me is not worthy of me," and the second, more strongly, "If any man come to me and hate not his father, and mother, and wife, and children, and brethren, and sisters, yea and his own life also, he cannot be my disciple."[51] These texts were generally interpreted in the Middle Ages in the context of religious conversion, which might require leaving behind earthly parents without rejecting them entirely.[52] But if parents blocked their offspring's conversion, then their authority was to be utterly rejected. In the words of the reforming cardinal and exegete Bruno of Segni, "If your father or mother or any of your kin wishes to separate you from the faith of Christ, flee him, fear him as an enemy, and hate him as a member of Satan."[53] This was precisely the attitude expressed in Alfanus of Salerno's *Life and Passion of Christina*.

Alfanus wrote this work for his "brothers," either at Montecassino, where he first entered the monastic life, or more likely at San Benedetto of Salerno, where he served as abbot before he ended his career as archbishop of the city (1058–85). "The Lord," he wrote, "has offered us a model in the feminine sex, so that, challenged by the virtue of women, we may regain the toughness of the virile soul which we have lost through sinful living ...".[54] One rather surprising aspect of that model, however, was a total disregard for paternal authority or filial piety. Christina begins by rejecting her father's commands, courts martyrdom (as we have seen, over her mother's anguished protests), then reengages with her father in a theological debate before his death. Her obligations towards her earthly parents are canceled out in this text, entirely replaced by her loyalty to her heavenly Father.

---

[50] Baschet (2000), 30–32.
[51] Matthew 19:29 was also frequently cited: "And every one that hath forsaken houses, or brethren, or sisters, or father, or mother, or wife, or children, or lands, for my name's sake shall receive an hundredfold, and shall inherit everlasting life."
[52] Search in the PL database for words from Matthew 10:37 and Luke 14:26.
[53] Bruno of Segni, *Commentaria in Lucam*, 2.14 (PL 165: 410).
[54] Alfanus of Salerno, *Vita et passio sanctae Christinae* (PL 147: 1282).

Alfanus' virgin martyr is an erudite (*erudita*) as well as a virtuous young woman. Shut up by her pagan father, Urbanus, in a high tower to serve as a vestal virgin, she uses references to pagan authors to prove to her twelve companions the impotence of the Roman gods, thus converting them to Christianity. Led by Christina, the virgins demolish the idols left in their care, toss the fragments out of the window, and give the offerings to the poor. When Urbanus discovers what has happened, he becomes "more violent than is fitting for parents" – slapping and kicking his daughter. His soldiers try to restrain him, suggesting that he treat Christina in a "fatherly" manner. They also claim that it seems very unlikely that a woman as clever and learned in Roman law as Christina would behave towards her father in such a way as to justify her disinheritance under civil law – for after all, this would only injure herself. Yet this association between paternal authority and inheritance becomes the very path by which Christina asserts her independence from Urbanus. She declares,

> If the laws determine – wish – aim to deprive of their possessions those who earn the disapproval of their parents, then *you* should be lawfully punished under your own sentence, for, separated from your Creator, who created you in His own likeness, you have shown yourself to be amenable to demons. However, *I* will lawfully obtain His inheritance, in that Christ is my co-heir, the angels my fellow citizens, the apostles my consorts, the martyrs my comrades, the confessors my friends, the virgins my in-laws. There [i.e. in heaven] no heir will ever be substituted for me, no praetor will be able to carry off the property, no tax collector will dare trouble me with fiscal demands.[55]

This formulation decisively undermines Urbanus' claim to paternal authority and reestablishes Christina as a dutiful daughter – of God. But Alfanus has already paved the way for this transfer of allegiance by constructing Urbanus as an unsuitable father, not only because of his pagan beliefs but also because of his behavior. He has to be urged to act in a "fatherly" manner; he becomes "more violent than is fitting for parents." There is repeated stress throughout the *vita* on his "fury" at his daughter's disobedience, and on the irrational brutality of his response to her behavior.

Christina's claim to a heavenly inheritance so enrages Urbanus that he has her imprisoned in an underground cell; when his wife sees her daughter there in chains, she goes nearly wild with grief.[56] We have already seen how the martyr-to-be rebuffed the delegation of matrons who begged her to take pity on her mother.[57] After their intervention fails, Urbanus

---

[55] Alfanus of Salerno, *Vita et passio sanctae Christinae* (PL 147: 1275), emphasis added.
[56] Alfanus of Salerno, *Vita et passio sanctae Christinae* (PL 147: 1275–76).
[57] See above, Chapter 3.

decides to call for his daughter's death. He has Christina brought out of her prison, before a group of onlookers, and enters into a debate with her, presumably designed to prove her guilt. As one might expect, however, Urbanus does not prevail. The young woman's opening salvo is a simple but devastating attack on her father's authority: "Not everything which seems true to you is necessarily so."[58] She then proceeds to demonstrate with irrefutable logic that Christ, rather than Jove, is truly God. Further enraged by her success in debate, Urbanus has Christina tortured and finally cast into the sea. However, she is carried safely back to shore by angels, while her father, seized by a demon, is the one who ultimately perishes.[59] Alfanus continues the story of Christina, describing further torments, her triumph over two dragons, and her eventual martyr's death. Our concern, however, is with the first – and longest – part of his account, which outlines Christina's conflict with Urbanus. This is the dramatic heart of the story, in which Alfanus attempts to resolve the powerful tension his eleventh-century readers and listeners must have felt between the demands of a father's authority and the obligation of obedience to God.

Alfanus was a close friend of Gregory VII. Indeed, it was at his court in Salerno that the exiled pope died in 1085. Alfanus' account of Christina's martyrdom in some ways exemplifies the attitude of the more radical reformers of the late eleventh century towards any form of earthly authority, including the paternal. On the one hand, like other churchmen, they urged sons to obey their fathers in obedience to divine law.[60] On the other, they were more willing than most of their contemporaries to rationalize rebellion against earthly fathers – whether biological, spiritual, or political – in order to protect the Church.[61] Nevertheless, these efforts always jostled uneasily with the overwhelmingly powerful emotional and ideological associations with the paternal in their society.

Absalom, Absalom

The complex and powerful tensions involved in the father–son relationship during the central Middle Ages are especially evident in accounts of the deeply troubled relationship between the Emperor Henry IV and his two rebellious sons. Chroniclers and polemicists devote considerable space to the dramatic events associated with these rebellions, and

---

[58] Alfanus of Salerno, *Vita et passio sanctae Christinae* (PL 147: 1277).
[59] Alfanus of Salerno, *Vita et passio sanctae Christinae* (PL 147: 1278–79).
[60] E.g. Gregory VII, *Register*, 7.27, p. 508; trans. Cowdrey, pp. 358–59.
[61] Monastic reformers were especially prone to this outlook, e.g. Raoul Glaber, 3.14, pp. 116–19; Peter Damian, 102, vol. 3: 133–34; trans. Blum, 4: 137.

considerable art to justifying the behavior of either the imperial father or his sons – depending on their own political positions. They also situate the struggle within the context of the ruling family's dynastic concerns.

Recent research has underlined the growing importance of such concerns in Germany during the "Salian century."[62] To a much greater extent than their predecessors, the Salian emperors were conscious of the transpersonal nature of kingship, the extent to which power and its appurtenances did not perish with the death of a king, but were passed down from one king to another.[63] In their view, good order required that the lands and privileges on which royal power was based, as well as the virtues through which it was exercised, be transmitted from father to son within a divinely chosen dynasty.[64] The new emphasis on inherited kingship in eleventh-century Germany is reflected in the new prominence of family groups, including not just the ruling emperor, but also his wife and – most importantly – his heir, in visual representations from the period.[65] A well-known image, from the earliest manuscript of Ekkehard of Aura's chronicle, depicts a father–son line of emperors, held in Conrad II's hand.[66]

The Salians and their court were, then, deeply concerned with father–son relationships within their dynasty. Hence the insistence of imperial polemicists in the last quarter of the eleventh century on the rights which Henry IV had inherited from his father. The Italian lawyer Peter Crassus, for example, uses the Roman law on inheritance to support Henry's claim to the his throne.[67] And hence, too, the anguish with which such polemicists greeted the rebellions of the emperor's two sons, Conrad and Henry V, which threatened both succession within the ruling family and peace within the kingdom.

Henry's eldest surviving son, Conrad, was born in 1074.[68] In 1087, at the age of thirteen, he was raised to the status of king and co-ruler, with special responsibility for the Italian kingdom – although initially, at least,

---

[62] Weinfurter (1991), pp. 29–43, 87–89, 156–58, 165–68.

[63] Hence Wipo, *Gesta Chuonradi II imperatoris*, 7, MGH SS 11: 263; trans. Mommsen and Morrison, p. 73. And see Bagge (2002), pp. 200–204.

[64] On inherited virtue, see Wipo's dedicatory letter to Henry III in *Gesta Chuonradi II imperatoris*, MGH SS 11: 254; trans. Mommsen and Morrison, p. 53.

[65] For example, a fresco in the apse of the cathedral of Aquileia features Conrad accompanied by the Empress Gisela and their young son Henry III: see Wolfram (2000), pp. 155–56.

[66] Berlin, Stiftung Preussischer Kulturbesitz, Cod. Lat. 295, f. 81v.

[67] Peter Crassus, *Defensio Heinrici IV. regis*, MGH, LL 1: 433–53. On this work, see Robinson (1978), pp. 75–83; Anton (1988); Melve (2007), 2: 349–422.

[68] On Conrad's life and career, see Goez (1996), pp. 1–49; Robinson (1999), pp. 286–301; Althoff (2006), pp. 211–13. The most detailed account of the rebellions may be found in Meyer von Knonau (1890–1909), vols. 4 and 5.

the actual government of Italy was confided to officials. Along with his father, Conrad entered Italy in 1090 to combat the forces supporting Pope Urban II – principally the redoubtable Countess Matilda of Tuscany. Three years later, however, the nineteen-year-old Conrad abandoned his father, and allied himself with Urban, Matilda, and her husband, young Welf V of Bavaria. Why Conrad rebelled against his father we cannot know for sure, but it seems likely that he chafed under Henry's renewed presence in Italy and his own relative insignificance in his father's court in the early 1090s. Goez has noted that, in the documents Henry issued in Italy in 1091, Conrad is not even listed first among those involved in the emperor's decisions.[69] Well on his way to becoming a fully adult male, within his own kingdom at least, the young king was now forced back into adolescence. The effects, on his own future status, of the ongoing papal schism and of Henry's weakness in Italy may also have worried Conrad.[70]

Soon after the rebellion began, Conrad was captured by his father's forces, but he managed to escape and made it to Milan, where, late in 1093, he was crowned king of Italy by the reforming Archbishop Anselm. In Milan, Conrad gained the allegiance of some of the most important Lombard cities, compelling the emperor and his entourage to withdraw from Lombardy to the March of Verona. Between them, Conrad and Matilda of Tuscany dominated most of northern Italy in 1094 and 1095, allowing Pope Urban II to pursue his reform agenda there. Urban held an important church council at Piacenza in March of 1095, at which Henry's second wife, Eupraxia, provided shocking testimony about her relationship with her husband.[71] She claimed that he had forced her to have sex with other men – testimony that, as we shall see, would be picked up and developed by writers hostile to Henry. One month later, at Cremona, Conrad performed the *officium stratoris* for Urban, ritually holding the pope's reins and stirrup as he dismounted from his horse.[72] In response, Urban recognized Conrad as a "son of the Roman Church," promised to crown him emperor, and arranged for his marriage to the daughter of another papal ally, Count Roger I of Sicily.

While the Pope headed north to France for a further series of reforming councils, Conrad remained in Italy; but by the middle of 1095, the pro-reform alliance was beginning to unravel. Matilda's marriage collapsed and young Welf returned to his father in Bavaria; the elder Welf then sought reconciliation with the emperor. A friendly Bavaria provided

---

[69] Goez (1996), pp. 22–23.   [70] Goez (1996), pp. 24; Robinson (1999), p. 288.
[71] See below, Chapter 6.
[72] The significance of this gesture will be discussed in the next chapter.

Henry IV with an escape route from northeastern Italy, where he had been hemmed in, and in the spring of 1097 the emperor crossed the Alps and returned to Germany for the first time in seven years. There, in May of 1098, he arranged for the German princes to depose Conrad and accept his younger son, Henry V, as co-ruler in Germany and heir to the imperial title. (Young Henry was obliged to promise never to usurp his father's power and seize his possessions as long as he lived – a promise he signally failed to keep.) Conrad, meanwhile, had not acquired the hoped-for dowry from his bride, and – having few resources of his own – became almost completely dependent on Countess Matilda. The pope, preoccupied with other matters (notably the crusade), and probably aware that Conrad was now a negligible factor even in Italian politics, never crowned him emperor. The young king died at the age of twenty-seven, in July of 1101.

Only a few years after Conrad's death, Henry IV was faced with another uprising, this time led by his younger son and namesake. When his rebellion began, Henry V was eighteen years old and had been associated on the throne with his father for six years.[73] While accompanying the emperor on a military expedition in the north of Germany in December of 1104, the young king suddenly left his father's camp and fled south to Bavaria, the land of the Welfs, who had earlier supported his brother Conrad. While young Henry's motives, like his elder brother's, are far from clear, the young king was probably worried that his father – whose health had been precarious for some time – might die suddenly. He wanted to establish his own independent authority before that event.[74] It has also been plausibly suggested that Henry was concerned about the damage being done to imperial power by the long-lasting conflict between empire and papacy; wanting to end the conflict, he turned against his father.

Historians have generally rejected Henry V's own claims that he rose against his father simply because the latter was excommunicate. However, soon after the rebellion began, the young king did seek absolution from Pope Pascal II for the sin of having associated with his excommunicated father, even as he encouraged German princes hostile to the emperor and his policies to join him. By the summer of 1105, the rebel forces were in a position to undertake an expedition against the emperor. Despite the aging monarch's best military and diplomatic efforts, he gradually lost control of his realm over the course of the autumn. The dramatic confrontation at Regensburg, described by Otto of Freising, ended with the emperor's flight.

---

[73] Robinson (1999), pp. 323–36; Althoff (2006), pp. 228–50.
[74] Robinson (1999), p. 327; Althoff (2006), pp. 234–35.

Then, in December of 1105, father and son reached an agreement. The emperor would attend an assembly of "all the princes of the kingdom" to be held at Mainz at Christmastime, and would submit to their decision about his future; in return, Henry V guaranteed his father's safety. But the agreement was not honored. Instead of conducting his father to Mainz, young Henry imprisoned him in the castle of Böckelheim, where he was treated not with the honor due to an emperor, but with the austerity suited to a sinner. Henry IV was forced to hand over the royal insignia, surrender his strongest fortresses, and even renounce his claim to the throne. In January 1106, his son was invested at Mainz with the symbols of royal authority and received the homage of most of the German princes and bishops.

But this was not the end of the story, for his father managed to escape from his captors, rally his few remaining supporters, and make a final bid for power. The indomitable emperor spent the last months of his life presenting his own version of recent events to both the German princes and a wider public and unsuccessfully seeking absolution from the pope. He died at Liège on August 7, 1106, and had his funeral there, but was finally buried in Speyer, at the cathedral which also served as the family mausoleum. According to one account, the poor and helpless of his kingdom wept "that they have been orphaned of their father," but his exequies lacked the solemnity that had marked his grandfather Conrad's funeral.[75] There is no indication that his one surviving son, Henry V, ever "bent his shoulders" beneath his father's coffin.[76]

Henry IV was far from the only high-ranking father to be faced with a rebellious son in this period. Fulk of Anjou quarreled with Geoffrey, William the Conqueror with Robert Curthose, and many other powerful men with the "youths" in their families. Yet Henry IV's situation was unusual, first because he had to face two uprisings, one after the other; second because Henry V actually succeeded in toppling his father from the throne; and third because of the significance attributed to these rebellions by the clerical writers of the period. Historians, letter writers, and polemicists within Germany and throughout Europe were fascinated by the family troubles of Henry IV, and set out to discover what those troubles meant, for the imperial family, for the empire, and for the Church.

For the emperor's supporters, the rebellions of Conrad and Henry V were personal and national tragedies, in which the most sacred of bonds, that uniting father and son, exploded in betrayal. Sigebert of Gembloux

---

[75] *Vita Heinrici IV.*, 13, p. 43; trans. Mommsen and Morrison, p. 136.

[76] At least not at the initial funeral, which was followed by several exhumations and a forced removal of the corpse to an unconsecrated chapel in Speyer. Henry IV's reburial in 1111 was more impressive; see Robinson (1999), pp. 343–44.

depicted Conrad "offering" himself "to his father's enemies"; Cosmas of Prague saw Henry V's assumption of arms against his father as the work of the devil.[77] To the annalist of Rosenveld, Henry V was "another Absalom," who plotted against his father even after taking over the kingdom.[78] Not surprisingly, though, the themes of filial disobedience and immorality sound most painfully in accounts written by the emperor himself and by his biographer.

In his final letters, composed during the months leading up to his death in 1106, Henry IV constantly returns to these issues. Describing how his son falsely promised him safe-conduct to Mainz, he complains, "this he promised in that attitude of truth and fidelity with which God orders a father to be honored by his son and a son to be loved by his father."[79] Young Henry's behavior was not only deeply immoral, but manifestly illegal:

We have been dealt with unjustly, inhumanly, and cruelly, having trusted in that fidelity which we ought not to have had to doubt. Against divine and human law and to the shame and abuse of the kingdom, we have been so despoiled of the honor of kingship, of our lands, and of everything else we had, that on the whole nothing but life alone has been left us.[80]

This theme was picked up by other writers sympathetic to the emperor, including Sigebert of Gembloux, who – perhaps influenced by Henry's own rhetoric – described the son's behavior as "against the law of nature and against what is permitted by [human] law."[81]

The immorality of a son rising against his father is most fully developed, however, in the strongly partisan biography of Henry IV, composed soon after his death by a skillful rhetorician, perhaps a member of the imperial chancery.[82] The author began his account of Conrad's rebellion with this apostrophe:

What may enemies do when children themselves rise up against their parents? Or whence may one assure himself of security when he is not safe from him whom he begat? Let marriages now cease; let no one hope for an heir: your heir will be your enemy, for not only does he rob you of your house and lands, but he also makes haste to rob you of your life.[83]

---

[77] Sigebert of Gembloux, *Chronica*, a. 1092, MGH SS 5: 366; Cosmas of Prague, *Chronica Boemorum*, 3.18, MGH SRG, n.s. 2, p. 182.
[78] *Annales Rosenveldenses*, a. 1106, MGH SS 16: 102.
[79] Henry IV, *Briefe*, 39, p. 54; trans. Mommsen and Morrison, p. 192.
[80] Henry IV, *Briefe*, 41, p. 61; trans. Mommsen and Morrison, p. 197.
[81] Sigebert of Gembloux, *Chronica*, a. 1106, MGH, SS 6: 369. Sigebert knew and cited Henry's letters.
[82] The name of Erlung, imperial chancellor and later bishop of Würzburg, has been suggested; see "Praefatio" to *Vita Heinrici IV.*, pp. 1–6; see also Bagge (2002), pp. 314–15.
[83] *Vita Heinrici IV.*, 7, p. 26; trans. Mommsen and Morrison, p. 118.

Not only the imperial family's dynastic hopes, but the broader social expectations of the period are invoked here. Most men at this time entered into marriage precisely out of a desire for legitimate heirs, who would be their father's most reliable allies in protecting the patrimony and who would preserve it after he was gone. If an heir could be an enemy, everything of earthly importance was in danger: marriage, house, lands – even life itself.

Conrad had been left in Italy specifically to fight against Matilda of Tuscany – to take "out of the hand of a woman that kingdom which would be his in the future." Instead, he fell under the countess's influence – "for whom may not womanly guile corrupt or deceive?" As Conrad, under Matilda's influence, renounced his loyalty to his father, the biographer underlined the resulting disruption of all order:

> He set the crown upon his own head, usurped the royal office, profaned right, confounded order, fought against nature, and sought the blood of his father, since he would not have been able to reign save by the blood of his father.

But Matilda's presence in this account not only shows how the world has been turned upside down, it also brings Conrad's masculinity into question. He failed to rescue his kingdom "out of the hand of a woman" as his father had planned. Moreover, not he, but a woman, was the "chief mover of the deed" (*Aeneid* 1, 364), and the emperor's enemies, delighted by this turn of events, praised her more than they did Conrad.[84] Quite possibly this passage plays off the unspoken assumption that rebellious sons were seeking to assert their own adult masculinity. The biographer counters this belief with his own construction of the situation: the young king's unnatural behavior leads not to manhood, but to emasculation.

Similar references to monstrous and unnatural behavior are distributed throughout the biographer's very long account of the rebellion of 1104–6, in which Henry V's lack of natural affection for his father is contrasted with other people's sympathy. At one point, he has the emperor modestly admit that sin might have cost him his power. However, he insists that his son should not have been the one to cast him out: "Barbarous kingdoms condemn and disavow such an inhuman deed; the very pagans abhor it, and those who do not know God recognize what they should owe to nature in loving men."[85] The young king's behavior, then, is worse than barbarous, worse than pagan, because it ignores the demands of nature herself. When the emperor is forced to abdicate in January of 1106, his speech "moved many to laments and tears; not even nature itself, however, could move his son to pity."[86]

---

[84] *Vita Heinrici IV.*, 7, p. 26; trans. Mommsen and Morrison, p. 118–19.
[85] *Vita Heinrici IV.*, 11, p. 37; trans. Mommsen and Morrison, p. 129.
[86] *Vita Heinrici IV.*, 10, p. 34; trans. Mommsen and Morrison, p. 127.

Both divine and natural law are invoked to condemn young Henry's rebellion.[87] As a result, the biographer can ascribe the emperor's few successes in this period, such as his thrilling escape from Regensburg, to divine intervention: "You have been warned by this miracle, O son of the Emperor, if you could have been warned, to learn to revere your father, not to harry him …".[88] By the same token, divine wrath accounts for the son's setbacks. Henry V's loss of the royal insignia to a mob, for example, is seen as a divine punishment:

Come to your senses at last, good King, come to your senses, and recognize wrath from above in this which has fallen your lot. It is the judgment of the wrath of God that you should flee, who had put your father to flight, and that you should lose the insignia which you had stolen from your father.[89]

In this final section of the biography, the emperor himself pleads with his son to avoid scandal and obey God by returning to filial obedience:

the Emperor sent envoys after him and recalled him as much with tears as with commands, entreating him not to cause grief to his old father; rather, not to offend the Father of all, not to expose himself to the scorn of men, not to make himself a subject of idle talk for the world.[90]

Connecting the earthly father to the heavenly "Father of all," the biographer renders the young king's action both shameful and sinful.

The indispensable *obligato* constantly sounding behind these representations of filial betrayal is the story of David and Absalom.[91] For many readers, the analogy would have been enriched by a tradition of imperial rhetoric – highly developed at the court of Henry III – that likened the emperor to King David. While any father of a rebellious son might compare his sufferings to those of David, the emperor's sufferings took on a special cosmic significance, since he, like the Biblical king, was the "anointed of the Lord." Writing to his godfather, Abbot Hugh of Cluny, Henry IV complains that he had been betrayed not by some servant or enemy, but

even the son of our loins, signally beloved of us, impiously, inhumanly, and unworthily effected this against us in such a way that we can cry out to God, not without grief or immense wonderment, in the very voice of the Psalmist-King, fleeing from the face of a son not unlike ours, "Lord, how are they increased that trouble me!" [Psalm 3:1].[92]

---

[87] The emperor's messengers even cite Exodus 20:12: see *Vita Heinrici IV.*, 11, p. 36; trans. Mommsen and Morrison, p. 129.

[88] *Vita Heinrici IV.*, 9, p. 32; trans. Mommsen and Morrison, p. 124.

[89] *Vita Heinrici IV.*, 11, p. 36; trans. Mommsen and Morrison, p. 128.

[90] *Vita Heinrici IV.*, 9, p. 30; trans. Mommsen and Morrison, p. 123.

[91] And not only in the empire: William the Conqueror is said to have reminded his rebellious son to remember Absalom's fate. Orderic, 5.10, vol. 3: 98–99.

[92] Henry IV, *Briefe*, 37, p. 47; trans. Mommsen and Morrison, p. 185.

In a letter addressed to King Philip I of France, but widely circulated in Germany in 1106, Henry IV gave his fullest account of young Henry's perfidy. He recalls how his enemies "worked against the very law of nature – and this I cannot say without the greatest grief of heart and without many tears; now that it is said, I tremble violently – and they not only turned the mind of my son against me, I say the mind of my most beloved Absalom, but they also armed him with great fury."[93] Undoubtedly influenced by the emperor's own rhetoric, the anonymous author of the *Life of Henry IV* represents imperial actions, even those obviously forced by circumstances, as expressions of piety and paternal love, patterned after Biblical precedents. Thus Henry IV's flight from the confrontation at Regensburg becomes a positive choice, arising from his desire to prevent the young king from falling into sin: "after the fashion of David, he fled lest his son become a parricide."[94]

To Henry IV and his supporters, the emperor is a virtuous father betrayed by those he loved best, while his sons' disobedience is an affront to him, to God, and even to the Salian dynasty.[95] (Indeed, the *Life of Henry IV* suggests that Henry V was unworthy of inheritance, in that "impatient of delay, he had seized ahead of time the kingdom from that very man by whom he had been designated its inheritor."[96]) Such arguments were relatively easy to make, for they drew on the dominant discourse of their time, which identified the authority of earthly fathers – however unworthy they might be – with the ultimate authority of God, and vilified disobedient sons as inherently impious.

The emperor's opponents – whether associated with the papal reform or with local discontent within Germany – faced a more difficult task, for they had to reconcile their support for rebellion with the legitimate claims of fathers to obedience. The obvious solution (employed, for example, by the historian responsible for the fourth section of the *Annals of Hildesheim*[97]) was to invoke obedience to a heavenly father to justify resistance to an earthly one. Such an approach could be supported by Scripture, while a number of saints' lives – of which the *Passion of Christina* is only the most elaborate example – also offered models. However, most of Henry IV's opponents, rather surprisingly it seems to me, did not take advantage of this obvious approach. Perhaps – at least for those who wrote after 1111 – this was because Henry V's later behavior did not appear to reflect obedience to a heavenly father either. But even those

---

[93] Henry IV, *Briefe*, 39, p. 53; trans. Mommsen and Morrison, p. 191.
[94] *Vita Heinrici IV.*, 9, p. 32; trans. Mommsen and Morrison, p. 124; see also the description of Henry IV surrendering Nuremburg on p. 31 (trans. p. 123).
[95] Bagge (2002), pp. 344–46.
[96] *Vita Heinrici IV.*, 10, p. 35; trans. Mommsen and Morrison, p. 127.
[97] *Annales Hildesheimenses*, a. 1105, MGH SRG, 8, pp, 54–55.

writing immediately after Conrad's rebellion generally pursued other paths, more in keeping with their individual goals.

Cardinal Deusdedit, for example, completed his *Little Book against the Invaders* [*of Churches*]*, Simoniacs and Schismatics* around 1097. It was intended primarily as a response to the imperialist claim that "the Church of Christ is subject to royal power."[98] Deusdedit begins by systematically citing theological arguments and legal precedents against this claim, but in Book Two – which deals with the validity of the sacraments performed by simoniacs and schismatics – he suddenly switches to a narrative of recent events. He draws parallels between his own day, in which the simoniacs and schismatics, supported by the emperor, hold the overwhelming advantage, and the first century, when the young Church was similarly beset on all sides by the Roman emperors and by heretics. For the reforming cardinal, Gregory VII was a new St. Peter, while Henry IV represented Nero – the depraved emperor who finally caused Peter's death, and Wibert of Ravenna figured Simon Magus, Peter's enemy and the prototypical simoniac, whom eleventh-century clerics commonly believed to have been supported by Nero. Drawing on the recent rebellion by Conrad and the shocking accusations made by Eupraxia at the council of Piacenza, Deusdedit highlights Henry's similarity to Nero. Just as Nero's family life was notoriously marked by sexual perversion and cruelty, so Henry was "abandoned by his wife (whom he prostituted to many men, as God is my witness) and his sons because of his cruelty."[99] Conrad's rebellion (or, for that matter, Eupraxia's defection) did not greatly interest Deusdedit – his goal was rather to paint the most shocking picture possible of Henry's behavior. For Deusdedit, then, filial disobedience followed logically, if not necessarily honorably, from paternal depravity.

Something similar happens in the mid-twelfth-century *Annals of St. Disibod*. This account of Conrad's rebellion falls outside the temporal bounds of this study and is highly fanciful as well. I include it here, nevertheless, because of the way it illuminates the role of the close temporal association of Conrad's rebellion and Eupraxia's flight from her husband's court in shaping understanding of the son's behavior, and also because of its focus on dynastic continuity as a source of both closeness and tension between father and son.[100] The *Annals of St. Disibod* attributes Conrad's rebellion to the shocking and "insane" demand of

---

[98] Deusdedit, *Libellus contra invasores et symoniacos et reliquos schismaticos*, Prologue, MGH LL 2: 300.

[99] Deusdedit, *Libellus contra invasores et symoniacos et reliquos schismaticos*, 2.12, MGH LL 2: 330.

[100] On the temporal association of the two events, see also below, Chapter 6.

Henry IV (who had already subjected Eupraxia to the sexual advances of other men) that his son (in the Biblical phrase) "go in" to his wife as well. When the young man refused to "pollute his father's bed" in this way, Henry accused him of being not his own son, but the illegitimate offspring of the duke of Swabia, whom he claimed Conrad resembled.[101] In this text, then, Henry's *dementia* leads him not only to plumb new depths of sexual misconduct, but also to break the continuity of his own dynasty, by rejecting a son who refused to share in his own depravity.

A much more reliable account of the rebellions comes from the second recension of the chronicle of Abbot Ekkehard of Aura (d. 1126), an eyewitness to many of the events he describes. While it contains some of the same elements as the *Annals of St. Disibod*, Ekkehard's account is a much more balanced narrative. Again Henry IV figures as an unnatural father, whose own behavior was the source of his dynasty's disruption. However, the sons receive much more attention in this work than in any other account of the rebellions. The abbot of Aura provides an extremely sympathetic portrait of Conrad as a good man, a dutiful son, and a conscientious king, and a similar, if slightly less panegyrical, picture of Henry V – with whose court Ekkehard was associated. Both sons actually strive to protect their father and the legitimacy of Salian claims to power.

Ekkehard admits that he does not know why Conrad rebelled against his father.[102] However, his picture of Conrad's character suggests he had only the highest motives. While he held the "title and dignity of king" in Italy, "such tales of his good character spread throughout the Roman world that no religious or wise man in any way doubted that the wellbeing of the state depended on him." "Subject to the apostolic see in all things," Conrad was "more given to spiritual activities than to matters of authority or arms, although sufficiently endowed with fortitude and audacity." He was affable to all, and generous to the poor, especially to poor soldiers. Although he married the daughter of Roger of Sicily, "so chaste was his union with her that it is scarcely to be believed that he ever had intercourse with her."[103] In short, the young king of Italy shared many characteristics with the better-known "saintly" kings of this period, such as Henry II of Germany and Edward the Confessor of England.[104]

Most remarkable, however, is Ekkehard's description of Conrad's relationship with his father. Ironically, it constitutes our most detailed report

---

[101] *Annales sancti Disibodi*, a. 1093, MGH SS 17: 14. A similar account, with additional detail, can be found in the early thirteenth-century *Annales Stadenses*, a. 1093, MGH SS 16: 316–17.

[102] Ekkehard, *Chronicon*, a. 1099, p. 128: "Chunradus vero causam rebellationis sue paucis tantum sibique familiarissimis in regno detegens …".

[103] Ekkehard, *Chronicon*, a. 1099 pp. 128–30.   [104] Elliott (1993), pp. 113–131.

from the central Middle Ages of proper filial behavior, for despite his refusal to obey Henry IV, Conrad chooses not to dishonor him:

In keeping with the legal precept[s], "Thou shalt not uncover the nakedness of thy father," and "Honor your father," he would never listen to the rumors which ripped at his father's way of life throughout the Roman Empire, or to [the story that] offense to himself was the cause of the dissension between himself and his father. He himself always referred to his father as his lord and as Caesar or Emperor, and treated all those who came from his father's court, even the lowest, with friendly benevolence, as his fellow servants.[105]

Far from abusing his father, Conrad accepts his position as servant willingly – hence the continuing mystery about the reasons behind his rebellion.

Henry V is less saintly than his older brother in Ekkehard's chronicle, but still an exemplar of filial piety. Given Ekkehard's close association with the court of Henry V, we can, I think, assume that the speeches he puts into the mouth of the king as a young man echo Henry V's later self-presentation. And what we see in those speeches is the image of a dutiful son, regretfully taking action to correct an erring father, ready to submit to paternal authority if only his father will see reason. Thus Ekkehard has young Henry declare to the synod of Nordhausen in May of 1105, that "he did not usurp his father's authority out of lust for power and did not wish his father to be deposed from the Roman Empire," but rather promised that "if [his father] would submit to St. Peter and his successors according to Christian law, he [the young king] would either withdraw from the kingship or submit to him like a servant."[106]

In another speech, supposedly made by Henry V during the face-off at Regensburg, he paradoxically denies attacking his father at all:

... the young king, torn by emotion concerning his father, began to exclaim mournfully: "I am completely grateful, comrades in arms, for your affection towards me ... But no one should desire or assume that I will be beholden to him if he boasts that my lord and father has been killed by him, or if he judges that he is to be killed. Indeed, I do desire – if it please the Lord of All – to hold the realm pledged to me by Christian law, as heir and successor of the emperor. I do not wish to be called or to be a parricide. But if my father submits himself to the yoke of apostolic obedience, I will hereafter be content with only those things which he has, in his clemency, conceded to me; in the meantime, know that I am not the attacker of my father, but the defender of the paternal realm.[107]

Notice that the son rather than the father becomes the defender of the "paternal realm," which is also the realm "pledged" to him "by Christian

---

[105] Ekkehard, *Chronicon*, a. 1099, p. 130.
[106] Ekkehard, *Chronicon*, a. 1105, p. 192; cf. Robinson, p. 192.
[107] Ekkehard, *Chronicon*, a. 1105, p. 196.

law." Henry V is, then, the true representative of the Salian dynasty. As such, he explicitly rejects the possibility of parricide. He will use his military power to defend his inheritance and make his father submit to the pope, but he refuses to let the emperor be killed.

Whether sympathetic to Henry IV or to his sons, the polemicists of the central Middle Ages saw the rebellions of Conrad and Henry V as rich in domestic meaning. They devoted much space and powerful rhetoric to interpreting these events in terms of paternal authority, filial piety, and dynastic continuity, unlike modern historians, who have generally lumped the rebellions of Henry IV's sons together with the many other uprisings that punctuated the emperor's reign. In the historical literature of the nineteenth and early twentieth centuries, Conrad and Henry V were sometimes condemned as "unnatural" sons,[108] but more recent scholars have withheld such assessments, pointing out – quite correctly – that not only the polemics, but also most of the chronicles from this period had a strong propagandistic character, and were thus not reliable guides to the real character of either the emperor or his sons.[109] Modern scholars thus tend to focus on the "public" and "political" motivations of the protagonists, rather than on "private" family dynamics. With the brief but important exception of a recent article by Karl Heinrich Krüger, which devotes three pages to considering contemporary critiques of Henry V's behavior as a son, the latest works on the rebellions represent Conrad and Henry V as ambitious young kings, motivated by concerns about their own, somewhat precarious, political positions, not as sons, troubled by their father's behavior or anxious about their obligations to him.[110]

Such analyses help to explain what the emperor and his sons actually did, and why, but they fail to do justice to the cultural context within which the rebellions occurred, a context which influenced the emperor, the kings, their supporters, and those whose support they were trying to attract. The works described in the last part of this chapter were indeed propaganda, but this fact does not make their content any less significant. Henry IV spent the last few months of his life complaining about his son, not because he was a querulous old man, but because it was good politics to do so. An abbot like Ekkehard, with close ties to Henry V's court, depicted his king as a dutiful son because such a depiction supported that king's claims to power. In the "public" life of the central Middle Ages, political legitimacy could easily be compromised by what

---

[108] E.g. Bryce (1863; 1920), p. 160; Hampe (1916), p. 74.
[109] Notably Tellenbach (1988); Robinson (1998), pp. 345–69.
[110] Krüger (2002), pp. 233–36; Weinfurter (1991); Suchan (1997), pp. 166–72; Robinson (1999), pp. 323–43.

we might think of as "private" failures. There was, of course, considerable room to maneuver here, for the limits of paternal authority and the exact nature of filial obligation remained open to interpretation. Yet the politics of paternity were never negligible in the central Middle Ages, for they constantly intruded on – indeed, they could not be excluded from – the "public" politics of the period.

Ða of flæpe onbrægd· funu lamehes· þa þona
ongeat· þ him cyne godum· cham nepolde· þa him
pær ane þearf· æmge cyðan· hyldo Ᵹ cuþpa þæt
þam halgan pær· fan onmode· ongan þa hit fel
fæ· belyun· pondum pyngean· cpæð he psan rcolde·
heun und feo hleoþnum· hleo maga þeop· cham on þon
þan him þa cpyde· fyððan· 7 hir from cynne· fræc
ne rcodon· þa nyttade· noe fyððan· mid funum fmu
fidan fuch· dpiteo hund pintra· þyrs· lifeo· fylð men
æfteh· flode 7 fiftægeuc· þa he ford gepat·

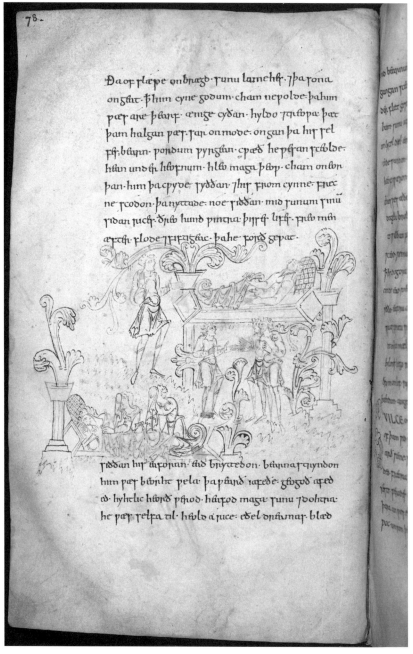

fidan hir æfopan· fud bryateðon· belynnas qynðon
him pær betonhte þela þa þfund iaxeðe· gfogod aftð
eð hyltelic hleored pfhod· harfoð maga funu 7 oohtna
he pær felfa til· heulo a fuce· eðel onfumay blæð

Figure 3. Oxford, Bodleian Library, Ms. Junius 11, p. 78. The
Drunkenness of Noah, from the Old English *Genesis*. Reproduced by
permission of the library.

6   Fathers in the spirit

> ... As a bishop is permitted to excommunicate a cleric who has
> seriously sinned, an abbot may do the same to a disobedient monk.
> For just as an actual father may disinherit a rebellious son, so may a
> spiritual father in a display of strict justice expel a disobedient subject
> from the Church. Hence the Apostle says, "We had earthly fathers
> and paid due respect to them; should we not submit even more readily
> to our spiritual father, and so attain life?" [Hebrews 12:9] And just a
> bit before that he said, "Can anyone be a son, who is not disciplined
> by his father? But if you escape the discipline in which all sons share,
> you must be bastards and no true sons" [Hebrews 12:7–8].[1]

A thousand years of history have accustomed even those of us who are
not Catholic to the practice of addressing bishops and ordinary priests as
"father," and the pope as "Holy Father." Such designations come easily
to our lips because they seem banal, almost entirely emptied of meaning.
This was not the case, however, in the eleventh century, when granting a
spiritual leader the title of father (or denying it to him) was still a political
statement. Paternal language increasingly pervaded political writing from
the middle of the eleventh century on, used in new ways to ground attacks
on simony, clerical marriage, and lay investiture; to support efforts at liberating bishops from lay control; and to assert papal primacy over those
bishops, as well as over the rest of the faithful. It was precisely because
images of fathers carried such a powerful rhetorical and emotional charge
that they were able to shape discussions of "right order" within the Church
and within Christian society during the central Middle Ages.

Yet the rich significance of paternal language in this period also
meant that its political use could never be simple or entirely straightforward. The popes of the eleventh and early twelfth centuries evidenced
some hesitation about asserting their paternal claims, most often making demands for filial obedience only indirectly. And because papal
correspondents, regardless of political position, normally accepted
the paternal authority of their *papa*, they had to wrestle with dilemmas

[1] Peter Damian, 56, vol. 2: 161; trans. Blum, 2: 367–68.

similar to those discussed in the last chapter – how to justify resistance to a spiritual father when they could not or would not accept his demands. So pervasive was the rhetoric of papal paternity in this period, however, that even those who resisted the papacy's new expectations found it difficult to dismiss their filial obligations out of hand.

Venerating him as a father

The image of the bishop as parent was already an old and well-established one by the eleventh century.[2] Bishops had been identified as spiritual fathers to the Christians under their jurisdiction since antiquity. Within a specifically Christian context, the fatherhood of God and the motherhood of the Church authorized such representations, but they were also derived from a general cultural tendency in both the ancient world and the Middle Ages to associate caretaking and leadership with paternity.[3] During the early Middle Ages, Christian authors continued to refer to bishops as the fathers of the faithful. The relationship between bishop and people was assumed to be one of affection, with the spiritual father caring tenderly for his children. Thus it might be said that the death of a bishop not only left his church a widow, but his people lamenting the loss of their father.[4] However, the political implications of episcopal paternity were as yet not spelled out particularly clearly, either in theology or in canon law. Curiously enough, the *Pastoral Care*, Gregory the Great's influential handbook for bishops, contains no reference to spiritual fatherhood at all.

In Pseudo-Isidore, whereas references to the Church as the Bride of Christ or the Mother of the faithful play an important role in regulating relationships between bishops and the behavior of individual prelates, the image of the bishop as father is seldom deployed. The only exception – and it would later prove an important one – occurs in reference to the problem of a bishop's subordinates making accusations against him.[5] Here, the story of Noah's drunkenness from Genesis 9:20–27 seemed relevant to Pseudo-Isidore's compilers. Hitherto, most exegetes had seen

---

[2] The fatherhood of ordinary priests is a separate subject, which I cannot pursue here.

[3] "The Church herself calls [bishops] 'fathers'; she gives birth to them and she installs them in the sees of their fathers [the apostles]." Augustine, *Enarrationes in psalmos* 44.32, CC, SL, vol. 38: 516. On episcopal paternity in antiquity, see Neuhäusler (1964); Lubac (1971), pp. 85–100; Thelamon (1997), pp. 543–44.

[4] E.g. Adalbero of Reims, *Epistolae*, 37 (PL 137: 516); Thangmar, *Vita Bernwardi*, 54, MGH SS 4: 781. Examples of orators addressing bishops as fathers: Landulf of Milan, *Historia Mediolanensis*, 2.32; 3.15; 3.17, MGH SS 8: 69, 83, 85.

[5] On the context within which these concerns were raised, see Reynolds (1983), pp. 326–27.

Noah as a prefiguration of Christ, whose humanity (his "shameful parts") was exposed on the cross. Ham, the son who not only failed to cover his father, but actually summoned his two brothers to view his shame, represented the Jews, who derided Christ's humanity and were therefore condemned to perpetual servitude.[6] Ham might also stand for heretics or infidels, who similarly mocked the Passion.[7] By the Carolingian period, however, another interpretation had developed, which turned the story into an admonition to subjects to conceal the misdeeds of those placed above them.[8] Pseudo-Isidore used it to protect bishops against attacks from below, warning the "sons" of a particular church – that is, subordinate clerics or the laity – not to defame or bring charges against their bishop. They could attempt to correct him if he deviated from the faith, but any other form of misbehavior was to be tolerated. For the story of Ham demonstrates "how great a condemnation, how great a curse threatens those who sin against their fathers."[9] An English manuscript created somewhere between 950 and 1000 vividly illustrates the difference between filial piety and impiety. It shows a smirking Ham pointing at Noah's exposed genitals, while his brothers, their faces averted, try to cover their father's "nakedness."[10] Whether the Junius manuscript was created at a monastery or a cathedral scriptorium, it would have carried much the same message about what was due to a spiritual father.

Early medieval bishops may have been important and powerful figures, but their position could nevertheless be quite precarious. If Pseudo-Isidore helped protect them from their subjects, it did nothing to protect them from manipulation and even intimidation from above. Intervention in church affairs by worldly powers was already the norm in the Carolingian period, and if anything it intensified with the passage of time. By the turn of the millennium, bishops were normally appointed, and sometimes removed from office, by members of the laity – emperors or kings in some places, lesser nobles elsewhere. They sometimes came from the same families as the rulers who appointed them, but often were

[6] Bede, *Hexaemeron*, 2, 3 (PL 91: 111, 121); cf. Hrabanus Maurus, *Commentariorum in Genesim*, 2.9 (PL 107: 525).

[7] Rupert of Deutz, *Commentaria in evangelium sancti Iohanni*, 11, CC, CM 9: 605; *idem*, *De divinis officiis*, CC, CM 7: 5; Honorius, *Speculum ecclesiae* (PL 172: 987).

[8] Stephen V, *Epistolae*, 16, MGH, EPP 7: 342 = JL 3434.

[9] Projekt Pseudoisidor, Teil 1, 2. Anacletus-Brief, pp. 134–35 (H. 38–39). Available at http://www.pseudoisidor.de/pdf/014_Anacletus_Benedictus_deus.pdf. Cf. Projekt Pseudoisidor, Teil 1, 2. Clemens-Brief, pp. 65–66, (H. 51). Available at http://www.pseudoisidor.de/pdf/008_Clemens_Quoniam_sicut.pdf. Projekt Pseudoisidor, Teil 1, 2. Fabianus-Brief, (H. 22). Available at http://www.pseudoisidor.mgh.de/html/042.htm.

[10] Oxford, Bodleian Library, Junius 11, f. 78. On this manuscript, see Karkov (2001), esp. pp. 14, 95, 166–67; on the problem of representing Noah's nakedness visually, see Deremble (2000); Caviness (2006).

younger – sometimes even illegitimate – sons.[11] A bishop's ability to correct or discipline his patron was very limited, and normally depended more on his persuasive powers than on the overt assertion of authority.[12] For it would have been undiplomatic, to say the least, for an early eleventh-century bishop to claim a father's authority over his elder brother or someone of higher social status. Moreover, asserting such a superior position conflicted with the ideal of Christian humility, to which most bishops paid at least lip service.

The hesitations bishops felt about their paternal role is reflected in the language of the letter Bishop Oliba of Vich sent to King Sancho of Navarre sometime around 1023, condemning incestuous marriages.[13] Bishop Oliba ended his letter with an appeal for the king's help in eradicating such unions: "We ask you as [our] lord, and we beg you as [our] father, and we admonish you as [our] son, not to refuse to believe our statements – or rather, these divine teachings."[14] Oliba ends by describing Sancho as his "son," but only after he has already characterized the king as "lord" and even as "father." If this is paternal authority, it is so fragile that the bishop has to hastily invoke "divine" teachings to justify his admonitions.[15]

What about the members of the bishop's flock? Did they see themselves as subject to a spiritual father's authority and discipline? Members of the lower classes may have – there is really no way to tell – but it seems unlikely that the powerful often viewed themselves as the "sons" of bishops who were actually under their control. Terms of address are important here. If we look at letters addressed by powerful laymen and laywomen to bishops from the early eleventh century, we rarely see paternal language used. While the pope – the bishop of Rome – was often addressed as "father," this undoubtedly reflects the pope's special prestige, as the successor of St. Peter. But nobles and kings – concerned about their status in

---

[11] On the social origins of bishops in this period, see Magnou-Nortier (1974), pp. 344–48; Guillemain (1974); Zielinski (1984), pp. 19–66; Bouchard (1987), pp. 67–74; Fanning (1988), pp. 19–43; Bührer-Thierry (1997), 151–52, 171–77. The situation appears to have been somewhat different in England, where the king generally chose bishops for reasons other than family connections. Barlow (1972), pp. 62–95.

[12] Bishops were also supposed to serve as moral exemplars; hence the formulaic admonition with which early eleventh-century popes recognized new archbishops, "let your life serve as a model [regula] for your sons." *Papsturkunden*, 534, 566, 595, 617, vol 2: 1016–17, 1072–73, 1121–22, 1158–59 = JL 4038, 4074, 4098, 4119.

[13] See above, Chapter 1.

[14] Oliba of Vich, *Epistolae*, 4 (PL 142, 604): "Rogamus vos ut dominum, et obsecramus ut patrem, et admonemus ut filium, quod nostris dictis, imo divinis assertinibus, credere non dedignemini."

[15] Even a severe critic of lay interference in ecclesiastical affairs like Geoffrey of Vendôme might sometimes find it politic to refer to a king as "father." Geoffrey of Vendôme, 152, p. 336.

a volatile political situation, and keenly aware of the danger of establishing legal precedents detrimental to that status – seem loath to concede even the title, let alone the authority, of "father" to lesser bishops.[16] When, for example, Duke William V of Aquitaine wrote to bishops, he sometimes addressed them as "friend," or even "brother," but never as "father."[17]

Narrative sources tell much the same tale. For example, in his life of Bishop Wulfstan of Worcester (1062–95), William of Malmesbury notes that King William the Conqueror "never caused [Wulfstan] any problems. Rather, he honoured and respected him, venerating him as a father and dignifying him by that name."[18] The fact that this is even mentioned suggests that Wulfstan had been singled out for an unusual honor that William did not normally accord to other bishops. During William the Conqueror's reign, however, a significant change – in which the reforming popes and their supporters played the leading role – was already under way. Hoping to bring an end to incestuous marriages, divorces, simony, and nicolaitism, the bishops of Rome sought to bolster the authority of their episcopal supporters.[19] One of their methods was to characterize *reforming* bishops as fathers, to whom all the laity, as well as the lesser clergy, owed filial obedience: the long-standing association of episcopal office with spiritual fatherhood was thus sharpened and turned in new directions in this period.[20]

This trend was already becoming apparent during the pontificate of Alexander II.[21] It was Gregory VII, however, who was most instrumental in promoting episcopal fatherhood.[22] For example, he wrote to the people of Tours and Angers: "You should faithfully and devotedly be obedient to [the archbishop of Tours, recently driven from his see] as your father, and should take care as good sons freely to assist his necessities."[23] Urban II, Pascal II, and Calixtus II issued similar warnings to individuals and groups within dioceses where there had been disputed

---

[16] Let alone to parish priests, many of whom were drawn in this period from the servile classes.
[17] William V of Aquitaine, *Epistolae*, 2, 4, 5 (PL 141: 829, 830, 830–31).
[18] William of Malmesbury, *Vita Wulfstani*, 2.1, in his *Saints' Lives*, pp. 60–61.
[19] In addition to their emphasis on bishops' paternal authority, discussed below, some Roman reformers also emphasized episcopal "fertility," their ability to "beget sons of God." Peter Damian, 40, vol. 1: 398; trans. Blum, 2: 118, and 112, vol. 3: 261; trans. Blum, 4: 259–60. McLaughlin (1999).
[20] Yet some hesitation was still evident: Lanfranc thanked Queen Margaret of Scotland for *asking* him to be her spiritual father. Lanfranc, 50, pp. 160–61.
[21] Alexander II, *Epistolae*, 97 (PL 146: 1384) = JL 4710. And see *Briefsammlungen*, p. 156.
[22] Gregory VII, *Register*, 8.10, 9.14, 9.16, and 9.23, pp. 529, 593, 596, and 604; trans. Cowdrey, pp. 375–76, 414–15, 416–17, 421–23. Gregory VII, *Epistolae Vagantes*, 4, 40, and 52, pp. 10, 100, and 126.
[23] Gregory VII, *Register*, 9.24, p. 606; trans. Cowdrey, p. 423.

elections, identifying the papally approved candidate, or to dioceses in which there had been resistance to a reforming bishop's authority.[24] On the other hand, simoniacal or incontinent bishops, or those who had resisted papal authority, might be denied the title of "father," and thus the obedience of their spiritual sons.[25]

This more aggressively paternal language was quickly picked up by members of the clergy – and not only by the reforming bishops' own cathedral canons and diocesan clergy. Monastic communities, which had a long tradition of submission to abbots (also characterized as fathers), readily accepted the idea of bishops wielding a father's power. Even monks from communities exempt from episcopal control still recognized episcopal paternity – perhaps because these communities were most likely to share the reforming papacy's ideas. Monks from exempt communities may have rejected the implications of their bishop's paternal role – that is, the necessity of submission to his authority – but they still accorded him the associated honor. Abbot Geoffrey of Vendôme, for example, had a sometimes difficult relationship with the bishops of Chartres. La Trinité of Vendôme was under direct papal control; as Geoffrey was fond of pointing out, the bishops of Chartres had no right to impose an interdict on La Trinité or its subject houses; he himself as abbot did not have to make profession to the bishop of Chartres.[26] At one point, Geoffrey even complained to the pope about the "injuries and persecutions" imposed by Ivo of Chartres on his monastery.[27] Yet he addressed Ivo as "lord and venerable father," promising him "what a subject son owes a beloved father and what a faithful servant owes his benevolent lord."[28]

A sign of wretched insanity

Clerics and monks might recognize the paternal authority of prelates, but kings and nobles were much more resistant. Such a concession might threaten their practical control over wealthy and influential bishoprics,

---

[24] Urban II, *Epistolae et privilegia*, 32 (PL 151: 316) = JL 5420; Pascal II, *Epistolae et diplomata*, 103, 132, 269, 320 (PL 163: 122, 141, 253, 288) = JL 5973, 5998, 6225, 6294; Calixtus II, *Epistolae et privilegia*, 64, 164, 215 (PL 163: 1152, 1229, 1277) = JL 6803, 6943, 7035.

[25] E.g. Peter Damian, 88, vol. 2: 538; trans. Blum, 3: 333 (on Cadalus of Parma as a cruel stepfather); Gregory VII, *Register*, 8.17, p. 539; trans. Cowdrey, pp. 382–83 (urging the people of Reims to elect a proper "father" for themselves, to replace the "pseudopastor" Manasses).

[26] Geoffrey of Vendôme, 10 and 81, pp. 18 and 154–58.

[27] Geoffrey of Vendôme, 74, pp. 138–40.

[28] Geoffrey of Vendôme, 38, p. 68; see also 121 and 180, pp. 236–38 and 412.

and – in the case of emperors and kings – the "symbolic capital" deriving from their unique social position.[29] By virtue of their anointing with holy oil when they were raised to the throne, such rulers claimed a status *sui generis*, somewhere between that of a cleric and a "mere" layman. Moreover, like the Biblical figures David and Solomon before them, they were the "anointed of the Lord," representing Christ himself on earth.[30] And this, of course, elevated them above any mere bishop. It was this set of assumptions about sacred kingship that the more radical reformers of the late eleventh century set out to undermine, firmly reducing anointed rulers to the status of ordinary layfolk. And the rhetoric of episcopal paternity played an important role in this endeavor.

In his famous second letter to Herman of Metz, Gregory VII spelled out the thinking behind the paternal allusions in his other letters, clarifying what he considered the proper relationship between *sacerdotes* – by whom he meant primarily bishops, although other members of the clergy were also included – and the laity, among whom he explicitly included kings and emperors:

Who may doubt that the priests of Christ are to be reckoned the fathers and masters of kings, of princes, and of all the faithful? Is it not acknowledged to be a sign of wretched insanity, if a son should try to subject to himself a father or a disciple a master, and to make subject to his power by wrongful obligations him by whom he believes that he can be bound and loosed not only on earth but also in heaven?[31]

Towards the end of his letter, Gregory invokes God's commandments concerning parents:

Let them [i.e. recalcitrant rulers] not seek to subject or subdue holy church to themselves like a handmaid, but before all else let them be concerned duly to honour her eyes, that is, the priests of the Lord, by acknowledging them as masters and fathers. For if we are commanded to obey our fathers and mothers after the flesh [Deuteronomy 5:16], how much more those after the spirit? And if he who shall curse father or mother is to be punished by death [Exodus 21:17], what does he deserve who curses his spiritual father or mother?[32]

Here *sacerdotes* are both the "eyes" of Mother Church and the fathers of the faithful. As such, they are entitled to pious obedience from their sons.

---

[29] Bourdieu (1972), esp. pp. 171–82.
[30] Bloch (1924); Tellenbach (1936), pp. 56–60; Kantorowicz (1957), pp. 42–86; Struve (1991).
[31] Gregory VII, *Register*, 8.21, p. 553; trans. Cowdrey, p. 390.
[32] Gregory VII, *Register*, 8.21, p. 562; trans. Cowdrey, p. 395.

In another letter, Gregory echoed and reworked the well-known dictum of Cyprian of Carthage, the early Church Father, that "someone cannot have God for a father who does not have the Church for a mother."[33] To a recalcitrant count he wrote, "it is clear that no one can have the love of God who is proved by the fault of his disobedience to have lost the grace and favor of a spiritual father [in this case, the local bishop]."[34] For Gregory, not kings, but bishops, in their paternal role, are the representatives of God on earth.

This new rhetorical strategy did important ideological work for the polemicists of the reform movement.[35] Cardinal Peter Damian, for example, used it in the fight against nicolaitism, condemning the marriage of bishops on the grounds that any sexual interaction between a bishop and a woman from his diocese was incestuous. Addressing a hypothetical bishop, he wrote,

All the children of the Church are undoubtedly your children. And it is also quite obvious that spiritual generation is something greater than carnal parenthood. Moreover, since you are the husband, the spouse of your church, symbolized by the ring of your betrothal and the staff of your mandate, all who are reborn in her by the sacrament of baptism must be ascribed to you as your children. Therefore, if you commit incest with your spiritual daughter, how in good conscience do you dare perform the mystery of the Lord's body?[36]

Here Peter is drawing not only on the identification of bishops with paternity, but also on contemporary understanding of other forms of spiritual kinship, notably godparenthood, which similarly precluded sexual relationships among such kin as "incestuous."[37]

Bruno of Segni attacked simony and irregular elections to clerical office though a reference to the Biblical story of Jacob, who received his father Isaac's blessing by deception, in place of his brother Esau (Genesis 27). Jacob's deception was seen as justified, because he had been sent to his father by his mother. In Bruno's treatise on simony, the Church is the Mother, the bishops take the role of fathers, and priests seeking ordination represent the sons:

They are not sent by the Mother, they are not sent by the Church, [those men] who deceive Isaac, who deceive the bishops, who wish to obtain the father's

---

[33] Cyprian of Carthage, *De ecclesiae catholicae unitate*, 6, in *Opera*, CC, SL 3: 253.

[34] Gregory VII, *Register*, 9.23, p. 604; trans. Cowdrey, pp. 421–23.

[35] See also Lanfranc, 9, pp. 68–69 on the relationship between King Guthric and Bishop Patrick of Dublin.

[36] Peter Damian, 61, vol. 2: 215; trans. Blum 3: 10–11. On the incestuous aspects of episcopal homosexuality, see Peter Damian, 31, vol. 1: 294–97, 299; trans. Blum, 2: 15–16, 19–20. Cf. McLaughlin (1998) and (1999).

[37] Lynch (1986); and see above, Chapter 1.

blessing deceptively and by theft. Therefore, and deservedly, a curse instead of a blessing is imposed on them. Only those are sent by the Mother, only those are sent by the Church, who – not because of money, not because of any promise, not through secular power, but solely through election by the clergy and people [of their city] (and that a clean election, without corruption) – are sent to the fathers, are sent to the bishops to be blessed and consecrated by them.[38]

The legitimacy of a priest's ordination thus depended on a proper relationship with his spiritual father.

Paternal imagery figured most prominently, however, in the debates about the investiture of bishops with ring and staff that raged at the beginning of the twelfth century, for investiture was intrinsically related to hierarchy. The person doing the investing – a noble or a king by custom, another bishop by the wish of the reformers – was understood as inherently superior to the person being invested, for he could only grant the symbols of episcopal office if he already possessed them. By emphasizing episcopal paternity, reformers could reverse the customary hierarchy, and undercut royal claims to grant bishops the symbols of office. Gregory VII, writing in the 1080s about a slightly different issue (whether a pope could excommunicate a king), had characterized kings as the sons of the clergy; by doing so, he made a radically new claim about the relative positions of kings and bishops, which his successors, writing about lay investiture, readily reasserted, and with which their opponents had to grapple.[39]

After William Rufus exiled him from England in 1097, Archbishop Anselm of Canterbury attended two reform councils held by Urban II, the first at Bari in 1098 and the second at Rome in 1099. The second featured an outburst by Bishop Ranger of Lucca (himself the author of a violently polemical treatise against lay investiture), directed against "secular tyrannies" in general, and against William Rufus in particular. Ranger condemned those who delayed action on Anselm's behalf. Possibly in response, Pope Urban concluded the council by excommunicating all laymen who gave investiture to clerics, and all clerics who received investiture from lay hands. In a novel move, he also declared any cleric who did homage to laymen for church property, and anyone who associated with such clerics, anathema.[40]

R. W. Southern has underlined the ambiguities surrounding this event – those who supported reform and the "liberty of the Church"

---

[38] Bruno of Segni, *Libellus de symoniacis*, MGH LL, 2: 555. Simoniacal priests represented as inheriting "leprosy" from their "fathers," the bishops who sold them their offices, can be found in Humbert, *Libri III adversus simoniacos*, 1.16, MGH LL 1: 129.

[39] E.g. Placidus of Nonantola, *Liber de honore ecclesiae*, 115, MGH LL 2: 621–22.

[40] Eadmer of Canterbury, *Historia novorum*, p. 114; trans. Bosanquet, pp. 117–18; and see Southern (1990), pp. 280–84.

may well have seen Urban's decrees of 1099 as "expressions of hope or at best long-term intention, rather than as strictly enforceable legislative acts."[41] Even members of the papal curia apparently thought of investiture and homage as two very different issues. Lay investiture had been repeatedly condemned since the time of Gregory VII; homage never, so its prohibition was legally more problematic, as well as vastly more difficult to enforce. Few churchmen, either in Rome or without, were willing to deny kings their right to homage in 1099. Anselm, however, in whose monastic background obedience to superiors was the preeminent virtue, immediately took the position that he was bound to follow both papal pronouncements to the letter.[42]

After Rufus' death, his younger brother took the English throne as Henry I. Anxious to show himself a good Christian, to resolve some of the many problems plaguing the English church, and to have his own wedding celebrated with suitable ceremony, Henry invited Anselm back to England. But when, as was customary, he asked Anselm to renew his homage, the archbishop refused. And if Henry attempted to invest new bishops, Anselm warned, he would have nothing to do either with the king or with those he had invested. This came as a considerable shock to Henry, who considered himself a supporter of reform – at least as it pertained to simony and nicolaitism. He wanted Anselm to remain in England, but he was equally unwilling to give up the privileges exercised by his forebears.

Intense negotiations continued between 1100 and 1103, with the new pope, Pascal II, expressing more willingness to compromise on the issue of homage than Archbishop Anselm. Nevertheless, all three – Pascal and Anselm on one side, Henry on the other – stuck stubbornly to their positions on investiture. In 1103, Anselm again traveled to Rome to consult with the pope; during his absence from England, both sides raised the stakes. Henry's envoys warned Anselm not to return unless he was willing to do homage; the king also seized Canterbury's temporal possessions. Pascal, for his part, responded by excommunicating the king's counselors and threatening the king himself with excommunication. Anselm added his own threat of excommunication in 1104. Apparently this was what led the king's sister, Countess Adela of Blois, to broker a meeting between king and archbishop in 1105, which led to a personal reconciliation. But it took another two years for a compromise on the most difficult issues to be reached and publicly promulgated, with the encouragement of the pope. In a council held at London in August 1107, Henry announced he would give up investiture, while Anselm – unwillingly – agreed to look the other way when other bishops did homage for the temporalities of their sees.

---

[41] Southern (1990), p. 282.   [42] Southern (1990), p. 283.

We have already seen the degree to which ideas about the authority of Mother Church informed Pascal II's letters to Henry I. Both sides of the controversy also relied heavily on ideas about paternity. In a letter from the late spring or early summer of 1101, Pascal reminded Henry to "render unto God the things which are God's and to Caesar the things which are Caesar's" (Matthew 22:21) – reversing the usual order of the phrases, perhaps to suggest the priority of the "things which are God's."[43] Recalling that a bishop is the husband of his church, and that a church not "properly married" is an adulteress, Pascal relegates the king to what the pope considered his proper place:

> Do you see, O King, how ignominious, how perilous it is for a mother to be polluted by adultery through her sons? If, therefore, you are a son of the Church – as every catholic Christian is – allow your mother to enter into legitimate matrimony, so that the Church may be joined to a legitimate spouse, not through man, but through God and Christ the Man ...

This reference to his duty towards his Mother also reminds Henry what he owes to his spiritual father. Pascal points out that any effort by the king (now established as "son") to "make" a bishop is unnatural: "Really, it is monstrous for a son to generate a father, for a man to create God. (It is clear that in Holy Scripture priests are called 'gods,' since they are God's vicars.)"[44] A cascade of similitudes – God/bishop/father and man/king/son – streams through this letter (like Gregory VII's), to show that royal investiture of bishops destroys the right order of the world. But the father–son relationship is the lynchpin, providing the crucial link between terms. Because the bishop is almost automatically identified as a spiritual father, Pascal can easily associate him with God (as in Gregory's letter, with masters), leaving the king (who might otherwise have been able to claim the role of God/master) in the subordinate position of man/disciple. And this, in turn, makes royal efforts to control bishops "monstrous"; that is, contrary to nature (for Gregory, "insane").

Anselm himself was reluctant to act the father, addressing Henry not imperiously, but humbly (as befitted a monk, perhaps more than an archbishop). While he refuses to acquiesce to Henry's demands for homage and investiture, his rhetoric always remains submissive: "As a faithful archbishop to his lord and king, I pray and counsel you ...";[45] "as a faithful servant and bishop, I advise, beg, and ... entreat ...";[46] "I beseech you to let me know your will if it pleases you, whether I may return to

---

[43] Pascal II, *Epistolae*, 49, (PL 163: 71) = JL 5868.
[44] Pascal II, *Epistolae*, 49 (PL 163: 71) = JL 5868; cf. 101 (PL 163: 120) = JL 5956.
[45] Anselm, 265, vol. 4 : 180; trans. Fröhlich, vol. 2 : 264.
[46] Anselm, 294, vol. 4 : 214; trans. Fröhlich, vol. 2: 310.

England …";[47] "I beseech you as my dearest lord, whose soul I love more than the present life of my body, and I advise you as a true friend of your body and soul …".[48]

Eadmer, Anselm's friend and biographer, was less squeamish. References to fatherhood pepper his account of these events. Some have to do with Anselm's relationship with his monks. Thus, traveling incognito in France, Anselm and his two companions agree to pass themselves off as three simple monks, concealing Anselm's paternal authority: "We went just as if we three were equals, our Father dropping in the presence of others any right of command."[49] However, Eadmer also consistently represented the archbishop's relationship with the king as a father–son bond. When Anselm quarreled with William Rufus, the king no longer recognized Anselm "as either archbishop or as his spiritual father."[50] Yet before Anselm left for Rome, Rufus allowed the archbishop to bless him, "as a spiritual father to a beloved son."[51] Eadmer, then, does not hesitate to place Anselm squarely in the paternal position, with the right both to bless and to command his spiritual sons.

Of course, Anselm's opponents had their own views on the relative position of bishops and kings in God's household. Sometime between 1102 and 1105, these were spelled out in a treatise *On Royal Power and Sacerdotal Dignity*, which Hugh, a monk of Fleury, addressed to Henry I. It is not entirely clear how a French monk got interested in events in England. Perhaps Hugh was encouraged to write by his friend and teacher, Bishop Ivo of Chartres, or by King Henry's sister, Adela of Blois (a friend of Ivo's and the patron of Hugh's monastery of Fleury) – the same woman who helped orchestrate the ultimate reconciliation between Anselm and Henry.[52] In any case, Hugh's treatise responds not to Pascal II directly, but to the claim Gregory VII had made two decades earlier, in his second letter to Herman of Metz (apparently made available to Hugh by the Gregorian chronicler, Hugh of Flavigny), that royal power was not ordained by God, and so must be inferior to that of priests.[53] Hugh of Fleury's retort that "there is no power but of God" (Romans 13:1) suggests that royal power

[47] Anselm, 308, vol. 4 : 231; trans. Fröhlich, vol. 2: 334.
[48] Anselm, 391, vol. 5: 336; trans. Fröhlich, vol. 3: 151.
[49] Eadmer, *Historia novorum*, p. 95; trans. Bosanquet, p. 99.
[50] Eadmer, *Historia novorum*, p. 63; trans. Bosanquet, p. 64.
[51] Eadmer, *Historia novorum*, p. 87; trans. Bosanquet, p. 91. Eadmer applied paternal language to the relationship between kings and archbishops elsewhere in this work: see pp. 11, 40; he also represented Anselm as a father to the English people in general: see pp. 61, 119, 147, 162.
[52] Hugh composed other works for Adela. See Ferrante (1997), pp. 96–98.
[53] Gregory VII, *Register*, 8. 21, esp. pp. 552–53; trans. Cowdrey, esp. p. 390. Cited by Hugh of Flavigny, *Chronicon*, 2, MGH SS 8: 453–58.

and priestly authority both have divine backing; they should work together for the good of the kingdom.

Nevertheless, at the beginning of Book One of his treatise, Hugh allows that divine order requires a single ruler: just as one man (Adam) originally had dominion over all the animals, just as one head governs all members of the human body, and just as God himself is the sole king of all creation.[54] Even in more complex systems, one power is always superior. Thus, while man and woman are of one substance, yet woman was created from man, and therefore man is greater in degree (*gradu*). And while within the Trinity, God the Father and Christ the Son are also of one substance, yet the Father is greater, not by nature, but by rank (*ordo*).[55] So, within the "body" of a kingdom, Hugh argues, the king represents (literally, "is in the image of") God the Father, while the bishop stands for Christ, the Son. And therefore, "rightly all the bishops of this kingdom are subject to the king, just as the Son is understood to be subject to the Father, not by nature, but by rank [*ordo*, again] – so that the entire kingdom may be reduced to a single root [*ad unum redigatur principium*]."[56] (This last sentence is repeated almost verbatim in the final section of the treatise, underlining its centrality in Hugh's thought.[57]) Hugh, like Pascal II, lines up a series of similitudes (Adam/head/God/man vs. animals/members/creation/ woman), but here apparently in a last-ditch effort to resist what by now was an almost irresistible trope – that of the bishop as father.

Between the middle of the eleventh century and 1100, a major change had taken place, if not in the actual relationship between kings and bishops, at least in how that relationship was articulated. Even kings (and their supporters) increasingly acknowledged the paternal authority of bishops. Whereas William the Conqueror calling Wulfstan "father" was a sign of special favor, Henry I regularly recognized Anselm as "father" in his letters.[58] Only during their periods of estrangement did he fail to address Anselm in this way – and even then, his wife, the queen, attempting to intervene in the quarrel, continued to appeal to her "spiritual father."[59]

---

[54] Hugh of Fleury, *De regia potestate et sacerdotali dignitate*, 1.1, MGH, LL 2: 467.
[55] Hugh of Fleury, *De regia potestate*, 1.2, MGH LL 2: 468.
[56] Hugh of Fleury, *De regia potestate*, 1.3, MGH LL 2: 468.
[57] Hugh of Fleury, *De regia potestate*, 2.4, MGH LL 2: 490.
[58] Henry's letters are included among those of Anselm. The relevant numbers are: 212, 367, 370, 371, 377, 396, 399, 401, 461, 470, vol. 4: 109–10, and vol. 5: 311, 314, 320–21, 340, 343–44, 345, 410–11, 418–19; trans. Fröhlich, vol. 2: 162–63, and vol. 3: 116, 120–21, 130, 156, 162, 164, 251–52, 263.
[59] Matilda's letters, included among those of Anselm: 242, 317, 400, vol. 4: 150–52 and vol. 5: 244–46, 344; trans. Fröhlich, vol. 2: 221–24 and vol. 3: 22–24, 163. See also the queen's letter to Pascal II: Anselm, 323, vol. 5: 253–54; trans. Fröhlich, vol. 3: 34–36.

In the end, even Hugh of Fleury was forced to admit that the relationship he envisioned between kings and bishops might sometimes be reversed, with bishops in the superior role. Bishops, he says, have the right and the duty to correct erring kings. Someone who fails to show obedience to "holy" bishops (the adjective is, perhaps, significant – indicating that less holy bishops might *not* be owed obedience) shows disdain for God. As a result, "every Christian should rightly seek to escape from the bonds of sin through their aid, and should honor and revere them *as fathers and as lords*."[60] In matters of sin, then, kings should account bishops their fathers, and render them honor – as hard as he tries, Hugh cannot completely evade Gregory VII's net.

The best of sons

Within the general trend just described, the popes represent a special case. From at least the fourth century on, the successors of St. Peter had been recognized as exercising a kind of universal fatherhood among the faithful. It was in that period that the Roman pontiff came to be addressed by Christians not only within, but also outside his own diocese with the title *papa* or "pope" (a term with Greek roots for a revered and beloved father).[61] At first this title was by no means restricted to the bishop of Rome. John Moorhead has shown that until the sixth century even members of the Roman Church sometimes addressed other bishops as *papa*, while Christians from Gaul sometimes referred to bishops from their own region as "popes" well into the ninth century.[62] Nevertheless, within the western church, the bishop of Rome soon came to be seen as the topmost (at least on earth) in a hierarchy of spiritual fathers.

This does not mean, however, that he used his paternal position to dominate either important members of the laity or other bishops. The ideal of episcopal humility would have made this very difficult in any case. From the time of Gregory I (590–604) on, the popes began to refer to themselves as the "servants of the servants of God" – how could they, at the same time, insist they were the spiritual heads of the ecclesiastical household? It is significant that when Gregory I uses the rhetoric of paternity or filiation in his letters to rulers, it is to speak of his concern, love, or affection for them.[63] A barbarian ruler of Britain, Gaul, or Italy might be addressed as "most excellent son," "most glorious

---

[60] Hugh of Fleury, *De regia potestate*, 2.2, MGH LL 2: 487. Added emphasis.
[61] On early occurrences of the term, see Pietri (1976), 2: 1608–11; Moorhead (1985).
[62] Moorhead (1985), pp. 337–38, 347–49. Moorhead also notes that in the modern Eastern Orthodox Church, the Patriarch of Alexandria continues to use the title "pope."
[63] On Gregory's letters, see Jasper and Fuhrmann (2001), pp. 70–81.

son," and so on, thereby invoking the bonds of charity between them, while still reassuring his correspondent that the pope recognized his exalted position.[64] Gregory greeted such rulers, recommended travelers to them, made requests of them, responded to their queries, and even offered advice with "fatherly love" or "fatherly sweetness."[65] However, he never took advantage of his position as their spiritual father to issue commands.

The difficulties Gregory I felt in asserting paternal authority over kings are evident from a letter he sent to the Frankish king Theudebert in 601. The pope wanted Theudebert to call a synod to legislate against simony in the Frankish church, and in this letter he came very close to making his wish a command: "Whoever adopts the words of paternal encouragement with a willing mind, and embraces them in the depths of his heart, without doubt declares that he will be a corrector of vices," the letter begins, reminding the king to follow the pope's advice. Gregory then goes further, asking Theudebert to "adhere to the orders of our God," and "deign to ensure," for his own (heavenly) reward, that a synod be held. "And," he continues,

because, indeed, we are saying this for your sake, we do not cease to threaten you more often, for the reason that we might be able to benefit our most excellent and most charming sons, even by incivility. For it is an advantage for your kingdom in every way, if what is done contrary to God in those parts is corrected by the reproof of your Excellency.[66]

In pushing even as hard as he does in this letter, Gregory recognizes that he might be guilty of "incivility." He therefore introduces an apologetic tone and rapidly effaces the more assertive paternal self that had crept into the letter. First, he attributes his own orders to God, then reminds Theudebert that he makes his demand for the synod for the king's own sake. Finally, he reestablishes the king (presumably along with his brother, Theodoric) in the enviable role of "our most excellent and most charming [!] sons."

The only other early medieval pope whose register of letters survives (albeit in fragmentary form) is John VIII (872–82).[67] His use of paternal rhetoric is very different from Gregory I's, anticipating that of his successors in the late eleventh century. It is, perhaps, not an accident

---

[64] E.g. Gregory I, *Registrum epistolarum*, 5.60, 9.216, 11.35, 11.37, CC, SL vol. 140: 360–62; vol. 140A: 776–79, 923–24, 929–32.

[65] E.g. Gregory I, *Registrum epistolarum*, 5.60, 6.51, 9, 214, 11.51, CC, SL vol. 140: 360–62, 423–24, vol. 140A: 772–73, 950–51.

[66] Gregory I, *Registrum epistolarum*, 11.50, CC, SL vol. 140A: 949–50.

[67] All of John VIII letters, including the register and the *vagantes*, are published in MGH, EPP, 7: 1–329. On the register, see Jasper and Fuhrmann (2001), pp. 127–30.

that John's register survives in a copy made during the eleventh century at a dependency of Montecassino – that center of reform activity, which produced Gregory VII's successor as pope, Victor III (1087).[68] Presumably it was copied for the privileges for Montecassino it contains. However, John's more aggressive rhetoric probably appealed to these supporters of reform, and may have shaped their ideas about the papal role.

Unlike any of his predecessors, John VIII often referred to himself as "Our Paternity" (*paternitas nostra*) in official documents. Most likely this reflects John's ambition, and forms part of his pattern of efforts to raise the status of the Roman see.[69] His letters are rich in references to Biblical fathers and to spiritual fatherhood, which he sometimes used to assert his authority over bishops, nobles, and rulers.[70] Yet unlike Gregory I, John VIII was never revered either as a theologian or as a spiritual leader, and his letters never had as wide a circulation. His ambitious rhetoric appears to have had little impact on his immediate successors, for the phrase "Our Paternity" virtually disappears from papal documents after his pontificate.[71] At the beginning of the eleventh century, it is Gregory I's rhetorical model that is being followed, not John VIII's.

Early eleventh-century popes refer to only a small number of rulers – primarily the Holy Roman Emperors – as "sons," and normal protocol in this period apparently still called for qualifying these references in ways that weakened any suggestion of hierarchy between papal father and imperial child. Thus Pope Benedict VIII addressed a letter to "always his most beloved lord in Christ, and most serene highness, Henry [II of Germany], crowned by God, and his own spiritual son."[72] In letters between popes and emperors (or, for that matter, other rulers), paternal rhetoric was still primarily limited to the granting of requests with

---

[68] On Montecassino during the reform period, see Cowdrey (1983).

[69] Scholz (2006), pp. 224–39.

[70] Many of these letters simply express fatherly affection for the recipient, but others praise high-ranking individuals, including the Byzantine emperor, for their devotion to "our paternity" (suggesting that the recipient has recognized the pope's even higher status): e.g. John VIII, *Epistolae*, 249, 255, 259, MGH EPP 7: 217, 222, 229 = JL 3307, 3319, 3323. Still other letters use the phrase "our paternity" in issuing commands to nobles and bishops: *Epistolae* 83, 175, 273, MGH EPP 7: 78, 141, 241 = JL 3119, 3237, 3343. John VIII's more assertive rhetoric reflects, of course, the changing claims of the papacy described above in Chapter 4, as well as the changes that had occurred in the eight century in the relationship between the papacy and the Carolingian family in particular. see Angenendt (1980).

[71] Search in the PL database for *paternitas nostra* and variants.

[72] *Papsturkunden*, 478, vol. 2: 907 = JL 3996; cf. 435, 484, 548, 581, vol. 2: 832, 919, 1040, 1098 = JL 3954, 4001, 4059, 4087.

"paternal love" and so on. The surviving letters of the early eleventh-century popes contain no direct commands to rulers at all.

From the middle of the eleventh century on, however, papal use of paternal rhetoric accelerated and changed. As the reforming popes crafted a stronger paternal role for bishops, they did the same for themselves. The strongest language comes not directly from the popes, but from their closest supporters. Thus, in *The Debate at the Synod*, his carefully worded criticism of the imperial court for its support of the wrong candidate in the disputed election of 1061, Peter Damian not only represents the Roman Church as the true mother of the child-emperor; he also baldly asserts that the pope is the emperor's father, and thus ultimately his superior: "as a father, [he] should always enjoy paramount dignity by reason of his paternal rights."[73] In their own letters, on the other hand, the reforming popes were generally more circumspect, their claims to paternal authority often muted. Projecting the role of parent onto either the Roman Church or the figure of St. Peter, they imply – but never explicitly state – their own position as father.

As Mother Rome began to play a more assertive role herself in the letters of the reforming popes, her earthly bridegroom, the pope, increasingly emerged as father of the faithful. In a letter to Sweyn of Denmark, Gregory VII praised the king and his people for showing proper reverence to the "Mother of all churches," and then "charges" Sweyn, "our most beloved son," "with fatherly affection" to ask if the pope can help him in any way.[74] Gregory's early eleventh-century predecessors had sent the same kind of letters to rulers, offering them favors out of paternal love. What makes this one different is its opening:

Among our predecessors it was a matter of right and custom by caritative embassies to teach the way of the Lord to all nations, to reprove kings and princes in matters that called for accusation, and by lawful disciplines to invite all men to eternal blessedness.

By framing the rest of the letter in terms of the power to teach, reprove, and discipline, this passage establishes the pope, as father, as well as Mother Rome, in positions of clear superiority to the Danish king.

Always looming behind the paternal figure of the pope was that of St. Peter. The prince of the apostles was, of course, central to papal ideology in many ways in this period.[75] But emphasizing his paternity allowed the

---

[73] Peter Damian, 89, vol. 2: 572; trans. Blum, 3: 368; cf. 46, vol. 2: 41; trans. Blum 2: 251.

[74] Gregory VII, *Register*, 2.75, p. 238; trans. Cowdrey, pp. 170–71.

[75] Meulenberg (1965), pp. 20, 124; Maccarrone (1974), p. 98, and (1989); Cowdrey (1998a), pp. 521–23.

reforming popes to highlight his, and thus their, authority in a particularly concrete way. The enlarged significance of Peter's paternity during the reform period is reflected in the custom – apparently new at this time – of recognizing certain individuals as "sons" or "daughters" of St. Peter.[76] In a polite letter to the Empress Agnes, dated to 1060, Peter Damian wrote, "For many years the Roman Church has not been in greater debt to anyone of imperial majesty than to your honor, from whose active and holy devotion it has received many great benefits. Thus, indeed, you are rightly called the daughter of blessed Peter, the prince of the apostles ...".[77] In 1066–67, Countess Matilda of Tuscany helped her husband drive the Normans out of Campania. Bonizo of Sutri noted that "not long afterwards," "for this and many services pleasing to God," she was also designated a "daughter of St. Peter."[78] This, then, seems a special honorific, bestowed on important women and men who had done outstanding services for the papacy.[79] Apparently, too, this form of recognition had a wide circulation – that is, people outside of Rome heard about it, whether through the papacy itself or through the person being honored. The anti-Gregorian Wenrich of Trier – writing far from Rome – noted that the anti-king Rudolf of Swabia had had several divorces – yet despite this "crime," Wenrich remarked sarcastically, "he is called the son of St. Peter."[80]

If they were hesitant to assert their own paternal authority, the popes apparently felt no compunction about characterizing Peter as a father, who could discipline kings, as well as ordinary layfolk.[81] And of course, as his successors, they shared – if only indirectly – in his power to command. When Gregory VII wrote to chide Henry IV for associating with his excommunicated counselors, he opened his letter by offering the king

[76] A search of the PL database reveals no occurrence of the phrase *filia(us) beati(sancti) Petri* before the mid-eleventh century.

[77] Peter Damian, 71, vol. 2: 323–24; trans. Blum3: 113; cf. Alexander II, *Epistolae*, 145 (PL 146: 1417) = JL 4767.

[78] Bonizo of Sutri, *Liber ad amicum*, 50, MGH LL 1: 599; cf. 75, p. 620. From this point on, Matilda was repeatedly referred to in this way. See Gregory VII, *Register*, 1.11, 1.47, and 2.9, pp. 18, 73, and 139; trans. Cowdrey, pp. 11–12, 51–53, 103–04. Gregory VII, *Epistolae vagantes*, 19, p. 50; Urban II, *Epistolae*, 51, 63, 143, 267 (PL 151: 330, 344, 419, 527) = JL 5449, 5464, 5567, 5738; Pascal II, *Epistolae*, 166 (PL 163: 177) = JL 6052; Calixtus II, *Epistolae*, 203 (PL 163: 1266) = JL 7017; Hugh of Lyons (papal legate), *Epistolae*, 9 (PL 157: 514); Bernold of St. Blasien, *Chronicon*, a. 1093, MGH SS 5: 455.

[79] E.g. on Rudolf of Swabia: Gregory VII, *Register*, 2.45, p. 185; trans. Cowdrey, pp. 135–36.

[80] Wenrich of Trier, *Epistola sub Theoderici episcopi Virdunensis nomina composita*, 7, MGH LL 1: 294.

[81] E.g. Calixtus II, *Epistolae*, 275 (PL 163: 1324) = JL 7166, on Peter as the "common father of all Christians."

his blessings only if "he shall show himself obedient to the apostolic see as befits a Christian king." Recalling how Henry has called himself "a son of holy Mother Church and ourself," Gregory places himself in the paternal role. But he also delicately suggests that his authority comes through St. Peter, head of the spiritual household of the Church: "It would have befitted your royal position, since you declare yourself a son of the church, to have regarded more respectfully the master of the church, that is, blessed Peter, the prince of the apostles."[82] Though Gregory carefully avoids any direct demand for filial obedience to himself here, it is clear that the subservience of early eleventh-century popes has given way to a confident assertion of their *patriapotestas*.

Elsewhere, the identification of St. Peter with the pope is played off against the paternity of an earthly progenitor. In November of 1077, Gregory VII wrote to Harald Hein, who had recently succeeded his father, Sweyn, as king of the Danes.[83] At first he invokes the Roman Church as Sweyn's mother:

With what persistent affection and love our holy and universal mother, namely the Roman Church, maintained her concern for your father and her solicitude for his honor you clearly know, nor do we fear that this has been lost to your memory, since you will be able to remember how he always exhibited in all things pure reverence in subjection and due obedience towards the honor of the blessed apostle Peter. We know that in his time he was, as the apostolic church testifies, a son so devout, so faithful, so unparalleled in the zeal of his love, that he was found second to none among kings.

Sweyn is identified as a "son" in the second sentence, and presumably a son not only of the Mother Church of Rome but also of St. Peter, since it is to Peter that he has shown proper filial obedience.

This is made explicit in the next paragraph, as an elaborate interplay between secular and spiritual fatherhood begins.[84] It is Harald's duty to atone for his father's sins:

We also urge you to help him with generous grants of alms and with the prayers of churches, as befits the best of sons. It is fitting indeed that he who, as a good father, left you the heir of his corporal and secular kingdom or honor, not seem to be defrauded of as much spiritual assistance as possible, since those goods which the honor of your father's kingdom provides for you, once given into the

---

[82] Gregory VII, *Register*, 3.10, pp. 263–64; trans. Cowdrey, pp. 187–90.
[83] Gregory VII, *Register*, 5.10, pp. 361–63; trans. Cowdrey, pp. 255–56. On the background of this letter, see Cowdrey (1998a), pp. 456–57.
[84] Something similar occurs in a series of letters from Lanfranc to Earl Roger of Hereford. Lanfranc, 31–33, pp. 118–23.

hands of the poor, will confer the assistance of eternal repose on your father in heaven.

Harald owes it to his father to provide him with alms and prayers to assist him in the next world. But he also owes it to Sweyn to become a son of St. Peter, and thereby of the pope:

Now, truly, beloved son, we urge you at our apostolic invitation, that the faith and love which your father showed towards the apostolic church, you now provide in your heart; extend [that faith and love] by faith, mentally turn towards [them], and thus show yourself to be the son of the Apostle Peter, so that regarding you with a serene countenance, he [i.e. Peter] may introduce you into your inheritance in the heavenly kingdom, into the place of due reward, as a worthy offspring.

After exhorting Harald to rule his kingdom with justice and mercy, Gregory reminds him that the Church – "our mother and mistress" – is in great danger in Denmark, as elsewhere. He urges the king "paternally" to help and defend her, thus reestablishing himself as the king's current father, taking the place of both Sweyn and St. Peter. Designation as a "son of St. Peter," this letter suggests, implies Harald's obligation to obey the pope.

In his letters, Gregory VII provided a rhetorical model for later popes who hoped to claim the same kind of position. Urban II also used St. Peter as an authoritative stand-in. Writing to the bishops of France, Urban explained how "his dear son," King Philip I, had pledged "in our hands, or rather, through us, in the hands of blessed Peter," never again to have "carnal relations" with Bertrade, Philip's notorious partner in adultery.[85] However, the pope found additional ways to establish himself as a father. Writing early in his pontificate to King Alfonso VI of Castile, Urban cites the famous letter of Pope Gelasius to the fifth-century Emperor Anastasius: "Two there are … by which this world is chiefly ruled, the sacred authority of the priesthood and the royal power." "But the priestly dignity, beloved son, so far excels royal power," Urban continues, "that we shall have to answer to the King of the Universe for these same kings. And therefore, pastoral duty compels us to provide for the salvation not only of ordinary people, but also of the great." Gelasius had used no paternal or filial imagery in writing to Anastasius, except to designate him as "son." Urban, on the other hand, writing to his "most beloved son," urges Alfonso to pay more attention to the wishes of the primate of Spain, Archbishop Bernard of Toledo: "Listen to him, as a beloved father, and whatever he conveys to you on behalf of the Lord, take care to obey."[86] This very delicately worded letter presents

---

[85] Urban II, *Epistolae*, 285 (PL 151: 538–39) = JL 5774.

the pope as the affectionate father, careful of his spiritual son's well-being, while only insinuating – both through the reference to Gelasius and by representing one of the pope's subordinates as a father in his own right – the king's filial duty to obey Urban himself.

It is within the context of this kind of cautious papal/paternal "self-fashioning" that we may return to the events that occurred at Cremona in the spring of 1095.[87] Conrad had rebelled against his father, the Emperor Henry IV, two years earlier; now his alliance with the reforming papacy was sealed through a series of ceremonies. As the official account of the papal curia put it:

> on April 10, as Pope Urban came to Cremona, King Conrad II went out to him and performed the *officium stratoris* [groom service]. Later, on April 15, he swore an oath of security to him in good faith, without fraud or evil intent, concerning his life and limbs, or injury, and concerning the acquisition, tenure and defence of the Roman papacy and the regalia of St. Peter – both within Rome and without – against all men.[88]

Scholars have long wrangled over the meaning of Conrad's oath, as reported in this and other sources – did it, for example, imply vassalage to the pope? Considerable research has also been devoted to the significance of the *officium stratoris*, a curious ceremony (possibly based on the description of an encounter between Constantine and Pope Sylvester I in the forged *Donation of Constantine*) in which the young king held the pope's stirrup for him.[89]

What has not received a great deal of attention is the event which followed Conrad's performance of the *officium stratoris*. Contemporary chroniclers, as well as the curial account, agree that the pope "received" Conrad as "a son of the Roman Church" and promised to help him in

> acquiring and holding and defending the kingdom, and when God granted him to come for his crown, to give him the crown of the empire and to help him in other matters to the honor of God and of St. Peter and of the Roman Church, that is to say, saving the justice of this Church and the papal decrees, especially concerning investiture.[90]

Modern historians have noted the papal promise to support Conrad in his quest for the imperial title, as well as the conditions attached to that promise. However, they have tended to ignore the preceding

---

[86] Urban II, *Epistolae*, 6 (PL 151: 289–90) = JL 5367.

[87] See above, Chapter 5.

[88] *Urbani II et Conradi regis conventus*, MGH Constitutiones, 1: 564.

[89] Much of the discussion is summarized by Becker (1964–88), 1: 133–36.

[90] *Urbani II et Conradi regis conventus*, MGH Constitutiones, 1: 564; cf. Bernold of St. Blasien, *Chronicon*, a. 1095, MGH SS, 5: 463.

statement: that Pope Urban "received" (*assumpsit* or *recepit*) Conrad as a "son of the Roman Church." Was this merely a rhetorical flourish, of no particular significance? Probably not, for other people were similarly identified as special "sons" or "daughters" of the Roman Church during this period.[91] Was this equivalent to the honor, discussed earlier, of being designated the "son" or "daughter" of St. Peter? (If the Roman Church was their mother, then presumably Peter would be the father.) Whatever the exact meaning of the phrase, there seems to have been some sort cere- mony involved. In both the curial account and the chronicles, Conrad's "reception" as a "son of the Roman Church" is treated as a kind of par- allel to the *officium stratoris*. Just as Conrad performed the groom service, and then swore his oath to the pope, so Urban – in a physical enactment of the reforming popes' claim to be the "fathers" of kings – received Conrad as a son, and then made him a promise of aid.

Some indications concerning Urban's state of mind on this occasion may be gleaned from a letter he wrote a year later to Koloman, the new king of Hungary, reminding him of Hungary's traditionally close asso- ciation with the reformed papacy, which dated back to the time of King Stephen: "Dearest son, you should obey the princes of divine power, Peter and Paul, and faithfully exhibit that subjection and honor towards their Church which was instituted by the aforesaid ruler."[92] Here Urban invokes the king's duty towards the two patron saints of Rome, while also calling Koloman "son," in an indirect bid for the same "subjection and honor." The pope also urges Koloman to avoid contact with Henry IV, framing his admonition in such a way as to contrast his own paternal role with that of two "bad fathers."

Twelve years earlier, Henry had driven Gregory VII from Rome and installed an antipope on the throne of St. Peter. Wibert, formerly arch- bishop of Ravenna, now claiming to be pope and therefore father of the faithful, is the first of the "bad fathers." Urban highlights Wibert's role in a classic Oedipal drama, in which the antipope usurps the place of his own spiritual father:

We believe it is not unknown to you how the heresiarch Wibert (excommuni- cated and condemned by all catholics everywhere), against divine law – note it well – against the law of the gospel, against the decrees of the sacred canons, came into the marriage bed of a living father and lord, invaded the pontifical

---

[91] Urban II, *Epistolae*, 18 (PL 151: 302) = JL 5398; cf. 40 (PL 151: 322) = 5433. In these two cases, the designation *speciali electione* as "sons of the Roman Church" provides religious communities with exemption from the control of their diocesan bishop. On exemption, see above, Chapter 4.

[92] Urban II, *Epistolae*, 207 (PL 151: 481) = JL 5662.

chair of Gregory VII of apostolic memory, and committed incest [*incestavit*] with the Roman Church, the Mother of all the faithful.

Joining his colleague Anselm of Lucca, who attacked Wibert on similar grounds, Urban unveils the antipope's crime as incest – as an intrusion into the marriage bed of his father, the pope, and his mother, the Roman Church.

Ultimately, however, it was Henry IV – the other "bad father" – who was to blame for Wibert's crimes. Henry was the "author of this iniquity and presumption," but divine justice had already imposed a punishment on him:

> Given over to wicked sensuality, and doing things which are not only unseemly, but indeed which are execrable to God and men, he was exposed to public ignominy ... Indeed, those whom he held most intimate, whom he loved as his own flesh, not only his closest associates, but even his own son, despised him for his abominable practices, and removed themselves from his company. Already, through the mercy and judgment of God, he has lost the principal part of his kingdom, that in which the Roman Church lies.

The son who abandoned Henry was, of course, young Conrad, who – in becoming king of Italy – deprived his father of what a pope would naturally see as the "principal part of his kingdom."

But this was not all of Henry's punishment; he had also been exposed to "public ignominy." Urban is clearly thinking of the council held at Piacenza in March 1095 – just a month before Conrad's meeting with the pope. At Piacenza, Henry's second wife, the Empress Eupraxia, already separated from her husband, complained to the pope and council about what some modern historians coyly refer to as "maltreatment." In fact, the sources tell us she described "unheard-of, filthy fornication," sexual sins which she claimed Henry not only performed himself, but forced her to perform, and for which she asked absolution from the pope.[93] Conrad clearly did not rebel against his father because of these shocking revelations. In the first place, Eupraxia was his stepmother, not his biological mother, and he seems to have had little contact with her. Moreover, Conrad was crowned king of Italy in 1093, long before she made her allegations about Henry. Still, Urban's letter to Koloman of Hungary, like Cardinal Deusdedit's *Little Book* and the *Annals of St. Disibod*, links

---

[93] Bernold of St. Blasien, *Chronicon*, a. 1095, MGH SS, 5: 462: "conquesta est de inauditis fornicationum spurciciis." Cardinal Deusdedit provided further details, reporting that Eupraxia had been forced to sleep with men other than her husband. Deusdedit, *Libellus contra invasores et symoniacos et reliquos scismaticos*, 1, MGH LL, 2: 300. Recent scholarship suggests that Eupraxia had been married by Henry essentially as a hostage for the good behavior of the Saxons; when the Saxons rebelled again, Henry retaliated by turning his wife over to his men for gang rape. Althoff (2006), pp. 216–17.

the mistreatment of Conrad's stepmother and his revolt. The young king is represented as rightly despising his father, whose debauchery parallels Wibert of Ravenna's "incest" with his father's "wife."

Urban never explicitly says Conrad turned away from these two wicked fathers to seek another, better, one in Urban himself. But surely that was how the pope, at least, must have understood Conrad's reception as a "son of the Roman Church" in 1095. The events at Cremona took their meaning as much from the reforming papacy's own growing assertion of paternal authority, and from its attack on the paternal claims of Henry IV and Wibert of Ravenna, as from the specific details of a young king's quarrel with his father.

The development of the theme of papal paternity made it easy to characterize rulers who opposed the popes not only as bad rulers, but also as treacherous sons (or sometimes as evil fathers). In his final letters, Henry IV had compared himself to King David and complained of betrayal by his beloved "Absalom." A few decades later, the English chronicler Orderic Vitalis turned Henry's own language of troubled fatherhood against him, this time characterizing Gregory VII as David, and Henry IV, the pope's spiritual son, as Absalom:

It had, I think, totally escaped [Henry's] memory how Absalom gathered great forces against his father David, waged war by the advice of Achitophel the Gileonite, attacked Jerusalem while his father withdrew his forces, and finally destroyed many thousand warriors; but nevertheless, after he had wrought his evil will on many, himself died a wretched death. Similarly Henry took up arms against his father [Gregory] and afterwards endured harsh persecution at the hands of his own son.[94]

According to Orderic, then, Henry V's rebellion was just retribution for Henry IV's unfilial behavior towards the pope.

In fact, the rebellion of 1104–6 was welcomed at first by reformers; however, after Henry V forced Pascal II to rescind the ban on lay investiture in 1111, it, too, was reinterpreted as a sign of his inherent impiety. Several polemicists compared Henry V's attacks on his earthly and spiritual fathers (Henry IV and Pascal II), and argued that in both cases he had ignored divine commandments to honor and not to curse his parents.[95] The anonymous author of one of these treatises laid out precisely what Henry's crimes were:

The mouth of the Lord has spoken: He that curses his father or mother shall surely be put to death [Exodus 21:17]. And so imperial law commands the

---

[94] Orderic, 7.4, vol. 4: 8–11.
[95] See the two *Epistolae de Paschali papa*, one by an anonymous German cleric and the other by Hildebert of Le Mans: MGH LL 2: 668.

disinheritance of an ungrateful son [*filium propter ingratitudinem iubet exheredandum*] [cf. Iuliani Ep. Novell. CVII] But King Henry, that enemy of the Church, ignoring what divine law says, not only saddened the teacher of truth, not only cursed both his carnal and spiritual fathers, but violently forced the carnal one to abdicate kingdom and rule, and the other, spiritual one, to depart from justice.[96]

Here, Roman law is adduced in support of papal as well as earthly paternity.[97]

If the papacy increasingly utilized paternal rather than maternal rhetoric to assert its power over the laity in this period, it may well have been because paternal authority had such clear support: secular as well as religious law supported a father's claim to obedience, whereas secular law had little to say about mothers. Moreover, paternal authority was more clearly identifiable with the pope personally. The exact identity of Mother Rome may have sometimes been in question, but even the enemies of the reforming popes never questioned their right to be called "father." Royal and imperial chanceries had been politely addressing popes as "fathers" for centuries; the title could not be denied to them now, simply because they chose to assert their paternal rights more vigorously.[98]

The best the emperors and kings who resisted increasingly radical papal demands in the late eleventh and early twelfth centuries could do was to characterize particular popes as unnatural fathers who treated their loving sons with hostility. Henry IV opens one of his letters to Gregory VII with just this theme: "Although hitherto I hoped for those things from you which are expected of a father and obeyed you in all respects to the great indignation of our vassals, I have received from you a requital suitable from one who was the most pernicious enemy of our life and kingly office."[99] Henry represents himself as a good son – even to the "indignation" of his vassals – and Gregory as a wicked father. Using a similar argument, Peter Crassus – one of the few laymen to leave us an account of the quarrel between Gregory VII and Henry IV – supported Henry's decision to replace Gregory with another pope in 1084. Peter was a lawyer, and he – like the anonymous author who attacked Henry V – cited Roman law on the relationship between fathers and sons, this time to justify Henry IV's behavior. Justinian's Code forbids a son to take legal action against his father unless he has been properly emancipated first. Peter argues that, by trying to "kill" Henry spiritually, Gregory has emancipated him from his control: such is Gregory's cruelty, that he can no longer be called a

---

[96] *Disputatio vel defensio Paschalis papae*, MGH LL 2: 665.
[97] Cf. the text by Peter Damian cited at the beginning of this chapter.
[98] Hauck (1977), pp. 45–47.
[99] Henry IV, *Briefe*, 11, p. 14; trans. Mommsen and Morrison, p. 146.

"father." The emancipated Henry thus has the legal right to move against Gregory. Indeed, Peter argues, Gregory himself is guilty of "parricide," the killing of close kin, and should suffer the horrible penalty the Romans laid out for that crime.[100]

Pater patrum

If lay rulers had come to accept the papacy's claims to a special paternal authority, what about other spiritual leaders? Western bishops had, of course, long recognized the primacy of the bishop of Rome, and had often described that primacy using paternal imagery. By the central Middle Ages, the pope had become the "father of all churches," the "universal father," the "father of all the faithful."[101] Unlike other prelates, whose responsibilities ended at the boundaries of their diocese, the pope was thought to have duties towards, and authority over, Christians in every part of Europe, and indeed, throughout the world: " ... as he [the pope] is aware that he is the father of the whole world, he must not grow weary in promoting eternal salvation for so many children," wrote Peter Damian to Pope Alexander II in 1064.[102] Even as bishops themselves were increasingly recognized as fathers during the central Middle Ages, they continued to represent themselves as the pope's "sons." The phrase *pater patrum*, "father of fathers," neatly summed up both the special status of the bishop of Rome and their own position.

On the other hand, early medieval popes had tended to display the same complex blend of authority and humility towards bishops as they did towards rulers. Gregory I, for example, seldom characterizes himself as a father in letters to other bishops.[103] When he issues a command, it is said to come from St. Peter – as apostle, not father – or, more often, no justification is given at all. Normally Gregory refers to his fellow bishops as "brothers," implying not hierarchy but equality. On those infrequent occasions when he does use paternal rhetoric, it is to speak of his concern, love, or affection for them. The rhetoric of the early eleventh-century popes is equally egalitarian. When they write to their fellow bishops, they, too, normally address "brothers" rather than "sons." And in virtually all the cases in which they call bishops sons, or describe themselves as feeling "paternal affection" for

---

[100] Peter Crassus, *Defensio Heinrici IV. regis*, 4, MGH LL 1: 441. Another "unnatural" father is suggested when Sigebert of Gembloux refers to Pascal II as "the father of all churches," and then describes how Pascal supported an attack on the church of Cambrai. Sigebert of Gembloux, *Leodicensium epistola*, MGH LL 2: 451.

[101] E.g. Raoul Glaber, 4.3, pp. 174–75; Eadmer, *Vita sancti Anselmi*, 2.32, p. 111.

[102] Peter Damian, 108, vol. 3: 192; trans. Blum, 4: 198.

[103] Search in the CETEDOC Library of Latin Texts database for *pater* and variants in Gregory I's Register.

bishops, they are conferring favors on their correspondents – granting them the pallium, confirming elections, issuing privileges, and so on. Seldom do they issue commands or reprimands to other bishops, and then in the name of St. Peter or Mother Church. The popes from the year 1000 to 1046, like Gregory I, employed images of fatherhood to underline their close ties to and affection for, not their authority over, their correspondents.

By the middle of the eleventh century, the reforming popes had begun to do just the opposite when addressing the laity. However, when asserting Rome's primacy over other episcopal sees, their paternal rhetoric remained muted. Like their predecessors, they normally refer to other bishops as brothers, most often deploying the language of paternity or filiation to confer favors out of "paternal affection." Paternal language does occasionally begin to slip into letters of admonition to "problem" bishops – but as in letters to lay rulers, authority is often projected onto St. Peter or Mother Church.[104] Perhaps displacing the demand for obedience made papal self-assertion less jarring to other bishops. Yet sometimes the reforming popes demanded filial obedience quite directly.[105]

Sometimes, too, they tried to encourage such obedience from other bishops by calling them dutiful sons – regardless of their actual behavior. Here is Nicholas II, writing to the rebellious archbishop Gervase of Reims: "Since we know that you maintain your fidelity to blessed Peter, and reverently defer to his authority in all things, we embrace you with paternal love as our most dear son, and in embracing you, love you with our whole heart." John VIII's phrase, *nostra paternitas*, made one of its rare appearances in this letter: "So long as you show yourself to be a faithful son, our paternity shall never fail you."[106] This is a warning to Gervase to toe the line, but it also allows the archbishop to save face by accepting Nicholas' characterization of him as an obedient son. Bishops brought to heel by the papacy picked up on this language, acknowledging that the pope, as father, had the right to discipline them. "You were concerned to rebuke me – gently as a father," wrote Archbishop Lanfranc of Canterbury to Gregory VII.[107] When Bishop Reinhard of Halberstadt, who had been suspended from office by Pascal II, sought absolution,

---

[104] On Peter as father, in relation to bishops, see Gregory VII, *Register*, 2.25 and 8.7, pp. 156–57 and 525; trans. Cowdrey, pp. 116 and 372–73. On Mother Rome as a foil for papal paternity, see Calixtus II, *Epistolae*, 161 (PL 163: 1225) = JL 6936. On paternal language in this period, see Meulenberg (1965), p. 55; Maccarrone (1974), p. 98.

[105] Gregory VII, *Register*, 6.5, 6.16, pp. 398–99, 421–23; trans. Cowdrey, pp. 280–81, 297–98; *Epistolae vagantes*, 10, 38, pp. 22–27, 94–97; Urban II, *Epistolae*, 57 (PL 151: 336–37) = JL 5458.

[106] Nicholas II, *Epistolae et diplomata*, 29 (PL 143: 1349) = JL 4445.

[107] Lanfranc, 38, pp. 128–31.

he wrote, "It is the duty of a good father to correct every son whom he loves, and to flagellate every one he receives" (Proverbs 3:12; Hebrews 12:6).[108]

However, the reforming popes' high-handed interference in the affairs of local churches also raised the hackles of many. In 1076, Henry IV, certainly acting upon his bishops' complaints, directed an inflammatory letter to Gregory VII, which was clearly intended for public consumption: "Not only have you dared to touch the rectors of the Holy Church – the archbishops, the bishops, and the priests, anointed of the Lord as they are – but you have trodden them underfoot like slaves who know not what their lord may do."[109] The German prelates assembled at Worms in the same year renounced their allegiance to Gregory; to them especially (but not exclusively), Gregory VII was a "dangerous man," who trampled on the long-established rights of local bishops.[110]

Even some of the Roman cardinals eventually rebelled against Gregory VII and Urban II. A collection of their letters, assembled at the very end of the eleventh century, includes many references to papal paternity. Cardinal Deacon Hugh cited the fourth commandment on honoring one's parents, and the passage from Exodus 21 invoking a curse on anyone who cursed his father or mother. "But," Hugh wrote, "where faith is lacking [laeditur], it is impiety to honor a father who is – despite much correction – an irrevocable enemy of the faith."[111] Like the reformers encouraging rebellion against unworthy earthly fathers, Hugh also cited Matthew 10:37 and 19:29 against Gregory VII. Rebels like Hugh could represent themselves as choosing a higher father (God) when their papal father resisted God's will. But what about the loyal supporters of the reforming popes and their policies? Confronted with their "father's" mistakes, what were faithful sons to do?

Uncovering his nakedness

In April 1111, under intense pressure, Pope Pascal II agreed to grant Henry V the right to invest bishops with ring and staff before consecration. Henry was widely attacked, by conservatives as well as reformers, for his treatment of the pope. But the supporters of reform were also deeply troubled by Pascal's capitulation on this key issue. They labeled his grant to Henry V a *pravilegium*, a "wicked privilege." However, they criticized Pascal himself only tentatively, as they strove to reconcile their

---

[108] *Diversorum ad Paschalem papam epistolae*, 14 (PL 163: 459); cf. 21 (PL 163: 464).
[109] Henry IV, *Briefe*, 12, p. 15; trans. Mommsen and Morrison, pp. 150–51.
[110] Robinson (1978b).   [111] *Benonis … scripta*, 1, MGH LL 2: 403–04.

disagreement with his policies with the commandment to honor their own spiritual father.

Here we return to the story of Noah and his three sons, which had long been interpreted as a warning to subordinates not to criticize their superiors. The story was everywhere in the reform period. Polemicists regularly deployed it to attack opponents who criticized particular passages from ancient history or canon law.[112] Hugh of Fleury used it to argue that subjects should tolerate, and not try to resist, even bad kings.[113] Geoffrey of Vendôme cleverly twisted its usual construction to demand a "blessing" from his spiritual father, the bishop of Chartres.[114] Most often, however, it was used to defend bishops from criticism from below.[115] The passages from Pseudo-Isidore cited above reappeared in many of the important collections of canon law from this period.[116]

But if subordinates should avoid exposing the "shameful parts" of their spiritual fathers, the diocesan bishops, how much more should they avoid criticizing the "father of fathers." A number of Gregory VII's supporters cited Pseudo-Isidore against the pope's opponents.[117] Clearly, too, the cardinals who rebelled against Gregory faced comparison of themselves with Noah's wicked son, Ham, for one of them alluded to the story, arguing that while Ham sinfully laughed at his earthly father's "shameful parts," it was virtuous for a spiritual son to lay bare a "demonic father's" "irrevocable madness."[118] It was in conjunction with the events of 1111, however, and in particular in reference to the *pravilegium*, that references to Noah's sons played the most important role.

Abbot Geoffrey of Vendôme continued to address the pope in 1111, as in earlier and later letters, as "dearest father," while nevertheless finding fault with what Pascal had done.[119] Geoffrey's position was that Pascal had indeed acted as a loving father – agreeing to Henry V's demands to prevent him from killing the pope's "sons," that is, the members of the papal curia imprisoned alongside the pope. However, Geoffrey argued, this had been a mistake. A father should value his sons' salvation more than their lives, preventing any "degenerate sons" from "step[ping] back from the

---

[112] Bernold of St. Blasien, *Libelli*, 1, MGH LL 2: 12, 14.

[113] Hugh of Fleury, *De regia potestate*, 1.4, MGH LL 2: 469.

[114] Geoffrey of Vendôme, 179, pp. 410–12.

[115] E.g., *Briefsammlungen*, pp. 45–46; the passage could also be cited to defend abbots from criticism by their monks. Geoffrey of Vendôme, 186, p. 435.

[116] *Diversorum partum sententie*, 74, pp. 58–59; trans. Gilchrist, pp. 111–12; Bonizo of Sutri, *Liber de vita Christiana*, 3.36, p. 83; Ivo, *Decretum*, 5.239 (PL 161: 396).

[117] Bernold of St. Blasien, *Libelli*, 2, MGH LL 2: 50; Manegold of Lautenbach, *Ad Gebehardum*, 44, MGH LL 1: 386.

[118] *Benonis ... scripta*, 2, MGH LL 2: 404.

[119] Geoffrey of Vendôme, 134, p. 272. Earlier letters to the "best of fathers" include 35, 43, 125, pp. 64–66, 76, 248.

Gate of Paradise," but instead, by his own constancy, encouraging them if necessary to die for the truth.[120] There are bishops, Geoffrey continues, who claim lay investiture is not a heresy – but they have themselves been invested by laymen. Their outrageous claim only lays open their own "shameful parts," making their "thighs" bare.[121] Geoffrey thus projects the scandal away from himself and even from Pascal, onto the bishops who defend the *pravilegium*. Like drunken Noahs, they themselves publicize what they have done wrong. Geoffrey, on the other hand, manages to present himself as a dutiful son, while still attacking Pascal's behavior.

Geoffrey criticizes Pascal privately, while still honoring him as a father. But could the pope's behavior be discussed publicly, in synod? The noted canonist Ivo of Chartres thought not – and his reasoning was also ultimately based on Pseudo-Isidore. When Archbishop Josceran of Lyons proposed a gathering of French bishops to discuss Pascal's actions, Ivo of Chartres wrote back that Josceran had no authority to summon the bishops, and that even if he did, they should avoid discussing lay investiture – "which some count among the heresies" – or risk laying bare the "shameful parts" of their father, the pope, exposing them to derision. Pseudo-Isidore did permit subordinates to criticize heretical bishops, but only "some" considered Pascal's actions heretical. Therefore, filial piety should prevail. The bishops, writes Ivo, can only hope for a "paternal blessing" if they "cover up" Pascal's actions, while (like Shem and Japheth) walking backwards.[122] In another letter, Ivo argues that the bishops will be exposing their own "shameful parts" to their enemies, thereby weakening their efforts to reform the Church, if they publicly criticize Pascal.[123] Josceran replies that he too would prefer to be blessed with the piety of the modest sons than cursed with the shamelessness of an irreverent son. However, he hopes that the pope himself will bring up the issue, so that the Church can deal with it and bring criticism to an end: "Would that the father would expose these shameful parts, as you say, to be covered up by our will."[124]

Other responses to the events of 1111 made no reference to Noah and his sons, but left the pope's paternity at the center of their arguments. "I love you, as I should love a father and lord," writes Bruno of Segni to Pascal, "and I wish to have no other pontiff while you live." But Jesus has said, "he who loves father or mother more than me, is not worthy of me" (Matthew 10:37). While Bruno loves Pascal, he loves still

---

[120] Geoffrey of Vendôme, 134, pp. 274–76.   [121] Geoffrey of Vendôme, 134, p. 278.

[122] Ivo of Chartres, *Epistolae ad litem investiturarum spectantes*, 1, MGH LL 2: 650.

[123] Ivo of Chartres, *Epistolae ad litem*, 1, MGH LL 2: 652.

[124] Josceran of Lyons, in Ivo of Chartres, *Epistolae ad litem*, 2, MGH LL 2: 656; cf. Ivo, *Epistolae*, 89 (PL 162: 109–11).

more the God who made them both, and so he feels compelled to reject Pascal's agreement with Henry.[125] The theme of preferring a heavenly to an earthly father appears here, as in the *Passion of Christina* and the *Annals of Hildesheim*. In this case, however, the "earthly" father is still a spiritual one – and he is never rejected completely. It is clear, then, that the events of 1111 presented the supporters of Pascal II with a crisis of paternity, as well as a crisis of primacy.[126] And their responses were in some ways akin to those Ekkehard of Aura attributed to the young king Conrad. While reforming abbots, bishops, and cardinals rejected Pascal's authority, insofar as it supported the *pravilegium*, they nevertheless continued to revere him as "father and lord," and were reluctant to "uncover his nakedness" by openly debating what he had done.

Paternity and primacy

The eleventh century has long been recognized as a turning point in the history of papal primacy.[127] The pope's authority over the faithful, while generally acknowledged (at least in the west), had only limited practical application in the early Middle Ages. Lack of resources and the difficulties of communication meant that the papacy was simply unable to intervene very regularly or very effectively in the affairs of local churches. (One jealously guarded exception was the papal privilege of confirming new archbishops by conferring the pallium, the ceremonial stole of office.) Over the course of the eleventh century, however, the papacy itself took a renewed lead in asserting its own primacy.[128] The multiplication of reforming councils called by papal authority, the more widespread use of legates to carry the papal agenda into various parts of the west, and the increase in papal correspondence (an aspect of the increasing importance of written records at this time) began to give the pope's claim to authority real meaning in a much wider range of matters than ever before.[129] The reforming popes of the eleventh and early twelfth centuries excommunicated adulterous nobles and rebellious kings, summoned scholars to defend their doctrines in Rome, and ordered unruly monks and nuns to submit to their diocesan bishops. And, increasingly, bishops themselves found themselves bending to the pope's will. We have seen how the language of paternity was deployed by the popes and their

---

[125] Bruno of Segni, *Epistolae quatuor*, 2, MGH LL 2: 564.
[126] For Pascal's own views on papal primacy, see Blumenthal (1978b).
[127] Congar (1961); Meulenberg (1965); Maccarrone (1974); Cantarella (1982); Schatz (1990).
[128] Schieffer (2002a).
[129] Southern (1970), pp. 105–25; Hartmann (1993b).

supporters, sometimes hesitantly and sometimes more forcefully, to achieve these goals.[130]

However, the change was one of conception as well as practice. The authority Rome exercised within the Church now came to be attributed less to the Roman Church as an institution, than to the pope as an individual.[131] This shift has often been illustrated by reference to Gregory VII's *Dictatus Papae*, which attributes unique status and powers to the pope himself. But it is even more clearly – and much more widely – evidenced in the hesitant but unmistakable move in the eleventh century from reliance on maternal authority, located in a vaguely defined "Roman Church," to the assertion of paternal authority. This was vested, perhaps, more in St. Peter than in the pope himself, but nevertheless increasingly highlighted the special position of the man who was at once the "servant of the servants of God" and the "father of all the faithful" throughout the world.

---

[130] The paternal claim was, of course, related to increased demands for obedience: see Robinson (1978c); Benz (1990).
[131] Congar (1961); Maccarrone (1974); Blumenthal (1978b), pp. 82–90; Cowdrey (1998a), pp. 523–25.

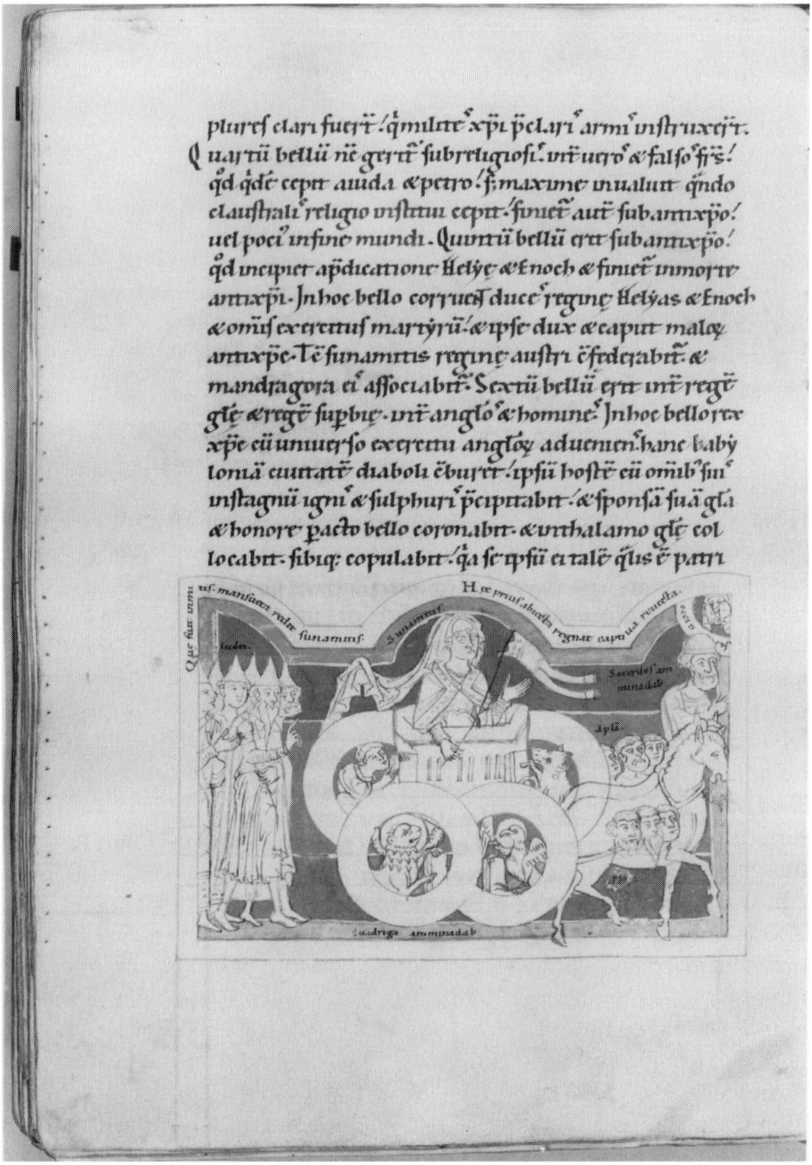

plures clari fuer̃t ᷑q̃milit̃e xp̃i p̃clari armi inſtruxer̃t.
Q uar̃tu bellũ nc̃ gerr̃t ſubr̃religioſi · ur̃t uer̃o ᷑falſo fr̃ē ·
q̃d q̃dē cepit auida ᷑petro · f̃ maxime inualuit q̃n̄do
clauſtrali religio inſtitui cepit · fin̄iet aut̃ ſub antixp̃o ·
uel poci̅ infin̄e mundi · Quar̃tũ bellũ err̃t ſub antixp̃o ·
q̃d incipier apdicationc̃ Helye ᷑Enoch ᷑finiet inmor̃tt̃
antixp̄i · Jnhoc bello cor̃ruet̃ duce ᷑regin̄e Helyas ᷑Enoch
᷑om̃ıſ exer̃cituſ mar̃tyr̃ũ · ᷑ipſe dux ᷑caput mala᷑
antixp̃e · T̃e ſunamitis regin̄e auſtr̄i c̃ſderabr̃ũ ᷑
mandr̃agora ei aſſociabr̃ · Sextũ bellũ err̃t int̃ rege᷑
gl̃e ᷑rege᷑ ſupbie · int̃ anglo ᷑homine᷑ Jnhoc bello rex
xp̃e cũ uniuer̃ſo exer̃citu anglo᷑ aduenient̃ hanc baby̅
lon̄ıã ciuitatt̃ diaboli c̃bur̃it̃ · ipſũ hoſt̃e cũ om̃ıb̃ ſui̅
inſtagnũ igni᷑ ſulphuri᷑ p̃cipitabit · ᷑ſponſã ſuã gl̃a
᷑honore᷑ pacto bello coronabit · ᷑ur̃thalamo gl̃e col
locabit · ſibıq᷑ copulabit · q̃a ſe ipſũ ei tale᷑ q̃lıs ē p̃tri

Figure 4. Baltimore, Walters Art Museum, Ms. 29, f. 89v. The
Sunamite, from Honorius, *Expositio in Cantica canticorum.*
Reproduced by permission of the museum.

Conclusion: the stumbling block

The scholar was afraid – or so he claimed. His brothers had asked him to resolve a "question published throughout the world, one discussed almost daily by everyone." But doing so would expose him, a "lamb," to the "savage wolves" who held different views. He trembled at the thought, but summoning up his courage, wrote a response to serve him as a shield – a "stumbling block" (*offendiculum*) on which his opponents would "blunt their envious teeth."[1] *On the Stumbling Block* is the title Honorius Augustodunensis himself gave to his treatise against clerical marriage, probably written in the first decade of the twelfth century, and most likely in England.[2] The title refers, however, to something more than the scholar's desire for protection from criticism. The question being "discussed almost daily by everyone" was whether priests could marry after ordination. There was a second question, too, just as widely debated: could the faithful gain any benefit from the masses and other sacraments married priests performed? Unspoken in *On the Stumbling Block*, but equally pressing for Honorius and his contemporaries, was a third question: was it even appropriate for the faithful to discuss publicly the sexual behavior of the clergy?

In the central Middle Ages, as today, sex was one of the most private aspects of human life. To ridicule the idea that intercourse was necessary for a valid marriage, Peter Damian sarcastically asked, "Should a man, then, mount his wife in public?"[3] The answer was obviously no. Even within the bounds of lawful matrimony, sex still engendered feelings of embarrassment and shame, and the desire to hide from public view. Clerical writers of the central Middle Ages, influenced by the thinking of Augustine of Hippo, saw this as a consequence of the Fall. Augustine had argued that erotic desire was a marker of sin: the disobedience of the genitals to human will during arousal was the penalty God had imposed on the human race

---

[1] Honorius, *De offendiculo*, 1, 55, MGH LL 3: 38–39, 57.
[2] Flint (1995), pp. 132–34,
[3] Peter Damian, 172, vol. 4: 259; trans. Blum, 6(7): 256.

for Adam and Eve's disobedience. In a postlapsarian world, sex and the sexual organs symbolize the loss of grace. They are always associated with shame, hence the universal custom of covering them up.[4] And this characteristic made sexual sins effectively representative of a much wider range of crimes, also characterized as "shameful." It also made it particularly inappropriate, however, to discuss openly the sexual behavior of individuals, especially those of high rank or authority. While the rules of intimate behavior could be and, as we saw in Chapter 1, often were debated publicly, the details of what individual women and men did in their beds remained private, certainly not to be "published throughout the world."

And yet that was precisely what reformers like Honorius were doing. Not only did they develop general policies directed against adultery, incest, divorce, and clerical marriage, they also implemented those policies by commenting on the misbehavior of individuals. The sex lives of emperors and kings were trotted out for public scrutiny – sometimes accompanied by highly improbable claims about what they were supposed to have done.[5] The unseemly interactions of priests and even bishops with sexual partners came in for similarly open criticism.[6] To the horror of conservatives, moreover, ordinary men and women were sometimes informed about their pastors' lustful activities, and even invited to exert their own pressure towards reform, by boycotting the masses and other sacraments of "fornicating" priests.[7] These were dangerous strategies, however: they opened up the reformers to just the kind of attack Honorius claimed to fear.

The Latin words *offendiculum* ("stumbling block") and *scandalum* were often treated as synonymous by Christian writers. Those who created a scandal within the Church placed a "stumbling block" in the way of the faithful striving to reach heaven. But scandal had two sources. On the one hand, there were the individuals who committed notorious, public crimes. They damaged not only themselves, but those around them, by setting a bad example. Scripture warned such sinners that they would be punished for both their sins and their pernicious influence. "But whoso shall offend one of these little ones that believe in me," Christ had said, "it were better for him that a millstone were hanged about his neck, and that he were drowned in the depth of the sea" (Matthew 18:6).

By spreading stories about their fellow Christians, scandalmongers, as well as those who behaved scandalously, "offended" the "little ones." St. Paul had warned the faithful not to judge one another, not to "put a stumbling block" in their brothers' way (Romans 14:13).[8] Not

[4] Augustine, *De civitate Dei*, 14, 17–20, CC, SL 48: 439–43.
[5] McLaughlin (forthcoming).   [6] McLaughlin (2010).
[7] See above, Chapter 1.   [8] See also 1 Corinthians 8:9.

works – good or bad – but faith was what mattered. Dependence upon the "works of the law" had proven the downfall, the "stumbling block," for the Jews (Romans 9:32). And it could be for Christians as well. Those who advertised the sexual sins of priests and bishops were often attacked on precisely these grounds, for their scandalous accusations undermined clerical authority.[9] Laymen, "given over to public mockery," were insulting their priests; the latter were defamed, losing their good name.[10] One anonymous author claimed that opposition to clerical marriage threatened to create a schism, a divorce between the Bride and her heavenly Spouse.[11] And another unknown author claimed that when priestly life was "publicly defamed," the "nakedness" of Mother Church was uncovered, in obvious contravention of divine law.[12]

It was the general consensus that even when accusations of clerical misconduct were well founded, it was always better to make them quietly. A discreet, private reprimand was more likely to be effective, less likely to scandalize others, and also less likely to humiliate prominent members of society. Bishop Fulbert of Chartres hesitated to bring Abbot Tetfrid of Bonneval to trial for immorality (*turpitudo*):

> Like filth the more [such immorality] is stirred up the worse it smells. Indeed, not only does [this case] involve immorality, it is also dangerous so much so that if he comes to trial, either he or his accusers must be degraded to his great dishonour … I held off, anxiously waiting and hoping that the Lord would rid his church of such a great disgrace without public discussion or derision.[13]

As a conscientious bishop, Fulbert was anxious to correct sins, but also to avoid "public discussion or derision." Thus he held off from pursuing the matter. In the end, Tetfrid himself demanded that the case be brought to trial.

But discretion was not always possible. Proponents of reform were particularly fond of citing Pope Gregory I's dictum that "it is better … for offence [*scandalum*] to be given than for truth to be abandoned."[14]

---

[9] Landulf of Milan, *Historia Mediolanensis*, 3.7–12, MGH SS 8: 78–82.

[10] Sigebert of Gembloux, *Apologia contra eos qui calumpniantur missas coniugatorum sacerdotum*, and *Die Brief der Kleriker von Cambrai und Noyon*, both in Frauenknecht (1997), pp. 220, 247.

[11] *Rescriptio beati Udelrici episcopi*, in Frauenknecht (1997), p. 215.

[12] *Cum sub liberi arbitrii potestate creati simus*, in Frauenknecht (1997), p. 286. Cf. Peter Damian 114, vol. 3: 296; trans. Blum, 4: 294.

[13] Fulbert, *Letters*, 75, pp. 134–35.

[14] Gregory I, *Homilia VII in Ezechielem* (PL 76: 842). Cited by Rather of Verona, *Briefe*, 29, MGH, Briefe des deutschen Kaiserzeit, 1: 164; trans. Reid, pp. 494–95; Anonymous (attributed to Rupert of Deutz), *De vita vere apostolica*, 1.18 (PL 170: 620). Cf. Projekt Pseudoisidor, Teil 1, 3. Clemens-Brief. p. 94. Available at http://www.pseudoisidor.de/pdf/009_Clemens_Urget_nos_fratres.pdf. Cited by Placidus of Nonantola, *Liber de honore ecclesiae*, 128, MGH LL 2, 628.

Clerical marriage – like incest, divorce and adultery, and, for that matter, simony – was such a terrible crime, they believed, that it had to be stopped, regardless of the cost. Only as a last resort, when they saw no other way of achieving their goal, did reformers publicize clerical misconduct and appeal to the laity to step in against incontinent priests.[15] Nevertheless, their opponents could – and frequently did – accuse them of "offending the little ones."

One way out of this dilemma for the reformers was to represent the people they accused as notorious sinners, their crimes widely known. Thus they could argue that the scandal already existed, and that they were merely trying to put a stop to it. Here is Peter Damian on the problem of married bishops:

If this evil were secret, silence could perhaps somehow be condoned. But what a criminal situation! Shamelessly, this epidemic has been so audaciously revealed that everyone knows the houses of prostitution, the names of the mistresses, the fathers-in-law and mothers-in-law, brothers, and other close relatives; and lest anything be lacking in these assertions, they give evidence of messengers running to and fro, of the sending of presents, of the jokes they laughed at, and of their private conversation. And lastly, to remove all doubt, you have the obvious pregnancies and the squalling babies. Therefore, because of the ignominy involved, I do not see how something that is everywhere publicly discussed can be suppressed at the synod ...[16]

A problem so public had to be dealt with openly as well.

Honorius Augustodunensis takes a similar position, arguing that "canonical censure keeps those who are held guilty of public crimes [publicis criminibus] at a distance from the priesthood." Those "whose sins are hidden [crimina latent], the Church tolerates and reserves their judgment for her Spouse, the searcher of hearts."[17] But priests today, he claims, "rejecting both the fear of God and human modesty," "impudently pollute themselves, in the manner of dogs, with any old harlot," and "publicly and insatiably undertake to wallow in uncleanness, like pigs in a sty."[18] When Honorius entitled his reforming treatise On the Stumbling Block, then, he prepared a defense for himself by turning his enemies' own charges against them. Not he, but they – by engaging openly in lewd behavior or by publicly defending it – placed a "stumbling block" before the faithful.

All of this appears, at first glance, very familiar to the modern historian. Honorius, Peter Damian and their opponents were distinguishing between the "public" and the "private," just as we do today, and they

---

[15] E.g. *Vita Altmanni episcopi Pataviensis*, 5, 11, MGH SS 12: 231, 232.
[16] Peter Damian, 61, vol. 2: 208; trans. Blum, 3: 4.
[17] Honorius, *De offendiculo*, 15, MGH LL 3: 42.
[18] Honorius, *De offendiculo*, 27, MGH LL 3: 46; cf. p. 53.

also seem to have assumed, as we do, that "private" business should not normally be discussed "publicly." Yet while "public" and "private" were theoretically distinguishable in the central Middle Ages, in practice they often flowed into one another, in ways almost unimaginable to us today. No real privacy, at least in the modern sense of the word, existed during the eleventh and early twelfth centuries.[19] The vast majority of the population had no separate bedrooms. And the few who did were seldom alone in them.[20] We know that royal bedchambers were normally full of attendants, "chamberlains" and ladies-in-waiting. Even when a sexual encounter took place, the king and queen might still be surrounded by others.[21] Bishops, for their part, were supposed to have clerical attendants present in their bedchambers at all times. This was required by canon law, the intention being to provide reliable witnesses – either to support the bishop against slanderous attacks, or simply to testify to his saintly behavior. And this helps to account for the remarkable amount of information we have about both episcopal celibacy and illicit episcopal sexuality in this period.[22]

The lack of complete privacy, then, sometimes made it hard to draw the line between the "public" and the "private" sides of life. There is, however, another sense in which public and private flowed into one another at this time, specifically in the realm of political discourse. Gerd Althoff has recently argued, against Habermas, that a "public sphere" of sorts did exist in the Middle Ages.[23] It was an elite public sphere, dominated not so much by verbal argument as by nonverbal forms of communication – ritual actions and visual images. Habermas assumed that premodern political rituals and images were rigid, unchanging representations of power, created by rulers and their servants, which their subjects viewed passively. Althoff, however, contends that while medieval rituals and images had to be unambiguous and easily understandable by their audience, they could also – paradoxically – serve as a highly flexible means of public communication. Political actors had "rules of the game" to follow when they engaged in ritual action, but they could also change the message through subtle or even not-so-subtle changes in the elements of representation.

But who, exactly, were these political actors? In the past, their diversity has been too often ignored. The focus has been on powerful men,

---

[19] Among recent works on the public/private distinction, see Innes (2000), pp. 254–59; Nelson (2006).

[20] E.g. *Liber miraculorum*, 1.33, pp. 140–41; trans. Sheingorn, p. 105, describing a castellan sleeping in his chamber with his household.

[21] Bruno of Magdeburg, *De bello Saxonico*, MGH SS 5: 331–32, describes (probably unreliably) a farcical encounter between Henry IV, his wife Bertha, and her ladies.

[22] McLaughlin (2010).

[23] Althoff (1993), (2002), (2003); cf. *Formen und Funktionen*.

who did, indeed, usually occupy center stage. However, in the central Middle Ages, the institutional location of "public" life was the household, whether noble or royal. And as a result, women, children, and even servants also had their roles to play in dramatic "enactments" of power, recognition, submission, petition – or, for that matter, enmity. The wives and children (especially the eldest son) of a ruler appeared "publicly," wearing their own crowns, at the king's solemn crown-wearings.[24] The queen might play a role, as well, in the transition of power that followed a king's death, through her control of the insignia of royal power. Famously, it was the dowager empress Cunigunde who formally confirmed the election of Conrad II as emperor in 1024, transferring the regalia to him after consultation with the magnates.[25] (Another queen, Richilde, had invested her stepson, Louis the Stammerer, with his regalia in 877.[26])

Rituals of social solidarity regularly involved not only the head of the household, but others in the family. Wives (less often, daughters) played a crucial role in the banqueting that solidified social bonds and re-created social hierarchies in this period, by distributing "appropriate" gifts to members of the company and sometimes by carrying the "mead-cup" to distinguished guests, in order of rank.[27] When a noble or churchman looked for an intercessor to help him petition a powerful man for assistance, he routinely turned to the man's wife or mother, for they were considered to have the greatest influence over him.[28] But even very young children might play such a role, as they were reported to have done when St. Ulric of Augsburg petitioned God for relief from Magyar attacks, by lining up wailing infants around the altar of his church to add their pleas to his.[29]

Obviously, daughters – sometimes very young ones – played a crucial role in the weddings that so often sealed peace treaties, while wives and children also regularly performed the solemn acts of donation and consent that created and supported religious communities, thereby also solidifying social bonds with the religious and with the other patrons of the same communities.[30] Rituals related to crisis resolution sometimes

---

[24] E.g. Wipo, *Gesta Chuonradi II imperatoris*, 23, MGH SS 11: 268; trans. Mommsen and Morrison, p. 84. On crown-wearings, see Klewitz (1939).

[25] Wipo, *Gesta Chuonradi II imperatoris*, 2, MGH SS 11: 259; trans. Mommsen and Morrison, p. 65.

[26] *Annales Bertiniani*, a. 877, MGH SRG, 5: 137–38.

[27] Hincmar of Reims, *De ordine palatii*, 5, pp. 72–74; and see Enright (1988).

[28] Farmer (1986); Huneycutt (1995); Parsons (1995); Rabin (2009).

[29] Ekkehard of St. Gall, *Casus sancti Galli*, 60, pp. 130–32. Consider the role of children in relieving the siege of Troia: Raoul Glaber, 3.4, pp. 102–03.

[30] Schieffer (2002b).

involved women and children as well.[31] Wives could be found ritually "begging pardon and favor" for their husbands from an aggrieved lord, while children sometimes participated in the acts of submission that ended power struggles.[32] Even the hideous ritualized penalties handed out to traitors were not limited to adult men. Women, and even children, could be sometimes executed as well.[33]

The intermingling of domestic and political life during the central Middle Ages is evident not only in the actors involved in these public rituals, but also in the specific ways they acted out their relationships. The gestures involved in "public" communication were closely related to those involved in communication among members of the household. Kissing and joining hands created marital as well as political fidelity. Bending the knee or bowing the shoulders could express the deference of subjects to kings, but also of sons to fathers. Formal, ritualized greetings welcomed guests into a house, just as they welcomed kings into a city.[34] Students of medieval political ritual have not always noted to what degree the repertoire of political gesture in the central Middle Ages was actually drawn from the gestures of family life. The whole point of the *officium stratoris* performed by Conrad for Urban II at Cremona was, after all, that helping someone dismount from his horse was normally the function of a servant.

Philippe Buc has criticized much recent scholarship on political ritual in the Middle Ages. He points out the potential discrepancies between the rituals actually performed, and the descriptions we have of them – which were shaped by textual traditions and by authorial motives as much as by eyewitness accounts of "what really happened."[35] These are important concerns, but they do not undermine my claim that women and children played a significant role in those rituals – for that claim is based on multiple texts, by a variety of authors. And while Buc's arguments should make us wary of placing too much confidence in the specific details of particular events, they ultimately undermine neither the basic premise of most current scholarship on medieval political rituals, which is that those rituals were an important way of conveying political messages, nor Althoff's claim that they created a "public sphere."

---

[31] On the Empress Gisela as mediator between her husband and the king of Burgundy, see Wipo, *Gesta Chuonradi II imperatoris*, 21, MGH SS 11: 267; trans. Mommsen and Morrison, pp. 82–83.

[32] Iocundus, *Translatio sancti Servatii*, MGH SS 12: 98. On "begging pardon and favor," see Koziol (1992).

[33] *Chronicon sancti Petri vivi Senonensis*, a. 999, p. 104; *Liber miraculorum*, 4.3, p. 226; trans. Sheingorn, p. 184. Richer, *Historiarum libri IIII*, 3. 8–9, MGH SS 38: 174–75.

[34] Consider the fascinating interplay of domestic and public gestures in *Chronicon sancti Huberti Andaginensis*, 23–28, MGH SS 8: 580–87.

[35] Buc (2001).

What has not, perhaps, been fully appreciated by Althoff, Buc, or other scholars who writing on this subject, is the extent to which these non-verbal "speech acts" influenced verbal communication as well – especially in the central Middle Ages, before the full development of scholastic thought.[36] Political writings from the eleventh and early twelfth centuries often communicated their points through verbal imagery that textually reproduced political gestures and rituals, often subtly reworking them to convey new messages – albeit always in keeping with the "rules of the game." Indeed, this is precisely how the textual representations of the Church which I have explored in this book were intended to reach their readers. Using words (and sometimes manuscript illustrations as well), they picture the normally invisible relationships that linked bishops to their churches, metropolitans to their suffragans, layfolk to the clergy, and so forth. The discourse of honor and shame constructed in these texts alerts us to their kinship with political rituals employing the same vocabulary. In a sense, then, my argument is the opposite of Buc's – not that textual traditions affected representations of political ritual, but rather that rituals informed textual traditions.

Political writers in the central Middle Ages employed many languages, but very often – as we have seen – they chose a domestic one, comparing earthly households to the Household of God, using the gestures of family life – kissing and embracing, spurning and spitting, bowing and deferring – to enact political relationships. Bishops are represented marrying their ecclesiastical brides, kings submitting to their spiritual fathers, suffragans petitioning their spiritual mothers for help. Polemicists and other clerical authors, like the impresarios of political rituals, scored rhetorical points by manipulating particular elements in this verbal theater – the Bride becomes a prostitute, the father mistreats his son, the daughter's tears flow.

The authors whose works we have been examining were obviously familiar with other forms of argument, but allegory often played a crucially strategic role in their works. And here let us return for a moment to *On the Stumbling Block*. When he wrote this work, Honorius was still quite a young man, and he showed off his education by inserting passages of impeccable logic (each duly labeled "syllogism") into his work. Most of his argument in this treatise, however, is not so much logical as stunningly visual and emotional. Honorius represents himself, as a lamb, attacked by savage wolves.[37] Throughout the text, images of the faithful

---

[36] But see Karl Leyser (1993), p. 25, for a perceptive description of political rituals as a form of "political theory."

[37] Honorius, *De offendiculo*, 1, 55, MGH, LL 3: 38, 57.

as sheep and the proponents of clerical marriage as wolves recur, along with references to the latter as various unclean animals (especially dogs and pigs) and as lepers. More central to his goal, however, is Honorius' complex interpretation of various passages from the Old Testament. Through allegory he animates and dramatizes these passages, emphasizing that the elements in them are *figurae* – by which he meant that they are the shadows of New Testament realities, but which we can also take to mean that they are visible actors, whose highly ritualized actions convey meanings both theological and political.

Thus Honorius substitutes a kind of rhetorical ritual for the rather dry language of the Law, as expounded in Leviticus 21. His dramatization is dominated by two main characters: the Synagogue, a concubine, and the Church, the "Queen of the Supernal Emperor."[38] Both female figures refuse to accept any servant who does not meet their requirements; that is, who fails to conform to the rules set out for priests in Leviticus – that they be whole (without any bodily deformity), married to virgin wives, and so on. Of course, the Synagogue interprets these rules literally, "carnally," while the Church understands them in a "spiritual" sense – although there is a considerable slippage here, since Honorius also expects Christian priests to be literal virgins, if possible, and certainly – if they were ever married before ordination – to have had a literally virginal wife.[39] The importance of such physical purity is highlighted by language that evokes both the Biblical account of Christ driving the moneylenders from the Temple and the ritual expulsion of excommunicates from the Church: "Queen Church" "expels" those who live voluptuously from the priesthood and "rejects" them from her service. At the same time, her husband, Jesus, "ejects" them from his church with a "whip" and "repels" them, as thieves and robbers, from "his father's house."[40]

In general, however, Honorius interprets the Old Testament rules about whom a priest could marry in terms of a Christian priest's allegorical relationship with his own individual church. She (the priest's church) should not be a harlot – that is, not "debased with many simoniacs for money." She should not be a divorcee – that is, not abandoned by her own priest because of heresy, or vicious and incorrigible behavior. She should not be a widow – that is (rather oddly), a church whose priest has been expelled for the sake of true religion (a reference here to the churches whose reforming pastors had been expelled by hostile laymen).

---

[38] Honorius, *De offendiculo*, 2, MGH LL 3: 39. On the interactions of Ecclesia and Synagoga in Honorius, see Cohen (2004).
[39] Similar slippage occurs in Peter Damian, 28, vol. 1: 264–65; trans. Blum, 1: 272–73.
[40] Honorius, *De offendiculo*, 17, MGH LL 3: 43. Cf. Matthew 21:12–13; Mark 11:15–17; Luke 19:45–46; John 2:14–16.

She should, rather, be a virgin – that is, one consecrated by a catholic bishop and given to her priestly spouse without simony.[11] Here the evocation of visible ritual is more muted than in the passage discussed above. Nevertheless, it is easy to imagine a manuscript illumination representing these rules with figures of women variously dressed and in various poses to represent their different statuses – and indeed, several manuscripts of Honorius' works contain precisely this kind of illustration.[42]

On the Stumbling Block, then, exemplifies with particularly vividness the style of allegorical communication I have been exploring throughout this book, in which highly educated clerics conveyed messages concerning the "public" life of their day, through textual (and sometimes visual) images of the "private" life of the Church. The details of those images often appear unseemly or even disturbing to modern sensibilities: a bishop is accused of raping another man's bride, an antipope of incest, a king of prostituting his own mother. What can such sexualized and gendered descriptions possibly tell us about the regulation of episcopal elections, the duties of a suffragan towards his metropolitan, the relationship between *regnum* and *sacerdotium*?

In this Conclusion I have chosen to return to the campaign against nicolaitism, because that campaign was concerned with sexuality, and sexuality (whether clerical or lay) was – of all the different aspects of human life in the Middle Ages – the one most clearly labeled "private" by medieval writers. Texts about sexuality (such as Honorius' *On the Stumbling Block*) thus illustrate most clearly the point I have been trying to make throughout this book: that boundaries between the "public" and the "private" were extremely fluid in the central Middle Ages – in practice because of the realities of political life, and in theory because educated clerics (and perhaps the laity as well) imagined a profound and divinely ordained resonance between them. Few modern scholars have paid much attention to the highly sexualized and gendered images with which medieval clerics littered their larger arguments about "right order in the world," largely because we have not noticed the roles they play in those arguments, and perhaps, too, because they disturb our modern scholarly sensibilities. Gender and sexuality, then, have hitherto been "stumbling blocks" to a better understanding of medieval political discourse. It is my hope that this book has helped somewhat to clear them out of our way.

---

[41] Honorius, *De offendiculo*, 8–9, MGH LL 3: 40–41.
[42] See, for example, the image of a queenly Sunamite driving her chariot in Walters Art Museum, Ms. 29, f. 89v (late twelfth century). On this and related images, see Curschmann (1988).

Works Cited

PRIMARY SOURCES

Abbo of Fleury. *Apologeticus* (PL 139: 461–72).

Acta et scripta quae de controversiis ecclesiae graecae et latinae saeculo undecimo composita extant, ed. C. Will. Leipzig/Marburg, 1861.

Actus pontificum Cennomannis in urbe degentium, ed. G. Busson and A. Ledru. Publications de la Société des archives historiques du Maine. Le Mans, 1902.

Adalbero of Reims. *Epistolae* (PL 137: 505–18).

Adam of Bremen. *Gesta Hammaburgensis ecclesiae pontificum*, ed. V. Lappenberg. MGH SS 7: 267–389; *History of the Archbishops of Hamburg-Bremen*, trans. F. Tschan. Records of Civilization, 53. New York, 1959.

Agnellus of Ravenna. *Liber pontificalis* (PL 106: 431–750).

Alexander II. *Epistolae et diplomata* (PL 146: 1279–1430).

Alfanus of Salerno. *Vita et passio sanctae Christinae* (PL 147: 1269–82).

Amalar of Metz. *Opera liturgica omnia*, ed. I. Hanssens. Studi e testi, 138–40. 3 vols. Vatican City, 1948–50.

Ambrose of Milan. *Hexaemeron* (PL 14 : 123–274).
   De Tobia (PL 14: 759–94).

Andrew of Strumi. *Vita sancti Arialdi*, ed. F. Baethgen. MGH SS 30.2: 1047–75.

Analecta hymnica medii aevi, ed. C. Blume and G. Dreves. 55 vols. Leipzig, 1886–1922.

Annales Bertiniani, ed. G. Waitz. MGH SRG 5. Hanover, 1883.

Annales Hildesheimenses, ed. G. Waitz. MGH SRG, 8. Hanover, 1878.

Annales Rosenveldenses, ed. G. Pertz. MGH SS 16: 99–104.

Annales Stadenses, ed. M. Lappenberg. MGH SS 16: 271–379.

Annales sancti Disibodi, ed. G. Waitz. MGH SS 17: 4–30.

Anselm of Laon. *Sententie*. In *Anselms von Laon systematische Sentenzen*, ed. F. Bliemetzrieder. Beiträge zur Geschichte der Philosophie des Mittelalters, Texte und Untersuchungen, 18: 2–3. Münster, 1919. Pp. 47–153.

Anselm of Canterbury. *S. Anselmi Cantuariensis archiepiscopi opera omnia*, ed. F. S. Schmitt , 6 vols., Edinburgh, 1946–61. Partially translated as *The Letters of Saint Anselm of Canterbury*, trans. W. Fröhlich. 3 vols. Cistercian Studies Series, 96, 97, 142. Kalamazoo, MI, 1990–94.

Anselm of Lucca. *Liber contra Wibertum*, ed. E. Bernheim. MGH LL 1: 519–28.

Aselbod of Utrecht. *Vita sanctae Walburgis* (PL 140: 1091–1102).

Augustine of Hippo. *De civitate Dei*, ed. B. Dombart and A. Kalb. 2 vols. CC, SL 47–48. Turnhout, 1955.

De nuptiis et concupiscentia (PL 44: 413–74).

Enarrationes in psalmos, ed. E. Dekkers and J. Fraipont. CC, SL 38–40. Turnhout, 1956.

Epistulae, ed. A. Goldbacher. 5 vols. CSEL, 34.1, 34.2, 44, 57, 58. Vienna, 1895–98.

"B." *Vita sancti Dunstani*, ed. W. Stubbs. In *Memorials of St. Dunstan*. Pp. 3–52.

Bede. *Hexaemeron* (PL 91: 9–190).

Benonis aliorumque cardinalium schismaticorum contra Gregorium VII. et Urbanum II. scripta, ed. K. Francke. MGH LL 2: 369–422.

Berengar of Narbonne. *Querimonia adversus Guifredum* (PL 143: 837–44).

Bernhard of Hildesheim. *Liber canonum contra Heinricum IV.*, ed. F. Thaner. MGH LL 1: 471–516.

Bernold of St. Blasien. *Chronicon*, ed. G. Pertz. MGH SS 5: 385–467.

Libelli, ed. F. Thaner. MGH LL 2: 1–168.

Bertold of Reichenau. *Annales*, ed. G. Pertz. MGH SS 5: 264–326.

Bonizo of Sutri. *Liber ad amicum*, ed. E. Dümmler. MGH LL 1: 571–620. Trans. Robinson, in *The Papal Reform of the Eleventh Century*, pp. 158–261.

Liber de vita Christiana, ed. E. Perels, Texte zur Geschichte des römischen und kanonischen Rechts in Mittelalter, 1. Berlin, 1930.

Die Brief der Kleriker von Cambrai und Noyon. In Frauenknecht (1997), pp. 243–51.

Briefsammlungen der Zeit Heinrichs IV., ed. C. Erdmann and N. Fickermann. MGH, Die Briefe der deutschen Kaiserzeit, 5. Weimar, 1950.

Bruno of Magdeburg. *De bello saxonico*, no editor given. MGH SS 5: 327–84.

Bruno of Reims (?). *Expositio in epistolas Pauli* (PL 153: 11–565).

Bruno of Segni. *Commentaria in Lucam* (PL 165: 333–452).

Epistolae quatuor, ed. E. Sackur. MGH LL 2: 563–65.

Expositio in Apocalypsim (PL 165: 605–736).

Expositio in Cantica canticorum (PL 164: 1233–88).

Expositio in Deuteronomium (PL 164: 505–50).

Expositio in Exodum (PL 164: 233–378).

Libellus de symoniacis, ed. E. Sackur. MGH LL 2: 546–62.

Sententie (PL 165: 875–1078).

Tractatus de sacramentis ecclesiae (PL 165: 1089–1110).

Bruno of Würzburg. *Expositio psalmorum* (PL 142: 49–530).

Burchard of Worms. *Decretum* (PL 140: 537–1058).

Calixtus II. *Epistolae et privilegia* (PL 163: 1093–1338).

Carmen rhythmicum de captivitate Paschalis papae, ed. E. Dümmler. MGH LL 2: 673–75.

Cartulaire de l'abbaye de Gorze, ed. A. D'Herbomez. Mettensia, 2. Paris, 1898.

Cartulaire de l'abbaye cardinale de la Trinité de Vendôme, ed. C. Métais. 5 vols. Publications de la Société archéologique du Vendômois. Paris, 1893–1904.

Chronica monasterii Casinensis, ed. H. Hoffmann. MGH SS 34.

Chronicon sancti Hubert Andaginensis, ed. L. Bethmann and W. Wattenbach. MGH SS 8: 565–630.

Chronicon sancti Petri vivi Senonensis, ed. R.-H. Bautier, M. Gilles, and A.-M. Bautier. Sources d'histoire médiévale. Paris, 1979.

"Concerning the Betrothal of a Woman." Trans. Whitelock, in *English Historical Documents, Volume 1: ca. 500–1042*, p. 431

Conrad of Braunweiler. *Vita Wolphelmi* (PL 154: 405–33).

Constitutio de expeditione Beneventana (a. 866). In MGH, Capitularia, 2: 94–96.

Cosmas of Prague. *Chronica Boemorum*, ed. B. Bretholz. MGH SRG, n.s. 2. Berlin, 1923.

The Councils of Urban II, Volume I: Decreta Claromontensia, ed. R. Somerville. Annuarium historiae conciliorum, Supplementum, 1. Amsterdam, 1972.

Cum sub liberii arbitrii creati simus. In Frauenknecht (1997), pp. 269–88.

Cyprian of Carthage. *Opera*, various editors. 7 vols. to date. CC, SL 3. Turnhout, 1960–.

De investitura episcoporum, ed. E. Bernheim, MGH LL 2: 498–504.

De ordinando pontifice, ed. E. Dümmler. MGH LL 1: 8–14.

De unitate ecclesiae conservanda, ed. W. Schwenkenbecher MGH LL 2: 184–284.

De vita vere apostolica. (PL 170: 611–64).

Decretales Pseudo-Isidorianae. Cited from the ongoing Projekt Pseudoisidor. Available at http://www.pseudoisidor.mgh.de/.

Deusdedit. *Libellus contra invasores et symoniacos et reliquos schismaticos*, ed. E. Sackur. MGH LL 2: 300–65.

Disputatio vel defensio Paschalis papae, ed. E. Sackur. MGH LL 2: 659–66.

Diversorum ad Paschalem papam epistolae (PL 163: 447–70).

Diversorum patrum sententie sive Collectio in LXXIV titulos digesta, ed. J. Gilchrist. Monumenta iuris canonici, series B: Corps collectionum, 1. Vatican City, 1973. *The Collection in Seventy-Four Titles: A Canon Law Manual of the Gregorian Reform*, trans. J. Gilchrist. Mediaeval Sources in Translation, 22. Toronto, 1980.

Drogo of Bergues. *Vita sanctae Godelevae*. *AASS*, Jul. II (July 6): 402–9.

Eadmer. *Historia novorum in Anglia*, ed. M. Rule. RS, 81. London, 1884; *Eadmer's History of Recent Events in England*, trans. G. Bosanquet. London, 1964.

Eadmer. *Vita sancti Anselmi*, ed. and trans. R. W. Southern. OMT. Oxford, 1962.

Vita et liber miraculorum sancti Dunstani, ed. W. Stubbs. In *Memorials of St. Dunstan*, pp. 162–250.

Ekkehard of Aura, *Chronicon*, ed. and trans. (into German) F.-J. Schmale and I. Schmale-Ott, AQDGM, 15. Darmstadt, 1972. Pp. 124–208, 268–376.

Ekkehard of St. Gall, *Casus sancti Galli*, ed. and trans. (into German) by H. Haefele. AQDGM, 10. Darmstadt, 1980.

Encomium Emmae, ed. and trans. A. Campbell. Camden Third Series, 72. London, 1949.

English Historical Documents, Volume 1: ca. 500–1042, ed. and trans. D. Whitelock. Oxford and New York, 1955.

Everhelm. *Vita Popponis abbatis Stabulensis*, ed. D. Wattenbach. MGH SS 11: 291–316.

"Extracts from King Ethelred's 1014 Code." Trans. Whitelock, in *English Historical Documents, Volume 1: ca. 500–1042*, pp. 411–14.

Flodoard of Reims. *Historia Remensis ecclesiae*, ed. M. Statmann. MGH, SS 36.

Frutolf of Michelsberg. *Chronicon*, ed. and trans. (into German) F.-J. Schmale and I. Schmale-Ott. AQDGM, 15. Darmstadt, 1972. Pp. 48–121.

Fulbert of Chartres. *The Letters and Poems of Fulbert of Chartres*, ed., F. Behrends. OMT. Oxford, 1976.

Gelasius II. *Epistolae et privilegia* (PL 163: 487–514).

Geoffrey Malaterra. *De rebus gestis Rogerii Calabriae et Siciliae comitis et Roberti Guiscardi ducis fratris eius*, ed. Er. Pontieri. 2nd ed., RIS, 5.1. Bologna, 1927–28.

Geoffrey of Vendôme. *Oeuvres*, ed. and trans. (into French) G. Giordanengo. Sources d'histoire médiévale. Paris and Turnhout, 1996.

Gerard of Cambrai. *Acta synodi Atrebatensis* (PL 142: 1269–1312).

Gerbert (Sylvester II). *Die Briefsammlung Gerberts von Reims*, ed. F. Weigle, MGH, Die Briefe der deutschen Kaiserzeit, 2. Weimar, 1966; *The Letters of Gerbert, with his Papal Privileges as Sylvester II*, trans. H. Lattin. Records of Civilization, 60. New York, 1961.

Gesta episcoporum Autissiodorensium, ed. M. Sot, G. Lobrichon, M. Goullet, and P. Bonnerue. 2 vols. CHFMA, 42. Paris, 2002.

Gesta episcoporum Cameracensium, ed. L. Bethmann. MGH SS 7: 393–489.

Gesta Galcheri Cameracensis episcopi, ed. C. de Smedt. In *Gesta pontificum Cameracensium/Gestes des évêques de Cambrai de 1092 à 1138*. Publications de la Société de l'Histoire de France, 197. Paris, 1880. Pp. 1–108.

Goscelin of Canterbury. *De sancta Wereburga Virgine. AASS*, Feb. I (February 3): 386–90.

Gregory I. *Homiliae in Evangelia*, ed. R. Étaix. CC, SL, 141. Turnhout, 1999.
Homiliae in Ezechielem (PL 76: 785–1072).
Moralia in Iob, ed. M. Adriaen. 3 vols. CC, SL, 143–143B. Turnhout, 1979–85.
Registrum epistularum, ed. D. Norberg. 2 vols, CC, SL 140–140A. Turnhout, 1982.

Gregory VII. *The Epistolae Vagantes of Pope Gregory VII*, ed. and trans. H. E. J. Cowdrey. OMT. Oxford, 1972.
Das Register Gregors VII, ed. E. Caspar. MGH, Epistolae selectae, 2. Berlin, 1920–23; *The Register of Pope Gregory VIII, 1073–1085*, trans. H. Cowdrey Oxford, 2002.

Guibert of Nogent. *De laude sanctae Mariae* (PL 156: 537–78).
. *De vita sua*, ed. and trans. (into French) E.-R. Labande. CHFMA, 34. Paris, 1981; *Self and Society in Medieval France: The Memoirs of Abbot Guibert of Nogent*, trans. J. Benton. New York, 1970.

Guigo of La Chartreuse. *Vita sancti Hugonis episcopi Gratianopolitani* (PL 153: 761–84).

Hadrian II. *Epistolae*, ed. E. Perels. MGH EPP 6: 691–762.

Hariulf of Oldeburg and Lisiard of Soissons. *Vita sancti Arnulfi episcopi Suessionensis. AASS*, Aug. III (August 15): 230–59.

Henry IV. *Die Briefe Heinrichs IV.*, ed. C. Erdmann, MGH, Deutsches Mittelalter, 1. Leipzig, 1937. Trans. Mommsen and Morrison, in *Imperial Lives and Letters*, pp. 138–200.

Die Urkunden Heinrichs IV., ed. D. von Gladiss and A. Gawlik. 3 vols. MGH, Diplomata, 6. Berlin, Weimar, and Hanover, 1941–78.

Hermannus Contractus. *Historia sanctae Afrae martyris Augustensis*, ed. D. Hiley and W. Berschin. Wissenschaftliche Abhandlungen, Musicological Studies 65/10. Ottawa, 2004.

Hildebert of Le Mans. *Epistolae* (PL 171: 141–302).

Epistolae de Paschali papa, ed. E. Sackur. MGH LL 2: 668–72.

Sermones (PL 171: 343–964).

Vita beatae Mariae Aegypticae (PL 171: 1321–40).

Hincmar of Reims. *Capitulae*, ed. R. Pokorny, M. Stratmann, and W.-D. Runge. MGH Capit. episc., 2: 34–70.

Coronatio Judith Caroli filiae (PL 125: 811–14).

De ordine palatii, ed. T. Gross and R. Schieffer. MGH, Fontes iuris germanici antiqui in usum scholarum separatim editi, 3. Hanover, 1980.

Epistolae. MGH EPP 8.1: 1–228. This edition is incomplete; the later letters are cited from *Epistolae* (PL 126: 9–280)

Hincmar of Reims and Hincmar of Laon. *Die Streitschriften Hinkmars von Reims und Hinkmars von Laon, 869–871*, ed. R. Schieffer. MGH Concilia, 4, Sup. 2. Hanover, 2003.

Historia inventionis sancti Wulfranni. AASS, Mar. III (March 20): 148–61.

Honorius Augustodunensis. *De offendiculo*, ed. I. Dieterich. MGH LL 3: 38–57.

Gemma animae (PL 172: 541–738).

Sacramentarium (PL 172: 737–806).

Speculum ecclesiae (PL 172: 807–1107).

Hrabanus Maurus. *Commentaria in Genesim* (PL 107: 439–670).

Hrabanus Maurus. *De clericorum institutione* (PL 107: 293–420).

Epistolae, ed. E. Dümmler. MGH, EPP 5: 379–516.

Hrotsvit (Hrotswitha). *Opera omnia*, ed. W. Berschin. Bibliotheca scriptorum graecorum et romanorum Teubneriana. Munich and Leipzig, 2001.

Hubert of Brabant. *Vitae sanctae Gudilae. AASS*, Jan. I (January 8): 514–23.

Hugh of Flavigny. *Chronicon*, ed. G. Pertz. MGH SS 8: 280–502.

Hugh of Fleury. *De regia potestate et sacerdotali dignitate*, ed. E. Sackur. MGH, LL 2: 466–94.

Hugo. *Versus contra Manegoldum*, ed. E. Dümmler, MGH LL 1: 430–31.

Humbert of Silva Candida. *Adversus simoniacos libri tres*, ed. F. Thaner. MGH LL 1: 100–253.

Imperial Lives and Letters of the Eleventh Century, ed. T. Mommsen, trans. K. Morrison. Records of Civilization, 61. New York, 1962.

Iocundus. *Translatio sancti Servatii*, ed. R. Köpke. MGH SS 12: 85–126.

Isidore of Seville. *De ecclesiasticis officiis* (PL 83: 737–826).

Etymologiae (PL 82: 73–728).

Ivo of Chartres. *Decretum* (PL 161: 47–1022).

Epistolae (PL 162: 11–288). Letters 1–70 cited from *Correspondance*, ed. and trans. (into French) J. Leclercq. CHFMA, 22. Paris, 1949.

Sermones (PL 162: 505–610).

Ivo of Chartres and Josceran of Lyons. *Epistolae ad litem investiturarum spectantes*, ed. E. Sackur, MGH LL 2: 642–57.

John VIII. *Registrum, fragmenta registri, et epistolae passim collectae*, ed. E. Caspar and G. Laehr. MGH EPP 7: 1–329.

John of Fécamp. *Epistola ad Leonem papam* (PL 143: 799–800).

John of Lodi. *Vita beati Petri Damiani. AASS*, Feb. III (February 23): 416–27.

John of Mantua. *In Cantica canticorum et de sancta Maria tractatus ad comitissam Matildam*, ed. B. Bischoff and B. Taeger. Spicilegium Friburgense, 19. Freiburg, 1973.

Justinian. *The Digest*, ed. T. Mommsen and P. Krueger, trans. A. Watson. 4 vols. Philadelphia, 1985.

"King Ethelred's Code of 1008." Trans. Whitelock, in *English Historical Documents, Volume 1: ca. 500–1042.* Pp. 405–9.

Lambert of Arras. *Epistolae* (PL 162: 647–716).

Gesta quibus Atrebatensium civitas ... in antiquam reformatur dignitatem (PL 162: 627–48).

Lampert of Hersfeld. *Opera*, ed. O. Holder-Egger. MGH SRG n.s. 38. Hanover and Leipzig, 1894.

Landulf of Milan. *Historia Mediolanensis*, ed. L. Bethmann and W. Wattenbach, MGH SS 8: 32–100.

Lanfranc of Canterbury. *Commentarius in omnes epistolas Pauli* (PL 150: 101–406).

The Letters of Lanfranc, Archbishop of Canterbury, ed. and trans. H. Clover and M. Gibson. OMT. Oxford, 1979.

"The Law of the Northumbrian Priests." Trans. Whitelock, in *English Historical Documents, Volume 1: ca. 500–1042.* Pp. 434–39.

Leo I. *Epistolae* (PL 54: 593–1213); *Letters*, trans. E. Hunt. The Fathers of the Church. New York, 1957.

Liber miraculorum sancte Fidis, ed. L. Robertini. Biblioteca di medioevo latino, 10. Spoleto, 1994; *The Book of Sainte Foy*, trans. P. Sheingorn. MAS. Philadelphia, 1995.

Manegold of Lautenbach. *Ad Gebehardum liber*, ed. K. Francke, MGH LL 1: 308–430.

Mansi, J., et al. *Sacrorum conciliorum nova et amplissima collectio.* 53 vols. Florence, Venice, Paris, and Arnheim, 1759–1927.

Marbod of Rennes. *Thaisidis vita altera metrica. AASS*, Oct. IV (October 8): 226–28.

Vita sancti Roberti abbatis Casae-Dei (PL 171: 1505–32).

Memorials of St. Dunstan, Archbishop of Canterbury, ed. W. Stubbs. RS, 63. London, 1874.

Nicholas I. *Epistolae*, ed. E. Perels. MGH EPP 6: 257–690.

Nicholas II. *Epistolae et diplomata* (PL 143: 1301–62).

Nicholas of Soissons. *Vita sancti Godefridi episcopi Ambianensi. AASS*, Nov. III (November 8): 905–44.

Norman Anonymous. *Die Texte des normannischen Anonymus*, ed. K. Pellens. Veröffentlichungen des Instituts für Europäische Geschichte, Mainz, 42. Wiesbaden, 1966.

Odilo of Cluny. *Epitaphium Adalheidae* (PL 142: 981–92).

Odorannus of Sens. *Opera omnia*, ed. and trans. (into French) R.-H. Bautier and M. Gilles. Sources d'histoire médiévale, 4. Paris, 1972.

"Old English Marriage Agreement between Wulfric and Archbishop Wulfstan's Sister." Trans. Whitelock, in *English Historical Documents, Volume 1: ca. 500–1042*. Pp. 547–48.

"Old English Record of a Family Lawsuit." Trans. Whitelock, in *English Historical Documents, Volume 1: ca. 500–1042*, p. 556.

Oliba of Vich. *Conversio beatae Afrae* (PL 142: 591–98).

Epistolae (PL 142: 599–604).

Orderic Vitalis. *Historia aecclesiastica*, ed. and trans. M. Chibnall. 6 vols. OMT. Oxford, 1969–80.

Orthodoxa defensio imperialis, ed. L. de Heinemann. MGH LL 2: 535–42.

Osbern of Canterbury. *Vita et liber miraculorum sancti Dunstani*, ed. W. Stubbs. In *Memorials of St. Dunstan*. Pp. 69–161.

Othlo of St. Emmeram. *Dialogus de tribus quaestionibus* (PL 146: 59–134).

Liber de cursu spirituali (PL 146: 139–242).

Otto of Freising. *Chronica, sive Historia de duabus civitatibus*, ed. A. Hofmeister. MGH, SRG, 45. Hanover and Leipzig, 1912; *The Two Cities: A Chronicle of Universal History to the Year 1146*, trans. C. Mierow. Records of Civilization. New York, 1928.

The Papal Reform of the Eleventh Century: Lives of Pope Leo IX and Pope Gregory VII, ed. and trans. I. S. Robinson. Manchester Medieval Sources. Manchester and New York, 2004.

Papsturkunden 896–1046, ed. H. Zimmermann. 3 vols. Österreichische Akademie der Wissenschaften, Philosophisch-Historische Klasse, Denkschriften, 174, 177, 198. Vienna, 1984–89.

Pascal II. *Epistolae et privilegia* (PL 163: 31–444).

Paul of Bernreid. *Vita Gregorii VII papae* (PL 148: 39–104). Trans. Robinson, in *The Papal Reform of the Eleventh Century*, pp. 262–364.

Peter Crassus. *Defensio Heinrici IV. regis*, ed. L. de Heinemann. MGH LL 1: 433–53.

Peter Damian. *Die Briefe des Petrus Damiani*, ed. K. Reindel. 4 vols. MGH, Die Briefe der deutschen Kaiserzeit, 4. Munich, 1983–93; *The Letters of Peter Damian*, trans. O. Blum (vol. 6 with I. Resnick). 6 vols. The Fathers of the Church, Medieval Continuation. Washington, DC, 1989–2004.

Sermones, ed. G. Lucchesi. CC, CM 67. Turnhout, 1983.

Vita beati Romualdi, ed. G. Tabbaco. Fonti per la storia d'Italia, 94. Rome, 1957.

"Physiologus Latinus, versio Y," ed. F. Carmody. *University of California Publications in Classical Philology* 12 (1941): 95–134.

Placidus of Nonantola. *Liber de honore ecclesiae*, ed. L. de Heinemann. MGH LL 2: 568–639.

Le pontificale romain au moyen âge, tome 1: Le pontifical romain du XIIe siècle, ed. M. Andrieu. Studi e testi, 86. Rome, 1938.

Prudentius. *Hamartigenia*, ed. and trans. J. Stam. Amsterdam, 1940.

Pseudo-Anselm of Canterbury. *De nuptiis consanguineorum* (PL 158: 557–60).

Pseudo-Bede (Manegold of Lautenbach?). *In psalmorum libro exegesis* (PL 93: 477–1098).

Ranger of Lucca. *De anulo et baculo*, ed. E. Sackur. MGH LL 2: 508–33.

Raoul of Saint-Sépulchre. *Vita sancti Lietberti Cameracensis episcopi*, ed. A. Hofmeister. MGH SS 30.2: 838–66.

Raoul (Rodulfus) Glaber. *Historiarum libri quinque*, ed. and trans. J. France. In *Opera*. OMT. Oxford, 1989.

Rather of Verona. *Die Briefe des Bischofs Rather von Verona*, ed. F. Weigle. MGH, Die Briefe der deutschen Kaiserzeit, 1. Weimar, 1949. Trans. P. Reid, in *The Complete Works of Rather of Verona*. Medieval and Renaissance Texts and Studies, 76. Binghamton, NY, 1991. Pp. 209–535.

Praeloquiorum libri VI, ed. P. Reid. In *Opera*. CC, CM 46A. Turnhout, 1984. Trans. P. Reid, in *The Complete Works of Rather of Verona*. Medieval and Renaissance Texts and Studies, 76. Binghamton, NY, 1991. Pp. 21–208.

Recueil des chartes de l'abbaye de Cluny, ed. A. Bernard and A. Bruel. 6 vols. Paris, 1876–1903.

Remigius Curiensis. *Canones pro sua dioecesi* (PL 102: 1093–1112).

Rescriptio beati Udelrici episcopi. In Frauenknecht (1997), pp. 203–15.

The Ruodlieb, ed. and trans. C. Grocock. Warminster and Chicago, 1985.

Richer of Reims. *Historiarum libri III*, ed. H. Hoffmann. MGH SS 38.

Rimbert of Hamburg. *Vita Anskarii*, ed. G. Waitz. MGH SRG, 55. Hanover, 1884.

Robert of Tombelaine. *Commentarium in Cantica canticorum* (PL 150: 1361–70).

Rupert of Deutz. *Anulus sive dialogus inter Christianum et Judaeum* (PL 170: 561–610).

Commentaria in evangelium sancti Iohannis, ed. H. Haacke. CC, CM 9. Turnhout, 1969.

De divinis officiis, ed. H. Haacke. CC, CM 7. Turnhout, 1967.

De sancta Trinitate et operibus suis, ed. H. Haacke. 4 vols. CC, CM, 21–24. Turnhout, 1971–72.

Le sacramentaire grégorien: ses principales formes d'après les plus anciens manuscrits, ed. J. Deshusses. Spicilegium Friburgense, 16. Freiburg, 1971.

Sacramentarium Fuldense, saeculi X., ed. G. Kopp, G. Richter and A. Schonfelder. Fulda, 1912. Cited from the reprint: Henry Bradshaw Society Publications, 101. Farnborough, 1982.

The Sacramentary of Ratoldus, ed. N. Orchard. Henry Bradshaw Society Publications, 116. Woodbridge, 2005.

Sigebert of Gembloux. *Apologia contra eos qui calumpniantur missas coniugatorum sacerdotum*. In Frauenknecht (1997), pp. 219–39.

Chronica, ed. L. Bethmann. MGH SS 6: 300–74.

Gesta abbatum Gemblacensium, no editor given. MGH SS 8: 523–42.

Leodicensium epistola adversus Paschalem papam, ed. E. Sackur. MGH LL 2: pp. 451–64.

Vita sancti Maclovii (PL 160: 729–46).

Vita Wicberti, no editor given. MGH SS 8: 507–16.

Stephen V. *Epistolae*, ed. E. Caspar and G. Laehr. MGH EPP 7: 334–65.

Stephen of Fougères. *Vita beati Vitalis primi abbatis Saviniacensis*, ed. E. Sauvage. *Analecta Bollandiana* 1 (1882): 357–90.

Tertullian. *De carne Christi*, ed. E. Kroymann. In *Opera, pars II: Opera montanistica*. CC, SL 2. Turnhout, 1954. Pp. 871–917.

Thangmar. *Vita beati Bernwardi episcopi Hildesheimensis*, no editor named. MGH SS 4: 754–82.

Thietmar of Merseburg. *Chronicon*, ed. R. Holtzmann. MGH SRG, n.s. 9. Berlin, 1935; *Ottonian Germany: The Chronicon of Thietmar of Merseburg*, trans. D. Warner. Manchester Medieval Sources. Manchester, 2001.

Tractatus pro clericorum conubio. In Frauenknecht (1997), pp. 254–66.

Two Anglo-Saxon Pontificals, ed. H. Banting. Henry Bradshaw Society Publications, 104. London, 1989.

Urban II. *Epistolae et privilegia* (PL 151: 283–548).

Urbani II et Conradi regis conventus. MGH Constitutiones, 1: 564.

The Usatges of Barcelona: The Fundamental Law of Catalonia, trans. D. Kagay. MAS. Philadelphia, 1994.

Vita Aedwardi regis qui apud Westmonasterium requiescit, ed. and trans. F. Barlow. Medieval Texts. London, 1962.

Vita Altmanni episcopi Pataviensis, ed. W. Wattenbach. MGH SS 12: 226–43.

Vita Annonis archiepiscopi Coloniensis, ed. R. Koepke. MGH SS 11: 462–518.

Vita Guidonis abbatis Pomposiani. AASS Mar. III (March 31): 912–15.

Vita Heinrici IV. Imperatoris, ed. W. Eberhard. MGH, SRG, 58. Hanover and Leipzig, 1899. Trans. Mommsen and Morrison, in *Imperial Lives and Letters of the Eleventh Century*, pp. 101–37.

Vita Hildeburgis viduae. AASS, Jun. I (June 3): 362–63.

Vita Leonis noni, ed. and trans. (into French) M. Parisse. CHFMA, 38. Paris, 1997. Trans. Robinson, in *The Papal Reform of the Eleventh Century*, pp. 97–157.

Vita sanctae Idae comitissae Boloniensis. AASS, Apr. II (April 13): 141–45.

Walrami et Herrandi epistolae de causa Heinrici regis conscriptae, ed. E. Dümmler. MGH LL 2: 285–91.

Wenrich of Trier. *Epistola sub Theoderici episcopi Virdunensis nomine composita*, ed. K. Francke. MGH, LL 1: 282–99.

Wibert of Ravenna/Clement III. *Epistolae et privilegia* (PL 148: 827–42).

William V, Duke of Aquitaine. *Epistolae* (PL 141: 827–32).

William of Jumièges. *The Gesta Normannorum ducum of William of Jumièges, Orderic Vitalis and Robert of Torigni*, ed. and trans. E. van Houts. 2 vols OMT Oxford, 1992–95.

William of Malmesbury, *De gestis regum Anglorum*, ed. and trans. R. Mynors, R. Thomson, and M. Winterbottom. 2 vols. OMT. Oxford, 1998–99.

Saints' Lives: Lives of SS. Wulfstan, Dunstan, Patrick, Benignus and Indract, ed. M. Winterbottom and R. Thomson. OMT. Oxford, 2002.

Wipo. *Gesta Chuonradi II. imperatoris*, no editor given. MGH SS 11: 254–75. Trans. Mommsen and Morrison, in *Imperial Lives and Letters*, pp. 52–100.

SECONDARY WORKS

Ackelsberg, M., and Shanley, M. (1996). "Privacy, Publicity, and Power: A Feminist Rethinking of the Public–Private Distinction." In *Revisioning the Political: Feminist Reconstructions of Traditional Concepts in Western Political Theory*, ed. N. Hirschmann and C. Di Stefano. Boulder, Colorado. Pp. 213–33.

Adair, P. (2003). "Constance of Arles: A Study in Duty and Frustration." In *Capetian Women*. Pp. 9–26.

Aird, W. (1998). "Frustrated Masculinity: The Relationship between William the Conqueror and his Eldest Son." In *Masculinity in Medieval Europe*, ed. D. Hadley. Women and Men in History. London and New York. Pp. 39–55.

Airlie, S. (1998). "Private Bodies and the Body Politic in the Divorce Case of Lothar II." *Past & Present* 161: 3–38.

Althoff, G. (1993). "Demonstration und Inszenierung: Spielregeln der Kommunikation in mittelalterlicher Öffentlichkeit." *FS* 27: 27–50.

——— (2002). "Die Kultur der Zeichen und Symbole." *FS* 36: 1–17.

——— (2003). "Zum Inszenierungscharakter öffentlicher Kommunikation im Mittelalter." In *Von Fakten und Fiktionen: Mittelalterliche Geschichtsdarstellungen und ihre kritische Aufarbeitung*, ed. J. Laudage. Cologne. Pp. 79–93.

——— (2006). *Heinrich IV*. Gestalten des Mittelalters und der Renaissance. Darmstadt.

Amado, C. (2002). "Donation maritale et dot parentale: pratiques aristocratiques languedociennes aux Xe–XIe siècles." In *Dots et douaires*. Pp. 153–70.

Amann, E. and Dumas, E. (1940). *L'Église au pouvoir des laïques (888–1057)*. Histoire de l'Église des origines jusqu'à nos jours, ed. A. Fliche and V. Martin, 7. Paris.

Angenendt, A. (1980). "Das geistliche Bündnis der Päpste mit den Karolingern (754–796)." *Historisches Jahrbuch* 100: 1–94.

——— (1989). "Princeps imperii–Princeps apostolorum. Rom zwischen Universalismus und Gentilismus." In A. Angenendt and R. Schieffer, *Roma – Caput et Fons. Zwei Vorträge über das päpstliche Rom zwischen Altertum und Mittelalter*. Gerda Henkel Vorlesung. Opladen. Pp. 7–44.

Anton, H. (1982). *Der sogenannte Traktat "De ordinando pontifice": Ein Rechtsgutachten in Zusammenhang mit der Synode von Sutri (1046)*. Bonner Historische Forschungen, 48. Bonn.

——— (1988). "Beobachtungen zur heinrizianischen Publizistik: Die Defensio Heinrici IV regis." In *Historiographia Mediaevalis. Festschrift für Franz-Josef Schmale*, ed. D. Berg and H.-W. Goetz. Darmstadt. Pp. 149–67.

Arendt, H. (1958). *The Human Condition*. Chicago.

Aristocratic Women in Medieval France, ed. T. Evergates. MAS. Philadelphia, 1999.

Ashworth, H. (1956). "Urbs beata Ierusalem: Scriptural and Patristic Sources." *Ephemerides Liturgicae* 70: 238–41.

Atkinson, C. (1991). *The Oldest Vocation: Christian Motherhood in the Middle Ages*. Ithaca, New York.

Auerbach, E. (1938). "Figura." *Archivum Romanicum* 17: 320–41; cited in English translation by R. Mannheim from *Scenes from the Drama of European Literature: Six Essays*. New York, 1959. Pp. 11–76.

Aurell, M. (1995). *Les noces du comte: mariage et pouvoir en Catalogne (785–1213)*. Histoire ancienne et médiévale, 32. Paris.

(1997). "De nouveau sur les comtesses catalanes (IXe–XIIe siècles). *Annales du Midi* 109: 357–80.

(2000). "La parenté en l'an mil," *Cahiers de civilisation médiévale* 43: 125–42.

(2002). "Le douaire des comtesses catalanes de l'an mil." In *Dots et douaires*. Pp. 171–88.

Aus Kirche und Reich: Studien zu Theologie, Politik und Recht im Mittelalter. Festschrift für Friedrich Kempf zu seinem fünfundsiebzigsten Geburtstag und fünfzigjahrigen Doktorjubilaüm, ed. H. Mordek. Sigmaringen, 1983.

Bachrach, B. (1980). "Some Observations on the Medieval Nobility: A Review Essay." *Medieval Prosopography* 1: 15–33.

(1993). *Fulk Nerra, The Neo-Roman Consul, 987–1040: A Political Biography of the Angevin Count*. Berkeley and Los Angeles.

Bagge, S. (2002). *Kings, Politics and the Right Order of the World in German Historiography, c. 950–1150*. Studies in the History of Christian Thought, 103. Leiden, Boston, and Cologne.

Barlow, F. (1963). *The English Church, 1000–1066*. London. Cited from the second ed., 1979.

Barstow, A. (1982). *Married Priests and the Reforming Papacy: The Eleventh-Century Debates*. Lewiston, New York.

Barthélemy, D. (1992a). "La mutation féodale a-t-elle eu lieu? (Note critique)." *Annales, économies, sociétés, civilisations* 47: 767–77.

(1992b). *La société dans le comté de Vendôme de l'an mil au XIVe siècle*. Paris.

(1999). *La mutation de l'an Mil et la Paix de Dieu*. Paris, 1999.

Bartoli Langeli, A. (2002). "Après la 'Morgengabe'. Donations nuptiales et culture juridique dans l'Italie communale." In *Dots et douaires*. Pp. 123–30.

Baschet, J. (2000). *Le sein du père: Abraham et la paternité dans l'Occident médiéval*. Paris.

Bates, D. (1982). *Normandy before 1066*. London.

Bauduin, P. "Le bon usage de la *dos* dans la Normandie ducale (Xe–début du XIIe siècle)." In *Dots et douaires*. Pp. 429–55.

Baumgärtner, I. (2004). "Fürsprache, Rat und Tat, Erinnerung: Kunigundes Aufgaben als Herrscherin." In *Kunigunde, consors regni*. Pp. 47–69.

Beaudette, P. (1998). "'In the World but Not Of It': Clerical Celibacy as a Symbol of the Medieval Church." In *Medieval Purity and Piety*. Pp. 23–46.

Becher, M. (2001). "Cum lacrimis et gemitu. Vom Weinen der Sieger und der Besiegten im frühen und hohen Mittelalters." In *Formen and Funktionen*, pp. 25–52.

Becker, A. (1964–88). *Papst Urban II. (1088–1099)*, 2 vols. Schriften der Monumenta Germaniae Historica, 19. Stuttgart.

Bedard, W. (1951). *The Symbolism of the Baptismal Font in Early Christian Thought*. Catholic University of America Studies in Sacred Theology, 2nd series, 45. Washington, DC.

Bell, C. (1992). *Ritual Theory, Ritual Practice*. Oxford and New York.

Benson, R. (1967) "Plenitudo Potestatis: Evolution of a Formula from Gregory IV to Gratian." *Studia Gratiana*, 14 (Collectanea Stephan Kuttner): 195–217.

Benz, K. (1990). "Kirche und Gehorsam bei Papst Gregor VII: Neue Überlegungen zu einem alten Thema." In *Papsttum und Kirchenreform: Historische Beiträge: Festschrift für Georg Schwaiger zum 65. Geburtstag*, ed. M. Weitlauff and K. Hausberger. St. Ottilien. Pp. 97–150.

Bernards, M. (1971). "Die Frau in der Welt und die Kirche während des 11. Jahrhunderts." *Sacris Erudiri* 20: 39–100.

Berschin, W. (1972). *Bonizo von Sutri: Leben und Werk*. Beiträge zur Geschichte und Quellenkunde des Mittelalters, 2. Berlin and New York.

(1991). "Die Publizistische Reaktion auf den Tod Gregors VII. (nach fünf oberitalienischen Streitschriften." *SG* 14: 121–35.

Between Poverty and the Pyre: Moments in the History of Widowhood, ed. J. Bremmer and L. van den Bosch. London and New York, 1995.

Beulertz, S. (1991). *Das Verbot der Laieninvestitur im Investiturstreit*. MGH, Studien und Texte, 2. Hanover.

Beumann, H. (1991). "Die *Auctoritas* des Papstes und der Apostelfürsten in Urkunden der Bischofe von Halberstadt. Vom Wandel des bischöflichen Amtsverständnisses in der späten Salierzeit." In *Die Salier und das Reich*. Vol. 2: 333–53.

Bienvenu, J.-M. (1968). "Les caractères originaux de la réforme grégorienne dans le diocèse d'Angers." *Bulletin philologique et historique du Comité des travaux historiques et scientifiques* 2: 141–57.

Bischof Burchard von Worms, 1000–1025, ed. W. Hartmann. Quellen und Abhandlungen zur mittelrheinischen Kirchengeschichte, 100. Mainz, 2000.

The Bishop: Power and Piety at the First Millennium, ed. S. Gilsdorf. Neue Aspekte der europäischen Mittelalterforschung, 4. Münster, 2004.

The Bishop Reformed: Studies of Episcopal Power and Culture in the Central Middle Ages, ed. J. Ott and A. Jones. Aldershot, England and Burlington, Vermont, 2007.

Bisson, T. (1990). "Nobility and Family in Medieval France: A Review Essay." *French Historical Studies* 16: 597–613.

(1994). "The 'Feudal Revolution'." *Past & Present* 142: 6–42.

Bitel, L. (1996). "Reproduction and Production in Early Ireland." In *Portraits of Medieval and Renaissance Living*. Pp. 71–89.

Black-Veldtrup, M. (1995). *Kaiserin Agnes (1043–1077): Quellenkritische Studien*. Münstersche historische Forschungen, 7. Cologne, Weimar, and Vienna.

Bloch, M. (1924). *Les rois thaumaturges: Étude sur le charactère surnaturel attribué à la puissance royale, particulièrement en France et en Angleterre*. Publications de la Faculté des Lettres de l'Université de Strasbourg, 19. Strasburg and Paris. Cited from the English translation by J. Anderson, *The Royal Touch: Sacred Monarchy in France and England*. London, 1973.

(1939–40). *La société féodale*. 2 vols. Paris. Cited from the English translation by L. Manyon, *Feudal Society*. 2 vols. Chicago, 1963.

Blumenthal, U.-R. (1978a). *The Early Councils of Pope Pascal II, 1100–1110*. Studies and Texts, 43. Toronto.

(1978b). "Paschal II and the Roman Primacy." *Archivum historiae pontificiae* 16: 67–92.

(1982). *Der Investiturstreit*. Stuttgart. Cited from her own English translation, *The Investiture Controversy: Church and Monarchy from the Ninth to the Twelfth Century*. Philadelphia, 1988.

(1998). "Pope Gregory VII and the Prohibition of Nicolaitism." In *Medieval Purity and Piety*. Pp. 239–67.

(2001). *Gregor VII. Papst zwischen Canossa und Kirchenreform*. Darmstadt.

(2004a). "The Papacy, 1024–1122." In *The New Cambridge Medieval History, Volume 4*. Part 2: 8–37.

(2004b). "Humbert of Silva Candida." In *Medieval Italy: An Encyclopedia*, ed. C. Kleinherz. 2 vols. New York. Vol. 1: 518–19.

Boelens, M. (1968). *Die Klerikerehe in der Gesetzgebung der Kirche unter besonderere Berucksichtigung der Strafe: Eine rechtsgeschichtliche Untersuchung von den Anfangen der Kirche bis zum Jahre 1139*. Paderborn.

Bosl, K. (1975). "Die 'familia' als Grundstruktur der mittelalterlichen Gesellschaft." *Zeitschrift für Bayerische Landesgeschichte* 38: 403–23.

Boswell, J. (1980). *Christianity, Social Tolerance, and Homosexuality*. Chicago.

Bouchard, C. (1981a). "Consanguinity and Noble Marriages in the Tenth and Eleventh Centuries." *Speculum* 56: 268–87.

(1981b). "The Origins of the French Nobility: A Reassessment." *American Historical Review* 86: 501–32.

(1987). *Sword, Miter, and Cloister: Nobility and the Church in Burgundy, 980–1198*. Ithaca, New York.

(2001). *"Those of My Blood": Constructing Noble Families in Medieval Francia*. MAS. Philadelphia.

Bougard, F. (2002). "Dot et douaire en Italie centro-septentrionale, VIIIe–XIe siècle: un parcours documentaire." In *Dots et douaires*. Pp. 57–95.

Bourdieu, P. (1972). *Esquisse d'une théorie de la pratique*. Paris; cited from the English translation by R. Nice, *Outline of a Theory of Practice*. Cambridge, 1977.

Boynton, S. (2006). *Shaping a Monastic Identity: Liturgy and History at the Imperial Abbey of Farfa, 1000–1125*. Conjunctions of Religion and Power in the Medieval Past. Ithaca, New York.

Brakel, C. (1972). "Die vom Reformpapsttum geförderten Heiligenkulte." *SG* 9: 241–311.

Bremmer, J. (1995). "Widows in Anglo-Saxon England." In *Between Poverty and the Pyre*. Pp. 58–88.

Brennan, T., and Pateman, C. (1979). "'Mere Auxiliaries to the Commonwealth': Women and the Origins of Liberalism." *Political Studies* 27: 183–200.

Brett, M. (1975). *The English Church under Henry I*. Oxford Historical Monographs. Oxford.

Brooke, C. (1965). "Gregorian Reform in Action: Clerical Marriage in England, 1050–1200." *Cambridge Historical Journal* 12: 1–21.

(1989). *The Medieval Idea of Marriage*. Oxford.

Brooke, Z. (1931). *The English Church and the Papacy: From the Conquest to the Reign of John*. Cambridge.

Brown, P. (1988). *The Body and Society: Men, Women and Sexual Renunciation in Early Christianity*. New York.

Brundage, J. (1967a). "The Crusader's Wife: A Canonistic Quandry." *Studia Gratiana* 12: 425–42.

——— (1967b). "The Crusader's Wife Revisited." *Studia Gratiana* 14: 241–52.

——— (1976). "Prostitution in Medieval Canon Law." *Signs* 1: 825–45.

——— (1987). *Law, Sex, and Christian Society in Medieval Europe*. Chicago.

Buc, P. (1994). *L'ambiguité du livre: prince, pouvoir et peuple dans les commentaires de la Bible au moyen âge*. Théologie historique, 95. Paris.

——— (2001). *The Dangers of Ritual: Between Early Medieval Texts and Social Scientific Theory*. Princeton.

Bühler, A. (2001). "Kaiser Heinrich IV. und Bertha von Turin – Eine schwierige Ehe im Spiegel der Urkunden," *Archiv für Kulturgeschichte* 83: 38–61.

Bührer-Thierry, G. (1997). *Évêques et pouvoir dans le royaume de Germanie: Les églises de Bavière et Souabe, 876–973*. Paris.

Bulst-Thiele, M.-L. (1933). *Kaiserin Agnes*. Beiträge zur Kulturgeschichte des Mittelalters und der Renaissance, 52. Leipzig and Berlin.

Büsch, J. (1989). "'Landulfi Senioris Historia Mediolanensis' – Überlieferung, Datierung und Intention." *DA* 45: 1–30.

——— (1990). *Der Liber de Honore Ecclesiae des Placidus von Nonantola. Eine kanonistische Problemerörterung aus dem Jahre 1111: Die Arbeitsweise ihres Autors und seine Vorlagen*. Quellen und Forschungen zum Recht im Mittelalter, 5. Sigmaringen.

Butler, J. (1990). *Gender Trouble: Feminism and the Subversion of Identity*. New York.

——— (1993). *Bodies that Matter: On the Discursive Limits of Sex*. New York.

Bynum, C. (1982). "Jesus as Mother and Abbot as Mother: Some Themes in Twelfth-Century Cistercian Writing." In her *Jesus as Mother: Studies in the Spirituality of the High Middle Ages*. Berkeley and Los Angeles. Pp. 110–69.

Cabaniss, A. (1954). *Amalarius of Metz*. Amsterdam.

Cadden, J. (1993). *The Meaning of Sex Difference in the Middle Ages: Medicine, Science, and Culture*. Cambridge History of Medicine. Cambridge.

Cammarosano, P. (2006). "La disciplina della vita sessuale nel mondo carolingio." In *Comportamenti e immaginario della sessualità nell'alto medioevo*. Vol. 2: 817–35.

Cantarella, G. (1982). *Ecclesiologia e politica nel papato di Pasquale II: Linee di una interpretazione*. Studi storici, 131. Rome.

——— (1983). "Placido di Nonantola: un progetto di ideologia." *Rivista di storia della chiesa in Italia* 37: 117–42.

——— (1987). *La costruzione della verità. Pasquale II, un papa alle strette*. Studi storici, 178–79. Rome.

Cantor, N. (1958). *Church, Kingship and Lay Investiture in England, 1089–1135*. Princeton.

Capetian Women, ed. K. Nolan. The New Middle Ages. New York, 2003.

Capitani, O. (1964). "La figura del vescovo in alcune collezioni canoniche della seconda metà del secolo XI." In *Vescovi e diocesi in Italia nel medioevo (sec. IX–XIII). Atti del II convegno di storia della Chiesa in Italia*. Italia Sacra, 5. Rome. Pp. 161–91.

(1974). "Episcopato ed ecclesiologia nell' età gregoriana." In *Le istituzione ecclesiastiche della <<societas christiana>> dei secoli XI–XII.* Pp. 316–73.

(1975). "Problematica della *Disceptatio Synodalis.*" *SG* 10: 142–74.

Carpegna Falconieri, T. di (2002). *Il clero di Roma nel mediovo: Istituzioni e politica cittadina (secoli VIII–XIII).*

Carpentier, E. (2000). "Un couple tumultueux en Poitou à la fin du Xe siècle: Guillaume de Poitiers et Emma de Blois." In *Mariage et sexualité au moyen âge: Accord ou crise?* Pp. 203–15.

Caviness, M. (2006). "A Son's Gaze on Noah: Case or Cause of Virilophobia?" In *Comportamenti e immaginario della sessualità nell'alto medioevo.* Vol. 2: 981–1024.

Chavasse, C. (1940). *The Bride of Christ: An Enquiry into the Nuptial Element in Early Christianity.* London.

Chélini, J. (1991). *L'aube du moyen âge: Naissance de la chrétienté occidentale. La vie religieuse des laïcs dans l'Europe carolingienne (750–900).* Paris.

Chibnall, M. (1991). *The Empress Matilda: Queen Consort, Queen Mother and Lady of the English.* Oxford.

Le chiese nei regni dell'Europa occidentale e i loro rapporti con Roma sino all' 800. 2 vols. Settimane, 7. Spoleto, 1960.

Chodorow, S. (1989). "Paschal II, Henry V, and the Origins of the Crisis of 1111." In *Popes, Teachers, and Canon Law in the Middle Ages,* ed. J. Sweeney and S. Chodorow. Ithaca, New York. Pp. 3–25.

Christelow, S. (1996). "The Division of Inheritance and the Provision of Non-Inheriting Offspring among the Anglo-Norman Elite." *Medieval Prosopography* 17: 3–45.

Chrysos, E. (2004). "1054: Schism?" In *Cristianità d'occidente e cristianità d'oriente (secoli VI-XI).* 2 vols. Settimane, 51. Spoleto. Vol. 1: 547–67.

Claussen, M. (1996). "Fathers of Power and Mothers of Authority: Dhuoda and the 'Liber manualis'." *French Historical Studies* 19: 785–809.

Cohen, J. (2004). "Synagoga conversa: Honorius Augustodunensis, the Song of Songs, and Christianity's 'Eschatological Jew'." *Speculum* 79: 309–40.

Comportamenti e immaginario della sessualità nell'alto medioevo. 2 vols. Settimane, 53. Spoleto, 2006.

Congar, Y. (1961). "Der Platz des Papsttums in der Kirchenfrömmigkeit der Reformer des 11. Jahrhunderts." In *Sentire ecclesiam: das Bewusstsein von der Kirche als gestaltende Kraft der Frömmigkeit. Festschrift zum 60. Geburtstag von Hugo Rahner,* ed. J. Daniélou and H. Vorgrimler. Freiburg, Basel, and Vienna. Pp. 196–217.

(1967). "S. Nicolas Ier (†867): ses positions ecclésiologiques." *Rivista di storia della Chiesa in Italia* 21: 393–410.

(1968). *L'ecclésiologie du haut moyen âge, de Saint Grégoire le Grand à la désunion entre Byzance et Rome.* Paris.

Conte, P. (1971). *Chiesa e primato nelle lettere dei papi del secolo VII.* Pubblicazioni dell'Università Cattolica del Sacro Cuore, Saggi e ricerche, serie 3: Scienze storiche, 4. Milan.

Corbet, P. (1990). "Le mariage en Germanie ottonienne d'après Thietmar de Merseburg." In *La femme au moyen âge,* ed. M. Rouche and J. Heuclin. Maubeuge. Pp. 187–214.

(2001). *Autour de Burchard de Worms: l'Église allemande et les interdits de parenté (IXe–XIIe siècles)*. Ius Commune, Sonderhefte: Studien zur europäischen Rechtsgeschichte, 142. Frankfurt.

(2002). "Le douaire dans le droit canonique jusqu'à Gratien." In *Dos et douaires*. Pp. 43–55.

Coulson, C. (2003). *Castles in Medieval Society*. Oxford and New York.

Cowdrey, H. (1970). *The Cluniacs and the Gregorian Reform*. Oxford.

(1983). *The Age of Abbot Desiderius: Montecassino, the Papacy, and the Normans in the Eleventh and Early Twelfth Centuries*. Oxford.

(1998a). *Pope Gregory VII, 1073–85*. Oxford.

(1998b). "Pope Gregory VII and the Chastity of the Clergy." In *Medieval Purity and Piety*. Pp. 269–302.

(2004). "The Structure of the Church, 1024–1073." In *The New Cambridge Medieval History, Volume 4*. Part 1: 228–67.

Crick, J. (1999a). "Men, Women, and Widows: Widowhood in Pre-Conquest England." In *Widowhood in Medieval and Early Modern Europe*, ed. S. Cavallo and L. Warner. London. Pp. 24–36.

(1999b). "Women, Posthumous Benefaction, and Family Strategy in Pre-Conquest England." *Journal of British Studies* 38: 399–422.

Crouch, D. (2005). *The Birth of Nobility: Constructing Aristocracy in England and France 900–1300*. Harlow, England.

Curschmann, M. (1988). "Imagined Exegesis: Text and Picture in the Exegetical Works of Rupert of Deutz, Honorius Augustodunensis, and Gerhoch of Reichersberg." *Traditio* 44: 145–69.

Cushing, K. (1998). *Papacy and Law in the Gregorian Revolution: The Canonistic Work of Anselm of Lucca*. Oxford Historical Monographs. Oxford.

(2005). *Reform and the Papacy in the Eleventh Century: Spirituality and Social Change*. Manchester.

Dalarun, J. (1992). "La Madeleine dans l'ouest de la France au tournant des XIe et XIIe siècles." In *La Madeleine (VIIIe–XIIIe siècle)*, ed. G. Duby. Mélanges de l'École Française de Rome, 104. Rome. Pp. 71–119.

D'Avray, D. (2005). *Medieval Marriage: Symbolism and Society*. Oxford.

"Debate: The 'Feudal Revolution'." *Past & Present* 152 (1996), 196–223 and 155 (1997), 177–208: Contributions by D. Barthélemy, S. White, T. Reuter, C. Wickham.

Debord, A. (2000). *Aristocratie et pouvoir: le rôle du château dans la France médiévale*. Paris.

De Jong, M. (1992). "Power and Humility in Carolingian Society: The Public Penance of Louis the Pious," *Early Medieval Europe* 1: 29–52.

Delahaye, K. (1958). *Erneuerung der Seelsorgsformen, aus der Sicht der frühen Patristik. Ein Beitrag zur theologischen Grundlegung kirchlicher Seelsorge*. Freiburg.

Delmaire, B. (1994). *Le diocèse d'Arras de 1093 au milieu du XIVe siècle: Recherches sur la vie religieuse dans le nord de la France au moyen âge*, 2 vols. Mémoires de la Commission départementale d'Histoire et d'Archéologie du Pas-de-Calais, 31. Arras.

Delogu, P. (2000). "The Papacy, Rome and the Wider World in the Seventh and Eighth Centuries." In *Early Medieval Rome and the Christian West: Essays in*

Honour of Donald A. Bullough, ed. J. Smith. Leiden, Boston, and Cologne. Pp. 197–220.

Denzler, G. (1973). *Das Papsttum und der Amtszölibat*. 2 vols. Päpste und Papsttum, 5. Stuttgart.

Depreux, P. (2002). "La dotation de l'épouse en Aquitaine septentrionale du IXe au XIIe siècle." In *Dots et douaires*. Pp. 219–44.

Deremble, J.-P. (2000). "La nudité de Noé ivre et ses relectures typologiques et iconographiques médiévales." In *Mariage et sexualité au moyen âge*. Pp. 147–55.

Dhondt, J. (1964–65). "Sept femmes et un trio de rois." *Contributions à l'histoire économique et sociale* 3: 35–70.

Dillard, H. (1984). *Daughters of the Reconquest: Women in Castilian Town Society, 1100–1300*. Cambridge Iberian and Latin American Studies. Cambridge.

Di Paola, L. (2002). "'Roma caput mundi' e 'natalis scientiae sedes.' Il recupero della centralità di Roma in epoca tardo-antica." In *Politica retorica e simbolismo del primato: Roma e Constantinopoli (secoli IV–VII)*, ed. F. Elia. Catania. Pp. 119–55.

Dixon, S. (1988). *The Roman Mother*. London and Sydney.

Dockray-Miller, M. (2000). *Motherhood and Mothering in Anglo-Saxon England*. The New Middle Ages. New York.

Dots et douaires dans le haut moyen âge, ed. F. Bougard, L. Feller, and R. Le Jan. Collection de l'École Française de Rome, 295. Rome, 2002.

Douglas, M. (1966). *Purity and Danger: An Analysis of Concepts of Pollution and Taboo*. London.

Drell, J. (2002). *Kinship and Conquest: Family Strategies in the Principality of Salerno during the Norman Period, 1077–1194*. Ithaca, New York.

Duby, G. (1953). *La société aux XIe et XIIe siècles dans la région mâconnaise*. Paris.

(1964). "Les 'jeunes' dans la société aristocratique dans la France du Nord-Ouest au XIIe siècle." *Annales: économies, sociétés, civilisations* 19: 835–46; rpt. in his *Hommes et structures au moyen âge*. Paris, 1973. Cited from the English translation by C. Postan, "Youth in Aristocratic Society," in G. Duby, *The Chivalrous Society*. London, 1977. Pp. 112–22.

(1973). *Hommes et structures au moyen âge*. Paris.

(1978) *Les trois ordres, ou l'imaginaire du féodalisme*. Paris. Cited from the English translation by A. Goldhammer, *The Three Orders: Feudal Society Imagined*. Chicago, 1980.

(1981). *Le Chevalier, la femme et le prêtre: le mariage dans la France féodale*. Paris. Cited from the English translation by B. Bray, *The Knight, the Lady, and the Priest: The Making of Modern Marriage in Medieval France*. Chicago, 1983.

(1988). *Mâle moyen âge: de l'amour et autres essais*. Paris. Cited from the English translation by J. Dunnett, *Love and Marriage in the Middle Ages*. Chicago, 1994.

(1995). "Women and Power." In *Cultures of Power: Lordship, Status, and Process in Twelfth-Century Europe*, ed. T. Bisson. MAS. Philadelphia. Pp. 69–85.

(1995–96). *Dames du douzième siècle*. 3 vols. Paris. Cited from the English translation by J. Birrell, *Women of the Twelfth Century*. 3 vols. Chicago, 1997–98.

Dunbabin, J. (1985). *France in the Making, 843–1180*. Oxford and New York.

Dvornik, F. (1964). *Byzance et la primauté romaine*. Unam Sanctam, 49. Paris. Cited from his English translation, *Byzantium and the Roman Primacy*. New York, 1966; rev. edn. 1979.

Elliott, D. (1993). *Spiritual Marriage: Sexual Abstinence in Medieval Wedlock*. Princeton.

—— (1999). *Fallen Bodies: Pollution, Sexuality, and Demonology in the Middle Ages*. MAS. Philadelphia.

Elstain, J. (1981). *Public Man, Private Woman: Women in Social and Political Thought*. Princeton.

Engelberger, J. (1996). *Gregor VII. und die Investiturfrage: Quellenkritische Studien zum angeblichen Investiturverbot von 1075*. Cologne.

—— (1998). "Gregor VII. und die Bischofserhebungen in Frankreich. Zur Entstehung des ersten römischen Investiturdekrets vom Herbst 1078." In *Die früh- und hochmittelalterliche Bischofserhebung*. Pp. 193–258.

Engels, O. (1987). "Der Pontifikatsantritt und seine Zeichen." In *Segni e riti nella chiesa altomedievale occidentale*. Vol. 2: 707–66.

—— (1998). "Bischofsherrschaft und Adel in Südfrankreich und Katalonien während des Hochmittelalters." In *Die früh- und hochmittelalterliche Bischofserhebung*. Pp. 259–85.

Enright, M. (1988). "Lady with the Meadcup: Ritual, Group Cohesion and Hierarchy in the Germanic Warband." *FS* 22: 170–203.

Erkens, F.-R. (1991). "Die Frau als Herrscherin in ottonisch-frühsalischer Zeit." In *Kaiserin Theophanu: Begegnung des Ostens und Westens um die Wende des ersten Jahrtausends: Gedenkschrift des Kölner Schnütgen-Museums zum 1000. Todesjahr der Kaiserin*, ed. A. Von Euw and P. Schreiner. 2 vols. Cologne. Vol. 2: 245–59.

—— (1998). "Die Bischofswahl im Spannungsfeld zwische weltlicher und geistlicher Gewalt. Ein tour d'horizont." In *Die früh- und hochmittelalterliche Bischofserhebung*. Pp. 1–32.

—— (2004). "Consortium regni – consecratio – sanctitas: Aspekte des Königinnentums im ottonisch-salischen Reich." In *Kunigunde, consors regni*. Pp. 71–82.

Esmyol, A. (2002). *Geliebte oder Ehefrau? Konkubinen in frühen Mittelalter*. Beihefte zum Archiv für Kulturgeschichte, 52. Cologne, Weimar, and Vienna.

The Experience of Power in Medieval Europe, 950–1350, ed. R. Berkhofer, A. Cooper and A. Kosko. Aldershot, England and Burlington, Vermont, 2005.

Exultet: rotoli liturgici del medioevo meridionale, ed. G. Cavallo, G. Orofino, and O. Pecere. Rome, 1994.

Die Exultetrolle: Codex Barberini Latinus 592, ed. G. Cavallo and L. Speciale. Zurich, 1988.

Facinger, M. (1968). "A Study of Medieval Queenship: Capetian France (987–1237)." *Studies in Medieval and Renaissance History* 5: 1–48.

Famille et parenté dans l'Occident médiéval, ed. G. Duby and J. Le Goff. Collection de l'École Française de Rome, 30. Rome, 1977.

Fanning, S. (1988). *A Bishop and His World before the Gregorian Reform: Hubert of Angers, 1006–1047.* Transactions of the American Philosophical Society, 78, no. 1. Philadelphia.

Farmer, S. (1986). "Persuasive Voices: Clerical Images of Medieval Wives." *Speculum* 61: 517–43.

Feller, L. (2002). "'Morgengabe,' dot, *tertia:* rapport introductif." In *Dots et douaires.* Pp. 1–25.

Feminism, the Public and the Private, ed. J. Landes. Oxford and New York, 1998.

Feminists Read Habermas: Gendering the Subject of Discourse, ed. J. Meehan. New York and London, 1995.

Femmes et pouvoirs des femmes à Byzance et en Occident (VIe–XIe siècles), ed. S. Lebecq, A. Dierkens, R. Le Jan, and J.-M. Sansterre. Publications du Centre de Recherche sur l'histoire de l'Europe du Nord-Ouest, 19. Lille, 1999.

Femmes, pouvoir et société dans le haut moyen âge, ed. R. Le Jan. Paris, 2001.

Ferrante, J. (1997). *To the Glory of Her Sex: Women's Roles in the Composition of Medieval Texts.* Bloomington, Indiana.

Fichtenau, H. (1983). "Vom Ansehen des Papsttums im zehnten Jahrhundert." In *Aus Kirche und Reich.* Pp. 117–24.

(1984). *Lebensordnung des 10. Jahrhunderts: Studien über Denkart und Existenz im einstigen Karolingerreich.* Stuttgart. Cited from the English translation by P. Geary, *Living in the Tenth Century: Mentalities and Social Orders.* Chicago, 1991.

Fliche, A. (1924–37). *La réforme grégorienne.* 3 vols. Paris.

Flint, V. (1995). *Honorius Augustodunensis of Regensburg.* Authors of the Middle Ages, 6. Aldershot, England and Brookfield, Vermont.

Foreville, R. (1974). "Royaumes, métropolitains et conciles provinciaux: France, Grande-Bretagne, Péninsule ibérique." In *Le istituzione ecclesiastiche della "societas christiana" dei secoli XI–XII.* Pp. 272–313.

Formen und Funktionen öffentlicher Kommunikation im Mittelalter, ed. G. Althoff. Vorträge und Forschungen, 51. Sigmaringen, 2001.

Fornasari, G. (1981). *Celibato sacerdotale e "autocoscienza" ecclesiale: per la storia della "Nicolaitica haeresis" nell'Occidente medievale.* Udine.

Fössel, A. (2000). *Die Königin im mittelalterlichen Reich: Herrschaftsausübung, Herrschaftsrechte, Handlungsspielräume.* Mittelalter-Forschungen, 4. Stuttgart.

Foucault, M. (1975). *Surveiller et punir: naissance de la prison.* Paris. Cited from the English translation by A. Sheridan, *Discipline and Punish: The Birth of the Prison.* New York, 1979.

(1976–84). *Histoire de la sexualité.* 3 vols. Paris. Cited from the English translation by R. Hurley, *The History of Sexuality.* 3 vols. New York, 1978–86.

Fournier, P., and Le Bras, G. (1931–32). *Histoire des collections canoniques en Occident.* 2 vols. Paris.

Fransen, G. (1977). "La rupture du mariage." In *Il matrimonio nella società altomedievale.* Vol. 2: 603–30.

Frauenknecht, E. (1997). *Die Verteidigung der Priesterehe in der Reformzeit.* Hanover.

Freed, J. (1986). "Reflections on the Medieval German Nobility. *American Historical Review* 91: 553–75.

Die früh- und hochmittelalterliche Bischofserhebung im europäischen Vergleich, ed. F.-R. Erkens. Beihefte zum Archiv für Kulturgeschichte, 48. Cologne, Weimar, and Vienna, 1998.

Fuchs, V. (1930). *Der Ordinationstitel von seiner Entstehung bis auf Innocenz III: Eine Untersuchung zur kirchlichen Rechtsgeschichte*. Kanonistische Studien und Texte, 4. Bonn.

Fuhrmann, H. (1972–73). *Einfluss und Verbreitung der pseudoisidorischen Fälschungen*. 3 vols. Schriften der Monumenta Germaniae Historica, 24. Stuttgart.

— (1991). "Widerstände gegen den päpstliche Primat im Abendland." In *Il primato del vescovo di Roma nel primo millennio*. Pp. 707–36.

— (1992). "Beobachtungen zur Schrift 'De ordinando pontifice'." In *Aus Archiven und Bibliotheken: Festschrift für Raymund Kottje zum 65. Geburtstag*, ed. H. Mordek. Frankfurt am Main, Bern, New York, and Paris. Pp. 223–37.

Fulton, R. (1996). "Mimetic Devotion, Marian Exegesis, and the Historical Sense of the Song of Songs." *Viator* 27: 85–116.

Gaudemet, J. (1978). "Note sur le symbolisme médiéval: le mariage de l'evêque." *L'année canonique* 22: 71–80.

— (1992). "La primauté pontificale dans le Décret de Gratien." In *Studia in honorem eminentissimi cardinali Alphonsi M. Stickler*, ed. R. Castillo Lara. Rome. Pp. 137–56.

Gaudemet, J., J. Dubois, A. Duval, and J. Champagne (1979) *Les élections dans l'église latine des origines au XVIe siècle*. Paris.

Geary, P. (1994). *Phantoms of Remembrance: Memory and Oblivion at the End of the First Millennium*. Princeton.

Georgi, W. (1998). "Die Bischöfe der Kirchenprovinz Magdeburg zwischen Königtum und Adel im 10. und 11. Jahrhundert." In *Die früh- und hochmittelalterliche Bischofserhebung*. Pp. 83–137.

Gilchrist, J. (1962). "Canon Law Aspects of the Eleventh-Century Gregorian Reform Programme." *Journal of Ecclesiastical History* 13: 21–38

— (1962/63). "Humbert of Silva Candida and the Political Concept of Ecclesia in the Eleventh-Century Reform Movement." *Journal of Religious History* 2: 13–28.

— (1965). "*Simoniaca haeresis* and the Problem of Orders from Leo IX to Gratian." *Proceedings of the Second Internal Congress of Medieval Canon Law, Boston College, 12–16 August, 1963*. ed. S. Kuttner and J. J. Ryan. Monumenta iuris canonici, Series S: Subsidia, 1. Vatican City.

Godefroy, L. (1926). "Le mariage au temps des pères." *DTC* 9: 2077–2123.

Goez, E. (1995). *Beatrix von Canossa und Tuszien: Eine Untersuchung zur Geschichte des XI. Jahrhunderts*. Sigmaringen.

— (1996). "Der Thronerbe als Rivale: König Konrad, Kaiser Heinrichs IV. älterer Sohn." *Historisches Jahrbuch* 116: 1–49.

Goez, W. (1970). "'Papa qui et episcopus': Zum Selbstverständnis des Reformpapsttums im Mittelalter." *Archivum historiae pontificiae* 8: 7–59.

Gold, P. (1982). "The Marriage of Mary and Joseph in the Medieval Ideology of Marriage." In *Sexual Practices and the Medieval Church*, ed. J. Brundage and V. Bullough. Buffalo, New York. Pp. 102–17.

Goldstaub, M. (1899–1901). "Der Physiologus und seine Weiterbildung, besonders in der lateinischen und in der byzantinischen Literatur." *Philologus*, Supplementband 8.3: 339–404.

Goody, J. (1983). *The Development of the Family and Marriage in Europe*. Cambridge.

Gorman, M. (1998). "The Argumenta and Explanationes on the Psalms Attributed to Bede." *Revue Bénédictine* 108: 214–39.

Gradowicz-Pancer, N. (1996). "Papa, mama, l'abbé et moi. 'Conversio morum' et pathologie familiale d'après les sources hagiographiques du haut moyen âge." *Le moyen âge* 102: 7–25.

Green, J. (2006). *Henry I: King of England and Duke of Normandy*. Cambridge.

Grégoire, R. (1965). *Bruno de Segni, exégète médiéval et théologien monastique*. Spoleto.

Gresser, G. (2007). *Clemens II. Der erste deutsche Reformpapst*. Paderborn, Munich, Vienna, and Zurich.

Guillemain, B. (1974). "Les origins des évêques en France au XIe et XIIe siècles." In *Le istituzione ecclesiastiche della <<societas christiana>> dei secoli XI–XII*. Pp. 374–407.

Guillot, O. (1972). *Le comte d'Anjou et son entourage au XIe siècle*. 2 vols. Paris.

Habermas, J. (1962). *Strukturwandel der Öffentlichkeit: Untersuchungen zu einer Kategorie des bürgerlichen Gesellschaft*. Darmstadt. Cited from the English translation by T. Burger, *The Structural Transformation of the Public Sphere: An Inquiry into a Category of Bourgeois Society*. Cambridge, Massachusetts, 1989.

Haluska-Rausch, E. (2005). "Transformations in the Powers of Wives and Widows near Montpellier, 985–1213." In *The Experience of Power in Medieval Europe*. Pp. 153–68.

Hamilton, S. (2001). *The Practice of Penance, 900–1050*. Royal Historical Society Studies in History, n.s., 20. Rochester, New York.

Hampe, K. (1909). *Deutsche Kaisergeschichte in der Zeit der Salier und Staufer*. Leipzig.

Hartmann, W. (1972). "Psalmenkommentare aus der Zeit der Reform und der Frühscholastik." *SG* 9: 313–66.

(1975). "Beziehung des normannischen Anonymus zu frühscholastischen Bildungszentren." *DA* 31: 108–43.

(1993a). *Der Investiturstreit*. Munich.

(1993b). "Verso il centralismo papale (Leone IX, Niccolò II, Gregorio VII, Urbano II." In *Il secolo XI: una svolta?* Pp. 99–130.

Hauck, K. (1954). "Haus- und sippengebundene Literatur mittelalterlichen Adelsgeschlechter, von Adelssatiren des 11. und 12. Jahrhunderts aus erläutert." *Mitteilungen des Instituts für österreichische Geschichtsforschung* 62: 121–45.

(1977). "Formes de parenté artificielle dans le haut moyen âge." In *Famille et parenté*, pp. 43–47.

Hauréau, B. (1870). "Une élection d'évêque au XIIe s., Rainaud de Martigné, évêque d'Angers." *Revue des deux mondes* 88: 548–62.

Heene, K. (1997.) *The Legacy of Paradise: Marriage, Motherhood, and Women in Carolingian Edifying Literature*. Frankfurt am Main and New York.

Hellmuth, D. (1998). *Frau und Besitz: Zum Handlungsspielraum von Frauen in Alamannien (700–940).* Vorträge und Forschungen, 42. Sigmaringen.

Henkel, N. (1976). *Studien zum Physiologus im Mittelalter.* Tübingen.

Herberhold, F. (1947). "Die Angriffe des Cadalus von Parma (Gegenpapst Honorius II.) auf Rome in den Jahren 1062 und 1063." *SG* 2: 477–503.

Herde, R. (1967). "Das Hohelied in der lateinischen Literatur des Mittelalters bis zum 12. Jahrhundert." *Studi Medievali*, ser. 3, 8: 957–1073.

Herlihy, D. (1962). "Land, Family and Women in Continental Europe, 701–1200." *Traditio* 18: 89–120.

——— (1985). *Medieval Households.* Cambridge, Massachusetts.

Herrmann, K.-J. (1973). *Das Tuskulaner Papsttum (1012–1046).* Päpste und Papsttum, 4. Stuttgart.

Hirsch, E. (1906). "Der Simoniebegriff und eine angebliche Erweiterung derselben im 11. Jahrhundert." *Archiv für katholisches Kirchenrecht* 86: 1–19.

Histoire des pères et de la paternité, ed. J. Delumeau and D. Roche. Paris, 1990.

Hoesch, H. (1970). *Die kanonischen Quellen im Werk Humberts von Moyenmoutier: Ein Beitrag zur Geschichte der vorgregorianischen Reform.* Forschungen zur kirchlichen Rechtsgeschichte und zum Kirchenrecht, 10. Cologne and Vienna.

Hoffmann, H. (2000). "Der König und seine Bischöfe in Frankreich und im deutschen Reich, 936–1060." In *Bischof Burchard von Worms, 1000–1025.* Pp. 79–127.

Hough, C. (1997). "Alfred's Domboc and the Language of Rape: A Reconsideration of Alfred Ch. 11." *Medium Aevum* 66: 1–27.

Hughes, D. (1978). "From Brideprice to Dowry in Mediterranean Europe." *Journal of Family History* 3: 262–96.

Hüls, R. (1977). *Kardinäle, Klerus und Kirchen Roms, 1049–1130.* Bibiothek des Deutschen Historischen Instituts in Rom, 48. Tübingen.

Huneycutt, L. (1995). "Intercession and the High-Medieval Queen: The Esther Topos." In *Power of the Weak.* Pp. 126–46.

Hunter, D. (2000). "The Virgin, the Bride, and the Church: Reading Psalm 45 in Ambrose, Jerome, and Augustine." *Church History* 69: 281–303

Huth, V. (1992). "Reichsinsignien und Herrschaftsentzug. Ein vergleichende Skizze zu Heinrich IV. und Heinrich (VII.) im Spiegel der Vorgänge von 1105/1106 und 1235." *FS* 26: 287–330.

Huyghebaert, N. (1981). "La mère de Godefroid de Boulogne: la comtesse Ide de Boulogne." *Publications de la Section Historique de l'Institut Grand-Ducal de Luxembourg* 95: 43–63.

Imbart de la Tour, P. (1891). *Les élections épiscopales dans l'église de France du IXe au XIIe siècle. Étude sur la décadence du principe électif (814–1150).* Paris.

Innes, M. (2000). *State and Society in the Early Middle Ages: The Middle Rhine Valley, 400–1000.* Cambridge Studies in Medieval Life and Thought, 47. Cambridge.

Le istituzione ecclesiastiche della <<societas christiana>> dei secoli XI–XII: papato, cardinalato ed episcopato. Pubblicazioni dell'Università Cattolica del Sacro Cuore: Miscellanea del Centro di studi medioevali, 7. Milan, 1974.

Jasper, D. (1986). *Das Papstwahldekret von 1059: Überlieferung und Textgestalt.* Beiträge zur Geschichte und Quellenkunde des Mittelalter, 12. Sigmaringen.

Jasper, D., and Fuhrmann, H. (2001). *Papal Letters in the Early Middle Ages.* History of Medieval Canon Law. Washington, DC.

Jäschke, K.-U. (1991). *Notwendige Gefährtinnen: Königinnen der Salierzeit als Herrscherinnen und Ehefrauen im römisch-deutschen Reich des 11. und beginnenden 12. Jahrhunderts.* Saarbrücken.

Jestice, P. (1998). "Why Celibacy? Odo of Cluny and the Development of a New Sexual Morality." In *Medieval Purity and Piety.* Pp. 81–115.

Jochens, J. (1987). "The Politics of Reproduction: Medieval Norwegian Kingship." *American Historical Review* 92: 327–49.

Johnson, P. (1981). *Prayer, Patronage and Power: The Abbey of la Trinité, Vendôme, 1032–1187.* New York and London.

Jones, A. (2007). "Lay Magnates, Religious Houses and the Role of the Bishop in Aquitaine (877–1050)." In *The Bishop Reformed.* Pp. 21–39.

Jordan, M. (1997). *The Invention of Sodomy in Christian Theology.* Chicago Series on Sexuality, History and Society. Chicago.

Jungmann, J. (1949). *Missarum sollemnia.* Rev. edn, Vienna. Cited from the English translation by F. Brunner, *The Mass of the Roman Rite.* 2 vols. New York, 1951.

Kaiser, R. (1981). *Bischofsherrschaft zwischen Königtum und Fürstenmacht: Studien zur bischöflichen Stadtherrschaft im westfränkisch-französischen Reich im frühen und hohen Mittelalter.* Pariser historische Studien, 17. Bonn.

Kantorowicz, E. (1957). *The King's Two Bodies: A Study in Medieval Political Theology.* Princeton.

Karkov, C. (2001). *Text and Picture in Anglo-Saxon England: Narrative Strategies in the Junius 11 Manuscript.* Cambridge and New York.

Karras, R. (1990). "Holy Harlots: Prostitute Saints in Medieval Legend." *Journal of the History of Sexuality* 1: 332.

(1996). *Common Women: Prostitution and Sexuality in Medieval England.* Studies in the History of Sexuality. Oxford.

Keller, H. (1993). "Die Investitur: Ein Beitrag zum Problem der 'Staatssymbolik' im Hochmittelalter." *FS* 27: 51–86.

Kelly, T. (1996). *The Exultet in Southern Italy.* New York and Oxford.

Kempf, F. (1978). "Primatiale und episkopal-synodale Struktur der Kirche vor der gregorianischen Reform." *Archivum historiae pontificiae* 16: 27–66.

Kienzle, B. and Nienhuis, N. (2004). "Battered Women and the Construction of Sanctity," *Journal of Feminist Studies in Religion* 17: 33–61.

Koch, H. (1930). *Cathedra Petri: neue Untersuchungen über die Anfänge der Primatslehre.* Beihefte zur Zeitschrift für die neutestamentliche Wissenschaft und die Kunde der älteren Kirche, 11. Giessen.

Kottje, R. (1975). "Konkubinat und Kommunionwürdigkeit im vorgratianischen Kirchen recht. Zu c. 12 der römischen Ostersynode von 1059." *Annuarium historiae conciliorum* 7: 159–65.

Koziol, G. (1992). *Begging Pardon and Favor: Ritual and Political Order in Early Medieval France.* Ithaca, New York.

Krause, H.-G. (1983). "Das Constitutum Constantini im Schisma von 1054." In *Aus Kirche und Reich.* Pp. 131–58.

Kreutz, B. (1996). "The Twilight of Morgengabe." In *Portraits of Medieval and Renaissance Living.* Pp. 131–47.

Krüger, K. (2002) "Herrschaftsnachfolge als Vater-Sohn Konflikt." *FS* 36: 225–40.

Kunigunde, consors regni: Vortragsreihe zum tausendjährige Jubiläum der Krönung Kunigundes in Paderborn, 1002–2002, ed. S. Dick, J. Jarnut, and M. Wemhoff. Mittelalter Studien, 5. Munich, 2004.

Kupper, J.-L. (2004). "L'oncle maternel et le neveu dans la société du moyen âge," *Académie royale de Belgique, Bulletin de la classe des lettres et des sciences morales et politiques,* ser. 6, 15: 7–12, pp. 247–62.

Lambert, M. (2002). *Medieval Heresy: Popular Movements from the Gregorian Reform to the Reformation.* 3rd edn. Oxford and Malden, Massachusetts.

Landgraf, A. (1938). "Probleme des Schrifttums Brunos des Kartäusers," *Collectanea Franciscana* 8: 542–90.

Lapidge, M. (1992). "B. and the *Vita S. Dunstani.*" In *St. Dunstan: His Life, Times and Cult,* ed. N. Ramsay, M. Sparks, and T. Tatton-Brown. Woodbridge. Pp. 247–59.

Lauchert, F. (1889). *Geschichte des Physiologus.* Strasburg.

Laudage, J. (1984). *Priesterbild und Reformpapsttum im 11. Jahrhundert.* Cologne and Vienna.

Lawson, M. (1992). "Archbishop Wulfstan and the Homiletic Element in the Laws of Aethelred II and Cnut." *English Historical Review* 107: 565–86.

Le Bras, G. (1926). "La doctrine du mariage chez les théologiens et les canonistes depuis l'an mil." *DTC* 9: 2123–2317.

Leclercq, J. (1947). "Simoniaca Haeresis." *SG* 1: 523–30.

(1957). *L'amour des lettres et le désir de Dieu.* Paris. Cited from the English translation by C. Misrahi, *The Love of Learning and the Desire for God.* New York, 1962.

Le Jan, R. (1995). *Famille et pouvoir dans le monde franc (VIIe–Xe siècle).* Histoire ancienne et médiévale, 33. Paris.

(2000). "Continuity and Change in the Tenth-Century Nobility." In *Nobles and Nobility in Medieval Europe: Concepts, Origins, Transformations,* ed. A. Duggan. Woodbridge, England. Pp. 53–68.

(2001). "L'épouse du comte du IXe au XIe siècle: transformation d'un modèle et idéologie du pouvoir." In *Femmes et pouvoir des femmes.* Pp. 65–73.

(2002). "Douaires et pouvoirs des reines en Francie et en Germanie (IXe–Xe siècle)." In *Dots et douaires.* Pp. 457–97.

Lesieur, T. (2003). *Devenir fou pour être sage: construction d'une raison chrétienne à l'aube de la réforme grégorienne.* Culture et sociétés médiévales. Turnhout.

Lesne, E. (1905). *La hiérarchie épiscopale. Provinces, métropolitains, primats en Gaule et en Germanie, 742–882.* Mémoires et travaux des Facultés catholiques de Lille, 1. Lille and Paris.

Leyser, K. (1970). "Maternal Kin in Early Medieval Germany: A Reply." *Past & Present* 49: 126–34.

(1979). *Rule and Conflict in an Early Medieval Society: Ottonian Saxony.* Oxford.

(1993) "Ritual, Zeremonie und Gestik: das ottonische Reich." *FS* 27: 1–26.

(1994). *Communications and Power in Medieval Europe*, ed. T. Reuter. 2 vols. London and Rio Grande, Ohio.

Lifshitz, F. (1996). "Is Mother Superior? Towards a History of Feminine *Amstcharisma*." In *Medieval Mothering*. Pp. 117–38.

Little, L. (1978). *Religious Poverty and the Profit Economy in Medieval Europe*. Ithaca, New York.

Livingstone, A. (1997). "Noblewomen's Control of Property in Early Twelfth-Century Blois-Chartres." *Medieval Prosopography* 18: 55–71.

LoPrete, K. (1996). "Adela of Blois as Mother and Countess." In *Medieval Mothering*. Pp. 313–33.

(2007a). *Adela of Blois: Countess and Lord (c. 1067–1137)*. Dublin.

(2007b). "Women, Gender and Lordship in France, c. 1050–1250." *History Compass* 5/6: 1921–41.

Lubac, H. de. (1959–64). *L'exégèse médiéval: les quatre sens de l'Écriture*. 2 vols. in 4. Théologie, 41–42, 59. Paris. Cited from the English translation by M. Sebanc and E. Macierowski, *Medieval Exegesis*. Grand Rapids, Michigan and Edinburgh, 2000.

(1971). *Les églises particulières dans l'Église universelle, suivi de La maternité de l'Église, et d'une interview recueillie par G. Jarczyk*. Paris. Cited from the English translation by S. Englund, *The Motherhood of the Church, followed by Particular Churches in the Universal Church, and an interview conducted by Gwendoline Jarczyk*. San Francisco, 1982.

Lynch, J. (1986). *Godparents and Kinship in Early Medieval Europe*. Princeton.

Lyotard, J.-F. (1979). *La condition postmoderne: rapport sur le savoir*. Paris. Cited from the English translation by G. Bennington and B. Massumi, *The Post-Modern Condition: A Report on Knowledge*. Minneapolis, 1984.

(1983). *Le différend*. Paris. Cited from the English translation by G. Van den Abbeele, *The Differend: Phrases in Dispute*. Minneapolis, 1988.

Maccarrone, M. (1960). "La dottrina del primato papale dal IV all'VIII secolo nelle relazioni con le chiese occidentali." In *Le chiese nei regni dell'Europa occidentale e i loro rapporti con Roma sino all' 800*. Vol. 2: 633–742.

(1974). "La teologia del primato romano del secolo XI." In *Le istituzione ecclesiastiche della <<societas christiana>> dei secoli XI–XII*. Pp. 21–122.

(1989). "I fondamenti 'Petrini' del primato romano in Gregorio VII." *SG* 13: 55–122.

(1991). "'Sedes apostolica – Vicarius Pietri.' La perpetuità del primato di Pietro nelle sede e nel vescovo di Roma (Secoli III–VIII)." In *Il primato del vescovo di Roma nel primo millennio*. Pp. 275–362.

McCulloch, F. (1962). *Medieval Latin and French Bestiaries*. University of North Carolina Studies in Romance Languages and Literatures, 33. Chapel Hill, North Carolina.

MacKinnon, C. (1989). *Toward a Feminist Theory of the State*. Cambridge, Massachusetts.

McKitterick, R. (1983). *The Frankish Kingdoms under the Carolingians, 751–987*. Harlow, England.

McLaughlin, M. (1990). "The Woman Warrior: Gender, Warfare and Society in Medieval Europe." *Women's Studies* 17: 193–209.

(1991). "Gender Paradox and the Otherness of God." *Gender and History* 3: 147–59.

(1994). *Consorting with Saints: Prayer for the Dead in Early Medieval France.* Ithaca, New York.

(1998). "The Bishop as Bridegroom: Marital Imagery and Clerical Celibacy in the Eleventh and Early Twelfth Centuries." In *Medieval Purity And Piety.* Pp. 209–37.

(1999). "Secular and Spiritual Fatherhood in the Eleventh Century." In *Conflicted Identitities and Multiple Masculinities: Men in the Medieval West,* ed. J. Murray. Garland Medieval Casebooks. New York. Pp. 25–43.

(2010). "The Bishop in the Bedroom: Witnessing Episcopal Sexuality in an Age of Reform." *Journal of the History of Sexuality* 19: 17–34.

(forthcoming). "'Disgusting Acts of Shamelessness': Sexual Misconduct and the Deconstruction of Royal Authority in the Eleventh Century." *Early Medieval Europe.*

MacLehose, W. (1996). "Nurturing Danger: High Medieval Medicine and the Problem(s) of the Child." In *Medieval Mothering.* Pp. 3–24.

McNamara, J. (1994). "The 'Herrenfrage': The Restructuring of the Gender System, 1050–1150." In *Medieval Masculinities: Regarding Men in the Middle Ages,* ed. C. Lees. Minneapolis. Pp. 3–29.

(1995). "Canossa and the Ungendering of the Public Man." In *Render Unto Caesar: The Religious Sphere in World Politics,* ed. S. Ramet and D. Treadgold. Washington, DC. Pp. 131–50.

(2003). "Women and Power through the Family Revisited." In *Gendering the Master Narrative: Women and Power in the Middle Ages,* ed. M. Erler and M. Kowaleski. Ithaca, New York. Pp. 17–30.

McNamara, J. and Wemple, S. (1973). "The Power of Women through the Family in Medieval Europe, 500–1100." *Feminist Studies* 1: 126–42.

Magnani Soares-Christen, E. (2002). "Alliances matrimoniales et circulation des biens à travers les chartes provencales (Xe–début du XIIe siècle.). In *Dots et douaires.* Pp. 131–52.

Magnou-Nortier, E. (1974). *La société laïque et l'église dans la province ecclésias-tique de Narbonne (zone cispyrénéenne) de la fin du VIIIe à la fin du XIe siècle.* Publications de l'Université de Toulouse-Le Mirail, série A, 20. Toulouse.

(2000). "Realité juridique et sociale du couple d'après les sources du Bas Languedoc avant 1100." In *Mariage et sexualité au moyen âge.* Pp. 157–84.

Mansfield, M. (1995). *The Humiliation of Sinners: Public Penance in Thirteenth-Century France.* Ithaca, New York.

Marchetto, A. (1971). *Episcopato e primato pontificio nelle decretali pseudo-isidori-ane: ricerca storico-giuridica.* Rome.

Mariage et sexualité au moyen âge: Accord ou crise?, ed. M. Rouches. Cultures et civilisations médiévales, 21. Paris, 2000.

Martindale, J. (1977). "The French Aristocracy in the Early Middle Ages: A Reappraisal." *Past & Present* 75: 5–45.

Märtl, C. (1990). "Aus dem Umkreis Bernolds von Konstanz." *DA* 46: 531–42.

Masschaele, J. (2002). "The Public Space of the Marketplace in Medieval England." *Speculum* 77: 383–421.

Il matrimonio nella società altomedievale. 2 vols. Settimane, 24. Spoleto, 1977.

Matter, E. A. (1990). *The Voice of My Beloved: The Song of Songs in Western Medieval Christianity.* MAS. Philadelphia.

Medieval Concepts of the Past: Ritual, Memory, Historiography, ed. G. Althoff, J. Fried, and P. Geary. Cambridge, 2002.

Medieval Mothering, ed. J. Parsons and B. Wheeler. The New Middle Ages. New York, 1996.

Medieval Purity and Piety: Essays on Medieval Clerical Celibacy and Religious Reform, ed. M. Frassetto. Garland Medieval Casebooks, 19. New York, 1998.

Medieval Queenship, ed. J. Parsons. New York, 1993.

Meier, T. (2000). "Die Rebellion Heinrichs V. (1104/06) im Diskurs über Religion und Lüge." In *Lügen und Betrügen. Das Falsche in der Geschichte von der Antike bis zur Moderne*, ed. O. Hochadel and U. Kocher. Cologne, Weimar, and Vienna. Pp. 33–50.

Meier-Welcker, H. (1952/53). "Die Simonie im frühen Mittelalter." *Zeitschrift für Kirchengeschichte* 64: 61–93.

Melve, L. (2007). *Inventing the Public Sphere: The Public Debate during the Investiture Contest (c. 1030–1122).* 2 vols. Brill's Studies in Intellectual History, 154. Leiden and Boston.

Meulenberg, L. (1965). *Der Primat der Römischen Kirche im Denken und Handeln Gregors VII.* The Hague.

Meyer von Knonau, G. (1890–1909). *Jahrbücher des deutchen Reiches unter Heinrich IV. und Heinrich V.* 7 vols. Leipzig.

Michel, A. (1924–30). *Humbert und Kerullarios.* 2 vols. Quellen und Forschungen aus dem Gebiete der Geschichte in Verbindung mit ihrem historischen Institut in Rom herausgegeben von der Görres-Gesellschaft, 21 and 23. Paderborn.

Miccoli, G. (1966). *Chiesa gregoriana.* Florence.

Miller, M. (1993). *The Formation of a Medieval Church: Ecclesiastical Change in Verona, 950–1150.* Ithaca, New York.

(1998). "Clerical Identity and Reform: Notarial Descriptions of the Secular Clergy in the Po Valley, 750–1200." In *Medieval Purity and Piety.* Pp. 305–35.

(2003). "Masculinity, Reform and Clerical Culture: Narratives of Episcopal Holiness in the Gregorian Era." *Church History* 72: 25–52.

Minnerath, R. (2003). "Le project réformateur de Léon IX." In *Le millénaire du pape Saint Léon IX*, ed. J. Doré. Strasburg. Pp. 109–37.

Mirbt, C. (1894) *Die Publizistik im Zeitalter Gregors VII.* Leipzig.

Moore, R. (1980). "Family, Community and Cult on the Eve of the Gregorian Reform." *TRHS*, 5th series, 30: 49–69.

(1998). "Property, Marriage, and the Eleventh-Century Revolution: A Context for Early Medieval Communism." In *Medieval Purity and Piety.* Pp. 179–208.

Moorhead, J. (1985) "*Papa* as 'Bishop of Rome'." *Journal of Ecclesiastical History* 36: 337–50.

Mordek, H. (1991). "Der römische Primat in den Kirchenrechtssammlungen des Westens vom IV. bis VIII. Jahrhunderts." In *Il primato del vescovo di Roma nel primo millennio.* Pp. 523–66.

Morin, G. (1911). "Le Pseudo-Bède sur les Psaumes, et l'Opus super Psalterium de maître Manegold de Lautenbach." *Revue Bénédictine* 28: 331–40.

Morrison, K. (1964). *The Two Kingdoms: Ecclesiology in Carolingian Political Thought*. Princeton.

Murray, A. (1978). *Reason and Society in the Middle Ages*. Oxford. Cited from the revised ed. (1990), published electronically in 2002.

Nelson, J. (2006). "Did Charlemagne have a Private Life?" In *Writing Medieval Biography, 750–1250: Essays in Honour of Frank Barlow*, ed. D. Bates, J. Crick, and S. Hamilton. Woodbridge. Pp. 15–28.

Neuhäusler, E. (1964). *Der Bischof als geistlicher Vater nach den frühchristlichen Schriften*. Munich.

The New Cambridge Medieval History, Volume 4, ed. D. Luscombe and J. Riley-Smith. 2 vols. Cambridge, 2004.

Newhauser, R. (2003). "Avarice and the Apocalypse." In *The Apocalyptic Year 1000: Religious Expectations and Social Change, 950–1050*, ed. R. Landes, A. Gow, and D. Van Meter. Oxford. Pp. 109–19.

Newton, F. (1995). "Constantine the African and Monte Cassino: New Elements and the Text of the Isagoge." In *Constantine the African and 'Ali Ibn Al-Abbas Al-Magusi: The Pantegni and Related Texts*, ed. C. Burnett and D. Jacquart. Leiden. Pp. 16–47.

Nicholas, K. (1999). "Countesses as Rulers in Flanders." In *Aristocratic Women in Medieval France*. Pp. 111–37.

Nip, R. (1995a). "The Canonization of Godelieve of Gistel." *Hagiographica* 2: 145–55.

(1995b). "Godelieve of Gistel and Ida of Boulogne." In *Sanctity and Motherhood*. Pp. 191–223

Nirenberg, D. (1996). *Communities of Violence: Persecution of Minorities in the Middle Ages*. Princeton.

Nolan, K. (1996). "*Ploratus et ululatus*: The Mothers in the Massacre of the Innocents at Chartres Cathedral." *Studies in Iconography* 17: 95–141.

Ohly, F. (1958). *Hohelied-Studien: Grundzüge einer Geschichte der Hoheliedausle-gung des Abendlandes bis um 1200*. Wiesbaden.

Ott, J. (2005). "Writing Godfrey of Amiens: Guibert of Nogent and Nicholas of Saint-Crépin between Sanctity, Ideology and Society." *Mediaeval Studies* 67: 317–65.

(2007). "'Both Mary and Martha': Bishop Lietbert of Cambrai and the Construction of Episcopal Sanctity in a Border Diocese around 1100." In *The Bishop Reformed*. Pp. 137–60.

Ott, J. and Jones, A. (2007). "Introduction: The Bishop Reformed." In *The Bishop Reformed*. Pp. 1–20.

Parisse, M. (2004a). "The Bishop: Prince and Prelate." In *The Bishop: Power and Piety*. Pp. 8–22.

(2004b). "Sigefroid, abbé de Gorze, et le mariage du roi Henri III avec Agnès de Poitou (1043). Un aspect de la réforme lotharingienne." *Revue du Nord* 86: 543–66.

Parsons, J. (1995). "The Queen's Intercession in Thirteenth-Century England." In *Power of the Weak*. Pp. 147–77.

Pateman, C. (1989). "Feminist Critiques of the Public/Private Dichotomy." In her *The Disorder of Women: Democracy, Feminism, and Political Theory.* Stanford, California. Pp. 118–40.

Pellens, K. (1973). *Das Kirchendenken des normannischen Anonymus.* Veröffentlichungen des Instituts für europäische Geschichte, Mainz, 69. Wiesbaden.

Petrucci, E. (1973). *Rapporti di Leone IX con Constantinopoli, Parte 1: Per la storia della scisma del 1054.* Studi medievali, ser. 3, 14. Rome.

——— (1977). *Ecclesiologia e politica di Leone IX: momenti di storia del papato medievale.* Rome.

Pietri, C. (1976). *Roma christiana: recherches sur l'Église de Rome, son organization, sa politique, son idéologie, de Miltiade à Sexte III (311–440).* Bibliothèque des Écoles d'Athènes et de Rome, 224. Rome.

Plumpe, J. (1943). *Mater Ecclesia: An Inquiry into the Concept of the Church as Mother in Early Christianity.* Catholic University of America Studies in Christian Antiquity, 5. Washington, DC.

Poly, J.-P., and Bournazel, E. (1980). *La mutation féodale, Xe–XIIe siècles.* Paris. Cited from the English translation by C. Higgitt, *The Feudal Transformation, 900–1200.* New York and London, 1991.

——— (1994). "Que faut-il préferer au 'mutationnisme'? ou le problème du changement social." *Revue historique de droit français et étranger* 72: 401–12.

Portraits of Medieval and Renaissance Living: Essays in Honor of David Herlihy, ed. S. Cohn and S. Epstein. Ann Arbor, 1996.

Power of the Weak: Studies on Medieval Women, ed. J. Carpenter and S.-B. MacLean. Urbana, Illinois, 1995.

Il primato del vescovo di Roma nel primo millennio, ed. M. Maccarrone. Pontificio comitato di scienzi storiche, Atti e documenti, 4. Rome, 1991.

Queens and Queenship in Medieval Europe, ed. A. Duggan. Woodbridge, England, 1996.

Quirk, K. (2001). "Men, Women, and Miracles in Normandy, 1050–1150." In *Medieval Memories: Men, Women, and the Past, 700–1300,* ed. E. van Houts. Women and Men in History. London. Pp. 53–71.

Quivy, P., and Thiron, J. (1967). "Robert de Tombelaine et son commentaire sur le Cantique des Cantiques." In *Millénaire monastique du Mont Saint-Michel.* 2 vols. Paris. Vol. 2: 347–56.

Rabin, A. (2009). "Female Advocacy and Royal Protection in Tenth-Century England: The Legal Career of Queen Aelfthryth." *Speculum* 84: 261–88.

Rahner, H. (1944). *Mater Ecclesia: Lobpreis der Kirche aus dem ersten Jahrtausend christliche Literatur.* Einsiedeln.

Remensnyder, A. (1992). "Pollution, Purity, and Peace: An Aspect of Social Reform between the Late Tenth Century and 1076." In *The Peace of God: Social Violence and Religious Response in France around the Year 1000,* ed. T. Head and R. Landes. Ithaca, New York. Pp. 280–307.

Resnick, I. (2000). "Marriage in Medieval Culture: Consent Theory and the Case of Joseph and Mary." *Church History* 69: 350–71.

Reuter, T. (2000). "Ein Europa der Bischöfe. Das Zeitalter Burchards von Worms." In *Bischof Burchard von Worms, 1000–1025.* Pp. 1–28.

(2001). "Gifts and Simony." In *Medieval Transformations: Texts, Power, and Gifts in Context*, ed. E. Cohen and M. De Jong. Cultures, Beliefs and Traditions : Medieval and Early Modern Peoples. Leiden. Pp. 157–68.

Reynolds, P. (1994). *Marriage in the Western Church: The Christianization of Marriage during the Patristic and Early Medieval Periods.* Supplements to *Vigiliae Christianae*, 24. Leiden.

Reynolds, R. (1983). "Patristic 'Presbyterianism' in the Early Medieval Theology of Sacred Orders." *Mediaeval Studies* 45: 310–42.

Riché, P. (1987). *Gerbert d'Aurillac: le pape de l'an mil.* Paris.

Riedlinger, H. (1958). *Die Makellosigkeit der Kirche in den lateinischen Hoheliedkommentaren des Mittelalters.* Beiträge zur Geschichte der Philosophie und Theologie des Mittelalters, 38.3. Münster.

Robinson, I. S. (1978a). "The Friendship Network of Gregory VII." *History* 63: 1–22.

(1978b). "'Periculosus Homo': Pope Gregory VII and Episcopal Authority." *Viator* 9: 103–31.

(1978c). *Authority and Resistance in the Investiture Contest.* Manchester.

(1979). "Pope Gregory VII, the Princes and the Pactum, 1077–80." *English Historical Review* 373: 721–56.

(1983). "'Political Allegory' in the Biblical Exegesis of Bruno of Segni." *Recherches de théologie ancienne et médiévale* 50: 69–98.

(1988). "Church and Papacy." In *The Cambridge History of Medieval Political Thought, c. 350–c. 1450*, ed. J. Burns. Cambridge. Pp. 252–305.

(1990). *The Papacy, 1073–1198: Continuity and Innovation.* Cambridge Medieval Textbooks. Cambridge.

(1999). *Henry IV of Germany, 1056–1106.* Cambridge.

(2004). "Reform and the Church, 1073–1122." In *The New Cambridge Medieval History, Volume 4.* Part 1: 268–334.

Rosenwein, B. (1989). *To Be the Neighbor of St. Peter: The Social Meaning of Cluny's Property, 909–1049.* Ithaca, New York.

(1999). *Negotiating Space: Power, Restraint, and Privileges of Immunity in Early Medieval Europe.* Manchester.

Ross, M. (1985). "Concubinage in Anglo-Saxon England." *Past & Present* 108: 3–34.

Rossetti, G. (1977). "Il celibato del clero nella società altomedievale." In *Il matrimonio nella società altomedievale.* Vol. 1: 473–576.

Rouche, M. (1974). "La matricule des pauvres: évolution d'une institution de charité du bas-Empire jusqu'à la fin du haut moyen âge." In *Études sur l'histoire de la pauvreté*, ed. M. Mollat. 2 vols. Paris. Vol. 1: 83–110.

(1987). "Des mariages païens au mariage chrétien, sacré et sacrement." In *Segni e riti nella chiesa altomedievale occidentale.* Vol. 2: 835–80.

(2006). "La sexualité dans le mariage durant le haut moyen âge." In *Comportamenti e immaginario della sessualità nell'alto medioevo.* Vol. 1: 381–415.

Rubenstein, J. (1995). "The Life and Writings of Osbern of Canterbury." In *Canterbury and the Norman Conquest: Churches, Saints and Scholars, 1066–1109*, ed. R. Eales and R. Sharpe. London and Rio Grande, Ohio. Pp. 27–40.

Runciman, S. (1955). *The Eastern Schism: A Study of the Papacy and the Eastern Churches during the XIth and XIIth Centuries.* Oxford.

Ryan, J. (1956). *Saint Peter Damiani and His Canonical Sources: A Preliminary Study in the Antecedents of the Gregorian Reform.* Pontifical Institute of Mediaeval Studies, Studies and Texts, 2. Toronto.

Die Salier und das Reich, ed. S. Weinfurter. 3 vols. Sigmaringen, 1991.

Sanctity and Motherhood: Essays on Holy Mothers in the Middle Ages, ed. A. Mulder-Bakker. Garland Medieval Casebooks, 14. New York, 1995.

Sansterre, J.-M. (1999). "Mère du roi, épouse du Christ et fille de Saint Pierre: les dernières années de l'impératrice Agnès de Poitou, entre image et réalité." In *Femmes et pouvoirs.* Pp. 163–74.

Santinelli, E. (1999). "La veuve du prince au tournant de l'an mil: l'exemple de Berthe de Bourgogne. In *Femmes et pouvoirs.* Pp. 75–89.

(2002). "Ni 'Morgengabe' ni *tertia* mais *dos* et dispositions en faveur du dernier vivant: les échanges patrimoniaux entre époux dans la Loire moyenne (VIIe–XIe siècle)." In *Dots et douaires.* Pp. 245–75.

(2003). *Des femmes éplorées? Les veuves dans la société aristocratique du haut Moyen Âge.* Lille.

Saxer, V. (1959). *Le culte de Marie Madeleine en Occident des origines à la fin du moyen âge.* 2 vols. Cahiers d'archéologie et d'histoire, 3. Auxerre and Paris.

Schatz, K. (1990). *Der päpstliche Primat: Seine Geschichte von den Ursprungen bis zum Gegenwart.* Würzburg. Cited from the English translation by J. Otto and L. Maloney, *Papal Primacy from Its Origins to the Present.* Collegeville, Minnesota, 1996.

Schieffer, R. (1972). "Spirituales Latrones: Zu den Hintergründen der Simonieprozesse in Deutschland zwischen 1069 und 1075." *Historisches Jahrbuch* 92: 19–60.

(1981). *Die Entstehung des päpstlichen Investiturverbots für den deutschen König.* Schriften der MGH, 28. Stuttgart.

(1990). "Väter und Söhne im Karolingerreich." In *Beiträge zur Geschichte des Regnum Francorum*, ed. R. Schieffer. Beihefte der Francia, 22. Sigmaringen. Pp. 149–64.

(1991). "Der Papst als Patriarch von Rom." In *Il primato del vescovo di Roma nel primo millennio.* Pp. 433–51.

(1998). "Bischofserhebung im westfränkisch-französischen Bereich im späten 9. und im 10. Jahrhundert." In *Die früh- und hochmittelalterliche Bischofserhebung.* Pp. 59–82.

(2002a). "Motu Proprio: Über die Papstgeschichtliche Wende im 11. Jahrhundert." *Historisches Jahrbuch* 122: 27–41.

(2002b). "Otto II. und sein Vater." *FS* 36: 255–69.

Schimmelpfennig, B. (1978). "Zölibat und Lage der 'Priestersöhne' vom 11. bis 14. Jahrhundert." *Historische Zeitschrift* 227: 1–44.

(2002). "Vestments, Pope's Liturgical." In *The Papacy: An Encyclopedia*, ed. P. Villain. 3 vols. New York and London. Pp. 1607–8.

Schmale, F. J. (1979). "Die 'Absetzung' Gregors VI. in Sutri und die synodale Tradition." *Annuarium historiae conciliorum* 11: 55–103.

Schmid, K. (1957). "Zur Problematik von Familie, Sippe und Geschlecht, Haus und Dynastie beim mittelalterlichen Adel." *Zeitschrift für die Geschichte des Oberrheins* 105: 1–62.

(1959). "Über die Struktur des Adels im früheren Mittelalters." *Jahrbuch für fränkische Landesforschung* 19: 1–23.

(1983). *Gebetsgedenken und adliges Selbstverständnis im Mittelalter.* Sigmaringen.

Schmid, P. (1926). *Der Begriff der kanonischen Wahl in den Anfängen des Investiturstreits.* Stuttgart.

Schmidt, T. (1977). *Alexander II. (1061–1073) und die römische Reformgruppe seiner Zeit.* Päpste und Papsttum, 11. Stuttgart.

Schmitt, E. (1983). *Le mariage chrétien dans l'oeuvre de saint Augustin: une théologie baptismale de la vie conjugale.* Paris.

Scholz, S. (1992). *Transmigration und Translation: Studien zum Bistumswechsel der Bischöfe von der Spätantike bis zum Hohen Mittelalter.* Kölner Historische Abhandlungen, 37. Cologne, Weimar, and Vienna.

(2006). *Politik-Selbstverständnis-Selbstdarstellung: Die Päpste in karolingischer und ottonischer Zeit.* Historische Forschungen, 26. Stuttgart.

Schramm, P. (1968–71). *Kaiser, Könige und Päpste: Ausgewählte Aufsätze zur Geschichte des Mittelalters.* 4 vols. Stuttgart.

Schreiner, K. (1990). "'Er küsse mich mit dem Kuss seines Mundes' (Osculetur me osculo oris sui, Cant. 1, 1). Metaphorik, kommunikative und herrschaftliche Funktionen einer symbolischen Handlung." In *Höfische Repräsentation. Das Zeremoniell und die Zeichen*, ed. H. Ragotzky and H. Wenzel. Wiesbaden. Pp. 89–132.

(2001). "Nudis pedibus. Barfüssigkeit als religiöses und politisches Ritual." In *Formen und Funktionen*, pp. 53–124.

Searle, E. (1988). *Predatory Kinship and the Creation of Norman Power, 840–1066.* Berkeley and Los Angeles.

Il secolo XI: una svolta?, ed. C. Violante and J. Fried. Annali dell'Istituto storico italo-germanico, 35. Bologna, 1993.

Segni e riti nella chiesa altomedievale occidentale. 2 vols. Settimane, 33. Spoleto, 1987.

Sergi, G. (1993). "Le istituzioni politiche del secolo XI: transformazioni dell'apparato pubblico e nuove forme di potere." In *Il secolo XI: una svolta?* Pp. 73–97.

Servatius, C. (1979). *Paschalis II. (1099–1118): Studien zu seiner Person und seiner Politik.* Päpste und Papsttum, 14. Stuttgart.

Shaffern, R. (2001). "Mater et Magistra: Gendered Images and Church Authority in the Thought of Pope Innocent III." *Logos: A Journal of Catholic Thought and Culture* 4: 65–88.

Sheehan, M. (1988). "Theory and Practice: Marriage of the Unfree and the Poor in Medieval Society." *Mediaeval Studies* 50: 457–87.

Sheridan, M. (2005). "Mothers and Sons: Emma of Normandy's Role in the English Succession Crisis, 1035–42." In *Studies on Medieval and Early Modern Women, 4: Victims or Viragos?*, ed. C. Meek and C. Lawless. Dublin. Pp. 39–48.

Skinner, P. (1993). "Women, Wills and Wealth in Medieval Southern Italy." *Early Medieval Europe* 2: 133–52.

(1997). "'The Light of My Eyes': Medieval Motherhood in the Mediterranean." *Women's History Review* 6: 391–410.

(1999a). "And Her Name Was …? Gender and Naming in Medieval Southern Italy." *Medieval Prosopography* 20: 23–49.

(1999b). "The Widow's Options in Medieval Southern Italy." In *Widowhood in Medieval and Early Modern Europe*, ed. S. Cavallo and L. Warner. London. Pp. 57–65.

(2001). *Women in Medieval Italian Society, 500–1200.* Women and Men in History. Harlow, England.

Southern, R. W. (1953). *The Making of the Middle Ages.* New Haven and London.

(1963). *Saint Anselm and His Biographer: A Study in Monastic Life and Thought, 1059-c.1130.* Cambridge.

(1970). *Western Society and the Church in the Middle Ages.* Harmondsworth.

(1990). *Saint Anselm: A Portrait in a Landscape.* Cambridge.

Stafford, P. (1981). "The King's Wife in Wessex, 800–1066." *Past & Present* 91: 3–27.

(1983). *Queens, Concubines, and Dowagers: The King's Wife in the Early Middle Ages.* Athens, Georgia.

(1994). "Women and the Norman Conquest." *Transactions of the Royal Historical Society*, 6th series, 4: 221–49.

(1997). *Queen Emma and Queen Edith: Queenship and Women's Power in Eleventh-Century England.* Oxford.

(1998). "La Mutation Familiale: A Suitable Case for Caution." In *The Community, The Family and the Saint: Patterns of Power in Early Medieval Europe*, ed. J. Hill and M. Swan. Turnhout. Pp. 105–25.

Stiernon, D. (1991). "Interprétations, résistances et oppositions en Orient." In *Il primato del vescovo di Roma nel primo millennio.* Pp. 661–705.

Struve, T. (1985). "Die Romreise der Kaiserin Agnes." *Historisches Jahrbuch* 105: 1–29.

(1991). "Die Stellung des Königtums in der politischen Theorie der Salierzeit." In *Die Salier und das Reich.* Vol. 3: 217–44.

(1995). "Mathilde von Tuszien-Canossa und Heinrich IV. Der Wandel ihrer Beziehungen vor dem Hintergrund des Investiturstreites." *Historisches Jahrbuch* 115: 41–84.

Suchan, M. (1997). *Königsherrschaft im Streit: Konfliktaustragung in der Regierungszeit Heinrichs IV. Zwischen Gewalt, Gespräche und Schriftlichkeit.* Monographien zur Geschichte des Mittelalters, 42. Stuttgart.

Symes, C. (2007). *A Common Stage: Theater and Public Life in Medieval Arras.* Ithaca, New York.

Szabó-Bechstein, B. (1985). *Libertas Ecclesiae: Ein Schlüsselbegriff des Investiturstreits und seine Vorgeschichte, 4.–11. Jahrhundert.* SG, 12. Rome.

Tabacco, G. (1977). "Le rapport de parenté comme instrument de domination consortiale: quelques exemples piémontais." In *Famille et parenté.* Pp. 153–58.

(2004). "Northern and Central Italy in the Eleventh Century." In *The New Cambridge Medieval History, Volume 4.* Part 2: 72–93.

Tanner, H. (2004). *Families, Friends and Allies: Boulogne and Politics in Northern France and England, c. 879–1160.* The Northern World, 6. Leiden and Boston.

Tasioulas, J. (1996). "The Mother's Lament: 'Wulf and Eadwacer' Reconsidered." *Medium Aevum* 65: 1–18.

Tellenbach, G. (1936). *Libertas. Kirche und Weltordnung im Zeitalter des Investiturstreites.* Stuttgart. Cited from the English translation by R. Bennett, *Church, State and Christian Society at the Time of the Investiture Contest.* Studies in Mediaeval History. Oxford, 1940.

(1939). *Königtum und Stämme in der Werdezeit des deutschen Reiches.* Weimar.

(1943). "Vom karolingischen Reichsadel zum deutschen Reichsfürstenstand." In *Adel und Bauern im deutschen Staat des Mittelalters,* ed. T. Mayer. Leipzig. Pp. 22–73.

(1957). *Studien und Vorarbeiten zur Geschichte des grossfränkischen Adels.* Freiburg.

(1988). *Die westliche Kirche vom 10. bis zum frühen 12 Jahrhundert.* Göttingen. Cited from the English translation by T. Reuter, *The Church in Western Europe from the Tenth to the Early Twelfth Century.* Cambridge Medieval Textbooks. Cambridge, 1993.

Thelamon, F. (1997). "*Homo Dei:* L'Évêque agent de l'histoire du salut dans *l'Histoire ecclésiastique* de Rufin d'Aquilée." In *Vescovi e pastori in epoca Teodosiana, XXV Incontro di studiosi dell'antichità cristiana.* 2 vols. Studia Ephemeridis Augustinianum, 58. Rome. Pp. 531–49.

Therel, M.-L. (1973). *Les Symboles de l'Ecclesia dans la création iconographique de l'art chrétien du IIIe au VIe siècle.* Rome.

Thomas, H. (1977). "Zur Kritik an der Ehe Heinrichs III. mit Agnes von Poitou." In *Festschrift für Helmut Beumann zum 65. Geburtstag,* ed. K.-U. Jäschke and R. Wenskus. Sigmaringen. Pp. 224–35.

Thompson, K. (1996). "Dowry and Inheritance Patterns: Some Examples from the Descendants of King Henry I of England." *Medieval Prosopography* 17: 45–61.

Toubert, H. (1990). *Un art dirigé: Réforme grégorienne et iconographie.* Paris.

Toubert, P. (1973). *Les structures du Latium médiévale: le Latium méridionale et le Sabine du IXe siècle à la fin du XIIe siècle.* 2 vols. Bibliothèque des Écoles françaises d'Athènes et de Rome, 221. Rome.

(1977). "La théorie du mariage chez les moralistes carolingiens." In *Il matrimonio nella società altomedievale.* Vol. 1: 233–82.

(1986). "Le moment carolingien (VIIIe–IXe siècle)." In *Histoire de la famille, I: mondes lointains, mondes anciens,* ed. A. Burgière, C. Klapisch-Zuber, M. Segalen, and F. Zonabend. Paris. Pp. 333–60.

(1998). "L'institution du mariage chrétien, de l'antiquité tardive à l'an mil." In *Morfologie sociali e culturali in Europa fra tarda antichità e alto medioevo.* 2 vols. Settimane, 45. Spoleto. Vol. 1: 503–49.

Turner, D. (1995). *Eros and Allegory: Medieval Exegesis of the Song of Songs.* Cistercian Studies Series, 156. Kalamazoo, Michigan, and Spenser, Massachusetts.

Turner, R. (1990). "The Children of Anglo-Norman Royalty and Their Upbringing." *Medieval Prosopography* 11: 17–52,

Twyman, S. (2002). *Papal Ceremonial at Rome in the Twelfth Century.* London.

Ullmann, W. (1955). *The Growth of Papal Government in the Middle Ages: A Study in the Ideological Relation of Clerical to Lay Power.* Cited from the 3rd ed., Oxford, 1970.

Van Meter, D. (1998). "Eschatological Order and the Moral Arguments for Clerical Celibacy in Francia around the Year 1000." In *Medieval Purity and Piety.* Pp. 149–75.

Vaughn, S. (1980). "St. Anselm and the English Investiture Controversy Reconsidered." *Journal of Medieval History* 6: 61–86.

Verdon, J. (1973). "Les femmes et la politique en France au Xe siècle." In *Économies et sociétés au moyen âge: Mélanges offerts à Edouard Perroy.* Publications de la Sorbonne, Études, 5. Paris. Pp. 108–19.

Violante, C. (1977). "Quelques caractéristiques des structures familiales en Lombardie, Émilie et Toscane aux XIe et XIIe siècles." In *Famille et parenté.* Pp. 87–148.

Virtue, N. (1998). "Another Look at Medieval Rape Legislation." *Mediaevalia* 22: 79–94.

Vogelsang, T. (1954). *Die Frau als Herrscherin im höhen Mittelalter: Studien zur "Consors Regni" Formel.* Göttinger Bausteine zur Geschichtswissenschaft, 7. Göttingen, Frankfurt, and Berlin.

Vogtherr, T. (1998). "Zwischen Benediktinerabtei und bischöflicher Cathedra. Zu Auswahl und Amtsantritt englischer Bischöfe im 9.-11. Jahrhundert." In *Die früh- und hochmittelalterliche Bischofserhebung.* Pp. 287–320.

Vollrath, H. (1993). "L'accusa di simonia tra le fazioni contrapposte nella lotta per le investiture." In *Il secolo XI: una svolta?* Pp. 131–56.

Wareham, A. (2001). "The Transformation of Kinship and the Family in Late Anglo-Saxon England." *Early Medieval Europe* 10: 375–99.

Weinfurter, S. (1991). *Herrschaft und Reich der Salier: Grundlinien einer Umbruchzeit.* Sigmaringen. Cited from the English translation by B. Bowlus, *The Salian Century: Main Currents in an Age of Transition.* MAS. Philadelphia, 1999.

White, S. (1988). *Custom, Kinship, and Gifts to Saints: The Laudatio Parentum in Western France, 1050–1150.* Chapel Hill and London.

Williams, G. (1951). *The Norman Anonymous of 1100 A.D.: Towards the Identification and Evaluation of the So-Called Anonymous of York.* Harvard Theological Studies, 18. Cambridge, Massachusetts.

Williams, J. (1954). "The Cathedral School of Rheims in the Eleventh Century." *Speculum* 29: 661–77.

Wolfram, H. (2000). *Konrad, II, 990–1039: Kaiser dreier Reiche.* Munich. Cited from the English translation by D. Kaiser, *Conrad II, 990–1039: Emperor of Three Kingdoms.* University Park, Pennsylvania, 2006.

Woll, C. (2002). *Die Königinnen des hochmittelalterlichen Frankreich, 987–1237/38.* Stuttgart.

Wood, S. (2006). *The Proprietary Church in the Medieval West.* Oxford.

Zechiel-Eckes, K. (2001). "Ein Blick in Pseudoisidors Werkstatt: Studien zum Entstehungsprozess der falschen Dekretalen." *Francia* 28: 37–90.

Zielinski, H. (1984). *Der Reichsepiskopat in spätottonischer und salischer Zeit (1002–1125).* Stuttgart.

Ziese, J. (1982). *Wibert von Ravenna: Der Gegenpapst Clemens III. (1084–1100)*. Päpste und Papsttum, 20. Stuttgart.

Zieulewicz, W. (1991). "The School of Chartres and Reform Influences before the Pontificate of Leo IX." *Catholic Historical Review* 77: 383–402.

Zimmermann, H. (1968). *Papstabsetzungen des Mittelalters*. Graz, Vienna, and Cologne.

    (1991). "Der Bischof von Rom im saeculum obscurum." In *Il primato del vescovo di Roma nel primo millennio*. Pp. 643–60.

Index of Biblical references

Genesis
  2:21–23 52–53
  2:24 23
  9:20–27 168, 188
  14:18–20 62
  16:1–6 99
  17:15–16 127
  21:1–10 27, 99
  27 194
  38:15–29 72
Exodus
  20:12 97, 110–11, 116, 129,
    157, 158, 168,
    183, 214
  21:17 125–26, 129, 135, 157, 158, 168,
    169, 193, 198, 210, 214
Leviticus
  10:1–2 35
  18:6–19 30, 168, 183
  18:24–29 30
  20:9 168
  21 229
  21:7 33
  21:17–23 47
Deuteronomy
  21:18–21 130
  23:18 73
  28:30 84
Joshua
  2 72
Ruth
  2–4 72
1 Samuel
  2:22–34 35
  4:17 35
2 Samuel
  6:6–7 35
  15–18 169, 210
Psalms
  3:1 179
  45 (Vulgate 44) 52, 53, 91, 154
  113 (Vulgate 112):9 127, 156

Proverbs
  3:12 214
  7:5–27 73
  9:13–18 73
  13:24 161
  23:14 161
  31:19 127
Song of Songs
  as a whole 53–56, 71, 123
  1:1 54, 59
  1:6–7 55, 75
  2:1 54
  2:3 86
  4:8 55
  5:2–7 55
  6:9 54
  8:3 88
Jeremiah
  2:16 67, 75, 158
Amos
  7:17 84
Sirach
  30:1 161
  30:8–10 161
Matthew
  2:16–18 112
  3:7 75
  5:9 158
  5:28 34
  10:8 70
  10:37 111, 170, 214, 216
  18:6 222
  19:9 45
  19:29 214
  19:30 156
  20:16 156
  21:12–13 229
  22:21 197
Mark
  10:11–12 45
  10:31 156
  11:15–17 229

General Index

abandonment of spouse 44
  and abandonment of episcopal see 65,
    89
Adam 23, 47, 52, 53, 199, 222
Adam of Bremen 37
Adela, countess of Blois 94, 115, 196, 198
adultery 36–42, 45 46
  episcopal marriage as 90
  invasion of church as 66–67, 129, 158
  lay investiture as 84, 197
  simony as 155, 156
Aethelraed, king of England 28, 102
Agnellus of Ravenna 139, 140
Agnes, empress, wife of Henry III 117–21,
    204
  and Roman schism of 1061 66, 118–19,
    130–31
  maternal Authority of 120–21
  vulnerability of 121
Alexander II, pope 66, 118–19, 131, 150,
    212
Alfanus of Salerno 96, 130–33, 170–72,
    180
Alfonso VI, king of Léon-Castile 150,
    206–07
Allegory
  and political theory 228–30
  compared to metaphor 5–7, 9–10
  sources for those used in this book 7
Amalar of Metz 58–59
Annals of Hildesheim (*Annales*
    Hildesheimenses) 180, 217
Annals of Rosenveld (*Annales Rosenveldenses*)
    177
Annals of St. Disibod (*Annales sancti*
    Disibodi) 181–82, 209
Anne of Kiev, queen of France, wife of
    Henry I 56
annulment 25
Anselm, archbishop of Canterbury
  encouraged to become archbishop 61
  invested by William Rufus 81, 82

  on the primacy of Canterbury 143
  quarrel with Henry I 81–82, 129,
    195–98, 199
Anselm II, bishop of Lucca 26
  on "blessed" persecution 152–53
  on Sarah and Hagar 152–53
  on Wibert of Ravenna 67, 134–58, 209
Aphra, saint 40, 100–01
Ariald, Milanese preacher 34
Arras, see of 141–42, 152
Augustine of Hippo 1, 23, 39, 128, 152,
    221–22
authority, maternal 13
  as negotiable 92–93, 99–101
  as situational 92–93, 132, 133
    derived from paternal authority 95,
      97–99, 128
  economic basis of 96–97, 105–10
  emotional basis of 92, 96, 101–05
  legal basis 98–99, 109, 132, 157
  of Church – *see* Church, as mother;
    Roman Church, as mother
  parameters of 93–95
  religious basis of 97, 110–11
authority, paternal 13
  and fear 162–64
  as "natural" 168, 177–79, 180, 184
  associated with authority of God
    168–69, 179, 180
  emotional basis of 162–64
  legal basis of 168–72, 177–79, 211
  parameters of 162–67, 185
  religious basis of 168–69, 177–79, 211
  represents other forms of authority
    160–62

"B." (author) 123–24, 141
"bad fathers" 171–72
  Gregory VII as 211–12, 214, 215
  Henry IV as 208–10
  reforming popes as 211–12
  Wibert of Ravenna as 208–09, 210